D0204174
P9-EEB-399

ABBOT GEORGE BURKE

Simply Heavenly!

The Monastery Vegetarian Cookbook

Saint George Press
Route 1, Box 75
Geneva, Nebraska 68361

COPYRIGHT ©1991 by Saint George Press

ISBN 0-932104-00-2

Contents

Foreword i
Salad Dressings 1
Salads 22
Bread and Such 42
Soups 54
Crackers 77
Dairy Substitutes 79
Gluten–For Goodness' Sake! 86
Beef Substitutes and Dishes 98
Pork Substitutes and Dishes 104
Poultry Substitutes and Dishes 114
Seafood Substitutes and Dishes 123
Flavoring Broths 132
Vegetables 134
Casseroles 171
Dried Beans and Lentils 201
Grains 223
Tofu Dishes 230
Gravies and Sauces 235
Pasta 251
Pizza 261
Sandwiches and Spreads 265
Square Meals 270
Pickles, Relish, Salsa, Etc. 277
N'eggs 285
Seasonings 286
Desserts 288
N'Ice Cream 295
Cake 297
Cookies 304
Pies 313
Sweet Pastry 319
Etc. 323
HEAVENLY SIMPLE! 331

FOREWORD

Originally Christians–like their Jewish spiritual antecedents, the Essenes–were vegetarians, but in time the insistence on a vegetarian diet became confined to the monasteries. One of the most interesting monastic "relics" of the early Christian era is a letter written by a monk of Egypt to one of his disciples who had gone to Alexandria on some project and there had begun to eat meat. Learning of this, the monk immediately wrote to him, exhorting him to return to his vegetarian ways, reminding him that in Paradise Adam and Eve had been told: "Behold, I have given you every herb bearing seed, which is upon the face of all the earth, and every tree, in the which is the fruit of a tree yielding seed; to you it shall be for meat" (Gen 1:29). This being so, the monk wrote, those who aspire to return to that pristine state of purity and communion with God must eat the diet of Paradise while on the earth in order to prepare themselves to regain that lost blessedness.

Although at times–especially in the West–this ideal was forgotten, whenever there was a resurgence of spiritual consciousness and reform among the monastics the absolute first principle would be that of total abstinence from animal flesh (including eggs) in all forms. Usually this abstinence would be extended to dairy products as well.

In the Eastern and Oriental Orthodox Churches this principle is still evident in the requirement for all Orthodox Christians–lay as well as monastic–to totally abstain from meat, fish, eggs, and dairy products on nearly all Wednesdays and Fridays as well as all days in the seasons of abstinence such as the forty days of Lent and Advent. In the Oriental Orthodox Churches these days of abstinence comprise more than half of the calendar year.

But many of the Eastern Christian monastics–and some non-monastics as well–prefer to observe this abstinence all the time. This is because in the Eastern Church such abstinence is not regarded as penitential self-denial or "mortification of the flesh," but rather as an aid to interior prayer (*Hesychia*–The Silence). The Fathers of the East taught that diet had a formative influence on the mind–which they saw as a field of energy, not merely the physical brain which they considered to be only the organ of the mind. They observed that some foods made the mental processes (movements of noetic energies) heavy, whereas other foods made the mind light and quick in movement. Topping the list of "heavy" foods were all animal proteins, including dairy. In contrast, vegetables, grains, and fruits–the food of Paradise–were seen to make the mind fluid and able to grasp the subtleties of spiritual thought and experience (*theoria*).

In this approach to vegetarianism they were maintaining the principle to be found in the Aramaic text of the *Evangelion Da-Mepharreshe*, the oldest text of the Gospels known to exist. There, in the Gospel of Luke (21:34), Jesus says most forthrightly: "See that you do not make your minds heavy, *by never eating meat* or drinking wine." In our own century, Saint John of Kronstadt (+1908) wrote that the more we live in the spirit the less will we live on animal flesh–the implication being that those who live fully in the spirit abstain completely from animal food. Saint John, a non-monastic parish priest, insisted that his spiritual children abstain at all times from animal foods, thus keeping a perpetual lent. Those priests who were under his spiritual aegis did the same in relation to those under their spiritual care.

Now that more detailed–and honest–research and information regarding diet and health are becoming widely spread, many clergy and laity of the Orthodox Church who had previously held an indifferent attitude toward observance of the traditional rules of abstinence are realizing the wisdom of the ancient ways.

So much excellent material has been written on the material and spiritual "why" of vegetarianism that I will not add any more here. (I would, though, like to recommend four publications: *What's Wrong With Eating Meat*, by Vistara Parham, *Diet For A New America*, by John Robbins, and my two booklets–*The Four Soul Killers*, and *Spiritual Vegetarianism*.)

But I do want to say a word about the quality of vegetarian food–at least what I think it should be.

From the first day I became a vegetarian I have been convinced that vegetarian food should not just be healthy in a theoretical sense and eaten like medicine, but that it should be really *good* food–in taste and appearance. In fact, since it is better for us than non-vegetarian food, it should taste even *better* than non-vegetarian food. Accomplishing that is not so simple. This cookbook is a result of more than twenty years' endeavor to do so.

One of the best ways to motivate others to consider becoming vegetarian is to feed them good vegetarian food. I am glad to say that by means of the recipes in this book our monastery has done so for many years. And so can you. Every recipe in this book has been put to the ultimate test: eating!

So much has been written on the subject of vegetarian and vegan diet that there is no need for it here. The proof is in the eating and in the resulting health benefits.

Following are a few comments regarding some of the ingredients you will find in these recipes.

APPLES

We prefer to use Granny Smith apples in the recipes that call for apples. They are a bit tart, and the recipes reflect this in the amount of Sucanat used, so you might want to experiment with cutting it down when you use other kinds of apples.

FLOUR

Most recipes in this book call for unbleached white flour. This may be surprising to some, but whole wheat flour is often simply too strong in its taste and interferes with the desired flavor. Although unbleached white flour does not contain all the nutrients of whole wheat flour, it is not devoid of food value. Bleached flour, however is both worthless and poisonous.

JALAPEÑO PEPPERS

You will often find jalapeño peppers listed as an ingredient. If you don't like them, just leave them out. Also, keep in mind that throughout the growing season jalapeños vary in their degree of hotness, so the amount may have to be adjusted some. You may find it simpler to use cayenne pepper instead since it is consistent. But the distinctive taste of jalapeños is worth the trouble in my opinion.

KITCHEN BOUQUET

Kitchen Bouquet has been around for many decades. I know, because as a child attracted by the name and the smell I took a gigantic swig from my "aunt" Suzy Snow's bottle! Brown lightning! It was my first introduction to flavorings that no kidding are supposed to be used sparingly! Only when I was a seasoned vegetarian did I drop my trauma and agree to try it in cooking.

Kitchen Bouquet imparts a richer flavor (and color) to dishes that accommodate a beef-like flavor. While it is no substitute for beef-like broth or other "beef" flavorings, it does sometimes give that added touch and body that makes a recipe just right.

You can buy Kitchen Bouquet at just about any grocery store.

LEA & PERRINS STEAK SAUCE

Many recipes need the boost that Worcestershire sauce can give, but the only two vegetarian versions I know of (unnamed out of Christian charity) taste terrible. Therefore I recommend

Lea & Perrins Steak Sauce (their Worcestershire sauce contains anchovies) as an excellent substitute. When you are cooking from another book and a recipe calls for Worcestershire sauce, use *twice* the amount of Lea & Perrins sauce as it is not as pungent as Worcestershire.

LIQUID SMOKE

I only recommend Wright's Liquid Smoke, as it alone is made from all natural ingredients.

LOUISIANA HOT SAUCE & TABASCO SAUCE

When the recipe calls for Louisiana Hot Sauce I mean the real Louisiana Hot Sauce made by Bruce Foods Corporation in New Iberia, Louisiana, not any of the imitations–all of which are poor. The purpose of this sauce is both to impart a red pepper "heat" and a good vinegary tang that brings out the other flavors in the dish. (If you are watching your salt intake, be aware that all hot pepper sauces of this type contain large amounts of salt.) Also, Louisiana Hot Sauce (the real thing, remember) does not mask any flavors, but only adds a dimension of its own.

Tabasco is of course known throughout the world, and rightly so. Tabasco, however, is much hotter than Louisiana Hot Sauce and tends to impart the heat of red pepper more than any tangy flavor. Yet there are times when that is needed in preference to the effect of Louisiana Hot Sauce. Therefore in these recipes the two are not interchangeable, but each is called for according to its characteristic effect on the dish. If you are in a pinch, however, use what you have, but remember: if the recipe calls for Louisiana Hot Sauce, use only *half* the amount of Tabasco; if the recipe calls for Tabasco, use *twice* the amount of Louisiana Hot Sauce.

LOW SODIUM SOY SAUCE

In the recipes I have always indicated *low sodium* soy sauce, for not only is it better for us (it has been estimated that in the "normal" American diet we eat twenty to thirty times more salt than we need), I find that the low sodium soy sauce has a stronger-bodied–and better–flavor. If possible a naturally brewed sauce should be used rather than the "common garden variety" brands we grew up with.

Angostura Low Sodium Soy Sauce is lower in sodium than any others I know of, and the flavor is incomparably better. Also, some other brands are much less flavorful, so the amount will have to be increased in the recipe to get the desired taste. However, this will increase the overall amount of sodium. So get Angostura if you can.

If you do use regular soy sauce you will no doubt need to decrease the amount to avoid the dish being too salty.

MEASUREMENTS

One of my pet peeves is the encountering a recipe in which I find terms like "a large bell pepper," "a medium potato," and "a small onion"–not to mention "a scant cup" or a "heaping spoon." Grrrrrrr! So I have not done this to you–unless it has slipped by me or refers to packages of frozen vegetables, raw grains or pasta. However, this may mean that you will have a little of some ingredient left over in the measuring. Put it in. Live!

MEASUREMENTS AND INGREDIENTS–ANOTHER WORD

God did not write this cookbook. Nor can I claim to be His instrument in the writing lest that prove me to be slightly bent if not broken. So don't think these recipes are infallible or inflexible. Feel free to use them as a basis for your own creativity. As Justin Wilson says, good cooking is a combination of imagination and common sense.

MILK SUBSTITUTES

In this book I give formulas for soy milk, cashew milk, and almond milk. But in the recipes you will see that I always recommend cashew milk. This is because I feel that soy and almond milks do not have the body or flavor I prefer in cooking. But go ahead and try the other two if cashew milk does not appeal to you. Try soy milk if you have an allergy to nuts.

MOLASSES

Barbados molasses is recommended in these recipes–unless you like the heavier taste of Blackstrap molasses. This really must be obtained from health food stores or suppliers. (Be warned: a very famous "natural" brand of "unsulphured molasses" found in regular supermarkets contains a high percentage of white sugar, but is not required to be so labeled since white sugar is considered "natural.")

MONOSODIUM GLUTAMATE (MSG)

Yep, the monster is here! But only when absolutely necessary–that is, when the flavor desired cannot be obtained any other way. If you want, in the soups you can substitute salt, but in a couple of the flavoring broths it is just not possible to get a satisfactory flavor without it.

When I eat at an oriental (Chinese, Vietnamese, etc.) restaurant, I frequently get an "MSG hangover," but I have never had such a thing happen with these recipes. I suppose it is because not much really goes into a serving since it is diluted in the broth which flavors the dish. And also it will only be in one dish at a meal, whereas nearly everything is loaded with it in many oriental restaurants.

Monosodium Glutamate does not come from animal sources, but is a derivative of wheat.

MUSHROOMS–A SUBSTITUTE

Those who do not care for mushrooms will find that in most recipes sliced or chopped black olives will substitute quite well.

NON-DAIRY MARGARINE

Read the labels of supposedly non-dairy margarine carefully, keeping in mind that ingredients such as sodium caseinate are really elements taken from milk.

Oil can be used if you do not have non-dairy margarine or prefer not to use it.

NUTRITIONAL YEAST

First of all, Nutritional Yeast is NOT Brewers Yeast. I put this in because friends of ours have wanted to try the recipes in this book and been told at health food stores that it is, and their culinary attempts were disasters! (Recently "Betty Crocker" assured readers of "her" column that the two were the same.) Nutritional Yeast (*Saccharomyces Cerevisiae*) is a food yeast grown in a molasses solution. It gives a "cheesy" taste to food, and is the basis for the Yeast "Cheese" recipe given in the Dairy Substitutes section. It can be stirred into or sprinkled on many things, and is especially good in adding flavor to soups. It contains several B Vitamins, including the elusive B12 that is so important for those who eat no dairy products.

Nutritional yeast can be obtained from a health food store or by mail from: The Farm, Summertown, Tennessee, 38483, or from the Red Star Yeast Company. There may be other sources, as well.

Foreword

OIL

Once a Theravadin Buddhist monk, commenting on a rival school of Buddhism, said to me: "It is a jungle!" So is the world of "healthy eating"! More so, I expect. The question of oil–how much, if any, and what kind–is a truly "vexed" question. Especially so since I have had the vexation of going through every recipe in this book and looking carefully at the quantities of oil prescribed!

As an Orthodox monk I have had much experience of totally oilless cooking, and am not interested, for I can say with Huck Finn: "I've done been there." However, I have tried to reduce the oil to the minimum that will still (to my palate) produce something that tastes good yet is not (to my mind) unhealthy. Some "ethnic" dishes, such as Indian ones, demand oiliness–otherwise they are just not the dish. But I have done what I could without violating their basic nature. There is also quite a good chance that I have managed to skip or overlook a recipe. If so, cut down the oil and forgive (and if you would let me know about it I would be most appreciative.) But believe me, I have gone through the jungle of this book with an oil-hacking machete and done my best.

Olive oil is an excellent food. It is the only monosaturate among oils, and has been found to actively remove cholesterol deposits from arteries. It is best used raw as in salad dressings, and in cooked dishes where its distinctive flavor is desired.

Corn oil is excellent in cooking, since it loses very little of its nutritional value from the heat. Mazola is the best brand beyond a doubt.

ONIONS

Onions, despite some medicinal elements, do contain some toxins that can affect the heart action. This is why the yogis of India avoid them. Red onions, however, contain the least of these elements and are also easier to digest, so I recommend that you try them. However, you can use any type of onions you prefer in the recipes. Chives, leeks, scallions or shallots are good substitutes for onions.

RECIPE COMMENTS

Under the heading of many recipes I have put some comments on the dish. This is because I am aware how easy it is to pass up a really good dish simply because it does not sound interesting. But please do not think that those without comments are not as good as those with them–they are! Sometimes I just could not think of anything clever to say about them. Often I have been tempted to put " Please try this! Please!" under many headings, because I know how much you will like it if you do.

RED PEPPER FLAKES

When the ingredients list says "red pepper flakes" I mean crushed *hot* red pepper flakes, not red *bell* pepper flakes.

RICE

Whenever a recipe in this book calls for rice, ordinary "white" rice is intended. Those who prefer brown rice can substitute it, but should keep in mind that cooking time may then need to be adjusted since brown rice takes about four times longer to cook.

The white rice usually found in grocery stores has neither fragrance nor taste, whereas good rice has a definite fragrance and a distinct though delicate taste.

You can get good rice by buying it from Indian or Oriental grocery stores. The best rice from India is Basmati Rice. My favorite rice is Jasmine Rice from Thailand ("Jasmine" is a type of rice, not a brand name). Don't be disturbed if the bag says the rice is "scented." The producers (whose English is not the best) only mean that it smells good when cooked. Also be assured that the rice does *not* smell or taste like Jasmine–a pretty awful idea.

If you have no Indian or Oriental stores in your town from which to obtain good quality rice, there are quite a few Oriental food companies that will sell to you through the mail. Oriental cookbooks often list such companies, or your local library should be able to help you locate them.

SALT

Sea salt is always recommended in these recipes as being more easily assimilated by the body.

SOVEX AND VEGEX

Sovex and Vegex are the brand names for a dark, saltish paste that is a yeast extract used for flavoring. Some large grocery stores carry it in the section where they have boullion cubes, but usually it must be bought from health food stores.

SUCANAT

The latest–and best–word on sweeteners is a product called "granulated sugar cane juice" which, despite the odd name, is actually a sweetener made by dehydrating sugar cane juice. Completely unrefined, the resulting powder contains all the nutrients of the sugar cane juice with none of the negative qualities of refined sugar. The brand I am familiar with and use is Sucanat, which is produced by Pronatec International, Inc., P.O. Box 193, Peterborough, NH 03458.

In the Etc. Section I give the formula for making powdered Sucanat when powdered sugar is needed in a recipe.

TAHINI

Tahini is a paste made from sesame seeds. It has a "smoky" or "bacon" taste that adds much to recipes. You can buy it in health food and import grocery stores.

TOMATOES

Our ancestors thought tomatoes were deadly poison. They were mistaken, but tomatoes do contain some elements that are toxic to a degree. It has been my experience that these elements are not in Italian (sometimes called Roma) tomatoes, and that Italian tomatoes are better in flavor when cooked. Nor are they as acidic as other tomatoes. As with the onions, if you prefer–or do not have Italian tomatoes–simply use whatever is available.

ZATARAIN'S CRAB BOIL

"Crab Boil" is a mixture of spices put in the water used to boil crab or shrimp in Louisiana Creole and Cajun cooking. While it is not absolutely necessary to have it in making Gluten Shrimp according to the recipe given in the Seafood section, I greatly recommend it.

There are several brands of Crab Boil available in supermarkets, but I have found that Zatarain's is by far the best, and more than a century of satisfied users agree with me. If you cannot find it in a local store, telephone: 504-367-2950 and ask where it might be sold near you. If there is no store "within reach" that stocks it, don't worry–Zatarain's will sell it directly to you through the mail (UPS, actually) by the case. That may seem like a lot to buy, but when you taste "shrimp" made with it you will make so much that it won't take long to use it up. Or you can split a case with friends.

Foreword

Zatarain's sells three forms of Crab Boil: dry (whole spices in a bag), liquid, and preseasoned (powdered in a box). *Get the dry whole spices in the bag.*

THE GOOD FOOD KEEPS ON HAPPENING!

Even as this cookbook "goes to press" I have a humongous number of reicpes waiting to be tested in our kitchen–and on our palates! I want to get them out to you before a new edition of this cookbook is printed, so we are putting out *The Simply Heavenly! Recipe Newsletter.* The ten pages of each issue contain many new recipes–all of which our brotherhood has agreed are simply heavenly. Occasionally I will be sharing some of our cooking tips and other widgets of wisdom.

Don't lose out on any of the goodness–subscribe today! For four issues send check or money order for $16.00 to: Saint George Press, Route 1, Box 75, Geneva NE 68361.

Abbot George

Father Philaret and Father Arsenios show a friend how to cook vegetarian.

Salad Dressings

ALFALFA SPROUT DRESSING

1/2 c.	Alfalfa Sprouts
2 tsp.	Celery seed
1/4 c.	Olive oil
1/3 c.	Lemon juice or white vinegar
1/2 tsp.	Low sodium soy sauce
1 tsp.	Onion powder or 1 T. Scallion, shallot or leek
1 T.	Sesame seeds

Mix well by hand or blend in a blender–according to your taste.

ALMOND DRESSING

1/4 c.	Almonds
1/4 tsp.	Garlic powder
1/2 tsp.	Sea salt
1/2 c.	Tomato, chopped
2 T.	Lemon juice or white vinegar
3 T.	Olive oil

Mix well by hand or blend in a blender–according to your taste.

AVOCADO-CASHEW DRESSING

Blend until smooth:

1/2 c.	Raw cashews
1 1/2 c.	Hot water

Add and continue to blend:

2	Avocados
2 tsp.	Lemon juice or white vinegar
1/4 c.	Onions, chopped
1/2 tsp.	Sea salt

Cool before using.

AVOCADO DRESSING-1

1	Avocado, in chunks
1	Tomato, sliced
1/4 tsp.	Sea salt
2 T.	Lemon juice
1/4 c.	Onions, chopped
1 T.	Nutritional yeast
1 T.	Olive oil

Mix well by hand or blend in a blender–according to your taste.
VARIATION: Add 2/3 cup of Tofu Mayonnaise, Cashew Mayonnaise, or Miraculous Whip.

AVOCADO DRESSING-2

1/2 tsp.	Garlic powder
1/2	Medium avocado
2 T.	Lemon juice
4 T.	Tofu Mayonnaise, Cashew Mayonnaise, or Miraculous Whip

Mix well by hand or blend in a blender–according to your taste.
VARIATION: Add 1/4 tsp. of Dill weed.

AVOCADO DRESSING-3

This does not keep well. Use up at one meal, if possible.

4	Avocadoes, mashed
1 T.	Olive oil
1 1/2 T.	Low sodium soy sauce
1/4 tsp.	Onion powder
1/4 tsp.	Oregano
1/4 tsp.	Basil
1/4 tsp.	Garlic powder
1/4 tsp.	Sea salt

Mix well by hand or blend in a blender–according to your taste.

AVOCADO DRESSING-4

3	Avocados, mashed
1 c.	Tofu Sour Cream or Cashew Sour Cream
1 tsp.	Sea salt
2 T.	Lemon or lime juice

Mix well by hand or blend in a blender–according to your taste.

AVOCADO DRESSING-5

2	Avocados, mashed
1 1/3 c.	Tofu Sour Cream or Cashew Sour Cream
1 tsp.	Sea salt
1/2 tsp.	Chives
1/8 tsp.	Onion powder

4 tsp. Lemon juice or white vinegar

Mix well by hand or blend in a blender–according to your taste.

AVOCADO DRESSING-6

1 Avocado
1 T. Lemon juice or white vinegar
2 T. Onions, minced
2 T. Bell pepper or pimento, chopped
1/2 tsp. Sea salt
2 T. Tofu Sour Cream or Cashew Sour Cream
1/4 tsp. Dill

Mix well by hand or blend in a blender–according to your taste.

AVOCADO-OLIVE DRESSING

1 Medium avocado, mashed
1/4 c. Ripe olives, sliced or chopped
1 c. Tofu Mayonnaise, Cashew Mayonnaise, or Miraculous Whip or Tofu Sour Cream or Cashew Sour Cream

Mix well by hand or blend in a blender–according to your taste.

AVOCADO MAYONNAISE

1/4 c. Avocado, mashed
1 1/2 tsp. Lemon juice or white vinegar
1 T. Corn oil

Mix well by hand or blend in a blender–according to your taste.

SIMPLE AVOCADO DRESSING

Mash avocado(s) and gradually add lemon juice (or white vinegar, or tomato juice), beating until it is creamy.Mix well by hand or blend in a blender–according to your taste.

BITTERS DRESSING

3/4 c. Lime juice
3 T. Olive oil
1/4 tsp. Garlic powder
1 1/2 tsp. Sea salt
1 tsp. Aromatic bitters

Mix well by hand or blend in a blender–according to your taste.

CAPER FRENCH DRESSING

1 c. French Dressing
1/3 c. Capers, minced

Mix well by hand or blend in a blender–according to your taste.

CARAWAY DRESSING

1/3 c.	Tofu Mayonnaise, Cashew Mayonnaise, or Miraculous Whip or Tofu Sour Cream or Cashew Sour Cream
3/4 tsp.	Caraway seeds
1 T.	Sesame seeds
1 1/2 tsp.	Lemon juice or white vinegar
1/4 tsp.	Sea salt
1/4 tsp.	Paprika

Mix well by hand or blend in a blender–according to your taste.

CARROT DRESSING

4	Carrots, grated
2 T.	Olive oil
1/2 tsp.	Garlic powder
1/2 tsp.	Onion powder
1 c.	Water
1 T.	Low sodium soy sauce
2 T.	Tahini OR nut butter

Mix well by hand or blend in a blender–according to your taste.

CASHEW CHEESE DRESSING

Superb!

3/4 c.	Cashews
1/2 c.	Water
3/4 tsp.	Sea salt
3/4 tsp.	Onion powder
2 T.	Lemon juice or white vinegar
1/4 c.	Canned pimentos
4 1/2 tsp.	Olive oil

Put the nuts in a blender (Vita-Mix is best) and grind them as fine as possible. Add the rest of the ingredients and continue blending until everything is smooth–about 1 minute.

VARIATION: Add 3 tablespoons of Nutritional Yeast.

CASHEW MAYONNAISE

2 c.	Water
6 T.	Cornstarch or arrowroot powder
2 c.	Hot water
2 c.	Raw cashews
1/3 c.	Lemon juice or white vinegar
1 tsp.	Garlic powder
2 tsp.	Onion powder
1 T.	Sea salt
1 T.	Sucanat
1/8 tsp.	Paprika

Mix the 2 cups of water with the cornstarch or arrowroot and boil on the stove until it thickens.

Cool slightly. Blend the hot water and cashews well. Add the rest of the ingredients to the cashew liquid. Add this to the cornstarch mixture and combine thoroughly. Cool before using.

CHIVE DRESSING

2/3 c. French Dressing
1/4 c. Chives, chopped

Mix well by hand or blend in a blender–according to your taste.
VARIATION: Add 1/4 c. Tofu Mayonnaise, Cashew Mayonnaise, Miraculous Whip, Tofu Sour Cream, or Cashew Sour Cream.

CREAM FRENCH DRESSING

When French Dressing-1 is used this is marvellous: good enough to eat by the spoonful.

1/2 c. French Dressing
1/4 c. Tofu Mayonnaise, Cashew Mayonnaise, Miraculous Whip, or Tofu Sour Cream or Cashew Sour Cream

Mix well by hand or blend in a blender–according to your taste.

CRUNCHY CREAM DRESSING

1/2 c. Cucumber, finely chopped
2 T. Bell pepper, finely chopped
2 T. Chives, finely chopped
2 T. Radishes, thinly sliced
1 c. Tofu Sour Cream, or Cashew Sour Cream
1/2 tsp. Sea salt
1/4 tsp. Paprika

Mix well by hand or blend in a blender–according to your taste.
VARIATION: Add 1 or 2 teaspoons of low sodium soy sauce.

CUCUMBER DRESSING

1 c. Cucumbers, chopped
1/2 tsp. Sea salt
1 T. Lemon juice
1 T. Dill, minced or 1 tsp. dry
1 c. Tofu Mayonnaise, Cashew Mayonnaise, Miraculous Whip, or Tofu Sour Cream or Cashew Sour Cream

Mix well by hand or blend in a blender–according to your taste.
VARIATION: Add 2 or 3 tablespoons of finely chopped onions.

CURRY MAYONNAISE

1 1/2 c. Tofu Mayonnaise, Cashew Mayonnaise, or Miraculous Whip
1 1/2 tsp. Curry Powder.

Mix well by hand or blend in a blender–according to your taste.

DILL DRESSING

Outstanding!

3/4 c.	Tofu, mashed
2 T.	Corn oil
2 T.	Wine vinegar
1/2 tsp.	Sea salt
1 tsp.	Sucanat
1 tsp.	Dill weed
1/8 tsp.	Black pepper
1 T.	Onion, minced

Blend in a blender until smooth and creamy.

DRIED BEAN DRESSING

Unusual, but equally tasty.

1 c.	Dried beans, cooked
2 T.	Onions, minced
1 c.	Beef-like Broth
1 tsp.	Garlic powder
1/2 tsp.	Oregano
1/2 tsp.	Basil
1/2 tsp.	Paprika

Mix well by hand or blend in a blender–according to your taste.

FRENCH DRESSING–1

1/4 c.	Olive oil
1/4 c.	Corn oil
3 T.	Lemon juice
1/2 tsp.	Sea salt
1/4 c.	Raw cashews
1/2 tsp.	Paprika
1/4 tsp.	Garlic powder
1/2 tsp.	Onion powder
1/4 tsp.	Dill weed
1/4 tsp.	Basil

Mix well by hand or blend in a blender–according to your taste.

FRENCH DRESSING–2

1/4 c.	Corn oil
2 T.	Vinegar
2 T.	Lemon
2 tsp.	Sucanat
1/2 tsp.	Sea salt
1/2 tsp.	Dry mustard
1/2 tsp.	Paprika

Salad Dressings

Mix well by hand or blend in a blender–according to your taste.

FRENCH DRESSING–3

1 1/2 c.	Tomatoes, chopped
1/2 c.	Tahini
1/8 c.	Low sodium soy sauce
1/4 tsp.	Oregano
1/4 tsp.	Garlic powder
1/4 tsp.	Parsley
1/4 tsp.	Sea salt
1/4 tsp.	Basil

Mix well by hand or blend in a blender–according to your taste.

FRESH TOMATO DRESSING

1 1/2 c.	Tahini/Oil Dressing
3/4 c.	Tomatoes, chopped
2 T.	Bell peppers, chopped
3 T.	Black olives, chopped
2 T.	Onions, minced

Mix well by hand or blend in a blender–according to your taste.

FRESH VEGETABLE DRESSING

1 c.	Fresh Tomato sauce
1/4 c.	Spinach or other greens, chopped
2 T.	Squash, chopped
2 T.	Bean Sprouts, minced

Mix well by hand or blend in a blender–according to your taste.

GARLIC DRESSING

1 c.	Tofu, mashed
2 T.	Corn oil
2 T.	Lemon juice
1/2 tsp.	Sucanat
3/4 tsp.	Sea salt
2 tsp.	Garlic, minced

Blend in a blender until smooth and creamy.

GARLIC AND DILL DRESSING

1/4 c.	Red wine vinegar
2 T.	Water
1 tsp.	Sucanat
1/4 c.	Olive oil
1/8 tsp.	Garlic powder
2 T.	Chopped parsley
2 T.	Chopped chives

2 T. "Parmesan Cheese"
1/2 tsp. Dill weed
1/2 tsp. Sea salt
1/8 tsp. Black pepper

Put all ingredients in a glass jar with a tight-fitting lid and shake until blended. Refrigerate.

GREEN DRESSING–1

1 1/2 c. Tahini/Oil Dressing
2 T. Bell peppers
1/4 c. Spinach or Bok Choy
1 T. Parsley

Mix well by hand or blend in a blender–according to your taste.

GREEN DRESSING–2

1/4 c. Bell pepper, finely chopped
1/4 c. Parsley, finely chopped
2 T. Celery, finely chopped
1 T. Onions, finely chopped
1 T. Pimento, finely chopped
1 T. Capers, finely chopped
1/2 tsp. Sea salt
1/8 tsp. Basil
3 T. Olive oil

Mix well by hand or blend in a blender–according to your taste.

GREEN GAZPACHO DRESSING

2 T. Onions, chopped
1 tsp. Garlic powder
1/4 c. Bell pepper, chopped
1 T. Fresh basil, or 3/4 tsp. dried
2 tsp. Parsley, chopped
1 c. Tomatoes, quartered
3 T. Lemon juice or white vinegar
2 T. Olive oil
1/2 tsp. Sea salt

Mix well by hand or blend in a blender–according to your taste.

GREEN GODDESS DRESSING

For those who love both flavor and tang!

1 c. Tofu Mayonnaise, Cashew Mayonnaise, Miraculous Whip, or Tofu Sour Cream or Cashew Sour Cream
2 T. Corn oil
1/2 T. Dried chives
1/2 c. Parsley, fresh

2 T.	Tarragon vinegar
1 tsp.	Onion powder
1/8 tsp.	Black pepper
1/8 tsp.	Garlic powder
1/2 tsp.	Sea salt

Put all in a blender and blend until smooth and creamy.

HERB DRESSING–1

3 T.	Olive oil
2 T.	Lemon or lime juice
1/2 tsp.	Chervil
1/2 tsp.	Thyme
1/2 tsp.	Oregano
1/2 tsp.	Savory
1/4 tsp.	Coriander
1/8 tsp.	Sage
1/2 tsp.	Sea salt
1 T.	Tofu Sour Cream or Cashew Sour Cream

Mix well by hand or blend in a blender–according to your taste.

HERB DRESSING–2

1/4 c.	Celery, chopped fine
3 T.	Onions, chopped fine
2 T.	Parsley, chopped
1/2 tsp.	Sea salt
1 tsp.	Paprika
1/4 tsp.	Basil
1/8 tsp.	Marjoram or rosemary
2/3 c.	Olive oil
2/3 c.	Lemon juice or white vinegar

Mix well by hand or blend in a blender–according to your taste.

HERB MAYONNAISE DRESSING

1 1/2 c.	Tofu Mayonnaise, Cashew Mayonnaise, or Miraculous Whip
1/4 tsp.	Paprika
1 tsp.	Herbs
1/4 tsp.	Onion powder
1/8 tsp.	Curry powder

Mix well by hand or blend in a blender–according to your taste.

HOT "CHEESE" AND CIDER DRESSING

Something special!

1/2 c.	Apple cider
1 c.	Yeast or Pimento "Cheese"
1/2 tsp.	Sea salt

1/8 tsp. Cayenne pepper
1/4 tsp. Parsley or chives, finely chopped
Pinch Garlic salt

Heat the cider to the boiling point, then reduce to a simmer. Stir the "cheese" gradually into the cider until all is well blended. Add the seasonings.

HUMMUS DRESSING

An excellent way to boost protein when eating salad! Tastes good, too!

1 1/3 c. Garbanzos, DRY
2 T. Olive oil
1 T. Sea salt
1 T. Garlic, minced
1/4 c. Lemon juice or white vinegar
1 c. Tahini
Water from cooking the garbanzos

Pressure cook the garbanzos, drain and mash them. Add the remaining ingredients except the garbanzo water. Using the garbanzo water, blend all in a blender until smooth and of the consistency of a medium-thick sauce.

ITALIAN DRESSING–1

1/2 c. Olive oil
1/2 c. White vinegar or lemon juice
1/2 tsp. Sea salt
1/4 tsp. Celery seed
1/4 tsp. Basil
1/4 tsp. Oregano
1/4 tsp. Onion powder
1/8 tsp. Garlic powder

Mix well by hand or blend in a blender–according to your taste.

ITALIAN DRESSING–2

1/2 c. Olive oil
1/2 c. White vinegar or lemon juice
1/2 tsp. Sea salt
1/4 tsp. Basil
1/4 tsp. Oregano
2 T. Onions, minced

Mix well by hand or blend in a blender–according to your taste.

LEMON DRESSING

Combine:

1 tsp. Sea salt
1/8 tsp. Black pepper
1 Pinch of Cayenne pepper

1/4 tsp. Paprika

Add slowly and beat thoroughly:

1 1/2 T. Lemon juice
3 T. Olive oil

Chop until fine and add:

1 T. Pimento
1 T. Cucumber
3/4 T. Bell pepper
1/2 T. Parsley
1/4 c. Onions

Mix well by hand or blend in a blender–according to your taste.

LEMON GARLIC DRESSING

1/3 c. Olive oil
6 T. Lemon juice
2 T. Red wine vinegar
1/3 c. Finely chopped green onions
2 T. Chopped parsley
1 T. Garlic, minced
1 tsp. Dijon-style mustard
1/4 tsp. Sea salt
1/8 tsp. Black pepper

Combine all ingredients in a jar with a tight lid. Shake vigorously until the mixture is blended. Store in the refrigerator.

LORENZO DRESSING

1 c. French Dressing
4 T. Tomato Relish, semi-liquified
4 T. Parsley, chopped

Mix well by hand or blend in a blender–according to your taste.

MARINADE DRESSING

2 T. Olive oil
1/4 c. Lemon juice or white vinegar
1/2 c. Water
2 tsp. Low sodium soy sauce
3 T. Nutritional Yeast
2 T. Tahini
1/4 tsp. Onion powder
1/4 tsp. Garlic powder
1/2 tsp. Sea salt

Mix well by hand or blend in a blender–according to your taste.

MAYONNAISE DRESSING

1 c.	Tofu Mayonnaise, Cashew Mayonnaise, or Miraculous Whip
1 T.	Cucumber, chopped
1 T.	Pimento, chopped
1 T.	Bell pepper, chopped
1 T.	Parsley, chopped
2 T.	Black olives, chopped
2 T.	Onions, chopped
	Salt to taste

Mix well by hand or blend in a blender–according to your taste.

MEXICAN TOMATO DRESSING

1 c.	Tomato, chopped
2 T.	Onions, minced
2 T.	Lemon juice or white vinegar
2 T.	Olive oil
1 tsp.	Cayenne pepper
1 tsp.	Nutritional yeast flakes

Mix well by hand or blend in a blender–according to your taste.

MEXICAN TOMATO VINAIGRETTE

1/2 T.	Tomato paste
2 T.	Onions, minced
1 T.	Lemon juice or white vinegar
2 T.	Olive oil
1/2 tsp.	Chili powder

Mix well by hand or blend in a blender–according to your taste.

"MIRACULOUS WHIP"

Tastes as much like the real thing as the real thing itself!
Thank you, Brother Ron Pickarski!

1 1/2 c.	Firm tofu
6 T.	Corn oil
1 T.	Apple cider vinegar
1/2 c.	Water
1 1/2 tsp.	Prepared yellow mustard
1 tsp.	Garlic, minced
1/4 c.	Onion, minced
1/4 tsp.	White pepper
1 1/4 tsp.	Sea salt
1 T.	Lemon juice or white vinegar
1 T.	Cashew nuts ground fine

Put everything in a blender and blend until completely smoooth. Refrigerate.

VARIATION: For dishes such as fruit salads in which you do not want the flavors of onion, garlic, and mustard, leave them out.

Salad Dressings

NUT BUTTER DRESSING–1

1/2 c.	Nut Butter
1 c.	Water
1 T.	Lemon juice or white vinegar
1/4 tsp.	Sea salt

Mix well by hand or blend in a blender–according to your taste.

VARIATION: Add 1/4 cup of Tofu Mayonnaise, Cashew Mayonnaise, Miraculous Whip, or Cashew Cream.

NUT BUTTER DRESSING–2

1/4 c.	Nut butter
1/4 c.	Tofu Sour Cream or Cashew Sour Cream
1 tsp.	Lemon juice or white vinegar
1/4 tsp.	Basil or Parsley

Mix well by hand or blend in a blender–according to your taste.

NUT BUTTER DRESSING–3

1/4 c.	Nut butter
2 T.	Corn oil
2 T.	Lemon juice or white vinegar
2 T.	Water
1/2 tsp.	Sea salt
1/8 tsp.	Paprika

Mix well by hand or blend in a blender–according to your taste.

NUT BUTTER DRESSING–4

1/4 c.	Nut butter
1/3 c.	Tomato juice
2 T.	Corn oil
1/4 tsp.	Sea salt

Mix well by hand or blend in a blender–according to your taste.

NUTRITIONAL YEAST DRESSING

1/2 c.	Nutritional yeast
2 T.	Corn oil
1/2 c.	Beef-like Broth
1/2 tsp.	Onion powder
1/2 tsp.	Garlic powder
1/4 tsp.	Basil
1/4 tsp.	Oregano
1/4 tsp.	Paprika

Mix well by hand or blend in a blender–according to your taste.

OIL AND LEMON JUICE DRESSING

1/2 c. Lemon juice
1/2 c. Olive oil
1/4 tsp. Sea salt

Mix well by hand or blend in a blender–according to your taste.

OIL AND VINEGAR DRESSING

3/4 c. Olive oil
1/4 c. Red wine vinegar
1 Garlic clove, minced
1/4 tsp. Basil
1 tsp. Sucanat
1 tsp. Dijon style mustard
1/2 tsp. Sea salt
1/4 tsp. Black pepper

Combine all ingredients in a jar with a tight lid. Shake vigorously until the mixture is blended. Store in the refrigerator.

OLD FASHIONED BOILED DRESSING

1 T. Non-dairy margarine
2 T. Unbleached white flour
1 c. Cashew milk
1 tsp. Dry Mustard
1/8 tsp. Cayenne pepper
1/4 c. Cider vinegar

Heat the margarine in a saucepan until it melts. Sprinkle in the flour, stirring carefully until it is smoothly blended with the margarine. Add the cashew milk, 1/4 cup at a time, stirring briskly to avoid lumping. Stir in the mustard and a dash of cayenne pepper. Let the sauce bubble gently until it is thick, about 8 to 10 minutes. Slowly stir in the vinegar and bring the mixture to a gentle boil. Let the dressing cool before using. Makes about 1 cup.

OLIVE DRESSING

3/4 c. French dressing
1/4 c. Ripe olives

Mix well by hand or blend in a blender–according to your taste.

OREGANO-MINT DRESSING

3 T. Olive oil
1/4 c. Lemon juice or white vinegar
1/4 tsp. Mint, chopped
1/4 tsp. Oregano
1/3 c. Tofu Mayonnaise, Cashew Mayonnaise, Miraculous Whip, or Tofu Sour Cream or Cashew Sour Cream

Mix well by hand or blend in a blender–according to your taste.

Salad Dressings

PARSLEY DRESSING

2 T. Olive oil
2 T. Lemon juice or white vinegar
1/4 tsp. Sea salt
1/4 tsp. Onion powder
2 T. Parsley, chopped

Mix well by hand or blend in a blender–according to your taste.

POTATO DRESSING–1

1/2 c. French Dressing
1/3 c. Potato, baked and mashed

Mix well by hand or blend in a blender–according to your taste.

POTATO DRESSING–2

1 c. Tofu Sour Cream or Cashew Sour Cream
1 c. Potato, baked and mashed
2 T. Onions, minced

Mix well by hand or blend in a blender–according to your taste.

POTATO DRESSING–3

1/2 c. Onions, chopped
5 c. Potatoes, mashed
1 1/2 c. Flavoring Broth or water from cooking the potatoes
1/4 c. Olive oil
2 T. Lemon juice or white vinegar

Mix well by hand or blend in a blender–according to your taste.
VARIATION: Use 4 tsp. of garlic powder instead of onions.
Add 1/2 to 1 cup of chopped ripe olives.

POTATO MAYONNAISE

1 c. Tofu Mayonnaise, Cashew Mayonnaise, or Miraculous Whip
1 c. Potato, baked and mashed

Mix well by hand or blend in a blender–according to your taste.

RUSSIAN DRESSING–1

1 c. Tofu Mayonnaise, Cashew Mayonnaise, Miraculous Whip, or Tofu Sour Cream or Cashew Sour Cream
2 T. Bell pepper, finely chopped
2 T. Celery, finely chopped
2 T. Black olives, finely chopped
1 T. Pimento, finely chopped
4 T. Tomato Relish

Mix well by hand or blend in a blender–according to your taste.

RUSSIAN DRESSING–2

1 c.	Tomatoes
2 T.	Olive oil
1 T.	Lemon juice or white vinegar
2 T.	Onions, minced fine
1/2 tsp.	Sea salt
1 tsp.	Paprika
1 tsp.	Garlic powder

Mix well by hand or blend in a blender–according to your taste.

"SOUR CREAM" DRESSING–1

1/2 c.	Tofu Sour Cream or Cashew Sour Cream
1/4 c.	Corn oil
1/2 c.	Wine vinegar
2 T.	Sucanat
1/2 tsp.	Sea salt
2 T.	Onions, minced

Mix well by hand or blend in a blender–according to your taste.

"SOUR CREAM" DRESSING–2

1 c.	Tofu Sour Cream or Cashew Sour Cream
1 T.	Pimento, chopped
1 T.	Bell pepper, chopped
1 T.	Parsley, chopped
2 T.	Lemon juice or white vinegar
2 T.	Chopped black olives
2 T.	Onions, minced
	Sea salt to taste

Mix well by hand or blend in a blender–according to your taste.

SWEET BASIL DRESSING

1 c.	Hot water
1/2 c.	Raw cashews
1/4 c.	Onions, chopped
1/2 tsp.	Sea salt
1 tsp.	Basil
2 T.	Lemon juice or white vinegar
1/4 c.	Black olives, minced

Mix well by hand or blend in a blender–according to your taste.

TAHINI DRESSING–1

3 T.	Tahini
3 T.	Chicken-like or Beef-like Broth, or low sodium soy sauce

Mix well by hand or blend in a blender–according to your taste.

TAHINI DRESSING–2

1/4 c.	Tahini
2 T.	Lemon juice or white vinegar
3 T.	Olive oil
1/4 c.	Beef-like Broth
1/8 tsp.	Sea salt
1 T.	Parsley, chopped

Mix well by hand or blend in a blender–according to your taste.

TAHINI DRESSING–3

1/4 c.	Celery, chopped as finely as possible
1/2 c.	Tahini
1 T.	Lemon juice or white vinegar
	Water, if needed, to thin the dressing

Mix well by hand or blend in a blender–according to your taste.

TAHINI DRESSING–4

1 tsp.	Garlic powder
1 c.	Tahini
3/4 c.	Water
1/4 c.	Lemon juice or white vinegar
1 tsp.	Sea salt

Mix well by hand or blend in a blender–according to your taste.

TAHINI DRESSING–5

1/2 c.	Tahini
2/3 c.	Water
1 T.	Low sodium soy sauce
1/4 tsp.	Garlic powder
1/3 tsp.	Paprika
1/8 tsp.	Basil
1/8 tsp.	Oregano
1 tsp.	Onion powder

Mix well by hand or blend in a blender–according to your taste.

TAHINI/OIL DRESSING

2 c.	Tahini or olive oil
1 tsp.	Sea salt
3 T.	Onions
1/4 c.	Black olives
1/8 tsp.	Cayenne pepper
2 T.	Bell pepper, chopped very fine
1 T.	Lemon juice or white vinegar

1/2 tsp. Basil
1/2 tsp. Oregano
1 1/2 c. Water

Mix well by hand or blend in a blender–according to your taste.

TAHINI SALAD DRESSING

1 c. Tahini
1 c. Water
1 tsp. Sea salt
2 T. Onion, chopped very fine
1/4 c. Lemon juice or white vinegar
1/4 tsp. Basil
1/4 tsp. Oregano

Mix well by hand or blend in a blender–according to your taste.

TARTAR DRESSING

1 c. Tofu Mayonnaise, Cashew Mayonnaise, Miraculous Whip, or Tofu Sour Cream or Cashew Sour Cream
2 T. Ripe olives, chopped very fine
1 T. Cucumber, chopped very fine
1 T. Pimento, chopped very fine
1 T. Bell pepper, chopped very fine
2 T. Onions, chopped very fine
1 T. Parsley, chopped very fine
1/4 tsp. Sea salt

Mix well by hand or blend in a blender–according to your taste.
VARIATIONS: Add 1 tablespoon of capers, chopped very fine. Add 2 tablespoons of lemon juice or white vinegar.

THOUSAND ISLAND DRESSING–1

3 c. Tofu Mayonnaise, Cashew Mayonnaise, Miraculous Whip, or Tofu Sour Cream or Cashew Sour Cream
1/2 c. Catsup or Tomato Relish (liquified)
1/4 c. Bell pepper, chopped fine
4 tsp. Pimento, chopped
2 T. Onions, minced
2 T. Bkack olives, minced

Mix well by hand or blend in a blender–according to your taste.

THOUSAND ISLAND DRESSING–2

1 c. French Dressing
2 T. Bell pepper, chopped
3 T. Pimento, chopped
2 T. Black olives, chopped
1/2 tsp. Low sodium soy sauce

Mix well by hand or blend in a blender–according to your taste.

THOUSAND ISLAND DRESSING–3

1 c. Tofu Mayonnaise, Cashew Mayonnaise, or Miraculous Whip
3 T. Catsup
1 T. Bell pepper, chopped
1 tsp. Pimento, chopped
1 tsp. Chives

Mix well by hand or blend in a blender–according to your taste.

TOFU MAYONNAISE-1

Adding the lemon in stages, and the oil as slowly as possible, is the secret of making good thick mayonnaise with this recipe.

1 c. Firm tofu
1 tsp. Dijon mustard
1/2 tsp. Sea salt
Pinch Paprika
1 T. &
1 1/2 tsp. Lemon juice or white vinegar
2 T. Corn oil

Put the tofu, mustard, salt, and paprika in a blender with 1 tablespoon of the lemon juice (or vinegar). Blend at high speed, stopping frequently to scrape down the sides of the jar, until all is well combined. Still blending, add the oil a few drops at a time, increasing to a steady stream, until about 1/3 of the oil is used. Slowly add another teaspoon of lemon juice while blending. Dribble in another 1/3 of the oil. Add the rest of the lemon juice in the same way as before. Continue adding the oil until it is gone.

TOFU MAYONNAISE-2

1 1/2 c. Firm tofu
2 T. Corn oil
1 T. Cider vinegar
2 T. Water
1 1/2 tsp. Prepared mustard
1/2 tsp. Garlic, minced
1/4 c. Onion, minced
1/4 tsp. White pepper
1 1/4 tsp. Sea salt
1 T. Lemon juice or white vinegar
1 T. Cashew nuts, ground fine

Put everything in a blender and blend until smooth. Refrigerate.

TOFU MAYONNAISE-3

1 1/2 c. Firm tofu
1/2 tsp. Garlic powder
1 tsp. Prepared mustard
1 1/2 T. Lemon juice or white vinegar

3 T.	Corn oil
1 tsp.	Sea salt
1/8 tsp.	White pepper

Put everything in a blender and blend until smooth. Refrigerate.

TOMATO DRESSING–1

1/2 c.	Tomato puree (or blend raw tomatoes well)
1 T.	Dill weed
2 T.	Onion, minced
2 tsp.	Bell pepper, minced
2 T.	Lemon juice or white vinegar
1/4 tsp.	Tarragon
1 T.	Low sodium soy sauce
1/2 tsp.	Basil
1/2 tsp.	Garlic powder

Mix well by hand or blend in a blender–according to your taste.

TOMATO DRESSING–2

2 qts.	Tomatoes, chopped
1 c.	Celery, chopped
1/2 c.	Bell pepper, chopped
1 c.	Onions, chopped
1/4 tsp.	Garlic powder
2 tsp.	Sea salt
1 c.	Lemon juice or white vinegar

Blend all ingredients. Use up in a few days.

TOMATO-CASHEW DRESSING

1/2 c.	Raw cashews
1/2 c.	Onions, chopped
1 tsp.	Garlic powder
1 tsp.	Celery salt
1 tsp.	Paprika
1 tsp.	Marjoram
2 c.	Tomato juice
2 T.	Olive oil
	Sea salt, if needed

Mix well by hand or blend in a blender–according to your taste.

TOMATO MAYONNAISE

1 c.	Tofu Mayonnaise, Cashew Mayonnaise, Miraculous Whip, Tofu Sour Cream, or Cashew Sour Cream
1/3 c.	Tomato juice or puree
1 tsp.	Onions, minced
1/8 tsp.	Garlic powder
1/2 tsp.	Sea salt

Salad Dressings

Mix well by hand or blend in a blender–according to your taste.

TOMATO FRENCH DRESSING

1 c.	French Dressing
1/2 c.	Tomato juice
OR	
2 or 3	Tomatoes, chopped

Mix well by hand or blend in a blender–according to your taste.

"VINAIGRETTE" DRESSING–1

2 1/2 T.	White vinegar or lemon juice
2 1/2 T.	Olive oil
1 T.	Parsley, chopped
1/2 tsp.	Sea salt

Mix well by hand or blend in a blender–according to your taste.

"VINAIGRETTE" DRESSING–2

2 T.	Olive oil
2 T.	White vinegar or lemon juice
1/4 c.	Beef-like Broth
1 tsp.	Basil
1 tsp.	Oregano
1/2 tsp.	Garlic powder

Mix well by hand or blend in a blender–according to your taste.

ZESTY FRENCH DRESSING

1	Garlic clove, crushed
1/4 tsp.	Sea salt
2 T.	Olive oil
1 T.	Lemon juice
1/4 c.	Wine vinegar
4 tsp.	Lea & Perrins Steak Sauce
1/2 tsp.	Louisiana Hot Sauce

Blend together in a blender.

SALADS

I have not given any recipes for fruit salad, simply because fruit looks, smells and tastes wonderful just as it is. To my way of thinking, the trouble of cutting it up and mixing it seems pointless. Also, since the fruits have such natural good taste and juiciness it seems a shame to mask them with some kind of dressing—whereas vegetables need a dressing since they are so dry.

Another big "absent" in most of these recipes is lettuce. We should indeed eat lettuce, but a lot of people (including me) consider a salad that is mostly lettuce just plain uninteresting. Therefore I have listed the non-lettuce ingredients only, and you can put in the amount of lettuce you like, or leave it out altogether. But when you do use lettuce, be sure it is not iceberg or "head" lettuce. That stuff is wet cellulose not worth the trouble, a waste of time for your stomach which deserves something real. Romaine lettuce is the staple, but other types are good, too.

Consider sometimes using cabbage instead of lettuce. Bok choy, "Chinese cabbage," is excellent, too.

Also, I have not listed lettuce so you can exercise the option of using the recipes to make salads with grains–an option well worth the trying. Instead of lettuce, mix the salad ingredients with rice, tabouli wheat, cracked wheat, barley or millet. Tabouli wheat need not be cooked, just soaked adequately, but cracked–or bulghur–wheat must be cooked (see section on Grains).

In case you prefer your grain in another form, put the salad in pocket bread. Any salad goes well stuffed in fresh pocket bread. Haters of lettuce salad often find they like it very much when eaten this way as a sandwich.

So you can use these recipes four ways: (1) just as given, (2) with lettuce, (3) with grains and (4) in pocket bread.

Except for potatoes, grains, and beans, all the vegetables listed in these recipes should be raw. Peas should be frozen first, as this makes them soft and easy to eat–as well as especially delicious. But be sure to drain them or put them on paper towels so they won't be wet and clammy. To get them at room temperature in a hurry, run tap water over them, then drain and dry them.

Corn, if not frozen, may need to be lightly steamed before using.

If you are not familiar with the different types of bean sprouts, start out using alfalfa sprouts.

When good avocadoes are not available, substitute mashed green peas.

Most of these salads should be served with a dressing from the Salad Dressings section. Those that have their own dressing or one recommended can be varied by substituting another dressing.

Salads

AVOCADO SALAD–1

2	Large avocados, diced
2	Large tomatoes, diced
1/4 c.	Bell pepper, chopped rather fine
1/4 c.	Onions, chopped fine
2 T.	Lemon juice
1 T.	Olive oil
1/2 tsp.	Sea salt

AVOCADO SALAD–2

2	Avocados, mashed
1/4 c.	Onions, chopped
1/4 c.	Parsley, chopped
1/2 tsp.	Sea salt
2 T.	Lemon juice
1 1/4 c.	Tofu Sour Cream or Cashew Sour Cream
1 tsp.	Low sodium soy sauce

BARBECUE BEAN SALAD

Mix together 1 part of Barbecue Beans and 2 parts of "Cottage Cheese" Salad-1.

BEAN SPROUT SALAD–1

1/2 c.	Celery, chopped fine
1/2 c.	Bell pepper, chopped
2 1/2 c.	Bean sprouts
1/4 c.	Onions, chopped
1/2 c.	Cucumber, chopped
2 c.	Tomatoes, chopped
2 c.	Garbanzos, cooked
1 c.	French dressing

BEAN SPROUT SALAD–2

2 c.	Bean sprouts
1 c.	Carrots, shredded
1 c.	Avocado, diced

CABBAGE AND LIMA BEAN SALAD

1	Small head of cabbage, shredded
1/2 c.	Radishes, sliced
1/2 c.	Parsley, finely chopped
1	10 oz. pkg. of frozen green lima beans, thawed
1/2 c.	Scallions, shallots or leeks
1/2 tsp.	Sea salt

CABBAGE SLAW–1

4 c.	Cabbage, shredded
1 1/2 c.	Carrots, shredded

1 c.	Bell pepper, chopped
1 c.	Celery, chopped
1/2 c.	Onions, chopped
1 1/2 c.	Tofu Sour Cream or Cashew Sour Cream
1 1/4 T.	Lemon juice
1/2 tsp.	Dill
1/2 tsp.	Sea salt

VARIATIONS: Slice tomatoes and put the slaw on top of the slices. Sprinkle with chopped ripe olives.

Add 3 cups of cooked beans to the slaw.

Add 1/2 tsp. Caraway seed.

CABBAGE SLAW-2

5 c.	Cabbage, shredded
1 c.	Carrots, shredded
1 c.	Tofu Mayonnaise, Cashew Mayonnaise, or Miraculous Whip
2 1/2 T.	Vinegar
1 T.	Prepared mustard
1 T.	Celery seed
1 tsp.	Sea salt

Combine cabbage and carrots. Blend the mayonnaise, vinegar mustard, celery seed, and salt, and mix with the cabbage and carrots. Let sit for an hour or so for flavors to blend.

VARIATION: For extra zest, add 1/2 to 1 teaspoon of Louisiana Hot Sauce.

CAJUN COLE SLAW

Fun on the bayou, I tell you!

1/2 c.	"Mayonnaise"
3 T.	Prepared mustard
2 T.	Olive oil
2 T.	Lea & Perrins Steak Sauce
1 tsp.	Louisiana Hot Sauce
2 T.	Catsup
2 tsp.	Sea salt
1 tsp.	Garlic salt
1 T.	Wine vinegar
2 T.	Lemon juice
1	Large head of cabbage, very finely shredded
4	Bell peppers, shredded fine
2	Medium onions, shredded very thin

Put the mayonnaise and mustard in a bowl. Beat together with a fork until combined. Slowly add the olive oil, beating all the time, until the mixture has returned to the thickness of the original mayonnaise. Still beating, add the steak sauce, then the hot sauce, then the catsup, then the salt and garlic salt, then the vinegar, and then the lemon juice. Place the cabbage, peppers, and onion in a large bowl, pour the sauce over all and toss well.

This should sit at least an hour before serving, and tastes even better the next day.

Salads

CHEF'S BEAN SALAD

5 c.	White beans
1/2 tsp.	Garlic, minced
1/2 c.	Italian dressing
1/4 c.	Onions, minced
1/2 c.	Celery, diced
1/2 c.	Dill pickles, diced
1/4 c.	"Mayonnaise"
1/2 c.	Pimento cheese
1 tsp.	Jalapeños, minced
4 tsp.	White vinegar.

Combine all and chill for several hours or overnight.

CORN SALAD-1

2 c.	Corn
1/2 c.	Bell pepper, chopped fine
1/3 c.	Onions, chopped
1 c.	Tomatoes, chopped fine

VARIATIONS: Add 1 to 2 cups of shredded cabbage. Omit the tomatoes and put the Mexican Tomato Dressing over it.

CORN SALAD-2

3 c.	Corn
1 1/2 c.	Tomatoes, chopped
1/4 c.	Onions, chopped
1/3 c.	Tofu Sour Cream or Cashew Sour Cream
1 T.	Lemon juice
1/2 tsp.	Sea salt
1/4 tsp.	Mustard seed
1/4 tsp.	Celery seed

CORN, RICE, AND BEAN SALAD

1 1/2 c.	Corn
1/2 c.	Dried beans, pressure cooked and drained
2 c.	Tomatoes, chopped
2 T.	Parsley, chopped
1/4 c.	Bell pepper, chopped
1 tsp.	Sea salt
1/2 c.	Tofu Sour Cream, Cashew Sour Cream, or "mayonnaise" of choice
1 1/2 tsp.	Lemon juice
2 T.	Olive oil
1/4 tsp.	Cayenne pepper
2 c.	Rice, cooked

Mix the corn, beans, tomatoes, parsley, bell pepper, and salt. Let this sit for 30 minutes at room temperature. Combine the mayonnaise or sour cream, lemon juice, olive oil, and pepper. On a serving plate, place the rice, then the corn-bean mixture, and spoon the dressing over all.

MEXICAN CORN SALAD

2 1/2 c.	Corn
1/2 c.	Pimento, chopped
1 c.	Onions, chopped
1/2 c.	Bell pepper, chopped
1 c.	Cucumber, chopped

MEXICAN BEAN AND CORN SALAD

1 c.	Corn
1 1/2 c.	Kidney or pinto beans, cooked and drained
2 c.	Lettuce, shredded
1/4 c.	Black olives, sliced or chopped
2 T.	Bell pepper, chopped fine
3 T.	Onions, minced
1/2 c.	Mexican Tomato Vinaigrette

"COTTAGE CHEESE" SALAD–1

9 c.	Tofu Cottage Cheese
6 c.	Tomatoes, chopped small
1/2 c.	Onions, chopped
1 c.	Black olives, chopped
1 c.	Bell pepper, finely chopped
1 T.	Jalapeños, minced
1/2 tsp.	Basil
1/8 tsp.	Dill weed
1 T.	Sea salt

"COTTAGE CHEESE" SALAD–2

2 c.	Tofu Cottage Cheese
1 c.	Tofu Sour Cream or Cashew Sour Cream
1 c.	Frozen mixed vegetables, steamed and cooled
1/3 c.	Onions, minced fine
1/2 tsp.	Jalapeños, minced fine
1/2 tsp.	Sea salt
1/4 tsp.	Dill or Basil

CUCUMBER SALAD–1

3 c.	Cucumbers, sliced about 1/8 inch thick
1 tsp.	Sea salt
2 tsp.	Lemon juice
1 c.	Tofu Sour Cream or Cashew Sour Cream
1/4 tsp.	Dill weed

CUCUMBER SALAD–2

4 c.	Cucumbers, thinly sliced
2 c.	Tomatoes, chopped
1/3 c.	Onions, chopped
1/4 c.	Fresh Basil (or 1 tsp. dried)

2 T.	Olive oil
1 T.	Lemon juice
1/4 tsp.	Sea salt

VARIATIONS: Substitute dill or parsley for the basil.
Add 1/4 or 1/2 cup of chopped ripe olives.

DRIED BEAN SALAD

2 c.	Dried beans (one type or more), cooked and drained
1/4 c.	Onions, chopped
2 T.	Lemon juice
2 T.	Olive oil
1/2 tsp.	Oregano
1/4 tsp.	Cumin
1/2 tsp.	Sea salt
2 T.	Parsley, minced
1/4 c.	Bell pepper
2 c.	Tomatoes, diced
1/2 c.	Cucumbers, peeled and diced

GARBANZO BEAN SALAD-1

2 T.	Olive oil
4 T.	Lemon juice
1/2 tsp.	Sea salt
1 c.	Garbanzo beans, cooked
2 T.	Parsley, chopped
1 c.	Celery, chopped
1/4 c.	Onions, chopped

GARBANZO BEAN SALAD-2

1 c.	Garbanzos, DRY
2 T.	Parsley, finely chopped
2 T.	Onions, chopped
1/8 tsp.	Garlic powder
1 T.	Lemon juice
2 T.	Olive oil
1/2 tsp.	Sea salt

Pressure cook and drain the beans. Combine everything.

GARBANZO AND CABBAGE SALAD

2 c.	Cabbage, shredded
1 c.	Garbanzos, cooked
3 T.	Onions, chopped
1/4 c.	Pimento, chopped
2 tsp.	Fresh basil, or 1/2 tsp. dried
1/2 tsp.	Sea salt
3 T.	Lemon juice
2 T.	Olive oil
1/4 c.	Tofu Sour Cream or Cashew Sour Cream

GARBANZO SALAD–1

1 c.	Garbanzos, pressure cooked and drained
2 T.	Onions, chopped
1 T.	Parsley, minced
2 tsp.	Lemon juice
4 tsp.	Olive oil
1/4 tsp.	Cumin, ground
1/2 tsp.	Sea salt

In a glass or enamel bowl combine the beans, onions, and parsley. In a separate bowl, whisk the lemon juice with the oil, cumin, and salt. Pour over the bean mixture.

GARBANZO SALAD–2

1 c.	Garbanzos, cooked and drained
1 T.	Green onions (not the tops)
1/4 tsp.	Cumin, ground
1 T.	Parsley, minced
2 tsp.	Lemon juice
4 tsp.	Olive oil
1/2 tsp.	Sea salt

In a glass or enamel bowl combine the beans, onions, cumin seeds and parsley. In a separate bowl, whisk the lemon juice with the oil and salt. Pour over the bean mixture.

GARBANZO-TOMATO SALAD

2 T.	Olive oil
2 T.	Lemon juice
1 tsp.	Sea salt
1/2 tsp.	Oregano
1 c.	Garbanzos, cooked
2 c.	Tomatoes, chopped
3/4 c.	Bell pepper, chopped
12	Ripe olives, sliced
3/4 c.	Onions, chopped
1/4 c.	Parsley, chopped

GAZPACHO SALAD

1 c.	Bell peppers, chopped
4 c.	Tomatoes, chopped
2 c.	Cucumbers, chopped
1/3 c.	Onions, chopped
1/2 tsp.	Sea salt

Dressing:	3 T.	Olive oil
	2 T.	Lemon juice
	2 T.	Chopped parsley
	1/4 tsp.	Garlic powder

VARIATION: Add 3 cups of mashed avocado to the dressing and mix thoroughly.

GREEN PEA SALAD–1

2	10-oz. packages of frozen peas, thawed
1 1/2 c.	Medium tomatoes, coarsely chopped
1 c.	Tofu Mayonnaise, Cashew Mayonnaise, Miraculous Whip, Tofu Sour Cream, or Cashew Sour Cream
1/3 c.	Onions, chopped
1 1/2 T.	Lemon juice
1 tsp.	Sea salt

GREEN PEA SALAD–2

2	10 oz. pkgs. of frozen green peas, thawed.
1 c.	Celery, thinly sliced
1/2 tsp.	Dill weed (dried)
1/3 c.	French or Italian Dressing

GREEN VEGETABLE SALAD

1 c.	Peas
1 c.	Lima beans, cooked
1 c.	Celery, chopped
1/2 c.	Bell pepper, chopped
1/2 c.	Onions, finely chopped

I doubt that guacamole is really holy–but every one of these certainly is heavenly!

GUACAMOLE–1

2	Large, ripe avocados, peeled, seeded and mashed
1/4 c.	Onions
1/2 c.	Tomatoes, chopped
1/2 tsp.	Sea salt
1/8 tsp.	Pepper
2 1/2 tsp.	Lemon juice

GUACAMOLE–2

3	Avocados, mashed
1/3 c.	Tofu Mayonnaise, Cashew Mayonnaise, Miraculous Whip, Tofu Sour Cream, or Cashew Sour Cream
1 tsp.	Sea salt
1/4 tsp.	Garlic powder
2 T.	Lemon juice
1	Tomato, chopped
1/4 c.	Onions, chopped
1/3 c.	Celery, sliced
1/2 c.	Bell pepper, chopped

GUACAMOLE–3

2	Avocados, mashed
1/4 c.	Tofu Mayonnaise, Cashew Mayonnaise, Miraculous Whip, Tofu Sour Cream, or Cashew Sour Cream

2 T.	Onions, chopped
1/2 tsp.	Sea salt
1/2 tsp.	Garlic powder
4 tsp.	Lemon juice
2	Tomatoes, chopped

GUACAMOLE–4

4	Avocados, mashed
1/2 tsp.	Sea salt
2 T.	Lemon or lime juice
1/2 tsp.	Low sodium soy sauce
1 tsp.	Garlic powder

GUACAMOLE–5

2	Large ripe avocados, mashed to a puree
1 T.	Onions, finely chopped
1/2 c.	Tomatoes, chopped
1/2 tsp.	Sea salt
1/8 tsp.	Black pepper (freshly ground is best)
2 tsp.	Lemon juice
3 T.	Salsa or Taco Sauce

KIDNEY BEAN SALAD–1

This is almost a meal in itself, and is excellent in pocket bread.

2 1/2 c.	Kidney beans, dry
1/4 c.	Apple cider vinegar or lemon juice
3 T.	Olive oil
1 T.	Sea salt
1/2 tsp.	Dry mustard
1/4 tsp.	Black pepper
1/8 tsp.	Cayenne pepper
1/4 tsp.	Dill weed
3/4 c.	Onions, chopped
2 c.	Cucumbers, chopped
2 c.	Tomatoes, chopped
1/2 c.	Celery, chopped
1/2 c.	Bell pepper, chopped

Pressure cook the beans and drain them. Blend the vinegar (or lemon juice), oil and spices. Mix all ingredients. Serve cold.

VARIATIONS: Use some other type of beans other than kidney.

Use mayonnaise instead of vinegar (or lemon juice) and olive oil.

Add 1 cup of cooked lentils.

KIDNEY BEAN SALAD–2

1 c.	Kidney beans, dry
1	Lemon–juiced and the peel grated
1 T.	Corn or olive oil
1/4 tsp.	Sage

3 T.	Parsley, chopped
1/2 tsp.	Sea salt
1/4 tsp.	Cayenne pepper

Pressure cook the beans. Combine everything, cover, and marinate for several hours.

LENTIL SALAD-1

3 c.	Lentils, pressure cooked and chilled
3 T.	Onions, chopped
1 c.	Tomatoes, chopped
1/4 c.	Bell pepper, chopped
1/2 c.	Peas
2 T.	Lemon juice
1/2 c.	Tofu Mayonnaise, Cashew Mayonnaise, Miraculous Whip, Tofu Sour Cream, or Cashew Sour Cream
1/4 tsp.	Celery seed
1/4 tsp.	Sesame seed
1/4 tsp.	Sea salt
1/4 tsp.	Garlic powder
1/4 tsp.	Marjoram
1/4 tsp.	Basil

LENTIL SALAD-2

2 c.	Lentils, pressure cooked
1/2 c.	French Dressing
1/4 c.	Bell pepper, chopped
3/4 c.	Onions, chopped
1/2 c.	Celery, chopped
2 T.	Parsley, chopped

LENTIL SALAD-3

2 c.	Lentils, cooked and chilled
1/4 c.	Onions, chopped
1 c.	Carrots, grated
1/2 c.	Radishes, chopped

Dressing:	1 T.	Lemon juice
	2 T.	Olive oil
	1 tsp.	Sea salt
	1/8 tsp.	Garlic powder

LIMA BEAN SALAD-1

2 c.	Green lima beans, cooked, drained, and cooled
1 c.	Celery, chopped
2 c.	Frozen green peas, thawed
1/4 c.	Onions, chopped

Good with Potato Dressing-1.
VARIATION: Add 1 cup of chopped tomatoes and 1/2 cup of chopped bell pepper. Add 2 cups of corn.

LIMA BEAN SALAD–2

2	Pkgs. of frozen Lima beans, cooked, drained, and cooled
1 T.	Lemon juice
1/4 tsp.	Garlic powder
2 T.	Olive oil
2 T.	Parsley
1/2 tsp.	Sea salt
1 c.	Tofu Sour Cream or Cashew Sour Cream

VARIATION: Add 1/2 cup of chopped celery.
Add 1/2 cup of chopped bell pepper.

LIMA BEAN AND GARBANZO SALAD

1 1/2 c.	Cooked garbanzos
1 1/2 c.	Cooked lima beans
1/4 c.	Onions, chopped
1/4 c.	Pimento, chopped

LIMA BEAN GAZPACHO SALAD

2 c.	Cooked lima beans, fresh, frozen, or dried (cooked)
2 c.	Tomatoes, chopped
1/2 c.	Cucumber, chopped
1/2 c.	Bell pepper, chopped
1/2 c.	Celery, chopped
1/2 c.	Onions, chopped
1/2 tsp.	Garlic powder
1/2 tsp.	Oregano
1/2 tsp.	Basil
1/8 tsp.	Cumin
2 c.	French or Italian Dressing

MACARONI AND "CHEESE" SALAD

2 c.	Macaroni, cooked and drained
1 1/2 c.	Peas, cooked and drained
2 c.	Yeast or pimento cheese
1/2 c.	Black olives, chopped
1/2 c.	Tofu Mayonnaise, Cashew Mayonnaise, Miraculous Whip, Tofu Sour Cream, or Cashew Sour Cream
2 T.	Onions, chopped
1/2 tsp.	Sea salt

MIXED VEGETABLE SALAD–1

3/4 c.	Carrots, grated
3/4 c.	Cauliflower, chopped
1 c.	Peas
1/4 c.	Ripe olives, sliced

MIXED VEGETABLE SALAD–2

2 c. Potatoes, cooked and cubed
2 c. Peas
2 c. Corn
2 c. Lima beans
2 c. Carrots, cubed
1/2 c. Sunflower seeds

VARIATION: Add 2 or 3 cups of chopped tomatoes.

PASTA SALAD VINAIGRETTE

2 c. Vermicelli, cooked and chilled
2 c. Black olives, sliced
2 T. Olive oil
4 tsp. Wine vinegar
1 T. Lemon juice
1 tsp. Sea salt
2 tsp. Sucanat
1 tsp. Dill weed
1/2 c. Peas
1/2 c. Bell pepper, cut in strips
Lettuce or spinach

Toss together all the ingredients except the peas, bell pepper and greens. Let it marinate for 20 minutes in the refrigerator. Mix in the peas and bell pepper. Serve on the lettuce or spinach.

PEA AND POTATO SALAD

2 c. Peas
3 c. Potatoes, cubed and cooked
1/4 c. Onions, chopped
3/4 tsp. Sea salt
1 T. Parsley
1/3 c. Ripe olives, sliced or chopped
2 T. Olive oil
2 tsp. Lemon juice

PECOS BEAN SALAD

2 c. Dried beans, pressure cooked
1/3 c. Onions, chopped
1/4 tsp. Garlic powder
1/2 c. Bell pepper, chopped
2 T. Olive oil
1 T. Lemon juice
1/2 tsp. Oregano
1/2 tsp. Basil
1 tsp. Sea salt

PIQUANT CAULIFLOWER

2 c. Cauliflower flowerets

3 T.	Corn oil
3 T.	White vinegar
1/3 c.	Tomatoes, chopped
1 T. & 1 tsp.	Pimento, chopped
2 tsp.	Green olives, chopped
1 T.	Dill pickle, chopped
1 tsp.	Sucanat
1 tsp.	Sea salt
1 tsp.	Paprika
1/8 tsp.	Cayenne

Separate the cauliflower into flowerets and cook in boiling water until tender–about 10 minutes. Combine the rest of the ingredients and pour over the cauliflower. Chill 2 to 3 hours, stirring occasionally. At serving time drain off the excess liquid.

PINK BEANS AND RED CABBAGE SALAD

3 c.	Pink or pinto beans, cooked
1 c.	Celery, grated
1 c.	Radishes, grated
1 c.	Cucumber, grated
2 c.	Red cabbage, shredded
1/4 c.	Onions, chopped fine

POTATO SALAD–1

6 c.	Potatoes, cooked and cubed
1 c.	Cucumber, chopped
1/2 c.	Celery, finely diced
3/4 c.	Onions, chopped
1/2 c.	Bell pepper, finely chopped
1/4 c.	Chopped black olives
2-3 T.	Chopped fresh parsley or dill, or some of both
1 tsp.	Sea salt

Good with either Tofu Sour Cream, Cashew Sour Cream or French Dressing.
VARIATION: Add 1/2 head of cabbage.

POTATO SALAD–2

4 c.	Potatoes, boiled and sliced
1 c.	Celery, chopped
1/2 c.	Onions, chopped
1 T.	Pimento, chopped
2 T.	Parsley, chopped
1 tsp.	Sea salt
	Caper French Dressing

POTATO SALAD–3

8 c.	Potatoes, cooked and cubed
6 T.	Parsley, chopped fine
1/2 c.	Bell pepper, chopped fine

1/3 c.	Black olives, chopped fine
1/4 c.	Pimentos, chopped fine
3 T.	Onions, chopped fine
1/4 tsp.	Cayenne pepper
3 c.	Tofu Sour Cream or Cashew Sour Cream
2 T.	Corn oil
1 T.	Wine vinegar
1 1/2 tsp.	Sea salt

VARIATION: Use French Dressing, Tofu Mayonnaise, Cashew Mayonnaise, or Miraculous Whip instead of "sour cream."

AUSTRIAN POTATO SALAD

2 c.	Potatoes, cooked, sliced and chilled
1/3 c.	Onions, minced
1/2 tsp.	Garlic, minced
1/2 tsp.	Sea salt
1/4 tsp.	Cayenne or black pepper
1 T.	Parsley, minced
1 T.	Olive oil
4 tsp.	Tarragon vinegar
1/2 tsp.	Prepared mustard

Combine the potatoes in a bowl with the onion, garlic, salt, pepper, and parsley. Bring the oil, vinegar, and mustard to a boil and pour over the salad. Mix and serve cold.

CAJUN POTATO SALAD

A real zinger!
It is best to make this a day ahead of time so the flavor will develop.

10 c.	Potatoes
1 1/2 c.	"Mayonnaise" of choice
1/4 c.	Prepared yellow mustard (the "American" type)
2 1/2 tsp.	Sea salt
1/4 c.	Louisiana Hot Sauce
1 c.	Dill relish
1/2 c.	Sweet relish
1 c.	Green olives, chopped
1 c.	Onions, chopped fine
1/2 c.	Celery, chopped fine
1/2 c.	Parsley, chopped fine

Boil the potatoes in their skins, cool them, peel them, and chop them in large chunks. Mix the mayonnaise, mustard, salt, and hot sauce. Add this to the potatoes along with the rest of the ingredients and mix well.

FRENCH POTATO SALAD

4 c.	Potatoes, cooked and diced
1/2 c.	Onions, chopped
1 c.	French Dressing
4 T.	Parsley

1/2 tsp. Sea salt
1/2 tsp. Paprika

Combine, cover, and chill–except for the parsley. Just before serving, stir in the parsley.

GERMAN POTATO SALAD

1/2 c. Onions, chopped
3 T. Corn oil
2 T. Unbleached white flour
1 tsp. Celery seed
2 T. Sucanat
1 1/2 tsp. Sea salt
1/2 c. Wine vinegar
1 c. Water
6 c. Potatoes, cooked and sliced
1/4 c. Bacon Gluten, chopped fine, or imitation bacon bits
1/2 tsp. Paprika
1/4 c. Canned pimento, diced
1 T. Fresh parsley, chopped

Sauté the onions in the oil until tender. Blend in the flour, celery seed, Sucanat, and salt. Add the vinegar and water. Cook and stir until thickened and bubbly. Add the potatoes and gluten and heat thoroughly, tossing lightly. Garnish with paprika, pimento and parsley.

PARSLEYED POTATO SALAD

4 c. Potatoes, cooked and diced
1/4 c. Celery, chopped
1/4 c. Parsley, chopped
1/4 c. Bell pepper, chopped
1/2 c. Onions, chopped
1/4 c. Dill pickle, chopped
1 3/4 c. Soy mayonnaise
3/4 c. French Dressing–1
2 tsp. Prepared mustard
1 1/2 tsp. Sea salt

RICE SALAD

Basic, but never dull!

2 c. Rice, cooked
1 tsp. Sea salt
2 T. Olive oil
1 1/2 T. Lemon juice
1/4 c. Parsley, chopped
1/3 c. Onions, chopped
1 c. Tomatoes, chopped
1 c. Total of one or more the following (singly or in combination):
  Lima beans, cooked
  Dried beans, cooked
  Thin carrot slices
  Peas

Corn
Celery, diced
Cucumber, diced
Bell pepper, chopped
Cabbage, shredded
Green beans, cooked
Radishes, sliced or chopped
Bean sprouts
"Greens" of any type, chopped

Combine everying. If it seems too dry, add more oil and lemon. Let stand to develop flavor.
VARIATION: Cook the rice in a Flavoring Broth.

RICE AND AVOCADO SALAD

1 c.	Avocado, mashed
1/2 tsp.	Garlic, crushed
1 tsp.	Sea salt
4 1/2 tsp.	Olive oil
2 tsp.	Lemon juice
2 tsp.	Wine vinegar
2 tsp.	Louisiana Hot Sauce
4 tsp.	Lea & Perrins Steak Sauce
1 T.	Poupon mustard
1/2 c.	Parsley, chopped
1 c.	Tomatoes, chopped
3 c.	Rice, cooked and chilled

RICE AND BEAN SALAD

1/2 c.	Onions, chopped
1/2 c.	Cucumber, chopped
1/2 c.	Bell pepper, chopped
1/2 c.	Black olives, halved
1 1/2 c.	Beans, cooked
2 1/2 c.	Rice, cooked
1/2 tsp.	Sea salt
2 T.	Lemon juice
3 T.	Olive oil

RICE SALAD ESPECIAL

1 1/2 c.	Rice, uncooked
1 c.	Black olives, chopped
2 T.	Olive oil
1/4 c.	Pimentos
1 c.	Tomatoes, chopped
2 T.	Wine vinegar
1/2 tsp.	Oregano
1/2 tsp.	Marjoram

Cook the rice. Add the remaining ingredients, mixing well. Chill at least 2 hours.

RICE SALAD SOUTHERN STYLE

Even Yankees will like this!

2 c.	Rice, uncooked
1 c.	Green onions, chopped
1 c.	Dill pickles, chopped
1 c.	Sweet pickles
1 c.	Celery, chopped
1 c.	Bell pepper, chopped
1 c.	Green olives, stuffed with pimentos, chopped
1 1/4 c.	Tofu Mayonnaise, Cashew Mayonnaise, or Miraculous Whip
3 T.	Prepared mustard
1/4 tsp.	Cayenne pepper
1 T.	Olive oil
2 tsp.	Wine vinegar

Cook the rice, cool, and then combine with the vegetables. Combine the mayonnaise, mustard, pepper, oil, and vinegar. Mix well with the rice mixture. Refrigerate.

RICE SALAD WITH BLACKEYE PEAS

5 c.	Blackeye peas, cooked
3 T.	Olive oil
1/8 c.	Lemon juice
1 tsp.	Sea salt
3 c.	Rice, cooked
1/2 c.	Onions, finely chopped
3/4 c.	Celery, chopped
3/4 c.	Carrot, grated
1/2 c.	Bell pepper, chopped
1/3 c.	Pimento, chopped

SALAD NICOISE

Outstanding!

2 T.	Lemon juice
1 tsp.	Garlic, crushed
2 T.	Olive oil
1/2 tsp.	Sea salt
1 tsp.	Chives, minced
2 c.	Potatoes, cooked and sliced
1 c.	Tomatoes, chopped
3/4 c.	Onions, chopped
3/4 c.	Celery, chopped
1/2 c.	Bell pepper, chopped
1/4 c.	Black olives, chopped or sliced
4 c.	Romaine lettuce, chopped.

Blend the lemon juice, garlic, oil, and salt. Toss with all the ingredients except the lettuce. Just before serving, mix in the lettuce.

VARIATION: Add 1 cup of cooked white or northern beans.

Salads

SUNSHINE SALAD

2 c.	Garbanzos, cooked
2 c.	Corn
1 c.	Celery, diced
1/4 c.	Onions, chopped
1/4 c.	Bell pepper, chopped
3 T.	Pimento, diced

TABOULI SALAD

Put this in pocket bread and you have magic!

3 c.	Tabouli wheat (this is not cracked wheat–see Grains section)
1/2 c.	Lemon juice
1/4 c.	Olive oil
2 c.	Cucumbers, diced small
1/2 c.	Bell pepper, minced
1/4 c.	Parsley, chopped fine
4 c.	Tomatoes, diced
1 c.	Onions, chopped fine
1/2 tsp.	Cayenne pepper
2 tsp.	Sea salt

Place the cracked wheat in a bowl and cover with water. Let it soak for 15 minutes, then drain. Add the lemon juice to the wheat and combine all the ingredients and mix well.

THREE-BEAN SALAD–1

1 c.	Lima beans or green beans, cooked
1 c.	Kidney or pinto beans, pressure cooked, drained, and cooled
1 c.	Garbanzos or white beans, pressure cooked, drained, and cooled
1/3 c.	Onions, chopped
1/2 tsp.	Jalapeños, minced
2 T.	Lemon juice
2 T.	Olive oil
1/4 tsp.	Sea salt

Combine the beans, onions, and jalapeños. Blend the lemon juice, oil, and salt. Pour over the beans and let them marinate at room temperature for 30 minutes.

THREE-BEAN SALAD–2

2 c.	Garbanzo beans, cooked
1 c.	Kidney beans, cooked
1 c.	Lima beans or Green beans, cooked
1/4 c.	Bell pepper, chopped
1/2 c.	Celery, chopped
1/2 c.	Black olives, chopped
3/4 c.	Onions, chopped
2 T.	Olive oil
3 T.	Lemon juice
1 tsp.	Sea salt
1 tsp.	Celery seed

1 tsp.	Lemon peel, grated
1 tsp.	Mustard seed
1 tsp.	Garlic powder
1 tsp.	Dill seeds

TOMATO SALAD

As a lover of tomatoes this is my favorite!

4 c.	Tomatoes, diced
1 1/2 c.	Bell peppers, chopped
3/4 c.	Onions, chopped
2 T.	Olive oil
2 T.	Lemon juice
2 T.	Red wine vinegar
4 tsp.	Basil, fresh and chopped (1 tsp. if dried)
1 c.	Cucumber, thinly sliced
1 1/2 tsp.	Sea salt
1/4 tsp.	Pepper
1 tsp.	Paprika
1/2 tsp.	Celery seed

Put tomatoes, bell pepper, and onion into a bowl. Add the olive oil and toss to coat evenly. Add the remaining ingredients and toss well. Refrigerate 30 minutes before serving.

TOMATO AND BEAN SALAD

2 T.	Olive oil
4 1/2 tsp.	Lemon juice
1 tsp.	Sea salt
1/2 tsp.	Oregano
1 c.	Dried beans, cooked
1 1/2 c.	Tomatoes, chopped
3/4 c.	Bell pepper, chopped
12	Black olives, sliced
3 T.	Onions, chopped
2 T.	Parsley, chopped

TOMATO SLAW

2 c.	Cabbage, shredded
1 c.	Tomatoes, diced
1/4 c.	Bell pepper, chopped
1/4 c.	Cucumber, chopped
1 tsp.	Sea salt

TOSSED SALAD

2	Tomatoes, chopped
1	Bell pepper, chopped
1	Carrot, chopped
1	Celery stalk, chopped
1	Cucumber, chopped
1	Head of Romaine lettuce

VARIATION: Put in whatever you please. Experiment!

WHITE BEAN SALAD

5 c.	White beans, pressure cooked and cooled
3/4 c.	Italian Dressing
1/2 c.	Onions, chopped
1/2 c.	Bell pepper, chopped
1/4 c.	Parsley, chopped
1/4 c.	Tofu Sour Cream, Cashew Sour Cream, Tofu Mayonnaise, Cashew Mayonnaise, or Miraculous Whip
1 tsp.	Sea salt
1/2 tsp.	Louisiana Hot Sauce

VARIATION: Add 4 cups of Pimento Cheese.

The monks eating in the Monastery library.

Bread and Such

ANADAMA BREAD

You might as well know–I did not like bread. Then one day I tried this. Revelation! It was so good that we began baking and selling it in stores and from that came a successful bakery which we operated for several years.

1/2 c. Corn meal
3 T. Corn oil
1/4 c. Barbados molasses
2 tsp. Sea salt
3/4 c. Boiling water
1 pkg. Yeast
1/4 c. Warm water
3 c. Flour

Combine the corn meal, oil, molasses, salt and boiling water. Let stand until lukewarm. Sprinkle yeast over the 1/4 cup of warm water to dissolve. Stir yeast and half of the flour into the corn meal mix. Beat. Stir in remaining flour. Knead until smooth and elastic (about 10 minutes). Transfer to a greased loaf pan, cover with a cloth, and set in a warm place until dough is 1 inch above the top of the pan. Sprinkle with a little corn meal and salt, if desired. Bake at 350° for 50 to 60 minutes.

APPLE AND BANANA BREAD

1 Apple, chopped and steamed until tender, then puréed in a blender or food processor
4 c. Unbleached white flour
2 1/2 tsp. Dried yeast
1/2 c. Warm water
1 c. Sucanat
1 tsp. Sea salt
1 tsp. Ground cinnamon
1 tsp. Ground nutmeg
1/3 c. Golden seedless raisins, soaked in apple juice
2 Bananas, mashed
1/8 tsp. Grated lemon peel

Chop and steam the apple until tender. Press through a sieve to make a puree and let cool. Mix together 1 cup of flour, yeast, and warm water until smooth. Leave in a warm place until frothy. Combine remaining flour, Sucanat, salt, spices, and raisins in a bowl. Stir in yeast mixture, apple puree, mashed banana, and lemon rind and beat well. Divide the mixture between 2 greased loaf pans. Let rise in a warm place until mixture reaches top of pans. Bake at 375° for about 35 minutes.

APPLE ICING BREAD

3/4 c.	Warm water
2 1/2 tsp.	Sucanat
1 T.	Yeast
1 tsp.	Sea salt
1 T.	Corn oil
2 1/2 c.	Unbleached white flour
6 c.	Applesauce, slightly warm
1/4 c.	Unsweetened coconut

Mix the water, Sucanat, and yeast together and let it sit for 10 to 15 minutes. Then add in the rest of the ingredients and squeeze between your fingers until all is mixed and the dough begins to stop sticking to your fingers. (You may need to add more flour, but do not be too quick to do so.) Turn onto an oiled board and knead well. Roll the dough out 1/2" thick. Place in a large, flat baking pan, lining it, including the sides. Prick the dough with a fork. Pour in the warm applesauce. Sprinkle with the coconut. Cover with a flat pan or kneading board. Let rise until the dough is double in thickness. Bake 1 1/4 hours at 350°. Leave in the pan for one or more days. Heat before serving. Slice as a pie.

BAKING POWDER BISCUITS

4 c.	Unbleached white flour
2 T.	Baking Powder
1 tsp.	Sea salt
1 c.	Corn oil
1 1/2 c.	Water

Sift the dry ingredients into a bowl. Cut in the oil until the whole thing is like coarse crumbs. Make a depression in the mass and put in the water all at once. Stir quickly with a fork just until the dough follows the fork around the bowl. *Do not overmix!* The dough should be soft. Turn onto a lightly floured surface. Knead gently 10 to 12 strokes. Roll or pat the dough into a 1/2 inch thickness. Dip the cutter in flour and cut the dough straight down–no twisting! Bake on an ungreased baking sheet at 450° for 12 to 15 minutes.

BISCUIT DUMPLINGS

2 1/4 c.	Biscuit Mix (see below)
2/3 c.	Cashew milk or water

Mix into a soft dough. Drop by spoonfuls into boiling liquid. Cook uncovered over low heat for 10 minutes. Cover and cook 10 minutes more.

BISCUIT MIX

6 c.	Unbleached white flour
3 T.	Baking powder
3 T.	Sucanat
1 T.	Sea salt

1 c. Non-dairy margarine

In a large mixing bowl combine thoroughly the dry ingredients. Sift it all together 6 to 8 times. Work in the margarine with your fingers until the mixture is the consistency of very fine gravel. Store in a tightly covered container at room temperature for up to 4 months. Tape 2 or 3 whole bay leaves to the inside of the lid to keep away any bugs.

BISCUITS

2 c. Unbleached white flour
1 T. Baking Powder
1/2 tsp. Sea salt
1/4 c. Corn oil
3/4 c. Cashew Milk

Sift the dry ingredients into a bowl. Cut in the oil until the mixture is like coarse crumbs. Make a well in the mixture and add the cashew milk all at once. Stir quickly with a fork just till dough follows the fork around the bowl. Turn onto a lightly floured surface. (The dough should be soft.) Knead gently 10 to 12 strokes. Roll or pat the dough 1/2 inch thick. Dip a cutter in flour and cut the dough straight down–no twisting. Bake on an *un*greased baking sheet at 450° for 12 to 15 minutes.

BREADSTICKS

A satisfying change from ordinary bread or crackers. Also a great crunchy snack when you want that little something that is also good for you!

2 T. Yeast
1 c. Warm water
1 tsp. Sucanat
1/4 c. Corn oil
3 c. Unbleached white flour
1/2 tsp. Garlic powder
1 1/2 tsp. Sea salt
1/4 c. Nutritional Yeast
1/2 c. Onions, minced fine

Mix the yeast, water and Sucanat. Let stand in a warm place for 10-15 minutes until risen and foamy. Whisk in the oil. In another bowl sift together the flour, garlic powder, salt, and nutritional yeast, and mix well. Add this, in small amounts at a time, with a whisk, to the yeast mixture, alternating with pieces of chopped onion. Continue to mix it with a spoon till it is smooth. Knead it for a while, just until it is a nice soft ball. Roll it out to about pencil thickness, and cut in strips with a pizza cutter. Put strips in lightly oiled baking pans with some space between. Let stand in a warm place until they rise. Bake in a 400° oven for about 10 to 15 minutes, or until golden brown on both sides, turning them over once.

FOR HARD BREADSTICKS: Put breadsticks in a warm oven overnight or in a 200° oven for 2 to 3 hours, or until hard.

"BUTTERED" BREAD CRUMBS

Sauté 1 cup of bread crumbs in 1/3 cup of non-dairy margarine. You may add minced onions, if you like.

"CHEESE" BREAD

Make the recipe for White Bread, except put in 1 cup of Nutritional Yeast.

CORN BREAD–1

All as for White Bread, except for these ingredients:

4 c.	White flour
1 3/4 c.	Corn flour
2 3/4 c.	Water

The kneading time must be 15 minutes.

CORN BREAD–2

2 c.	Corn meal
2 c.	Unbleached white flour
5 tsp.	Baking powder
1 1/2 tsp.	Sea salt
2 T.	Sucanat
2 3/4 c.	Water
1/3 c.	Corn oil

Mix all dry ingredients, then add all liquid ingredients and mix. Pour into greased and floured pan. Bake at 425° for about 45 minutes or until top is browned.

VARIATION: For crispy corn bread, add water until a thin batter is formed, pour out until batter covers the bottom of the pan or cookie sheet, and then bake.

CORN BREAD–3

1/2 c.	Onions, chopped fine
1 1/4 c.	Unbleached white flour
3/4 c.	Cornmeal
2 T.	Sucanat
1 T.	Baking powder
1 tsp.	Sea salt
1 T.	Nutritional yeast
3 T.	Non-dairy margarine
1 c.	Cashew Milk
1/2 c.	Bacon Gluten, chopped fine

Sauté the onion in as little corn oil as possible. Mix the flour, cornmeal, Sucanat, baking powder, salt, and yeast together. Melt the margarine and add the cashew milk to it. Stir that into the dry ingredients. Add the onions and gluten.

CORN CHIPS

The commercial cardboards just cannot equal these!

1/2 c.	Cashew Milk or water
3 T.	Corn oil
1/2 c.	Yellow cornmeal
1/2 c.	Toasted cornmeal

1/2 c.	Unbleached white flour
3/4 tsp.	Sea salt
1/4 tsp.	Baking soda
1/8 tsp.	Cayenne pepper
1/2 tsp.	Chili powder
1/4 tsp.	Onion powder

Combine the cashew milk and oil. Stir the dry ingredients together in a mixing bowl. Add the cashew milk mixture and stir until the dough forms a ball. Knead on a floured board (adding a little more flour if necessary) about 5 minutes. Divide the dough in half. Roll each half into a 12-inch square. Cut into 1-inch squares. Sprinkle with salt or paprika. Bake on a lightly oiled baking sheet for 15 minutes or until lightly brown around the edges. Cool slightly before removing from the baking sheet, and transfer to a wire rack.

CORN TORTILLAS

3 c.	Unbleached white flour
3 c.	Corn *flour* (not meal)
1 tsp.	Sea salt
1 tsp.	Baking powder
1/4 c.	Corn oil or non-dairy margarine, melted
1 3/4 c.	Warm water

Mix the flours, salt and baking powder. Make a depression and put in the oil (or margarine). Mix with a spoon. Add 1/2 cup of warm water and mix again. Add about 3/4 cup more warm water, or enough to knead it into bread dough consistency. Let it rest for about 5 minutes. Form into balls about 1 1/2 inches in diameter and dip each ball into flour before rolling it out on a lightly floured board. Cook on a hot, dry griddle until bubbly and brown-flecked on each side. (This will not take long–only a few seconds on a really hot griddle.)

VARIATION: For deep-fried tortillas, omit the baking powder.

CRANBERRY BREAD

This makes a special gift, but bake some for yourself, too!

2 c.	Unbleached white flour, sifted
1 tsp.	Sea salt
1/2 tsp.	Baking soda
1 1/2 tsp.	Baking powder
1 c.	Sucanat
1/4 c.	Corn oil
1	N'egg
3/4 c.	Orange juice
1 T.	Grated orange rind (optional)
1/2 c.	Chopped nuts
1 c.	Chopped cranberries

Sift together the dry ingredients. Cut in the oil. Pour the n'egg, orange juice, and grated rind all at once into the dry ingredients, mixing just enough to dampen. Carefully fold in the nuts and cranberries. Spoon into a greased loaf pan. Spread the corners and sides slightly higher than the center. Bake at 350° about 1 hour.

DROP BISCUITS

2 1/4 c. Biscuit Mix
2/3 c. Cashew Milk or water

Mix into a dough and beat for 30 seconds. Drop by spoonfuls onto an ungreased baking sheet. Bake at 450° 8 to 10 minutes until golden brown.

FLAT BREAD

This doesn't look like much on the page, but it is excellent! We much prefer this to chapattis or puris when eating Indian food.

1 c. Rye flour
2 c. Unbleached white flour
2/3 c. Soy flour
1/3 c. Wheat bran
1 tsp. Sea salt
1/4 c. Corn oil
1 1/4 c. Boiling water

Mix the flours, bran, and salt in a bowl. Add the oil. Stir in only enough of the boiling water to make a stiff dough. Knead to mix thoroughly. Roll out small pieces of dough paper-thin to about 8 inches in diameter. Bake directly on top of an ungreased griddle, or place on an ungreased cookie sheet in an oven set at 250° until thoroughly dried and slightly browned.

FLOUR TORTILLAS

6 c. Unbleached white flour
1 tsp. Sea salt
1 tsp. Baking powder
1/4 c. Corn oil or non-dairy margarine, melted
1/2 c. Warm water
3/4 c. Warm water

Mix together the flour, salt, and baking powder. Make a well and pour in the oil or margarine and mix again with a spoon. Add 1/2 cup of warm water and mix again. Add about 3/4 cups more warm water–enough to knead it into bread dough consistency. Let it rest for 5 minutes. Form into balls about 1 1/2 inches in diameter and dip each ball into flour before rolling it out very thin on an unfloured board. Cook on a hot, dry griddle until bubbly and brown-flecked on each side.

FRENCH BREAD

1 pkg. Dry yeast
1 tsp. Sucanat
1/2 c. Warm water (100-103°)
1 1/2 c. Warm water (100-103°)
3 1/3 c. Flour
1 1/2 tsp. Salt
1 T. Oil

In a glass measuring cup, stir together the yeast, Sucanat, and 1/2 cup of warm water. Allow it to stand until foamy. In a large bowl of an electric mixer, place the yeast mixture, additional water, flour and salt, and beat for about 5 to 7 minutes or until the dough is smooth and elastic. It should be very soft and sticky. Drizzle the oil evenly over the dough. Cover the bowl with plastic wrap and then a towel and set it in a warm place (75-80°) until it is doubled in bulk. With a spatula, scrape the dough down into the bowl, cover it as before and let it rise again until doubled. Grease a 3-loaf baguette pan, 8 1/2x17 inches. With a large kitchen spoon, scoop out 1/3 of the dough into each section and spread it out evenly. Brush the tops with a little oil. Cover the pan loosely with plastic wrap and allow the dough to rise again until almost doubled. Remove the plastic wrap and bake in a preheated 425° oven about 25 minutes, until the tops are a beautiful golden brown and the bread sounds hollow when thumped. Remove the bread from the pan and cool on a rack.

FRIED CORNMEAL CAKES

Versatile. Can be a side dish to themselves or can take the place of cornbread, regular bread, biscuits, etc. Good with syrup, too!

2 T.	Non-dairy margarine, softened
2 c.	Cashew Milk
2 c.	Water
1 T.	Corn oil
1 1/3 c.	Yellow cornmeal
1 tsp.	Sea salt

Spread the margarine over the bottom and sides of a shallow baking dish with a pastry brush. Set aside. In a saucepan bring the "milk," water and corn oil to a boil. Stirring constantly with a wooden spoon, pour in the cornmeal in a slow, thin stream so the water continues to boil as the cornmeal is absorbed. Stir in the salt, reduce heat to low and, stirring frequently, simmer for 15 to 20 minutes, or until the cornmeal is so thick that the spoon will stand unsupported in the middle of the pan. While the cornmeal is still hot, spoon it into the baking dish, spreading it out to 1/2-inch thickness, smoothing the top with a spatula. Cover with wax paper and refigerate overnight or for at least 6 hours, or spread the cornmeal into a pan with sides and cool in a freezer for 15 or more minutes–until the cornmeal is firm to the touch. With a pastry wheel or sharp knife, divide the chilled cornmeal into 2-inch squares and carefully lift them out of the pan with a small metal spatula. In a skillet melt 2 tablespoons of non-dairy margarine. Fry 4 or 5 of the cornmeal squares for 2 or 3 minutes on each side, turning them over gently with a spatula until brown. Fry the remaining squares, adding more margarine as needed.

GARLIC BREAD

Melt two cups of non-dairy margarine with 1 tablespoon of garlic powder. Spread on bread slices. Toast the bread in the oven under the broiler.

GARLIC CROUTONS

1	Loaf of bread
2 c.	Non-dairy margarine
1 T.	Garlic powder

Cube the bread (about 1/2-inch cubes). Toast in the oven at 550°, turning often until the edges brown–about 10 minutes. Melt the margarine with the garlic powder. Roll the toasted bread cubes in the margarine.

HAMBURGER BUNS

Make Whole Wheat or White Bread recipe. Roll out dough thickly on a lightly floured surface and cut into six 4-inch rounds. Place on a baking sheet, brush lightly with apple juice, and bake at 400° for 20 to 25 minutes.

HERB BREAD

Make the recipe for White Bread, except put in 1 teaspoon of Oregano, 1 1/2 teaspoon of Rosemary, 1 teaspoon of Tumeric, and 1/2 teaspoon of Sage.

HERB AND ONION BREAD

Make the recipe for White Bread, except put in 1 cup of finely chopped onion and 1/2 teaspoon of dill weed.

HUSH PUPPIES

Even Yankees can like these!
Try using different kinds of chopped vegetables.

2 c.	Cornmeal
1 c.	Unbleached white flour
1 tsp.	Baking powder
1 tsp.	Sea salt
1/2 tsp.	Baking soda
1/2 tsp.	Garlic powder
1/2 c.	Parsley, finely chopped
1/4 tsp.	Cayenne pepper
2	N'eggs
1 c.	Cashew milk or Tofu Buttermilk
1 c.	Green onions, finely chopped
2 T.	Corn oil

Combine the cornmeal, flour, baking powder, salt, baking soda, and garlic powder. Add the rest of the ingredients and mix well. Drop by the spoonfuls into hot oil and deep fry until brown on all sides. Remove and drain on paper towels.

OATCAKES

Something truly different. I like these just by themselves, but they can be used in place of crackers, biscuits, and regular bread. A backpacker's delight!

1 3/4 c.	Oatmeal
1/4 tsp.	Baking powder
1/4 tsp.	Sea salt
1 T.	Non-dairy margarine, melted
5-8 tsp.	Hot water

Half a cup at a time, pulverize 1 cup of the oatmeal by blending at high speed in a blender until you have a gritty "flour." Combine the pulverized oatmeal, baking powder and salt in a bowl. Stir in the melted margarine. When all the margarine has been absorbed, add the hot water, a teaspoon at a time, stirring constantly, to make a smooth but firm paste. Gather the mixture into a ball and place it on a board or table lightly sprinkled with 1/4 cup of the remaining oatmeal. Roll the ball into the oatmeal until it is completely covered with the flakes. Spread another 1/4 cup of oatmeal evenly over the board and, with a rolling pin, roll the ball out into an 8-inch circle about 1/8-inch thick. With a pastry wheel or sharp knife, cut the circle into 8 pie-shaped wedges. Scatter the remaining 1/4 cup of oatmeal on a baking sheet and, with a large metal spatula, carefully transfer the wedges to the sheet. Bake the cakes in the middle of the oven for about 15 minutes at 350°. When the wedges are light brown, turn off the heat and open the door of the oven. Leave the oatcakes in the oven for 4 or 5 minutes, or until they become firm and crisp. Serve at once.

ONE-HOUR WHOLE WHEAT BREAD

Everything–including the flour must be measured, warm, and ready to go. (Warm the flour by putting it in a 275° oven for 3 to 5 minutes.)

1 c.	Warm water
3 pkg.	Yeast
1 T.	Molasses (unsulphured)
3 c.	Hot water
1/3 c.	Sucanat
1 1/2 c.	Whole wheat flour
1 1/2 T.	Salt
4 T.	Oil
	Approximately 7 1/2 cups whole wheat flour–just enough to make a soft dough consistency.

Combine the 1 cup of warm water, yeast, and molasses, and let is stand for 10 minutes. While the yeast mixture is standing, combine the 3 cups of hot water, Sucanat, and 1 1/2 c. of whole wheat flour. After the 10 minutes–or when this has cooled to lukewarm–add the yeast mixture and let it stand for 15 minutes. Add the salt, oil and flour. Mix so it makes a soft dough–not too stiff. If you want, you can knead it for up to 10 minutes, but you may knead it just until it is smooth. Put directly into loaf pans (3 or 4, according to the size of loaf you want.) Let sit in a warm place until doubled in bulk. Bake at 350° until done.

ONION BREAD

Make the recipe for White Bread, except put in 1 1/2 cups of chopped onions.

POCKET BREAD

We struggled for years to succeed in making pita (pocket) bread. And here is the sucess!

1 1/2 tsp.	Dry active yeast
1 1/2 c.	Warm water
1 T.	Sucanat or Barbados Molasses
1/4 c.	Corn oil
4 c.	Unbleached white flour
1/2 tsp.	Sea salt

Preheat your oven to 550°. Dissolve the yeast in warm water, and add the sweetener and oil. Set aside for a few minutes. It will (should) foam up. Sift together the flour and salt. Add the yeast mixture to the flour and salt and knead 5 minutes. Shape the dough into a ball and place it in an oiled bowl. Coat the dough ball lightly with oil. Cover the bowl with a dry towel and place it in a warm place until it is doubled in bulk—about one hour. Again knead for 5 minutes. Separate the dough into 4 parts. Divide each of those parts into 6 small balls, so you have 24 total. (If you desire a larger size pocket bread, divide the parts into larger balls.) Roll all of the balls out into round shapes about 1/8 to 1/4 inch in thickness. Then beginning again—in the order you originally rolled them out–roll the rounds out slightly thinner (somewhere between 1/4 and 1/8 inches thick). This may seem unnecessary, but it is important. Cover them all with a dry cloth and then with a damp cloth over the dry. Let the rounds rise for 20 minutes. While the rounds are rising, put your *ungreased* baking pans (or cookie sheets) in the oven so they will get hot. After twenty minutes, take the pans out of the oven and quickly *and gently* transfer the rounds to the pans. Place the pans ON THE BOTTOM RACK OF THE OVEN for about 2 minutes. Then transfer the pans to the middle of the oven for 1 to 2 minutes more. Remove the pans, cool the rounds and cut in half. If you are not going to serve the bread immediately, cover the rounds with a damp cloth so they will not dry out.

TIPS: If you wish the tops of the bread to be more browned, transfer the pans to a rack in the middle of the oven and leave them there for two more minutes. If the bread is a day or more old, you can steam it to soften it before serving.

PUMPERNICKEL BREAD

1 qt. Water, warm enough to warm up the molasses
1 c. Barbados molasses
1 T. Oil
1 T. Salt
1 Package of Yeast
3 c. Rye flour
6 c. Whole wheat flour

Mix the water, molasses, oil, salt and yeast, and let them stand for 10 minutes. Slightly warm the flour in the oven. Add the flour to the other ingredients. Mix. Let stand for 15 minutes. Knead until smooth and elastic. Cover and put in a warm place until it is doubled in bulk. Form into small loaves and place in pans. Let rise again until doubled in size. Bake for one hour at 350°.

PURIS

1/2 tsp. Sea salt
1 c. Whole wheat flour
1 c. Unbleached white flour
1 1/2 tsp. Non-dairy margarine
1 1/2 tsp. Corn oil
1 c. Warm water (all this may not be used)

Combine the salt, flour, margarine, and oil and mix until it looks like coarse meal. Add the minimum amount of water and knead well, adding water slowly. Use only enough water so as to form a firm compact ball. Knead about 7 minutes, or until the dough becomes smooth and elastic. Cover the dough with a damp towel and let it sit for at least 30 minutes. Break off pieces about 2 tablespoons in size. Roll out each piece on a lightly floured surface into a 5-or-6-inch circle. Deep fry until it starts to brown, turning occasionally. They will puff up some. Set to drain in a colander or on paper toweling. Keep them covered if they are to sit for any length of time. Taste-test the first few. If they are raw, either the oil is too hot or the puri is rolled too thick. If it is too crisp, then it has been rolled too thin.

SOY BREAD

7 c. Warm water
2 T. Barbados molasses

3 T. Yeast (dry; or 2 yeast cakes)
1/2 c. Barbados molasses
1/2 c. Corn oil
2 T. Sea salt
14 c. Unbleached white flour
4 c. Soy flour

Combine the water, 2 tablespoons of molasses, and yeast. Let it stand until dissolved. Add the 1/2 cup of molasses, oil, and salt. Stirring, slowly add the flours. Mix with a spoon and then knead for 10 minutes. Let rise in warm place until doubled. Shape into loaves. Brush with oil and let rise till very light. Bake at 350° for 1 hour or until brown on top.

SWEET MUFFINS

2 c. Biscuit Mix
1/3 c. Sucanat
2/3 c. Cashew milk
2 T. Corn oil

Mix all ingredients together until just moistened. Spoon into greased muffin pans and bake at 400° for about 15 minutes, until brown.

VARIATION: After mixing muffin batter, fold in 3/4 cup blueberries.

TOAST POINTS

Trim the crust from thin slices of bread. Cut the bread slices diagonally in half. Brush one side of each slice with melted margarine. Put the bread, margarine side up, on a baking sheet. Bake at 450° for 3 minutes. Turn the bread over and bake 2 to 3 minutes or until golden brown.

WHITE BREAD

1 pkg. Dry yeast
1/4 c. Warm water
2 c. Warm water
2 tsp. Sea salt
2 T. Corn oil
1 T. Sucanat or Barbados Molasses
6 1/4 c. Unbleached white flour (or a combination of white and whole wheat flours)

Soften the yeast in the 1/4 cup of warm water. Combine all the rest of the ingredients with the yeast. Turn out on floured board and knead until smooth and satiny–about 10 minutes. Cover and let sit in a warm place for about 20-30 minutes. Punch down and separate into three equal parts. Put the dough into loaf pans and shape. Wipe their tops with more oil and let rise 30-45 minutes. Bake in 400° oven until well brown so there will be a heavy crust.

WHOLE WHEAT BREAD

A lot of whole wheat bread ought to be sold to the roads department to fill holes in the pavement. But THIS is what it ought to be!

3 c. Warm (105°-110°) water
3 T. Yeast
3 T. Sucanat or Barbados molasses
3 tsp. Sea salt

3 T. Corn oil
8 c. Whole wheat flour (warmed in a 275° oven for 3 to 5 minutes)

Mix the water, yeast, and sweetener together. Add the salt, oil, and flour. Knead for 10 minutes. Let rise in the bowl in a warm place, covered, until double in bulk. Cut into 3 parts with a sharp knife, place in loaf pans, and shape. Allow to rise until doubled in bulk. Bake in a 425° oven for 15 minutes. Reduce heat to 350° and bake about 30 minutes more. Remove from pans and cool on a wire rack so the air can circulate around them.

VARIATIONS: For Raisin Bread, add 1 1/2 cups of raisins to the dough. For a single loaf, use only 1/3 of the ingredients, except use 2 1/2 cups of flour.

YEAST BISCUITS–1

A good idea!

1 1/3 c. Warm water
1 T. Yeast
4 c. Unbleached white flour
1 tsp. Sea salt
2 T. Sucanat
1/4 c. Corn oil

Mix all ingredients, but only BARELY ENOUGH to get them wet, as over-handling makes the biscuits more like rolls. Oil your hands and shape the biscuits. Place on an oiled pan 1/2" apart. Let them rise only about 1/4" or the texture will resemble buns instead of biscuits. Bake at 400° for 20 to 30 minutes.

YEAST BISCUITS–2

1 T. Dry yeast
1/2 c. Warm water
1 T. Sucanat or Barbados molasses
2 1/2 c. Unbleached white flour
1 tsp. Sea salt
5 T. Non-dairy margarine or corn oil
1/2 c. Warm water

Dissolve the yeast in the 1/2 cup of warm water with the sweetener. Sift together the flour and salt. Cut shortening and one more 1/2 cup of warm water into the flour and salt. Add the yeast mixture and mix *lightly*. Roll out 1-inch thick. Cut with biscuit cutter. Let rise 20 minutes. Bake at 400-425° for 25 to 30 minutes.

SOUPS

"ALMOST INSTANT" VEGETABLE SOUP-1

6 c.	Frozen vegetables of choice, thawed
1/8 tsp.	Black pepper
1/4 tsp.	Onion powder
1/8 tsp.	Garlic powder
3 T.	Corn oil
1/2 tsp.	Sea salt
1 tsp.	MSG
1/2 tsp.	Poultry seasoning
3 T.	Nutritional yeast

Combine all ingredients, heat, and serve.

VARIATIONS: Include 3 cups of canned tomatoes, blended slightly to break them up. Omit the MSG and add 1 teaspoon of salt.

"ALMOST INSTANT" VEGETABLE SOUP-2

3/4 c.	Onions, chopped
3 T.	Corn oil
4 c.	Frozen Vegetables
3 c.	Canned tomatoes, chopped (reserve liquid)
1 tsp.	Basil
3 T.	Low sodium soy sauce
1/2 tsp.	Cayenne pepper
4 c.	Beef-like Broth

Sauté the onions in the oil. Combine all ingredients and cook together for 20 to 30 minutes. If more liquid is needed, use the tomato liquid or more broth.

AVOCADO AND TOMATO SOUP

6	Medium tomatoes, chopped and pureed
2/3 c.	Tofu Sour Cream or Cashew Sour Cream
1/2 c.	Cashew Milk
3 T.	Lemon juice
2 T.	Italian tomato paste
1 T.	Olive oil

3 T.	Fresh parsley, chopped
1 1/2 tsp.	Sea salt
1/4 tsp.	White pepper
1	Small ripe avocado, pureed or mashed

Combine everything–except the avocado–until well blended. Cover tightly and refrigerate for at least 2 hours, until thoroughly chilled. Just before serving, blend the avocado into it.

BAKED BEAN SOUP

3 c.	Barbecue Baked Beans
1/2 c.	Canned tomatoes, blended
2 c.	Water
1 T.	Low sodium soy sauce
1/4 tsp.	Cayenne pepper

Combine everything and simmer for 30 minutes. Add more water or tomatoe juice if it gets too thick.

BORSCHT

Peeling the beets ensures that they will not have their usual "earthy" taste that many people dislike.

2 c.	Beets, peeled and diced
1 c.	Carrots, peeled and diced
4 c.	Potatoes, peeled and diced
1/2 c.	Celery, diced
1/2 c.	Onions, chopped
1/2 c.	Tomatoes, chopped
1	Bay leaf
1 tsp.	Sea salt
1/4 tsp.	Black pepper
4 c.	Beef-like Broth
1 T.	Corn oil

Boil the beets, carrots, potatoes, celery, and onions together in the broth for 10 minutes or until they are almost done. Add the rest of the ingredients and additional broth if needed. Simmer for at least 30 minutes more. Serve with Tofu Sour Cream or Cashew Sour Cream.

BROCCOLI, BEAN AND SPAGHETTI SOUP

1 c.	Dried beans, uncooked
1/3 c.	Onions, chopped
1/2 tsp.	Garlic, minced
3 T.	Corn oil
4 c.	Broccoli, chopped
6 c.	Tomatoes, chopped
1/2 tsp.	Basil
1/2 tsp.	Oregano
1/8 tsp.	Cayenne pepper
1/2 tsp.	Sea salt
2 c.	Chicken-like Broth
1 c.	Spaghetti, uncooked, broken in pieces

Pressure cook the beans. Sauté the onions and garlic in the oil. Combine all the ingredients–except the spaghetti–and cook for 30 minutes. While this is being done, cook and drain the spaghetti. When the soup has cooked for 30 minutes, add the spaghetti and cook for 5 minutes more.

CABBAGE AND "CHEESE" SOUP-1

2 T.	Non-dairy margarine
1 c.	Cabbage, shredded
1 1/2 c.	Potatoes, grated
2 c.	Cashew Milk
2 c.	Water
1/2 tsp.	Sea salt
1/4 tsp.	Black or cayenne pepper
1/4 c.	Pimento, Yeast, or Mozarella "Cheese"

Melt half of the margarine in a heavy pot with a tight-fitting lid. Cook the cabbage and potatoes in the margarine, covered, until they are soft. Mash the cooked cabbage and potatoes with the "milk" and the rest of the margarine. Gradually add all the liquid, the salt, and the pepper. Cook slowly for 15 minutes, stirring occasionally. Stir in the "cheese" just before serving.

VARIATION: Make the cashew milk with Chicken-like or Beef-like Broth and cut the salt in half.

CABBAGE AND "CHEESE" SOUP-2

2 T.	Non-dairy margarine
1/3 c.	Onions, chopped
1 c.	Cabbage, shredded
1 1/2 c.	Potatoes, grated
2 c.	Cashew Milk
2 c.	Chicken-like Broth
1/4 tsp.	Sea salt
1/4 tsp.	Cayenne pepper
1/4 c.	Pimento, Yeast, or Mozarella "Cheese"

Melt 1 tablespoon of the margarine in a heavy pot with a tight-fitting lid. Sauté the onions, cabbage and potatoes until they are soft. Mash them with the "milk" and the rest of the margarine. Gradually add the broth, salt, and pepper. Cook slowly for 15 minutes, stirring occasionally. Add the "cheese" and stir in well.

CABBAGE AND TOMATO SOUP

1 c.	Beef Gluten, chopped or ground
2 c.	Cabbage, grated or coarsely cut.
1/2 c.	Sauerkraut, drained
1 c.	Canned tomatoes, drained and chopped
2 c.	Chicken-like Broth
1/2 c.	Beef-like Broth
1 1/2 tsp.	Low sodium soy sauce
1 1/4 c.	Onions, chopped
3/4 tsp.	Garlic, minced
1/3 c.	Carrot, finely grated
1/8 tsp.	Black pepper

1 T. Corn oil

Combine all the ingredients, bring to a boil, lower the heat and simmer with the lid slightly off for about 1 hour.

CALSOUP

1/2 c. Bell pepper, chopped
1/3 c. Onions, chopped
2 T. Corn oil
6 c. Tomatoes
4 T. Flour
1-2 T. Lemon juice
1/2 tsp. Sea salt

Sauté the bell peppers and onions in the oil. Combine with rest of ingredients and cook.

CARROT SOUP

3/4 c. Onions, chopped
1 tsp. Garlic, minced
2 T. Non-dairy margarine
2 c. Carrots, chopped
2 c. Potatoes, chopped
1/4 tsp. Sage
1/4 tsp. Thyme
4 c. Beef-like or chicken-like Broth
1/4 tsp. Sea salt
1/4 tsp. Cayenne pepper

Sauté the onions and garlic in the margarine until the onions are transparent. Add the rest of ingredients. Bring to a boil, reduce heat, and simmer, covered, 30 minutes. Cool a bit, then blend in a blender. Reheat if need be.

"CHICKEN" NOODLE SOUP

1 c. Onions, chopped
1 tsp. Garlic, minced
2 T. Bell pepper, chopped
2 T. Corn oil
1 c. Chicken Gluten or "Chicken" Soy Grits
3 c. Mixed vegetables, chopped if need be
3 c. Chicken-like Broth
1/4 tsp. Black pepper
1/2 c. Spaghetti or other noodles

Sauté the onions, garlic, and bell pepper in the oil. Combine with the rest of the ingredients–except for the pasta–and cook together for 30 minutes. Meanwhile cook the pasta and drain it. At the end of the 30 minutes, add the pasta and cook for 5 more minutes.

VARIATION: For Chicken Rice Soup use 2 1/2 cups of cooked rice instead of pasta.

CREAM OF CARROT SOUP

1 1/2 c. Onions, chopped

1 tsp.	Garlic, minced
2 T.	Corn oil
3 c.	Carrots, chopped and cooked
4 c.	Chicken-like Broth made with Cashew Milk
1/2 tsp.	Sea salt
1/4 tsp.	Cayenne pepper

Sauté the onions and garlic in the oil until the onions are transparent. Combine all ingredients and run through a blender until smooth. Heat just to the boiling point.

"CHEESE" SOUP-1

1/2 c.	Bell peppers, chopped fine
1 c.	Mushrooms, sliced or chopped
3 T.	Onions, chopped
1/8 tsp.	Cayenne
4 1/2 tsp.	Non-dairy margarine
1 1/2 c.	Chicken-like Broth
3 c.	"Cheese" sauce, warm

Sauté the bell pepper, mushrooms, onions, and cayenne in the margarine. Add the broth and vegetables to the warm "cheese" sauce and stir in well.

VARIATIONS: Add 1 cup of chopped canned tomatoes. Add 1/3 cup of Cooked Tomato Salsa. Add Tofu Sour Cream.

"CHEESE" SOUP–2

3/4 c.	Onions, chopped
1 c.	Potatoes, chopped
1 c.	Carrots, chopped
2 T.	Non-dairy margarine
2 c.	Beef-like Broth
1/4 tsp.	Thyme
1 c.	Cashew milk
1 1/2 c.	Yeast or pimento cheese
1/4 tsp.	Sea salt
1/4 tsp.	Cayenne pepper

Sauté the vegetables until the onions are transparent. Add broth and herbs. Bring to a boil, reduce heat, cover, and simmer for 25 minutes. Add the rest of the ingredients and allow to cool slightly. Blend until smooth. Reheat, if need be, but do not boil.

"CHEESE "AND ONION SOUP

1 1/2 c.	Onions, chopped coarsely
1/2 tsp.	Garlic, minced
2 T.	Non-dairy margarine
2 T.	Unbleached white flour
2 c.	Cashew Milk–heated
1 tsp.	Sea salt
1/4 tsp.	Black or cayenne pepper
1/2 c.	Pimento, Yeast, or Mozarella "Cheese"

Sauté the onions and garlic in the margarine. Add the flour and blend. Add the heated "milk" slowly while stirring. Stir in the salt, pepper, and cheese.

CHILI

More than you can eat at one sitting, but the rest is terrific the second day in Chili-Mac!

2 c.	Beef-flavored gluten or Soy Grits Beef
1 1/2 c.	Onions, coarsely chopped
3 T.	Chili powder
1 tsp.	Garlic powder
3 T.	Corn oil
3 1/4 c.	Beef-like Broth
1 c.	Tomato paste
5 c.	Cooked kidney beans (other beans may be used)
1 qt.	Tomatoes, chopped
1/2 tsp.	Cayenne pepper
1/2 tsp.	Sea salt

Sauté the gluten (or grits), onions, chili powder, and garlic powder in the oil. Combine the broth and tomato paste (you might want to blend the paste in a blender with some of the broth). Combine all ingredients and cook for 1 hour.

CHILI WITH MUSHROOMS

Distinctively good. But be sure you use Mexican oregano, not Italian. It is not the same at all.

2 c.	Dried kidney beans
2 c.	Onions, coarsely chopped
1/2 c.	Bell pepper, chopped
3 T.	Corn oil
2 tsp.	Garlic, minced
1 1/2 c.	Mushrooms, shredded
3/4 tsp.	Cumin, powdered
1 1/2 tsp.	Sea salt
5 c.	Tomatoes, chopped
1/2 c.	Canned tomato sauce
2 tsp.	Dried cilantro
3/4 tsp.	Mexican oregano, powdered
1 tsp.	Cayenne pepper

Pressure cook the beans and set aside, saving the liquid. Sauté the onions and bell pepper in the oil. When the onions are transparent add the garlic and mushrooms and cook a little bit longer. Add the rest of the ingredients except for the beans–but including the bean cooking liquid. Simmer together for 45 minutes. Add the beans and simmer 30 more minutes.

COLD CREAM OF SQUASH SOUP

4 1/2 tsp.	Non-dairy margarine
3 T.	Onions, finely chopped
3/4 c.	Carrot, finely chopped
1 T.	Bell pepper, finely chopped
3 1/2 c.	Yellow crookneck squash, cut into 1/2-inch dice
1 c.	Potato, peeled and cut into 1/2- inch dice
4 c.	Chicken-like Broth made with Cashew Milk

1/2 tsp. Dill weed
1/4 tsp. Cayenne pepper

Melt the margarine and sauté the onions, carrot, and bell pepper, and cook for 5 to 6 minutes until the vegetables are soft but not brown. Stir in the diced squash and potato, and pour in the broth. Bring to a boil, reduce heat and simmer, partially covered, for about 20 minutes, or until the squash is tender and offers no resistance when pierced with the tip of a sharp knife. Strain through a fine sieve set over a large mixing bowl, and purée the vegetables through a food mill or by pushing them through the sieve with the back of a large wooden spoon. Combine the purée and the soup liquid and, when the soup has cooled to room temperature, stir in the dill. Cover tightly with plastic wrap and refrigerate for at least 2 hours, or until thoroughly chilled.

COUNTRYSIDE CHILI

For those who like mild chili–and for everybody else, too!

3 c. Beef gluten, ground
2 c. Onions, chopped
3/4 c. Bell pepper, chopped
1/4 c. Celery, chopped
3 T. Corn oil
6 c. Canned whole tomatoes, undrained
1/2 c. Canned tomato paste
1 T. Dried parsley flakes
2 T. Chili powder
1/2 tsp. Sea salt
1/2 tsp. Cayenne pepper
1/2 tsp. Garlic powder
2 c. Cooked kidney beans
1 c. Cooked pinto beans

Brown the gluten in a large skillet. Add the onions, bell pepper, and celery, and sauté until the onions are soft. Add the rest of the ingredients except for the beans, reduce heat, cover, and simmer for 1 hour. Stir in the beans (if needed, add tomato juice at this point to make it soupy) and cook, uncovered, for 30 more minutes.

COLD CREAM OF TOMATO SOUP

Unusual–and unusually good!

2 T. Olive oil (do not use "extra virgin" olive oil, as the taste will be too strong in this dish)
1 1/2 c. Onion, chopped
1 1/2 tsp. Garlic, minced
1/4 tsp. Ground mace
3 T. Unbleached white flour
3 c. Chicken-like Broth
4 c. Tomatoes, coarsely chopped
1/2 tsp. Sucanat
1/2 c. Tofu Sour Cream or Cashew Sour Cream
1/2 tsp. Sea salt
1/8 tsp. Black Pepper

Heat the oil in a heavy saucepan over low heat. Add the onion, garlic, and mace. Cook, covered, for 5 minutes. Do not let brown. Sprinkle the flour over the onion mixture, and cook while stirring for 2 minutes. Whisk in the broth. Add the tomatoes and Sucanat. Bring to a boil, reduce heat, and simmer, uncovered, for 20 minutes. Let cool to room temperature. Purée in a blender or food processor. Stir until smooth, then pour through a sieve into a bowl. Whisk in the sour cream, salt, and pepper. Chill thoroughly. Sprinkle with chopped chives before serving.

CORN AND POTATO CHOWDER–1

1/2 c.	Onions, chopped
2 T.	Corn oil
6 c.	Chicken-like Broth
2 c.	Potatoes, cooked and cubed
2 1/2 c.	Corn
1/8 tsp.	Cayenne pepper
1/2 tsp.	Savory

Sauté the onions in the oil. Combine with rest of ingredients and cook.

CORN AND POTATO CHOWDER–2

1/2 c.	Onions, diced
1/2 c.	Celery, diced
1/4 c.	Bell pepper, chopped
2 T.	Corn oil
1 c.	Potatoes, raw and cubed
3/4 c.	Beef-like Broth
2 c.	Creamed style corn
1 1/2 c.	Beef-like Broth made with Cashew Milk

Sauté the onions, celery, and bell pepper in the corn oil. Stir in the potatoes and plain broth. Heat to boiling. Reduce heat and simmer until tender, but do not overcook. Add the corn and milk-broth and heat to the boiling point.

CORN AND TOMATO CHOWDER

4 1/2 tsp.	Non-dairy margarine
2 T.	Onions, chopped
2 T.	Unbleached white flour
1 c.	Tomato juice
2 c.	Canned tomatoes
1 1/2 c.	Corn
1/2 tsp.	Sea salt
Pinch	Cayenne pepper
1/2 c.	Yeast , Pimento, or Mozzarella "Cheese"

Melt the margarine. Sauté the onions. Blend in the flour. Gradually add the tomato juice. Stir in the rest of the ingredients except for the "cheese." Simmer for 10 minutes. Stir in the "cheese" well.

CORN CHOWDER

1/4 c.	Bell peppers, chopped
3 T.	Onions, chopped
2 T.	Corn oil

1 c.	Potatoes, cooked and cubed
Pinch	Cayenne pepper
1/2 c.	Chicken-like Broth
2 c.	Creamed corn
1 1/2 c.	Corn milk (equal parts of corn and Chicken-like Broth well blended in a blender)
1/4 tsp.	Sea salt

Sauté the bell peppers and onions in the oil. Combine with rest of ingredients and cook until it thickens.

CORN SOUP

1 c.	Bell pepper
3 T.	Onions, minced
4 1/2 tsp.	Non-dairy margarine
4 c.	Corn
3 c.	Chicken-like Broth
1/4 tsp.	Cayenne pepper
1/2 tsp.	Sea salt

Sauté the bell peppers and onions in the margarine. Combine corn and broth in a blender, and blend slightly till "cream corn" consistency. Add rest of ingredients and cook for 20 minutes.

VARIATIONS: When done, add 2 cups of Yeast or Pimento "Cheese" and stir over low heat until the cheese is mixed in. Add 3 cups of cubed potatoes and 2 more cups of chicken-like broth to ingredients. Add 2 cups of squash or pumpkin to ingredients.

CREAM OF BROCCOLI SOUP

This tastes very much like oyster soup!

2 T.	Non-dairy margarine
4 c.	Cashew milk
1/4 tsp.	Garlic powder
1/4 tsp.	Onion salt
Dash	Cayenne pepper
3 c.	Broccoli, cooked in Chicken-like Broth and drained

Puree all ingredients together in a blender. Simmer for 5 minutes.

VARIATION: During the 5 minutes of simmering, stir in 1 cup of yeast or pimento cheese.

CREAM OF CAULIFLOWER SOUP

2 c.	Cauliflower, broken or cut into flowerets
2 T.	Onions, chopped
1/4 tsp.	Garlic, minced
1 c.	Celery, chopped
2 T.	Non-dairy margarine
1/4 c.	Unbleached white flour
4 c.	Chicken-like Broth
2 c.	Cashew Milk

Cook the cauliflower in boiling salted water until barely tender. Reserve 1/3 of the flowerets. Chop the rest of the cauliflower fine or run through a sieve or purée strainer. Sauté the onion, garlic, and celery in the margarine. Add the flour. Slowly add the broth. Add all the cauliflower and "milk" and heat through.

CREAM OF CELERY SOUP

1 1/2 c. Celery, diced
1/3 c. Onions, chopped
1/4 tsp. Garlic, minced
1 c. Salted boiling water
3 1/2 c. Medium White Sauce, made with Chicken-like Broth

Cook the celery, onion, and garlic, covered, in the cup of boiling water until tender–about 13 minutes. Drain off the water, stir in the white sauce, and heat through.

CREAM OF PEA SOUP

4 c. Peas (if frozen, thawed; if fresh, lightly steamed)
2 c. Chicken-like or Beef-like Broth made with cashew milk
4 1/2 tsp. Non-dairy margarine

Blend the peas with the broth and margarine. Heat and serve.
VARIATION: Use 2 cups of Thin White Sauce made with Chicken-like or Beef-like Broth.

CURRIED MUSHROOM SOUP

1/4 c. Unbleached white flour
2 c. Onions
2 tsp. Garlic, minced or crushed
2 T. Corn oil
3 c. Mushrooms, cleaned, stemmed, and sliced or chopped
4 1/2 tsp. Curry powder
1/4 tsp. Cayenne pepper
1/4 tsp. Sea salt
4 c. Chicken-like or Beef-like Broth

Put the flour in a heavy skillet, spreading it out. Put it on low heat. Stir with a wooden spoon occasionally. Within a few minutes the flour will turn a slightly darker shade and begin to smell "nutty." Then begin stirring continuously to prevent burning. When the flour has toasted and developed a rich aroma, remove it from the pan immediately and set aside. Sauté the onions and garlic in the oil over medium heat for 3 to 5 minutes. Add the mushrooms and sauté 2 to 3 minutes more. Sprinkle the curry powder, cayenne, and salt over the vegetables and stir gently. Add the toasted flour and stir to coat all the vegetables. Stir in the broth. Bring to a boil, lower the heat, and simmer for 15 to 20 minutes. When the vegetables are soft, transfer the soup–2 cups at a time–to a blender and purée it.
NOTE: Best made one day before so the flavors will mingle.
VARIATIONS: Instead of mushrooms, try cauliflower, broccoli or zucchini. Stir in 1/3 cup of cashew milk before serving.

CURRY STEW

Our version of a Vietnamese-Indian recipe!

1 1/2 c. Onions, cut in large chunks
1 tsp. Garlic, crushed

2 T.	Corn oil
3 T.	Curry powder
3 c.	Chicken-like Broth
2 c.	Potatoes, cubed small
1 1/2 c.	Carrots, sliced
1 1/2 c.	Coconut milk

Sauté the onions and garlic in the oil. When the onions are transparent, add the curry powder and sauté for 2 more minutes, stirring constantly. Add the rest of ingredients EXCEPT the coconut milk and cook until the vegetables are done. Add the coconut milk and cook for 10 more minutes.

DIETER'S BROTH

This is a tremendous help for those wanting to cut down on calories. However, if water retention is also a problem you might want to omit either the salt or soy sauce.

1/4 c.	Low sodium soy sauce
1/2 c.	Tomato juice
1 1/2 tsp.	Sea salt or salt substitute
1/2 tsp.	Garlic powder
4 c.	Cabbage
1 1/2 c.	Celery
2 c.	Onions
3/4 c.	Bell peppers
2 c.	Tomatoes
3 qt.	Water
1/4 tsp.	Cayenne pepper
1 1/2 tsp.	Nutritional Yeast Flakes

Combine everything except the nutritional yeast in a pot. Cook for 40 minutes. Take from heat and stir in the yeast. Purée in a blender or food processor if you like.

FRESH TOMATO SOUP

1 1/2 c.	Onions, chopped
2 T.	Non-dairy margarine
1 c.	Potatoes, chopped
2 c.	Tomatoes, chopped
1/2 tsp.	Basil
1	Bay leaf
2 T.	Tomato paste
2 c.	Beef-like Broth
1/2 tsp.	Sea salt
1/4 tsp.	Cayenne pepper
2 c.	Cashew Milk, hot

Sauté the onions in the margarine until transparent. Add the rest of the ingredients except for the cashew milk. Cover and simmer for 20 minutes. Remove from the heat, take out the bay leaf, and stir in the "milk."

VARIATION: Instead of Cashew Milk, use Beef-like, Chicken-like, or Sausage-like Broth, or plain water. If broth is used, cut the salt in half.

Soups

GAZPACHO-1

3 T.	Onions, minced
2 T.	Corn oil
3 T.	Low sodium soy sauce
1 tsp.	Kitchen Bouquet
1 T.	Nutritional Yeast
1/8 tsp.	Sage, rubbed
2 c.	Tomato juice
2 c.	Tomatoes, finely chopped
2 c.	Tomatoes, chopped and then pureed
3 T.	Onions, finely chopped
1/4 c.	Bell pepper, finely chopped
1/2 c.	Celery, finely chopped
1/4 c.	Cooked Tomato Salsa
1/4 tsp.	Sea salt

Sauté the onions in oil until transparent. Add soy sauce, Kitchen Bouquet, nutritional yeast, sage, and tomato juice. Simmer for 5 minutes. Cool to room temperature. Combine all ingredients and chill for a few hours. Serve with Tofu Sour Cream or Cashew Sour Cream.

GAZPACHO-2

1 c.	Canned tomatoes, crushed–or chopped fresh tomatoes
4 c.	Tomato juice
1/2 c.	Onions, finely chopped
1/2 c.	Cucumbers, finely chopped
1/2 c.	Bell pepper, finely chopped
1/2 c.	Salsa
1 T. & 1 tsp.	Low sodium soy sauce
1/8 tsp.	Garlic powder

Combine all (you may need to blend the garlic powder with some of the tomato juice in a blender to make sure it mixes) and chill for a few hours.

GOLDEN CORN SOUP

3/4 c.	Onions, chopped
2 T.	Non-dairy margarine
2 c.	Corn
3/4 c.	Chicken-like Broth made with Cashew Milk
1/2 tsp.	Sea salt
Pinch	Cayenne pepper
1 c.	Tomatoes, chopped
3/4 c.	Chicken-like Broth
1/2 tsp.	Oregano

Sauté the onions in the margarine, put all together and cook.

GREEN PEA SOUP

1/3 c.	Onions, coarsely chopped
1/2 tsp.	Garlic, minced

4 1/2 tsp.	Non-dairy margarine
1 1/2 c.	Green peas (if frozen, thawed, if fresh, lightly steamed)
1 c.	Potatoes, coarsely chopped
2 1/2 c.	Chicken-like or Beef-like Broth
1/8 tsp.	Sea salt
1/8 tsp.	Cayenne pepper
1/2 c.	Cashew Milk

Sauté the onions and garlic in the margarine until the onions are transparent. Add the peas, potatoes, broth, salt, and pepper, and bring to a boil. Reduce heat, cover and simmer for 20 minutes. Remove from heat and stir in the "milk." Cool a bit, then blend in a blender. Reheat if need be.

VARIATION: May be served chilled. If so, chill before adding the "milk," which should also be cold.

MINESTRONE

2 T.	Non-dairy margarine
1/2 c.	Peas
1/2 c.	Zucchini or other squash, scrubbed and sliced (not peeled)
1/2 c.	Potatoes, diced
1/2 c.	Carrots, diced
3 T.	Celery, thinly sliced
1/4 c.	Onions, chopped
1 1/2 tsp.	Garlic, minced
1 1/2 c.	Tomatoes, coarsely chopped
4 c.	Chicken-like Broth
1/2 tsp.	Basil, dried
1	Bay leaf
1 1/2 tsp.	Parsley, dried
1/8 tsp.	Sea salt
Dash	Black or cayenne pepper
2 T.	Uncooked spaghetti broken in 1-inch pieces
1/4 c.	Cooked dried beans of choice, drained
1/8 c.	Bacon Gluten, chopped fine
2 c.	Ham Gluten or Sausage Gluten, ground and fried

Melt half of the margarine in a skillet. Add peas, zucchini, potatoes, carrots, and celery. Tossing constantly with a wooden spoon, cook 2 to 3 minutes, until they are lightly coated with margarine, but not browned. Set aside. Melt the rest of the margarine, and sauté the onions and garlic, stirring constantly, for about 5 minutes until the onions are soft and lightly browned. Stir the vegetables from the skillet into the onions, and add the tomatoes, broth, basil, bay leaf, parsley, salt, and pepper. Bring to a boil, reduce heat and simmer partially covered for 25 minutes. Add spaghetti, beans, and gluten and cook for 15 to 20 more minutes until the spaghetti is done.

MOCK "CREAM OF MUSHROOM" SOUP

2 c.	Garbanzos, cooked
1 c.	Celery, minced
1/2 c.	Onions, minced
2 T.	Corn oil
2 T.	Unbleached white flour
4 c.	Thin white sauce

1/2 tsp.	Sea salt
1/4 c.	Parsley, minced
1 T.	Nutritional Yeast

Gently sauté the garbanzos, celery and onion in the oil until the onions and celery are tender. Stir in the flour well. Add the remaining ingredients and heat through.

MULLIGATAWNY SOUP

1 c.	Carrots, chopped
2 c.	Potatoes, chopped
1 1/2 c.	Onions, chopped
1 tsp.	Garlic, minced
2 tsp.	Curry powder (Madras style preferred)
2 T.	Corn oil
1 c.	Tomato juice
5 c.	Beef-like Broth
1/2 tsp.	Sea salt
1/4 tsp.	Cayenne pepper

Sauté the carrots, potaotes, onions, garlic, and curry powder in the oil until the onions are transparent. Add tomato juice, broth, salt, and pepper, and bring to a boil. Reduce heat, cover, and simmer for 30 minutes. Cool a bit, then blend in a blender. Reheat if need be.

ONION SOUP

1 T.	Non-dairy margarine
1 T.	Corn oil
4 c.	Onions, thinly sliced
2 tsp.	Garlic, minced
1 qt.	Beef-like, Chicken-like, Ham-like, or Sausage-like Broth

In a heavy saucepan or soup kettle, melt the margarine with the oil. Stir in the onions and garlic and cook uncovered over low heat, stirring occasionally, for 20 to 30 minutes, or until the onions are a rich golden brown. Add the broth and cook for 20 minutes or more–until done.

CREAMY ONION SOUP

2 3/4 c.	Onions, chopped
1 1/2 tsp.	Garlic, minced
2 T.	Non-dairy margarine
1 c.	Potato, chopped
2 c.	Cashew milk
1 c.	Beef-like, Chicken-like, Ham-like, or Sausage-like Broth
1	Bay leaf
1/4 tsp.	Sea salt
1/4 tsp.	Cayenne pepper

Sauté the onions and garlic in the margarine until transparent. Add rest of ingredients. Bring to a boil, reduce heat, cover, and simmer for 20 minutes. Remove the bay leaf. Cool slightly, then run through a blender. Reheat if need be.

POTATO SOUP

3/4 c.	Onions, chopped
1 tsp.	Garlic, minced
3 T.	Bell pepper, chopped
4 1/2 tsp.	Corn oil
3 c.	Potatoes, cubed
Pinch	Cayenne pepper
1/4 tsp.	Sea salt
3 c.	Beef-like Broth

Sauté the onions, garlic, and bell pepper in the oil. Combine ingredients and cook until the vegetables are done.

VARIATION: Add 2 cups of corn and omit the garlic.

CHILI POTATO SOUP

6 c.	Potatoes, peeled and diced
3 c.	Water
4 1/2 tsp.	Non-dairy margarine
4 1/2 tsp.	Olive oil
1 1/2 c.	Onion, chopped
1/4 c.	Green onions, finely chopped, including the tops
1 1/4 tsp.	Sea salt
1/2 tsp.	Cumin, ground
1 tsp.	Basil
1/2 tsp.	Black pepper
2	Garlic cloves, minced
3/4 c.	Bell pepper, finely diced
1/4 c.	Jalapeños, chopped, or 1 T. hot pepper flakes
2 c.	Cashew Milk

Cook the potatoes in the water until tender–about 20 minutes. Meanwhile, begin sautéeing both kinds of onions in the margarine and oil. Add the seasonings and bell pepper and continue to cook until the onions are soft. When the potatoes are tender, mash them in their water, then add the sautéed vegetables, jalapeños, and "milk." Stir to blend, then heat over very low heat, until very hot.

CREAM OF POTATO SOUP

1 c.	Onions, chopped fine
1 tsp.	Garlic, minced
2 T.	Bell pepper, chopped fine
2 T.	Celery, chopped fine
2 T.	Non-dairy margarine
1 T.	Unbleached white flour
4 c.	Chicken-like Broth made with Cashew Milk
3 c.	Potatoes, peeled, cooked, and cubed
1/4 c.	Gluten Bacon, minced, or imitation bacon bits
1 T.	Parsley, minced
1/8 tsp.	Black or cayenne pepper

Sauté the onion, garlic, bell pepper, and celery in the margarine. Stir in the flour and blend well. Gradually add the broth, stirring constantly. Add the rest of the ingredients and cook until the soup thickens–about 15 minutes.

MASHED POTATO AND "CHEESE" SOUP

1 c.	Bell pepper, chopped fine
1/4 c.	Onions, chopped
2 T.	Non-dairy margarine
3 c.	Mashed potatoes
4 c.	Beef-like or Chicken-like Broth
1/8 tsp.	Cayenne pepper
1/4 tsp.	Sea salt
1 c.	Yeast , Pimento, or Mozzarella "Cheese"

Sauté the bell pepper and onions in the margarine. Combine all ingredients except the "cheese," and simmer 30 minutes, adding more broth if needed. Add the "cheese" and stir in well.

VARIATION: Make the broth with Cashew Milk instead of water.

MONASTERY POTATO SOUP

3/4 c.	Onions, chopped
1 tsp.	Garlic, minced
1/4 c.	Celery, chopped fine
1 c.	Mushrooms, chopped
1 1/2 tsp.	Jalapeños, minced
2 T.	Corn oil
2 c.	Potatoes, cubed
1 c.	Carrots, chopped small
1/2 tsp.	Sea salt
2 c.	Water
1/4 c.	Nutritional yeast

Sauté the onions, garlic, celery, mushrooms, and jalapeños in the oil until the onions are transparent. Combine with rest of ingredients, bring to a boil, reduce heat, and simmer for 30 minutes. Take off the heat and stir in the nutritional yeast.

VARIATION: When sautéing the vegetables, add 2 tablespoons of curry powder, and do not add the nutritional yeast at the end.

POTATO & MUSHROOM SOUP

6 c.	Potatoes, diced
2 qt.	Water
2 tsp.	Sea salt
1 c.	Red onions, chopped well
2 tsp.	Garlic, minced
2 c.	Mushrooms, sliced
3 T.	Non-dairy margarine
2 T.	Unbleached white flour
1/2 tsp.	Black pepper
2 tsp.	Poultry seasoning
3 T.	MSG
2/3 c.	Nutritional yeast flakes
1/2 tsp.	Caraway seed

Begin to boil the potatoes in the water with the salt. Sauté the onions, garlic, and mushrooms in the margarine. Add the flour and stir it in well. Add this and all the rest of the ingredients to the boiling potatoes. Cook until the potatoes start to fall apart.

POTATO-CABBAGE SOUP

1/2 c.	Bell pepper, chopped
1/4 c.	Onions, chopped
2 T.	Corn oil
2 c.	Cabbage, chopped
2 c.	Potatoes, peeled and chopped in pieces no bigger than 1 inch
1/4 tsp.	Sea salt
1/8 tsp.	Cayenne pepper
2 1/4 c.	Beef-like or Chicken-like Broth

Sauté the bell pepper and onion in the oil until the onion is soft. Combine with the rest of the ingredients and cook for about 30 minutes or until the potatoes are done.

VARIATION: Use squash instead of cabbage.

SHCHI-1

1 can	Loma Linda "Big Franks"
1 qt.	Sauerkraut, drained
1 c.	Onions, finely minced
4 c.	Beef-like Broth
1/3 c.	Corn oil
1	Bay leaf
1/4 tsp.	Black pepper
2 c.	Potatoes, diced
1/2 tsp.	Caraway seeds
1 T.	Corn oil
	Liquid from the "Big Franks"

Pour off the liquid from the Big Franks and reserve it. Grind the Franks in a food processor or grinder. Add all the ingredients, including the Big Frank liquid, and cook for 45 minutes.

VARIATION: Instead of Big Franks use 2 cups of Gluten Sausage, but retain the Beef-like Broth.

SHCHI-2

2 c.	Cabbage, coarsely shredded
1/3 c.	Wine vinegar
1 tsp.	Sea salt
2 c.	Water
1/2 c.	Onions, chopped
2 T.	Corn oil
2 c.	Canned tomatoes
5 c.	Beef-like Broth
1	Bay leaf
1/2 c.	Carrot, grated
1 tsp.	Caraway seeds
1/8 tsp.	White pepper
2 c.	Potatoes, diced

Combine the cabbage, vinegar, salt, and water. Bring to a boil and cook, partially covered, for 20 minutes. While cabbage is cooking, sauté onions in the oil. Add tomatoes, broth, bay leaf, carrot, caraway and pepper. Simmer. When cabbage is done, drain it, saving the liquid. Add it to simmering soup along withthe potatoes. Simmer at least 30 to 45 minutes. If soup is not tart enough, add some of the reserved cabbage juice. Serve with Tofu Sour Cream or Cashew Sour Cream.

SOUP THICKENER

For each 2 cups of soup, melt 1 tablespoon of margarine and stir in 1 tablespoon of unbleached white flour or 1 teaspoon of potato flour (this is best). Cook slowly until smooth, stirring constantly–about 5 minutes. Add a little of the hot soup, stir well and pour into the rest of the soup. Reheat the soup, stirring constantly.

SOUR CREAM TOMATO SOUP

2 T.	Onions, minced fine
1 T.	Corn oil
2 c.	Tomato juice
1/4 tsp.	Sea salt
Pinch	Cayenne pepper
Pinch	Dill weed
1 c.	Tofu Sour Cream or Cashew Sour Cream

Sauté the onions in the oil. Add rest of ingredients except the "sour cream" and simmer for 30 minutes. Just before serving blend in the "sour cream."

SPICY TOMATO SOUP

1/4 c.	Onions, chopped
1/4 tsp.	Garlic, minced
1 tsp.	Jalapeños, minced
2 T.	Bell pepper, chopped
1 T.	Non-dairy margarine
1 T.	Unbleached white flour
2 c.	Hot water
1 c.	Tomatoes, chopped
1/4 tsp.	Sea salt

Sauté the onions, garlic, jalapeños, and bell pepper in the margarine for 6 minutes. Add flour and blend, then add the hot water gradually while stirring. Add tomatoes and salt. Simmer for 15 minutes.

SPINACH SOUP

3 /4 c.	Onions, chopped
1 tsp.	Garlic, minced
2 T.	Non-dairy margarine
1/2 c.	Potatoes, chopped
1/4 c.	Carrots, chopped
1 c.	Tomatoes, chopped
2 T.	Parsley
1	Bay leaf
2 1/2 c.	Beef-like or Chicken-like Broth

1/8 tsp.	Sea salt
1/4 tsp.	Cayenne pepper
2 c.	Spinach, finely shredded

Sauté the onions and garlic in the margarine until transparent. Add everything else except the spinach. Bring to a boil, reduce heat, cover and simmer for 30 minutes. Let cool a bit, then run through a blender until smooth. Return to saucepan, add the spinach and simmer for 10 minutes.

SPLIT PEA SOUP–1

2 1/2 c.	Dry split peas
	Enough Beef-like or Chicken-like Broth to cover the peas with 2 inches of broth.
1 c.	Bell pepper, chopped
3 T.	Onions, chopped
3 T.	Corn oil
3/4 tsp.	Sea salt
1/8 tsp.	Cayenne pepper
2 c.	Tomatoes, chopped
1/4 tsp.	Summer savory

Cook the peas in the broth for about 30 minutes until they are soft. Sauté the bell peppers and onions in the oil. Combine with rest of ingredients and cook about 30 minutes more. When done the peas will be "dissolved." If needed, add more broth or water to keep a soup consistency.

SPLIT PEA SOUP–2

2 c.	Split peas
1/3 c.	Onions, chopped
1/2 c.	Celery, chopped
1/2 tsp.	Garlic, minced
1/4 c.	Corn oil
1/8 tsp.	Italian Herb Seasoning
1/4 tsp.	Sage
1	Bay leaf
1/4 tsp.	Cayenne pepper
2 c.	Potatoes, cooked and diced
1 c.	Carrots, cooked and sliced into rounds
1 c.	Bacon Gluten, chopped fine
4 c.	Chicken-like Broth

Pressure cook the split peas. Sauté the onions, celery, and garlic in the corn oil. Combine all ingredients and cook for 30 minutes.

VARIATIONS: Omit the gluten and use Beef-like Broth instead. Use lentils instead of split peas.

SPLIT PEA SOUP–3

1 c.	Green split peas, dry
3/4 c.	Onions, chopped
2 T.	Non-dairy margarine
2 c.	Beef-like or Chicken-like Broth
1/4 tsp.	Cayenne pepper

Pressure cook the split peas. Sauté the onions in the margarine. Combine all ingredients and simmer for 1 hour.

"THREE SISTERS" SOUP

The American Indians understood the nutritive value of combining dried beans, corn, and squash–so much so that they referred to them as "the three sisters." I think you will agree.

3 T.	Onions, chopped
2 T.	Corn oil
2 c.	Cooked beans
2 c.	Corn
2 c.	Squash, chopped
1/2 tsp.	Sea salt
1/8 tsp.	Cayenne pepper
3 c.	Beef-like Broth

Sauté the onions in the oil. Combine with rest of ingredients and cook.

TOMATO SOUP–1

This is fabulous the first day and legendary a day or so later when the flavors have blended to perfection.

2 T.	Non-dairy margarine
1/4 tsp.	Rosemary
1/4 tsp.	Basil
1/4 tsp.	Sea salt
1/8 tsp.	Cayenne pepper
2 c.	Tomatoes, chopped
1 c.	Tomato sauce
1/3 c.	Onions, chopped
1 tsp.	Garlic, minced
1/2	Bay leaf
1 c.	Frozen lima beans, thawed
2 c.	Water

Combine all ingredients and cook for 30 minutes.

TOMATO SOUP–2

1/4 c.	Onions, chopped
2 T.	Non-dairy margarine
1 1/2 tsp.	Unbleached white flour
2 1/2 c.	Water
2 c.	Tomatoes, chopped
1 c.	Carrots, chopped
1/2 tsp.	Basil
2 T.	Parsley, minced
1 tsp.	Sea salt
1/4 tsp.	Black or cayenne pepper

Sauté the onions in the margarine until they are soft. Add the flour and stir in well. Gradually add the water, stirring constantly. Add the rest of the ingredients and cook together for 30 minutes.

TOMATO SOUP WITH RICE

1/2 c.	Bell peppers, chopped
1/3 c.	Onions, chopped
1/2 tsp.	Garlic, minced
2 T.	Corn oil
5 c.	Tomatoes, chopped
1 1/2 c.	Okra, sliced, or Green Beans, cut in 1-inch pieces
3/4 tsp.	Sea salt
1/2 tsp.	Basil
1/8 tsp.	Dill weed
1/4 tsp.	Cayenne pepper
1 1/2 c.	Cooked rice or barley
1 c.	Beef-like or Chicken-like Broth

Sauté the bell peppers, onions, garlic in the oil. Combine with rest of ingredients and cook.

TOMATO VEGETABLE CREAM SOUP

3 T.	Onions, chopped
1/2 tsp.	Garlic, minced
1 1/2 tsp.	Non-dairy margarine
1 c.	Tomatoes, chopped
1 1/2 c.	Mixed vegetables, chopped if need be
2 c.	Thin White Sauce
1/8 tsp.	Basil
Pinch	Dill weed
1 1/2 tsp.	Corn flour (not meal, though it can be used)
1/4 tsp.	Sea salt

Sauté the onions and garlic in the margarine. Combine all and cook.

VARIATION: Make the white sauce with Beef-like or Chicken-like Broth and cut the salt in half.

MONASTERY VEGETABLE SOUP

1 c.	Onions, chopped
1/4 c.	Celery, chopped fine
1/2 c.	Bell pepper, chopped
1 c.	Mushrooms, chopped
3 c.	Beef, Ham, or Sausage Gluten, cubed
3 T.	Corn oil
2 tsp.	Garlic, minced
3 c.	Potatoes, cubed
1 1/2 c.	Yellow squash, cubed
1 c.	Green beans
3/4 c.	Lima beans
3/4 c.	Carrots, chopped small
3/4 tsp.	Crushed red pepper flakes
6 c.	Water
3 c.	Canned tomatoes, mashed (use juice)
1/4 c.	Tomato paste

3 T.	Parsley, chopped
1/4 tsp.	Basil
1/4 tsp.	Oregano

Sauté the onions, celery, bell pepper, mushrooms, and gluten in the oil until the onions are transparent. Add the garlic and sauté a little more. Combine with rest of ingredients, bring to a boil, reduce heat, and simmer for 45 minutes or until the potatoes begin to fall apart.

RUSSIAN VEGETABLE SOUP

3 T.	Non-dairy margarine
1/3 c.	Onions, chopped
2 c.	Potatoes, chopped
1 c.	Parsnips, chopped (carrots, if none are available or you don't like parsnips)
1 c.	Carrots, chopped
2 T.	Parsley, chopped
1/4 tsp.	Basil
1/4 tsp.	Oregano
5 c.	Beef-like Broth
1/4 tsp.	Sea salt
1/4 tsp.	Cayenne pepper
1/2 c.	Cabbage, shredded

Melt half of the margarine and sauté the onions until they are transparent. Add the rest of the ingredients except the cabbage. Bring to a boil, reduce heat, cover, and simmer for 30 minutes. Let cool a bit, then run through a blender until smooth. Sauté the cabbage in the rest of the margarine until it is just tender. Add to the blended soup and simmer gently for 10 minutes.

WINTER HOT POT

1/3 c.	Onions, chopped
2 T.	Non-dairy margarine
5 c.	Mixed vegetables, chopped if need be
1/4 c.	Barley, soaked
3 3/4 c.	Beef-like Broth
1	Bay leaf
1/2 tsp.	Sea salt
1/4 tsp.	Cayenne pepper

Sauté the onions in the margarine until transparent. Add the rest of the ingredients. Bring to a boil, reduce heat, and simmer 15 to 20 minutes or until the vegetables are just tender.

ZUCCHINI-TOMATO STEW

3/4 c.	Onions, sliced
3/4 tsp.	Garlic, minced
3/4 c.	Bell pepper, chopped
2 T.	Corn oil
1/4 c.	Water
2 c.	Zucchini, in 1/2-inch slices
2 1/2 c.	Tomatoes, chopped
1 tsp.	Basil
1/4 tsp.	Cayenne pepper

Sauté the onions, garlic, and bell pepper in the oil. Combine everything and cook over low heat, covered, 20 minutes or until the squash is tender.

Father Philaret tills the garden, since the monks try to raise as much of their food as possible.

CRACKERS

CRACKERS

This makes good pizza dough, too.

1 1/2 T.	Yeast
1 c.	Warm water
1 tsp.	Sucanat
1/3 c.	Corn oil
1 tsp.	Sea salt
3 1/2 c.	Unbleached white flour

Combine the yeast, water, and Sucanat in a medium-sized bowl. Let sit until foamy. Add the oil, salt, and flour to the yeast mixture and knead lightly together. Let rise at least 5 minutes. Roll out thin. Put in a baking pan that has NOT been oiled. Cut or score into squares or diamonds. Bake at 450°-500° until light brown.

"CHEESE" CRACKERS

My favorite cracker to eat straight or in soup.
Make these good and crispy.

2 c.	Unbleached white flour
2 tsp.	Baking powder
1/2 tsp.	Sea salt
2 T.	Corn oil
3/4 c.	Water
1/2 c.	Nutritional yeast
1 tsp.	Garlic powder
1 tsp.	Chili powder (optional)

Mix all ingredients into a stiff dough, adding more water as needed. Knead lightly. Roll dough as thin as possible. Oil the top of the dough and sprinkle with salt. Cut into squares. Bake 5-7 minutes at 375° or until brown on both sides.

COCONUT CRACKERS

As good as they are unusual.

1/3 c. Coconut
1/4 c. Barbados Molasses
1 tsp. Sea salt
3 T. Corn oil
3/4 c. Water
3 c. Unbleached white flour

Blend the coconut, molasses, salt, oil, and water in a blender until the coconut is chopped. Pour this into the flour. Roll out very thin on cookie sheets. Score and prick. Bake at 275° until well browned–about 45 minutes.

GRAHAM CRACKERS

Better than the "real thing"!

2 c. Whole wheat flour
1 1/2 c. Unbleached white flour
2 T. Corn starch or arrowroot
1/2 tsp. Sea salt
1/2 c. Water
1/3 c. Corn oil
1/2 c. Barbados molasses

Mix all the dry ingredients. Mix all the wet ingredients in a blender. Combine. Knead a little. Roll out to 1/4-inch thick. Cut, and prick with a fork. Bake at 275° for 35 minutes.

RYE CRISPS

3 c. Rolled oats
1 c. Rye flour
1/2 tsp. Sea salt
1/4 c. Corn oil
1 c. Water

Grind the oats to a course flour in a blender. Mix the dry ingredients. Add the oil to the water in a blender and whirl to emulsify. Pour it over the dry mixture while stirring to distribute the moisture evenly. Divide into three equal portions and place each on an ungreased cookie sheet. Press out flat with your fingers. Sprinkle lightly with flour to prevent sticking to the rolling pin, and then roll out until thin and even. Cut into squares or diamond shapes. Bake at 300° for 50 minutes. Watch carefully when nearly done. OR: Bake at 250° for 1 1/4 hours to be sure the crisps do not burn.

Dairy Substitutes

The milk substitutes given here will keep only for two to three days, so it is best to make only as much as you need in a recipe or make sure to use the rest later that day or the next day.

Any other dairy substitutes that have vinegar or lemon juice in them will keep well for five days.

When storing these substitutes, use containers that will not have much "air space." This will ensure that they keep better and longer.

ALMOND MILK

This is very thin, but that is necessary to obtain the right flavor.

1 c.	Almonds
	Boiling water to cover
1/8 tsp.	Salt
1 T.	Vegetable oil
2 T.	Sucanat

Drop the almonds into boiling water. Boil for 10 seconds. Turn off the heat and let the almonds stand for 2 to 3 minutes. Drain water. Remove the skins and discard. Combine the almonds with the rest of the ingredients in a blender. Blend for 1 to 2 minutes. Strain through a cheesecloth.

CASHEW CREAM

Make Cashew Milk, as below, but with only 2 cups of water.

CASHEW MILK

1 c.	Raw cashew nuts
4 c.	Water
1/4 tsp.	Salt
1 1/2 tsp.	Sucanat

In a blender put the cashews and 1 cup of the water. Blend until smooth. Add the rest of the ingredients and blend for 30 more seconds.

NOTE: If the "milk" is to be used in a dessert or other sweet dish–or even on breakfast cereal–make it with double the Sucanat (i.e., 1 tablespoon of Sucanat).

VARIATION: For use in some "salty" dishes, use Beef-like or Chicken-like Broth instead of water and leave out the Sucanat altogether.

CASHEW SOUR CREAM

2 c. Water
6 T. Cornstarch or arrowroot powder
1 c. Hot water
2 c. Raw cashews
1/3 c. Lemon juice
1 tsp. Garlic powder
1 T. Sea salt
2 tsp. Onion powder

Mix the 2 cups of water with the cornstarch or arrowroot and boil on the stove until it thickens. Cool slightly. Blend the hot water and cashews well. Add the lemon juice, garlic powder, salt, and onion powder to the cashew liquid. Add this to the starch mixture and combine thoroughly. Cool before using.

MOCK CHEESECAKE

FILLING:

3 c. Pimento cheese
4 T. Green olives, chopped
1 T. Dried chives, or 2 T. fresh chives, chopped
1/2 tsp. Garlic powder
1 tsp. Lemon juice
1/2 tsp. Low sodium soy sauce
1/4 tsp. Paprika
1/2 tsp. Sea salt
1/4 tsp. Louisiana Hot Sauce

Combine everything.

CRUST:

1 1/4 c. Cheese cracker crumbs
1/4 c. &
2 T. Non-dairy margarine, melted

Combine crackers and margarine and press into a pie pan and bake at 375° for 6 to 8 minutes or until light brown. Put the filling in the crust and refrigerate until needed.

MOZZARELLA "CHEESE"

Not really "just like," but really good.

2 c. Water
2 1/4 tsp. Lemon juice
1/3 c. Nutritional yeast flakes
1/3 c. Quick oats

1/4 c. Arrowroot
1 1/2 tsp. Onion powder
3 T. Tahini
1 1/2 tsp. Sea salt

Blend all the ingredients on high for 1 minute. Pour into a saucepan and cook on medium heat, stirring constantly, until thickened. Put into a loaf pan or other container. Chill overnight. Remove from the pan and slice.

NOTE: For pizza use only 2 tablespoons of arrowroot.

PARMESAN "CHEESE"-1

This both is and is not like parmesan cheese, but it adds a lot to a recipe where parmesan cheese is needed. It is very strong in flavor, so be cautious in its use.
Refrigerated, this keeps at least one month.

1 c. Sesame seeds
1/4 c. Lemon juice
1 1/4 c. Nutritional Yeast
2 tsp. Garlic Powder
1 T. Onion Powder
3 T. Schilling's Vegetable Supreme Seasoning

Mix all together. Sprinkle on a cookie sheet. Cover with a piece of waxed paper. Roll out thin. Remove the waxed paper. Put in a 200° oven for 2 hours. Grind fine and store in a covered container in a cool place.

PARMESAN "CHEESE"-2

For those who find the first recipe too salty or can't get Butter Buds. To my taste this is more like powdered Yeast Cheese than Parmesan Cheese, but you may prefer it.
Refrigerated, this keeps at least one month.

1 c. Sesame seeds
2 tsp. Sea salt
1 c. Nutritional yeast flakes
2 tsp. Onion powder
1/2 tsp. Garlic powder
2 T. Special Seasoning (see Etc.)
2 T. Lemon juice

Toast the sesame seeds in a dry skillet on medium-high heat, stirring constantly until they are slightly browned and beginning to crackle–about 5 minutes. Remove from heat, put in a blender, and blend on high until it is ground fine. Pour into a bowl, add the rest of the ingredients, and mix together well. Keep refrigerated.

PIMENTO "CHEESE"-1

This cheese should not be grainy from the ground (blended) cashews. If this happens to yours, then you did not blend long enough or your blender lacks the power to do the job. We use a Vitamix, and it works perfectly.

1/4 c. Agar
1 c. Water

3/4 c. Cashews
1/4 c. Pimentos
1 tsp. Salt
1 tsp. Onion powder
2 T. Oil
2 T. Lemon juice

Soak the agar in water about 5 minutes and boil gently until clear. While the agar is boiling, place the nuts, pimentos, salt, onion powder and oil in a blender and whirl until smooth. Add the hot agar and whirl 1/2 minute. Add the lemon juice and mix for only a second. Pour immediately into a mold and set in the refrigerator to cool.

VARIATIONS: For a cheese sauce or spread, use only half the agar. Use cooked potatoes instead of cashews.

PIMENTO "CHEESE"-2

See what I have written above about grainy cheese.

1/4 c. Agar
1 c. Water
3/4 c. Cashews
1/4 c. Pimentos
1 1/4 tsp. Salt
1 tsp. Onion powder
2 T. Sesame seed
3 T. Nutritional yeast
Dash Garlic powder
Dash Dill seed
2 T. Oil
2 T. Lemon juice

Soak the agar in water about 5 minutes and boil gently until clear. Place the other ingredients–except for the oil and the lemon juice–in a blender with the agar and whirl. Add slowly the oil. Add the lemon juice last of all. Pour immediately into a mold and set in the refrigerator to cool.

VARIATIONS: For a cheese sauce or spread, use only half the agar. Use cooked potatoes instead of cashews.

PIZZA "CHEESE"

Makes 2 1/2 cups

1/2 c. Nutritional Yeast flakes
1/4 c. Cornstarch
1 tsp. Sea salt
1/2 tsp. Garlic powder
2 c. Water
1/4. Corn oil
1 tsp. Prepared mustard

Mix the dry ingredients in a saucepan. Whisk in the water. Cook over medium heat while whisking until it thickens and bubbles. Cook 30 seconds more and remove from heat. Whip in the oil and mustard. Add 1 cup or more of water to make a thick, smooth sauce that will pour easily. Pour on pizza, and for the last few minutes of baking, broil the pizza for a few minutes until the cheese is speckled.

SOY MILK

Sort dried soybeans and wash in cold water. Soak the beans until they double in size–about 4 hours. In warm weather, soak them in the refrigerator so they will not ferment and spoil. Using 2 1/2 cups of water to 1 cup of beans, liquefy in a blender or grind in a food grinder. Heat the mixture to a boil in a double boiler or heavy pot. Simmer for 40 minutes, stirring occasionally. Strain through a clean cloth (nylon, folded cheesecloth, etc.) placed in a colander or strainer. This only lasts a couple of days.

FLAVORING SOY MILK

4 c.	Soy milk
1 T.	Corn oil
1/4 & 1/8 tsp.	Sea salt
1/4 c. & 3 T.	Sucanat

Blend together in a blender.

SOY WHIPPED CREAM

3/4 c.	Soy milk
1 T.	Cornstarch
1/2 c.	Corn oil
1/4 c.	Sucanat
1/8 tsp.	Salt
2 tsp.	Vanilla

Put the soy milk and cornstarch in a blender. While running on high, slowly add the oil in a thin stream until the spinning funnel of soy milk closes and the mixture stops blending–the blender blades changing speed. Add the Sucanat, salt, and vanilla to the blender and blend again until the mixture thickens as before. If necessary, add a small amount of oil. Allow to set in the refrigerator for at least one hour before using. This lasts only two or three days.

TOFU BUTTERMILK

Make Tofu Sour Cream and add 2/3 cup of water.

TOFU COTTAGE CHEESE

1 1/2 c.	Firm tofu
1/4 c.	Miraculous Whip or other "Mayonnaise" recipe
2 T. & 1 1/2 tsp.	Lemon juice
2 tsp.	Low sodium soy sauce
1/4 tsp.	Garlic powder
Pinch	Paprika

Mash all together.

TOFU CREAM CHEESE–1

1 1/2 c.	Tofu, squeezed
2 T.	Corn oil
1/2 tsp.	Sea salt
Dash	White pepper
2 tsp.	Lemon juice
Pinch	Onion powder

Puree in a blender until smooth and thick.

TOFU CREAM CHEESE–2

1 c.	Tofu Cottage cheese
1/4 c.	Non-dairy margarine

Blend in a blender until smooth.

TOFU RICOTTA CHEESE

6 c.	Firm tofu, pressed to remove excess water
1/2 c.	Lemon juice
4 tsp.	Sucanat
2 tsp.	Sea salt
6 T.	Corn oil
4 tsp.	Basil
1 tsp.	Garlic powder

Mash the tofu. Mix the other ingredients into the mashed tofu–mixing well.

TOFU SOUR CREAM

1 c.	Tofu
2 T.	Corn oil
1 T.	Lemon juice
1/2 tsp.	Salt
1/4 tsp.	Sucanat

Combine and blend till smooth. Can be used in place of mayonnaise.

TOFU WHIPPED CREAM

1 1/2 c.	Tofu
3 T.	Maple syrup
1/8 tsp.	Sea salt
1/2 tsp.	Vanilla
1 T.	Corn oil

Purée in a blender until smooth.

TOFU YOGURT

Make Tofu Sour Cream, using 1 1/2 teaspoons more lemon juice, and add 1/3 cup of water.

YEAST "CHEESE"

This is a bit like "process cheese," but is distinctively itself. Make it and see what I mean.
Makes 2 1/2 cups

1/2 c.	Nutritional Yeast flakes
1/2 c.	Unbleached white flour
1 tsp.	Sea salt
1/2 tsp.	Garlic powder
2 c.	Water
2 T.	Non-dairy margarine
1/2 tsp.	Prepared mustard

Mix the dry ingredients in a saucepan. Whisk in the water. Cook over medium heat while whisking until it thickens and bubbles. Cook 30 seconds more and remove from heat. Whip in the margarine and mustard. This thickens when it cools, and thins when heated. Water can be added to thin it more. This keeps about five days.

The members of the Nebraska Theater Caravan enjoying breakfast at the Monastery. The star attraction was tofu "scrambled eggs."

Gluten - For Goodness' Sake!

Gluten is the protein of wheat (flour) that remains when the starch is washed away in water. Gluten is sometimes referred to as "seitan," although that is a Japanese term properly applied only to gluten that has been flavored with soy sauce.

Gluten can be made into a variety of meat substitutes that are an ideal means of supplying healthy protein to the diet–something all vegetarians need just as much as non-vegetarians.

Two-thirds of a cup of raw gluten supplies 56 grams of protein–a little more than the recommended daily allowance for a 167-pound man. Also they are a boon for those of us who are frustrated with the way so many commercial meat substitutes contain egg albumen. (And they are much, much less in cost than the commercial substitutes, too!)

Many vegetarians who feel an aversion for meat dislike the idea of eating non-meat substitutes that look or taste like meat. This is quite understandable, yet meat substitutes can be of great value. For one thing they can demonstrate to meat-eaters that there is an alternative to animal flesh. They also make it very easy for people to make the transition to vegetarianism, since they can keep on eating the kind of dishes they have been used to for much of their life.

Meat substitutes are often the only tactic a person has to convince spouse or children that vegetarianism does not mean grazing out in the back yard. For no matter how delicious and creative vegetarian dishes can be, there are some who just cannot believe they are eating "real food" if it does not include meat–or something very like it. I am not theorizing. Through the years we have helped many individuals and families to become vegetarian by means of these meat substitutes. Although our personal motives for diet are based on what we feel are bed-rock principles of health and spiritual development, not many share those ideals–at first. But serve them up a "meat" dish that is even better than "the real thing" and you have them more than halfway to taking what a friend of ours called "the first step to wisdom": a vegetarian diet. It is results that count.

With these recipes vegetarians can continue using the dishes they liked when they ate meat. As I have said, they are also excellent means of convincing non-vegetarians that they can "live" without meat and, they can help beginning vegetarians make the transition to a non-meat diet.

By using these meat substitutes the family cooks can also keep right on using the same recipes and the same cookbooks they have all along. When meat is called for–no problem!

Don't forget to look for other excellent recipes in the "beef," "pork," "poultry," and "seafood" sections as well as in this one.

Raw gluten, unflavored and uncooked, will keep only one day. It should not be frozen.

Once gluten is cooked, any that is not going to be used right away should be frozen. It will keep indefinitely and can also be refrozen.

Unfrozen cooked gluten can be kept, refrigerated, for up to one week.

Dishes containing gluten can only be kept as long as the "life" of the other ingredients.

Gluten should be stored in airtight containers.

BASIC GLUTEN

Don't let this intimidate you. It is easy after you have done it once.
Do not use pastry flour in this because it does not have enough gluten to work.

8 c. Whole wheat flour
8 c. White flour
6 c. Cold–not chilled–water

Mix the flour and water together and knead it for about 10 to 15 minutes, adding water or flour as (if) needed, until you have a very smooth ball of dough with no cracks in it. Kneading is what develops the gluten. It should bounce back when you punch it.

Put this ball of dough in a bowl large enough to hold it and add enough cold water to cover the ball completely. Let it soak under water for one-half hour at least, preferably one to two hours.

Then begin kneading it under water, kneading out all the starch and being careful to hold the gluten together. Change the water when it gets quite milky from the starch, and keep changing it until the water stays almost clear. The last part of the kneading should be done in a colander (not a strainer) under running water.

If the dough distintegrates in the kneading-washing you must try another brand of flour.

Cook according to one of the methods given below.

COOKING METHOD 1

Bring the Gluten Broth (not Flavoring Broth) given in a particular gluten recipe to a boil.
Tear the raw gluten into a small piece–about 2-3 inches long.
Press the gluten flat between your hands.
Drop into boiling broth.
Repeat with all the gluten.
A weight may be required to keep the gluten submersed while boiling.
When all the pieces are in the boiling broth, cook for 30 minutes.

If possible, let the cooked gluten soak overnight in the refrigerator for best flavor, though it can be used right away if need be.

If you simmer the gluten very slowly the texture will be more compact. If you boil it more vigorously it will be more spongy. We prefer the spongy type of gluten as it absorbs a higher degree of the flavorings.

COOKING METHOD 2

Oil a loaf pan. Place the raw gluten in the pan and bake at 450° for 45 minutes. The gluten will rise just like a loaf of bread and when done will have a shiny golden brown "skin."

Slice the gluten "loaf" into slices 3/8 inch to 1/2 inch thick. If chunks are desired, cut the slices into cubes or strips.

Place the slices or cubes in boiling Gluten Broth (not Flavoring Broth) of the type that is prescribed in the recipe, and boil for 30 minutes. A weight may be required to keep the gluten submersed while boiling.

If possible, let the cooked gluten soak overnight for best flavor, though it can be used right away if need be.

COOKING METHOD 3

The long, slow cooking time of this method permits the seasoning to penetrate the gluten and gives it a texture that enables it to be sliced very thin.

Shape 2 cups of raw gluten into an oval loaf and place it in an oiled loaf pan.

Pour 2 1/2 cups of the prescribed Gluten Broth (not Flavoring Broth) over the gluten.

Cover *tightly* with aluminum foil and bake in a 250° oven for 10 hours or overnight–turning the gluten over after 5 hours of baking so the flavoring will be evenly absorbed.

For a larger quantity of gluten, increase the amounts of raw gluten and broth proportionately. You may need to increase the baking time to give the increased amount of gluten adequate time to absorb the broth. You should be sure to bake it in a pan or dish that will be of a size that ensures the broth covers the gluten at the beginning of the baking.

"INSTANT" GLUTEN

I have good news for those who would like to cook with gluten but don't want to make it in the "old-fashioned" way. All you need do is obtain Vital Wheat Gluten (Instant Gluten Flour) from your local health foods store or order it from: The Farm, Summertown, Tennessee, 38483. Vital Wheat Gluten is pure gluten powder, it is *not* "high gluten flour." Don't mistake it!

IMPORTANT: Gluten made in this way and immediately used will be somewhat less soft or tender than gluten made the regular way, but if you have time, put the gluten in a bowl and cover it with warm water and let it sit for 30 minutes and then bake it.

Here is the formula for making one "loaf" of gluten from Vital Wheat gluten.

1 c. Vital Wheat Gluten
14 T. Water (this is 7/8 cup–measure out 1 cup of water (16 tablespoons) and then remove 2 tablespoons)

Mix the gluten and water by hand until it forms a spongy "dough"–no kneading is required. Put into an oiled loaf pan and bake at 375° for 1 hour and 15 minutes–or until dark brown on top. The gluten will rise just like a loaf of bread and when done will have a shiny golden brown "skin." However, after about 30 minutes of baking, check the gluten, and if it is starting to puff up more than 2 inches above the sides of the pan, pierce the top in 3 places with a knife.

When it is done, slice the gluten "loaf" into slices 3/8 inch to 1/2 inch thick. If chunks are desired, cut the slices into cubes or stips.

Place the slices or cubes in boiling Gluten Broth (not Flavoring Broth) of the type that is prescribed in the recipe, and boil for 30 minutes. A weight may be required to keep the gluten submersed while boiling.

If possible, let the cooked gluten soak overnight for best flavor, though it can be used right away if need be.

BAKED GLUTEN

2 c. Unbleached white flour
1/2 tsp. Sea salt
1/4 tsp. Cayenne pepper
6 c. Flavored gluten, sliced
2 c. Onions, chopped fine
1 c. Bell pepper, chopped
1 tsp. Garlic, minced
3 T. Corn oil
1 tsp. Sea salt
1 tsp. Dried mint
1/2 tsp. Cayenne pepper
4 c. Canned tomatoes, crushed
2 T. Parsley, chopped
1/4 tsp. Thyme, chopped

Combine the flour, salt and pepper. Coat the gluten with this mixture and brown it in some corn oil. Take the gluten from the skillet, but keep it hot–this is essential. In the skillet put the onions, bell pepper, garlic, and 3 tablespoons of corn oil. Sauté until the onions and pepper are tender. Put in the salt, mint, cayenne, tomatoes, parsley, and thyme. Cook for 15 minutes. Put the gluten in a casserole and pour this mixture over it. Cover the casserole tightly and bake at 325° for 45 minutes. Serve with rice.

BAKED CUBED GLUTEN

Fantastic is the word for this recipe. And don't worry about the hot sauce–it blends into the rest of the flavors and loses its bite.

3 T.	Corn oil
5 c.	Flavored gluten, cooked by Method 2 or 3, and cut in 1-inch cubes
2 T.	Unbleached white flour
1/2 tsp.	Kitchen Bouquet
3/4 c.	Onions, chopped
3/4 tsp.	Garlic, minced
1 1/2 c.	Flavoring Broth according to type of gluten being used
1/4 tsp.	Sea salt
1 T.	Lea and Perrins Steak Sauce
1 1/2 tsp.	Louisiana Hot Sauce

Put the oil in a skillet, heat it, and fry the gluten cubes until they are browned on all sides. Remove the gluten and put it in a baking dish or pan. Stir the flour into the oil in the skillet and turn the fire down so it will cook slowly. Add the Kitchen Bouquet and keep stirring the flour constantly, adding more oil if the mixture is too dry, until the mixture is a rich brown. Add the onions and garlic, stirring constantly. Add the broth and keep stirring until it starts to form a thick gravy. Add the salt, steak sauce, and hot sauce. Add more water if you need to, and bring all to a boil. Pour the sauce over the gluten cubes. Bake at 400° for 30 to 45 minutes, basting frequently and adding water if needed. This is good served on a bed of mashed potatoes.

BAKED CUBED GLUTEN CASSEROLE

By taking the foregoing recipe a step further we get this casserole that cannot fail to be appreciated.

3 T.	Corn oil
5 c.	Flavored gluten, cooked by Method 2 or 3, and cut in 1-inch cubes
3 c.	Potatoes, cut into 1/2-inch slices and boiled
1 c.	Carrots, sliced and boiled
1 1/3 c.	Onions, cut into 1/2-inch slices
1/4 c.	Unbleached white flour
1 1/4 tsp.	Kitchen Bouquet
3 c.	Mushrooms (fresh preferred), sliced thick
1 1/2 c.	Onions, chopped
1 1/2 tsp.	Garlic, minced
3 c.	Flavoring Broth according to type of gluten being used
3 T.	Lea and Perrins Steak Sauce
1 T.	Louisiana Hot Sauce

Put the oil in a skillet, heat it, and fry the gluten cubes until they are browned on all sides. Take the gluten and put it in a baking dish or pan along with the potatoes, carrots, and onion slices. Stir the flour into the oil in the skillet and turn the fire down so it will cook slowly. Add the Kitchen Bouquet and keep stirring the flour constantly, adding more oil if the mixture is too dry, until the mixture is a rich brown. Add the mushrooms, and onions, stirring constantly and cook till the onions are soft. Add the garlic and cook a little bit more. Add the broth and keep stirring until it starts to form a thick gravy. Add the steak sauce, and hot sauce. Add more water if you need to, and bring all to a boil. Pour the sauce over the gluten and vegetables in the baking dish. Cover and bake at 400° for 30 to 45 minutes, basting frequently and adding water if needed.

BARBECUE GLUTEN

This is something special!

2 c. Onions, chopped
3/4 c. Bell pepper, chopped
1/3 c. Celery, chopped
2 tsp. Garlic, minced
2 T. Corn oil
6 c. Flavored gluten, cut in thin slices
6 c. Barbecue Sauce of choice
1 tsp. Hot pepper flakes

Sauté the onions, bell pepper, celery, and garlic in the oil until the onions just start to get soft. Add the gluten and continue to sauté until the gluten begins to brown. Add the barbecue sauce and pepper flakes and simmer for 20 more minutes. If it gets too dry, add more barbecue sauce or some water.

GLUTEN AND CABBAGE CASSEROLE

1 c. Celery, chopped
1/2 c. Onions, chopped
1/2 tsp. Garlic, minced
1/2 c. Bell pepper, chopped
1 1/2 c. Flavored gluten of choice
1/2 c. Canned tomato sauce
1 T. Parsley
1/4 tsp. Oregano
1/4 tsp. Sea salt
1/4 tsp. Italian Herb Seasoning
5 c. Cabbage, chopped and parboiled until it is tender
1/2 c. Pimento or Yeast "Cheese"

Sauté the celery, onion, garlic, bell pepper, and gluten in a small amount of corn oil. Add the tomato sauce, parsley, oregano, salt, and Italian seasoning. In a baking dish alternate layers of cabbage and sauce mixture. Top with the "cheese." Bake uncovered at 350° for 30 minutes.

GLUTEN AND CORN CASSEROLE

1/2 c. Bell pepper, chopped
1/4 c. Onions, chopped
1 T. Corn oil
1 c. Flavored gluten or flavored soy grits
2 c. Medium White Sauce
1 tsp. Prepared mustard
2 c. Corn
1/2 c. Pimento or Yeast "Cheese"

Sauté the bell pepper and onion in the oil until tender. Add the gluten (or grits) and cook for 5 minutes. Blend the white sauce, mustard, and gluten mixture. Add the corn. Place in a casserole and top with "cheese." Bake at 350° for 30 minutes.

GLUTEN AND GREEN BEANS STIR-FRY

2 c.	Flavored gluten of choice
1/2 tsp.	Sea salt
1/3 tsp.	Black pepper
2 T.	Corn oil
1 c.	Green beans, cut into 1-inch lengths
1 c.	Onions, chopped
1 tsp.	Garlic, minced
3/4 c.	Flavoring Broth according to the type of gluten being used
1 tsp.	Basil (dried)
1/8 tsp.	Sea salt
1 T.	Cornstarch
2 T.	Water
1 1/2 c.	Tomatoes, chopped
1/2 tsp.	Kitchen Bouquet

Thinly slice the gluten into 2 1/2 x 1/2-inch strips and season them with the salt and pepper. Heat the oil in a skillet over medium heat until hot. Add the gluten and stir-fry 3 to 5 minutes. Remove the gluten from the skillet and put in 1 more tablespoon of oil and heat it until hot. Put the green beans, onions, and garlic in the skillet and sauté for a few minutes. Add the broth, basil and salt. Cover and simmer for 15 minutes or until the beans are tender. Combine the cornstarch and water in a small bowl and stir until blended. Add the cornstarch mixture, gluten, and tomatoes to the skillet. Stir in the Kitchen Bouquet. Cook, stirring constantly, until the mixture boils and thickens–about 2 minutes.

GLUTEN AND POTATO HASH

1 1/2 c.	Flavored gluten, ground
2 T.	Non-dairy margarine
1 c.	Onions, chopped
1 tsp.	Garlic, minced
2 T.	Browned flour
1 c.	Flavoring Broth according to the type of gluten being used
3 c.	Cold, boiled potatoes, diced
1/8 tsp.	Black pepper

Sauté the gluten in the margarine until it is browned. Just before the gluten is done, add the onions and garlic and sauté until the onions are soft. Add the flour. Gradually add the broth, stirring constantly. Add potatoes, gluten, and pepper and cook for 5 minutes. Transfer to a baking dish and bake at 375° about 30 minutes.

GLUTEN AND RICE CASSEROLE

2 c.	Onions, chopped
2 c.	Celery, chopped
3 T.	Corn oil
4 1/2 c.	Rice, cooked
3 c.	Tomato paste

4 c.	Pimento or Yeast "Cheese"
2 1/2 c.	Flavored gluten, ground
1 tsp.	Bell pepper flakes
1 tsp.	Garlic powder

Sauté the onion and celery in the oil. Combine all and bake in an oiled baking dish or pan at 400° for 45 minutes, covered.

VARIATION: Use flavored soy grits instead of gluten.

GLUTEN CHOW MEIN

1 1/2 c.	Celery, chopped
1/2 c.	Onions, chopped
1/2 c.	Bell pepper, chopped
1/2 c.	Snow peas
1 tsp.	Hot pepper flakes
2 T.	Corn oil
1/3 c.	Cold water
1/3 c.	Cornstarch
1 c.	Flavoring Broth according to the type of gluten being used
1/3 c.	Low sodium soy sauce
1 c.	Bean sprouts, blanched at 160° for 10 seconds
1/2 c.	Bamboo shoots
1/2 c.	Water chestnuts, sliced
1 1/2 c.	Flavored gluten, cubed

Sauté the celery, onions, bell pepper, peas, and pepper flakes in the oil until they are crisp-tender. Blend the water, corn starch, broth, and soy sauce together. Add the blended liquid to the vegetables along with the sprouts, bamboo shoots, water chestnuts, and gluten. Cook until thick–about 15 minutes.

GLUTEN CURRY

The aristocrat of curries!

1 T.	Corn oil
1/2 c.	Onion, chopped fine
1 T.	Garlic, minced
1/2 tsp.	Ginger, powdered
11/2 tsp.	Garam Masala
2 tsp.	Chili powder
3/4 tsp.	Tumeric
2 c.	Coconut milk
3/4 c.	Tomato, chopped
1 1/2 tsp.	Lemon juice
1/4 tsp.	Sea salt
2 c.	Flavored or unflavored gluten, cubed

In the oil sauté the onion, garlic, and ginger until the mixture is golden. Add the garam masala, chili powder, and tumeric, and sauté for 2 more minutes. Stir in the coconut milk, tomato, lemon juice, and salt. Boil, stirring occasionally, until thickened. Add the gluten and cook together for 1 minute.

GLUTEN DUMPLINGS

Unflavored gluten can often add a great deal to dishes that contain a lot of liquid for it will absorb the flavors of the vegetables and seasonings. When the dish is fully assembled or boiling, take the raw (uncooked) gluten, break off small 1/2-inch pieces, roll each between your thumb and fingers and drop them in. After dropping in 10 pieces stir so the gluten pieces will not stick to one another.

GLUTEN ENCHILADAS

You're always on target with this dish!

3 T.	Corn oil
4 c.	Flavored gluten, ground,
2 tsp.	Garlic, minced
2 c.	Onions, chopped
2 tsp.	Jalapeños, minced
3 T.	Chili powder
3/4 c.	Black olives, chopped
1/4 tsp.	Sea salt
10 c.	Spanish Tomato Sauce
1	Recipe of Corn Tortillas or Flour Tortillas
	Yeast or Pimento "Cheese" to cover

In 1 1/2 tablespoons of the oil, sauté the gluten until it begins to brown. Set aside. In rest of oil, sauté the garlic, onions, and jalapeños until the onions are transparent. Add the chili powder and sauté for 2 more minutes, stirring constantly. Add olives, salt, gluten, and 3 cups of the tomato sauce and cook for another 5 minutes. Dip a tortilla in the remaining tomato sauce, put some of the filling on it and roll it up and put it in a casserole pan. Do this with all the tortillas until the filling is used up. Cover the enchiladas with the remaining sauce. Spread a layer of "cheese" over that. Bake at 350° for 30 minutes.

VARIATION: Use flavored soy grits instead of gluten.

GLUTEN HASH

Don't think this is just a way of using up leftovers! It can stand on its own!

3 T.	Non-dairy margarine
3 c.	Onions, chopped
2 c.	Mushrooms, sliced
1/2 c.	Unbleached white flour
2 c.	Flavoring Broth of the type of gluten used
1/2 c.	Cashew Cream
3 c.	Flavored gluten, diced
1/3 c.	Parsley, chopped fine
2 T.	Lea & Perrins Steak Sauce
1/8 tsp.	Cayenne Pepper

Melt the margarine and sauté the onions until they are soft. Add the mushrooms and cook until most of the liquid is evaporated. Stir in the flour and then the broth and "cream," stirring constantly. Cook until thickened. Stir in the gluten, parsley, steak sauce, and pepper. Heat through.

Serve over Toast Points (see Bread and Such section).

GLUTEN JAMBALAYA

This is worth swimming the bayou for!
Even if you are not a rice fan you will love it in this dish, I garontee!

	Sea salt
	Black pepper
	Cayenne pepper
4 c.	Flavored gluten, sliced 1/4-inch thick
1/3 c.	Corn oil
3 c.	Onions, chopped
1 T.	Bell pepper, chopped fine
1 T.	Celery, chopped fine
1 c.	Mexican Chorizo Sausage Gluten, chopped fine
3 c.	Uncooked rice
1 1/2 tsp.	Sea salt
2 1/2 c.	Flavoring Broth of gluten type
2 1/2 c.	Water
1/8 tsp.	Liquid Smoke
2 tsp.	Garlic clove, chopped fine

Sprinkle the salt and both types of pepper on the gluten slices–both sides. Fry in the oil until brown. Lower the heat and add the onions, bell pepper, and celery. Sauté until the onions are transparent. Add the Sausage Gluten. Add the rice and salt. Cook over low heat for 15 minutes, stirring often. Add the broth, water, liquid smoke, and garlic. Stir and cover. *Do not stir any more.* Simmer over low heat for 20 or 30 minutes until the rice is done. Keep covered until served.

GLUTEN LOAF

2 1/2 c.	Flavored gluten, ground
1 c.	Rolled oats
1 c.	Bread crumbs
1 c.	Nuts, ground
1 c.	Onions, ground
1 1/4 c.	Mushroom soup made by using Basic 'Cream of' Soup recipe
1/2 tsp.	Sea salt
1/4 tsp.	Garlic, minced
2 T.	Water
2 T.	Corn oil

Mix the gluten, oats, crumbs, nuts, onions, soup, salt, and garlic together and form into a loaf. Put the loaf in a well-oiled baking dish or pan. Mix the water and oil and baste the loaf. Bake at 350° until the loaf is brown and firm.

VARIATION: Instead of gluten, use flavored soy grits.

GLUTEN PAPRIKA

You haven't lived until...

4 1/2 tsp.	Non-dairy margarine
4 1/2 tsp.	Corn oil
1 c.	Onion
3/4 tsp.	Garlic, chopped

3 tsp.	Paprika
5 c.	Flavored gluten, cut in 1-inch cubes
2 c.	Tomatoes, cubed
3/4 c.	Bell pepper, chopped
3 T.	Water
1 tsp.	Sea salt
1/4 tsp.	Cayenne pepper
3 T.	Unbleached white flour
1 1/2 c.	Tofu Sour Cream or Cashew Sour Cream
1 c.	Cashew Milk

Heat the oil and margarine together, and sauté the onion and garlic for 3 to 4 minutes until transparent. Stir in the paprika and cook a few more seconds. Add the gluten and sauté over high heat, lightly tossing, until it is lightly browned–about 15 minutes. Add the tomatoes and bell pepper along with the water, salt , and pepper. Mix well and cook over moderate heat for 12 to 15 minutes, stirring occasionally. Whisk in the flour. Combine the "sour cream" and "milk." Add to the gluten and stir. Cook for a few more minutes, stirring, until thickened.

GLUTEN PIQUANT

This is a "somewhat Cajun" recipe adapted for use by vegetarians from some recipes of Justin Wilson, the famous television Cajun cook.

2 T.	Olive oil
1/4 c.	Unbleached white flour
1 c.	Mushrooms, chopped
1 c.	Onions, chopped
1 c.	Green onions, chopped
1/4 c.	Bell pepper, chopped
2 T.	Celery, chopped
1/2 c.	Parsley, chopped
1 1/2 tsp.	Garlic, minced
3 c.	Cold (i.e., not hot) Flavoring Broth according to the type of gluten being used
3 c.	Flavored gluten, cooked by Method 2 or 3, and cut in 1-inch cubes
2 T.	Olive oil
2 T.	Louisiana Hot Sauce
1 1/2 c.	Canned tomato sauce
1/4 c.	Canned tomatoes, mashed
1 tsp.	Dried mint OR 1 bay leaf
1 T.	Lemon juice
2 T.	Lea & Perrins Steak Sauce
1/2 tsp.	Sea salt

Heat the oil in the skillet, stir in the flour, and turn the fire down so it will cook slowly, stirring constantly, adding more oil if the mixture is too dry, until it is a rich brown. Add the mushrooms, onions (both kinds) and bell pepper, and sauté until they are tender. Add the celery and parsley, and sauté until the celery is tender. Add the garlic and sauté a bit longer. Add the broth, *which should be cold, not heated,* and stir in well. Let simmer. While the above is simmering, brown the gluten in the oil and put it in a cooking pot. Add all the rest of the ingredients and mix well. Cover and bring to a boil. Lower the heat and simmer for 2 1/2 hours, adding more water if needed. Serve over spaghetti, rice, or potatoes.

GLUTEN POT PIE

This is a regular standby–but not dull!

1/2 c.	Pimentos or bell peppers, chopped
1/2 c.	Mushrooms, sliced
1/2 c.	Onions, minced
2 T.	Non-dairy margarine
1/2 c.	Unbleached white flour
3 c.	Flavoring Broth according to the type of gluten being used
6 c.	Mixed vegetables, cooked
3 c.	Flavored gluten
1 tsp.	Garlic, minced
1/4 tsp.	Cayenne pepper

Sauté the pimentos (or peppers), mushrooms, and onions in the margarine. Stir in the flour. Gradually add the broth. Add rest of ingredients and cook until it is thick and bubbly. Serve over biscuits.

VARIATIONS: With ham gluten use chicken-like broth. Serve over rice instead of biscuits.

GLUTEN SALAD

You can trust this to please every time!

2 1/2 c.	Flavored gluten, ground or chopped
1/4 c.	Celery, chopped fine
1/4 c.	Bell pepper, chopped fine
1/3 c.	Onions, chopped fine
3/4 c.	Dill or sweet pickle, chopped fine
1 T.	Parsley, chopped fine
2 c.	"Mayonnaise" or "sour cream"
1/4 tsp.	Louisiana Hot Sauce
1/8 tsp.	Garlic powder
1/8 tsp.	Black pepper
1 T.	White vinegar

Combine and chill for a few hours to let flavors mix.

VARIATION: Use frozen tofu that has been flavored beef, chicken, ham, sausage, or fish.

GLUTEN SANDWICH SPREAD

Try it and like it!

3 c.	Flavored gluten, coarsely ground
3/4 c.	Tofu Cream Cheese, 1 or 2
1 tsp.	Lemon juice
10	Green onions, minced
1 c.	"Mayonnaise"
4 tsp.	Louisiana Hot Sauce
3 T.	Lea & Perrins Steak Sauce

Combine everything.

GLUTEN-VEGETABLE CASSEROLE

2 c.	Potatoes, peeled and cut into 3/4-inch cubes
1 c.	Carrot, coarsely grated
1 c.	Peas
3 c.	Flavoring Broth of the type of gluten being used
1/4 c.	Corn oil
1/3 c.	Unbleached white flour
1/4 c.	Non-dairy margarine
2 c.	Flavored gluten, cooked according to Method 2 or 3, and cubed
2 c.	Onions, chopped coarsely
3 c.	Mushrooms
2 tsp.	Garlic, minced
1/4 c.	Parsley, chopped well
1/4 c.	Lea & Perrins Steak Sauce
1 T.	Louisiana Hot Sauce

In a saucepan combine the potatoes, carrots, peas, and broth. Simmer for 10 minutes or until the potatoes are done, drain and set aside, saving the broth. Put the oil in a skillet, stir in the flour, and cook, stirring constantly, until the flour is dark brown but not burned. Slowly stir in the reserved broth. Add the steak sauce and hot sauce. Melt the margarine in a frying pan and fry the gluten, onions, and mushrooms until the gluten starts to brown. Add the garlic and parsley and sauté 2 more minutes. Combine everything and simmer over low heat for 10 minutes. Put in a casserole and bake at 375° for 20 minutes.

HEARTY GLUTEN BAKE

A sure thing.

2 c.	Mashed potatoes
4 tsp.	Non-dairy margarine, melted
2 c.	Flavored gluten of choice, cubed small
1/2 c.	Onions, chopped
4 tsp.	Lea & Perrins Steak Sauce
1/2 tsp.	Sea salt
1/8 tsp.	Cayenne pepper
1 c.	Tofu Cottage Cheese
2	Medium tomatoes, sliced
1 c.	Pimento cheese

Mix the potatoes and margarine. Spread 1 1/2 cups of this in the bottom of a casserole and set aside. In some corn oil, sauté the gluten and onions until the gluten begins to brown. Add the steak sauce, salt, and pepper. Spoon the gluten mixture onto the potatoes in the casserole. Spread the "cottage cheese" over the gluten mixture. Cover with the tomato slices. Spread the "cheese" over all. Spread the remaining potatoes over that. Bake at 350° for 20 to 30 minutes.

Beef Substitutes and Dishes

For other "beef" dishes, look in the "Gluten–For Goodness' Sake" section and use beef gluten in those recipes.

Once flavored gluten is prepared, any that is not going to be used right away should be frozen. It will keep indefinitely. Gluten can also be refrozen.

BEEF GLUTEN

If you have regular soy sauce instead of low sodium soy sauce to use in this broth, then cut the amount you use in half.

Cook 2 cups of raw gluten according to Method 1, 2, or 3 in a broth made by combining and simmering together for 5 minutes:

1/4 c.	Low sodium soy sauce
2 tsp.	Kitchen Bouquet
2 T.	Nutritional Yeast
1/2 c.	Onions, chopped
1/4 tsp.	Sage, rubbed
1 T.	Corn oil
2 c.	Water

"BEEF" AND MUSHROOM ÉTOUFFÉE

4 c.	Beef Gluten, cubed
1/2 c.	Corn oil
1/2 c.	Unbleached white flour
3 1/2 c.	Tomato juice
3 c.	Onions, chopped
6 c.	Mushrooms, thickly sliced
1 c.	Bell pepper, chopped
1 T.	Garlic, chopped
3 T.	Parsley, chopped
1/4 tsp.	Cayenne pepper
4 1/2 tsp.	Louisiana Hot Sauce
1/3 c.	Lea & Perrins Steak Sauce
1 tsp.	Sea salt

Deep-fry the gluten and set it aside. Combine the oil and flour and cook until dark brown. Add the tomato juice and mix until it is absorbed by the flour-oil mixture. Add the onions, mushrooms, bell pepper, and garlic and cook for 10 minutes or until the onions are soft. Add the rest of the ingredients, including the gluten, and cook for 15 more minutes, adding more tomato juice is necessary to keep it from getting too thick. Transfer to a casserole and bake, uncovered, at 350° for 30 minutes. Serve with rice, spaghetti, or mashed potatoes.

"BEEF" WITH RICE AND TOMATOES

6	Beef Gluten slices, cut 1-inch thick
6	Large bell pepper rings
2 c.	Rice, cooked
6	Medium onion slices
6	Tomato slices
6 c.	Canned tomatoes with juice
1/2 tsp.	Sea salt
1/4 tsp.	Cayenne pepper
1 tsp.	Louisiana Hot Sauce

Sprinkle the gluten on both sides with some salt and pepper, and brown it in a skillet. Put the gluten slices in a large baking dish so they do not overlap. Put a bell pepper ring on each gluten slice. With an ice cream scoop or large spoon take some of the rice and put it in the pepper ring, patting to make it firm. Put an onion slice on each mound of rice. Put a tomato slice on each onion slice. Empty the canned tomatoes into a bowl and chop or squeeze them until they are all broken up fine. Season the tomatoes with the salt, pepper, and hot sauce and pour them around the gluten slices. Cover and bake 1 hour at 375°.

CHINESE PEPPER "STEAK"

Simple as this is, it delivers.

3 c.	Unflavored gluten cooked by Cooking Method 2 or 3
2 T.	Corn oil
1 tsp.	Sea salt
1 c.	Celery, sliced
1 c.	Bell peppers, sliced
1 c.	Onion, sliced
2 tsp.	Garlic, minced
2 c.	Tomatoes, sliced

Cut the gluten in thin strips. Sauté it in the oil, until slightly brown or deep-fry it (this is best). Remove from the pan. Sauté the vegetables and seasonings in the skillet, mixing gently but thoroughly. Cook until just tender. Add the gluten. Serve over rice. You can season this with soy sauce or some other condiment.

VARIATION: Use gluten made with Beef-like or Chicken-like Broth. Add 1 tablespoon of minced or sliced jalapeños.

COMPANY PRIDE HASH

Worthy of serving to guests–not just family!

2 T.	Non-dairy margarine
1 c.	Beef Gluten, chopped or ground
1 c.	Potatoes, cooked and diced

1 c.	Onion, diced
1 T.	Parsley, minced
1/2 c.	Cashew milk
1/4 tsp.	Salt
1/8 tsp.	Black pepper

In a skillet (or on a griddle) melt the margarine. Add all the ingredients and mix well. Cover and cook until the mixture is crisp on the bottom. Then turn and brown the other side.

CONTINENTAL STROGANOFF

2 1/2 c.	Beef Gluten, cut into strips
1/4 c.	Onions, chopped
2 T.	Non-dairy margarine
3 T.	Unbleached white flour
1/8 tsp.	Black pepper
1 c.	Cashew Milk
1/2 c.	Tofu Sour Cream or Cashew Sour Cream

Sauté the gluten and onions in the margarine until the gluten is browned. Add the flour and pepper and gradually stir in the "milk." Add the "sour cream" and heat through. Serve over rice or pasta with more "sour cream" on the side.

GLUTEN ROAST

A favorite. Excellent cold, and gets better with age. Chopped or ground this is a superb hamburger substitute.

6 c.	Raw gluten
1/4 c.	Corn oil
3/4 c.	Low sodium soy sauce
1 1/2 tsp.	Sea salt
1 1/2 tsp.	Garlic powder
1 T.	Onion powder
1/4 & 1/8 tsp.	Black pepper
1 1/2 c.	Roasted unsalted peanuts

Combine all the ingredients well. Put in an oiled casserole, and spread out to about 1-inch thick. Blend together equal parts of corn oil, low sodium soy sauce, and water–enough to cover the gluten well. Pour this into the loaf pan. Bake at 350°, covered, for 45 minutes. Uncover, and continue to bake until the gluten becomes dark brown on top.

GLUTEN ROAST "BEEF"

Make Beef Gluten cooked according to Method 3 given in the "Gluten–For Goodness' Sake!" section.

GOULASH

2 c.	Beef Gluten, cut into 1/2-inch cubes
1 c.	Bell pepper, diced
1 c.	Onion, chopped
1 tsp.	Garlic, minced

1 c.	Spaghetti sauce
1/2 tsp.	Paprika
1/4 tsp.	Sea salt
Pinch	Caraway seed, crushed
1/3 c.	Tofu Sour Cream or Cashew Sour Cream

Brown the gluten and set aside. Sauté the bell peppers, onion, and garlic until tender-crisp. Combine everything but the "sour cream" in a casserole and bake at 400° for 20 minutes. Stir in the "sour cream" and serve.

VARIATION: Use Chicken Gluten.

SAUCY "STEAK" SKILLET

2 c.	Beef Gluten, cut into large pieces
1/2 c.	Unbleached white flour mixed with 1/4 tsp. of black pepper
2 T.	Corn oil
1 c.	Onions, chopped
2 tsp.	Garlic, minced
1 c.	Potato water
1/4 c.	Catsup
1 T.	Kitchen Bouquet
2 T.	Bell pepper flakes
1 tsp.	Low sodium soy sauce
1/2 tsp.	Marjoram
1/4 tsp.	Black pepper
2 c.	Potatoes, peeled, boiled whole, and cut in chunks (reserving the cooking water)
1 1/4 c.	Green beans
1/4 c.	Sliced pimento

Coat the gluten pieces with flour-pepper and pound it into the gluten. Brown the gluten in the oil. Add the onions and garlic and sauté until they are tender. Mix the potato water, catsup, Kitchen Bouquet, bell pepper flakes, soy sauce, marjoram and pepper and pour it over the gluten and onions. Heat this to the boiling point, reduce heat, cover, and simmer 75 to 90 minutes. Add potatoes, beans, and pimento. Heat to boiling, reduce heat, cover, and simmer until the beans are tender–10 to 15 minutes.

SOY GRITS BEEF

1/2 c.	Soy grits
1 c.	Boiling Beef Gluten Broth (not Beef-like Broth)

Stir grits into the broth and cook for 5 minutes.

"STEAK" ÉTOUFFÉE

7	Beef gluten "steaks"
2 T.	Corn oil
1 1/2 c.	Mushroom Gravy
1 c.	Beef-like broth
1 c.	Onion, chopped
1/4 c.	Pimento, chopped
1 T.	Garlic, minced
1/2 tsp.	Celery seed
1 T.	Parsley, dried

1 T.	Low sodium soy sauce
1/2 tsp.	Angostura bitters
1/2 tsp.	Sea salt
1/4 tsp.	Black pepper
1 1/2 tsp.	Louisiana hot sauce or 3/4 tsp. Tabasco

Sauté the gluten in the oil. Cover the gluten with the rest of the ingredients. Cover and let cook over low heat for 45 minutes.

STIR-FRY "BEEF"

Good on rice or pasta

2 c.	Beef Gluten, thinly sliced
2 T.	Corn oil
2 c.	Broccoli flowerets
1/2 c.	Green onions, sliced
1/2 c.	Mushrooms, sliced
1 1/2 tsp.	Low sodium soy sauce
1/4 tsp.	Powdered ginger
1/4 tsp.	Black pepper

Sauté the gluten in the oil, take out, and set aside. Add 1 more tablespoon of oil to the skillet. Add the broccoli and sauté for 1 minute. Add the onions and sauté for 1 more minute. Add the mushrooms and sauté for 1 more minute. Add the gluten and the rest of the ingredients and sauté 2 or more minutes.

SWISS "STEAK"

This is an all-time favorite, the one that has won over the most meat-eaters to the idea that there is an alternative to meat. It's easy, too!

2 tsp.	Garlic, minced
2 c.	Onions, chopped
1 1/2 c.	Celery, chopped
1/4 c.	Corn oil
2 qt.	Tomatoes, pureed
1/2 tsp.	Cayenne pepper (black, if you prefer)
1 tsp.	Basil
1 tsp.	Sea salt
2 c.	Beef-like Broth
6 c.	Beef Gluten, sliced and deep fried
4 c.	Potatoes, peeled, sliced 1/2-inch thick, and boiled

Sauté the garlic, onions, and celery in the oil until the onions are transparent. Add the tomatoes, pepper, basil, salt and broth, and simmer together for 1 hour. Cover the bottom of a casserole with a small amount of this sauce. Put in the gluten in a layer, covering the bottom of the casserole. Layer the potatoes over the gluten. Top with the remaining sauce. Bake at 375° for 30 to 45 minutes.

TAMALE PIE

Oh, yes!

2 c.	Beef Gluten, ground
1 c.	Onions, chopped
1 c.	Bell pepper, chopped
3 T.	Corn oil
2 1/2 c.	Tomato sauce
1 1/2 c.	Corn
1/2 c.	Black olives, chopped
1 1/2 tsp.	Sucanat
1 tsp.	Sea salt
1 T. & 1 tsp.	Chili powder
1/2 tsp.	Garlic, minced
Dash	Cayenne pepper
1 c.	Yeast "Cheese"
3/4 c.	Cornmeal (yellow)
1/2 tsp.	Sea salt
2 c.	Cold water
1 T.	Non-dairy margarine

In a large skillet, sauté the gluten, onions, and bell pepper in the corn oil until tender. Stir in the tomato sauce, corn, olives, Sucanat, salt, chili powder, garlic, and pepper. Simmer 20 to 25 minutes, or until thick. Stir in the "cheese" and mix thoroughly. Put in an oiled 9x9x2 baking dish. Stir the cornmeal and salt into the cold water. Cook and stir until it is thick. Add the margarine and mix well. Spoon this over the "beef" mixture in the dish and bake at 375° about 40 minutes.

TANGY "MEATBALLS"

Flavoricious!

2 c.	Beef gluten, ground
1	All-purpose n'egg
1/4 c.	Chili sauce
1/4 c.	Onion, chopped fine
1/2 tsp.	Sea salt
1/4 tsp.	Cayenne pepper
1 1/2 c.	"Cheese" cracker crumbs
	Corn oil

Combine the gluten, n'egg, chili sauce, onions, salt, pepper, and 1 cup of the cracker crumbs and mix thoroughly. Shape into small balls and roll in the remaining crumbs. Put 1/2 inch of corn oil in a skillet and heat. Sauté the gluten balls 3 to 5 minutes, turning to brown on all sides.

Pork Substitutes and Dishes

For other "pork" dishes, look in the "Gluten–For Goodness' Sake" section and use one of the types of "pork" gluten in those recipes.

Once flavored gluten is prepared, any that is not going to be used right away should be frozen. It will keep indefinitely. Gluten can also be refrozen.

A NOTE ON COOKING "SAUSAGE" that applies to all the types of sausage whose recipes are given here: If the sausage is to be used in a dish, the recipe will tell you if it needs any prior preparation. If you are going to eat it "straight," you can either fry it, using a small amount of oil, or spray or brush on a small amount of oil (both sides) and lightly broil.

"BACON" GLUTEN–1

Cook 2 cups of raw gluten according to Method 3 in a broth made by combining and simmering together for 5 minutes:

1/4 c.	Low sodium soy sauce
2 tsp.	Kitchen Bouquet
2 T.	Nutritional Yeast
1/2 c.	Onions, chopped
1/4 tsp.	Sage, rubbed
1/2 tsp.	Black pepper
1/2 tsp.	Oregano
1 tsp.	Garlic powder
1 1/4 tsp.	Liquid smoke
2 T.	Corn oil
2 c.	Water
1 tsp.	Sea salt

Use in recipes as indicated. For crispy bacon, slice thinly, spray or coat lightly with oil and broil until it starts to turn brown. It gets crisp as it cools, so do not overbroil by having it get crispy under the broiler.

"BACON" GLUTEN–2

Cook 2 cups of raw gluten according to Method 3 in a broth made by combining and simmering together for 5 minutes:

1/2 c.	Onions, chopped
4 1/2 tsp.	Monosodium glutamate
1 tsp.	Sea salt
1 tsp.	Poultry seasoning
1/3 c.	Nutritional Yeast
1/2 tsp.	Black pepper
1 tsp.	Garlic, minced
1 tsp.	Coriander seed, ground
1/4 tsp.	Mace
1 tsp.	Liquid smoke
2 T.	Corn oil
2 c.	Water

Use in recipes as indicated. For crispy bacon, slice thinly, spray or coat lightly with oil and broil until it starts to turn brown. It gets crisp as it cools, so do not overbroil by having it get crispy under the broiler.

"BAKED HAM" GLUTEN

Cook 2 cups of raw gluten according to Method 3 in a broth made by combining and simmering together for 5 minutes:

1/2 c.	Onions, chopped
4 1/2 tsp.	Monosodium glutamate
1 tsp.	Sea salt
1 tsp.	Poultry seasoning
1/3 c.	Nutritional Yeast
2 T.	All Purpose Seasoning (see Etc.)
2 T.	Corn oil
2 T.	Low sodium soy sauce
2 T.	Liquid smoke
2 T.	Barley malt syrup
2 c.	Water

BARBECUE "SPARE RIBS"

This is a real gem. When we lived in the little town of Forest Park, Oklahoma, the police (dedicated carnivores) insisted that they be invited over for some every time we cooked this because they said these "ribs" were BETTER than the "real thing." They are!

1 c.	Onions, chopped
1/3 c.	Non-dairy margarine or corn oil
1/3 c.	Nutritional Yeast flakes
1/2 c.	Tahini
2 T.	Paprika
1 1/2 T.	Sea salt
4 c.	Raw gluten
1/4 c.	Corn oil

Sauté the onions in the margarine (or oil) until soft. Combine the nutritional yeast, tahini, paprika, and salt in a bowl. Add the onions along with the sautéeing margarine (or oil) to this and combine well. Take half of this seasoning mixture and half (2 cups) of the gluten (broken into several pieces) and blend together in a food processor using the metal blade, gradually adding the gluten. Set aside and repeat with the other half of the seasoning mixture and ingredients. Pour the corn oil into a 9x13 pan. Put the gluten mixture into the pan and pat it out flat so it covers the bottom of the pan. Bake, uncovered, at 350° for 45 minutes. Onto an oiled baking sheet pour 1/2 to 1 cup of Barbecue Spare Rib Sauce (see below) and spread it over the bottom. Cut the baked gluten into rib-like strips, dip them in the barbecue sauce, and arrange them on the baking sheet, leaving a little space between them. Pour 1 to 2 cups of barbecue sauce over them. Put back in the oven and bake at 375° for 20 minutes or until well done. Serve with extra barbecue sauce on the side.

BARBECUE "SPARE RIB" SAUCE

Be good to yourself. Don't use a store-bought brand of barbecue sauce on the ribs, but make this.

1/2 c.	Onion, chopped
1 tsp.	Garlic, minced
3 T.	Corn oil or non-dairy margarine
2 1/2 c.	Canned tomato sauce
1/4 c.	Water
1 c.	Sucanat
2 T.	Barbados molasses
1/2 c.	Prepared mustard
1 T. & 1 tsp.	Sea salt
1 tsp.	Allspice
2 tsp.	Hot pepper flakes
1 1/2 tsp.	Dried parsley OR 1 sprig of fresh parsley, chopped
1/4 c.	Water
1 T.	Low sodium soy sauce
2 T.	Lemon juice
1 tsp.	Liquid smoke

Sauté the onion and garlic in oil or margarine until the onions become clear and golden. Add tomato sauce, the first 1/4 cup of water, Sucanat, molasses, mustard, salt, allspice, pepper flakes and parsley. Bring to a boil, reduce heat and let simmer for about an hour. Add second 1/4 cup of water, soy sauce, lemon juice, and liquid smoke. Cook 10-15 minutes longer.

CHINESE "PORK" WITH WATER CHESTNUTS AND MUSHROOMS

2 T.	Corn oil
2 c.	Pork Gluten, minced fine
1/4 c.	Mushrooms, minced
10	Water chestnuts, drained and minced
1/3 c.	Green onions, sliced
2 tsp.	Jalapeños, sliced
1/2 tsp.	Sucanat
1/2 tsp.	Powdered ginger
2 T.	Low sodium soy sauce
1 T.	Cornstarch, mixed in 3 T. of cold water

In the oil, sauté the gluten, mushrooms, water chestnuts, onions, jalapeños, Sucanat, and ginger until the gluten browns. Add the soy sauce and cornstarch-cold water mixture and cook for 5 more minutes. Serve with rice.

BREAKFAST "SAUSAGE"

Nice and mild, yet flavorful.

Cook 2 cups of raw gluten according to Method 1, 2, or 3 in a broth made by combining and simmering together for 5 minutes:

1/2 c.	Onions, chopped
4 1/2 tsp.	Monosodium glutamate
1 tsp.	Sea salt
1 tsp.	Poultry seasoning
1/3 c.	Nutritional Yeast
1 tsp.	Dried crushed sage leaves
1/2 tsp.	Ground ginger
1/4 tsp.	Black pepper
1 tsp.	Liquid Smoke
2 T.	Corn oil
2 c.	Water

CAJUN "SAUSAGE"

This bites back!

Cook 2 cups of raw gluten according to Method 1, 2, or 3 in a broth made by combining and simmering together for 5 minutes:

1/2 c.	Onions, chopped
4 1/2 tsp.	Monosodium glutamate
1 tsp.	Sea salt
1 tsp.	Cayenne pepper
1/8 tsp.	Garlic powder
1 tsp.	Cumin
1 tsp.	Poultry seasoning
1/8 tsp.	Sage
1/8 tsp.	Curry powder
1 tsp.	Dried mint
1/3 c.	Nutritional Yeast
2 T.	Corn oil
2 c.	Water

FARMER'S "SAUSAGE"

Flavor galore!

Cook 2 cups of raw gluten according to Method 1, 2, or 3 in a broth made by combining and simmering together for 5 minutes:

1/2 c.	Onions, chopped
4 1/2 tsp.	Monosodium glutamate
1 tsp.	Sea salt
1 tsp.	Poultry seasoning
1/3 c.	Nutritional Yeast
3/4 tsp.	Fennel seed
1/2 tsp.	Black pepper

2 T.	Low sodium soy sauce
1 1/2 tsp.	Oregano
1/4 tsp.	Cayenne
1 T.	Sucanat
1 T.	Garlic powder
1 T.	Prepared mustard
1 tsp.	Allspice
2 T.	Corn oil
2 c.	Water

GARLIC "SAUSAGE"

A garlic lover's delight!

Cook 2 cups of raw gluten according to Method 1, 2, or 3 in a broth made by combining and simmering together for 5 minutes:

1 c.	Onions, chopped
4 1/2 tsp.	Monosodium glutamate
1 tsp.	Sea salt
1 tsp.	Poultry seasoning
1/3 c.	Nutritional Yeast
1/3 c.	Garlic powder
1/2 tsp.	Black pepper
2 T.	Corn oil
2 c.	Water

"HAM" GLUTEN

Cook 2 cups of raw gluten according to Method 1, 2, or 3 in a broth made by combining and simmering together for 5 minutes:

1/4 c.	Low sodium soy sauce
2 tsp.	Kitchen Bouquet
2 T.	Nutritional Yeast
1/2 c.	Onions, chopped
1/4 tsp.	Sage, rubbed
1/2 tsp.	Black pepper
1/2 tsp.	Oregano
1 tsp.	Garlic powder
1 1/4 tsp.	Liquid smoke
2 T.	Corn oil
2 c.	Water
1 tsp.	Sea salt

HERB "SAUSAGE"

This has been formulated for those who find the spices in regular sausage too hard to digest easily. But everybody will like it.

Cook 2 cups of raw gluten according to Method 1, 2, or 3 in a broth made by combining and simmering together for 5 minutes:

1/2 c.	Onions, chopped

4 1/2 tsp.	Monosodium glutamate
1/3 c.	Nutritional Yeast
1/2 tsp.	Garlic salt
1 tsp.	Dried parsley
1 tsp.	Dried sage
1/8 tsp.	Thyme leaves
1/2 tsp.	Black pepper
2 T.	Corn oil
2 c.	Water
1/4 tsp.	Allspice, ground

ITALIAN "SAUSAGE"

Pizza delight!

Make Basic gluten and cook it by Method 1, 2, or 3 in a broth made by combining and simmering together for 5 minutes:

1/2 c.	Onions, chopped
4 1/2 tsp.	Monosodium glutamate
1 tsp.	Sea salt
1 tsp.	Poultry seasoning
1/3 c.	Nutritional Yeast
1/2 tsp.	Sucanat
1/4 tsp.	Garlic powder
1/4 tsp.	Fennel seed
1/4 tsp.	Lemon pepper seasoning
1/4 tsp.	Paprika
1/8 tsp.	Celery salt
1/8 tsp.	Dried crushed sage leaves
1/8 tsp.	Cayenne pepper
1 1/2 tsp.	Low sodium soy sauce
1 tsp.	Lea and Perrins Steak Sauce
2 T.	Corn oil
2 c.	Water

ITALIAN "SAUSAGE,"PASTA, AND BEAN CASSEROLE

2 c.	Italian Sausage Gluten, ground
2 c.	Beef Gluten, ground
1 1/2 c.	Onion, chopped
1 T.	Garlic, chopped
1 tsp.	Oregano
1/2 tsp.	Thyme
3 1/2 c.	Canned tomatoes, drained and chopped
2 T.	Tomato paste
1/2 tsp.	Sea salt
1/2 tsp.	Pepper
2 c.	Cooked kidney beans, drained
3/4 lb.	Macaroni, cooked and drained
1/3 c.	"Parmesan 'Cheese'"
1/4 c.	Parsley, chopped
2 c.	Yeast, Pimento, or Mozzarella "Cheese"

Sauté the two types of gluten, onion, garlic, oregano, and thyme until the gluten is browned well. Add the tomatoes, tomato paste, salt, pepper, and beans, and heat through. Add the macaroni, "parmesan," and parsley and toss together well. Put into an oiled baking dish or pan. Spread the "cheese" on top and bake, uncovered, at 375° for 30 minutes.

MEXICAN CHORIZO "SAUSAGE"

Good and spicy!

Cook 2 cups of raw gluten according to Method 1, 2, or 3 in a broth made by combining and simmering together for 5 minutes:

1/2 c.	Onions, chopped
4 1/2 tsp.	Monosodium glutamate
1 tsp.	Sea salt
1 tsp.	Poultry seasoning
1/3 c.	Nutritional Yeast
1 1/2 tsp.	Paprika
1/2 tsp.	Black pepper
3/4 tsp.	Crushed red pepper flakes
1/4 tsp.	Sucanat
1/4 tsp.	Garlic powder
1/4 tsp.	Dried oregano leaves
1/8 tsp.	Cumin seed, powdered
1 T.	White vinegar
2 T.	Corn oil
2 c.	Water

PIZZA "SAUSAGE"

This is a milder version of Italian Sausage for those who prefer it.

Cook 2 cups of raw gluten according to Method 1, 2, or 3 in a broth made by combining and simmering together for 5 minutes:

1/2 c.	Onions, chopped
4 1/2 tsp.	Monosodium glutamate
1 tsp.	Sea salt
1 tsp.	Poultry seasoning
1/3 c.	Nutritional Yeast
1/4 tsp.	Black pepper
1/4 tsp.	Red pepper flakes
1/2 tsp.	Fennel seeds
2 T.	Corn oil
2 c.	Water

"PORK" GLUTEN-1

Cook 2 cups of raw gluten according to Method 1, 2, or 3 in a broth made by combining and simmering together for 5 minutes:

1/2 c.	Onions, chopped
4 1/2 tsp.	Monosodium glutamate
1 tsp.	Sea salt

1/3 c.	Nutritional Yeast
1/2 tsp.	Red pepper flakes
1/4 tsp.	Black pepper
3/4 tsp.	Sage
2 T.	Corn oil
2 c.	Water

"PORK" GLUTEN–2

Cook 2 cups of raw gluten according to Method 1, 2, or 3 in a broth made by combining and simmering together for 5 minutes:

1/2 c.	Onions, chopped
4 1/2 tsp.	Monosodium glutamate
1 tsp.	Sea salt
1 tsp.	Poultry seasoning
1/3 c.	Nutritional Yeast
2 T.	Corn oil
2 c.	Water
1/2 tsp.	Black pepper
1/2 tsp.	Mace

"PORK" GLUTEN–3

Cook 2 cups of raw gluten according to Method 1, 2, or 3 in a broth made by combining and simmering together for 5 minutes:

1/2 c.	Onions, chopped
4 1/2 tsp.	Monosodium glutamate
1 tsp.	Sea salt
1 tsp.	Poultry seasoning
1/3 c.	Nutritional Yeast
2 T.	Corn oil
2 c.	Water
1/2 tsp.	Black pepper
1 tsp.	Garlic, crushed
1/4 tsp.	Marjoram, powdered

"PORK" CHOPS

Cook 2 cups of raw gluten according to Method 1, 2, or 3 in a broth made by combining and simmering together for 5 minutes:

1/2 c.	Onions, chopped
4 1/2 tsp.	Monosodium glutamate
1 tsp.	Sea salt
1/3 c.	Nutritional Yeast
1/2 tsp.	Black pepper
1/4 tsp.	Paprika
1	Bay leaf
1/2 tsp.	Ground sage
2 T.	Corn oil
2 c.	Water

Cut the gluten into "chops."

ROSEMARY "SAUSAGE"

Different and delicious! Mild, too.

Cook 2 cups of raw gluten according to Method 1, 2, or 3 in a broth made by combining and simmering together for 5 minutes:

1/2 c.	Onions, chopped
4 1/2 tsp.	Monosodium glutamate
1 tsp.	Sea salt
1 tsp.	Poultry seasoning
1/3 c.	Nutritional Yeast
1/2 tsp.	Black pepper
3/4 tsp.	Rosemary, powdered
1/4 tsp.	Thyme
1/4 tsp.	Marjoram
1/4 tsp.	Freshly grated nutmeg
2 T.	Corn oil
2 c.	Water

"SAUSAGE" AND CABBAGE

Not for food snobs–but the rest of us love it!

1 T.	Corn oil
1 1/2 c.	Gluten Sausage of choice, cut into 1-inch cubes
4 c.	Cabbage, chopped
2 c.	Onion, sliced thin
1 1/2 c.	Broth of type of sausage used

Brown the gluten in the oil. Add the cabbage and onion and cook, stirring occasionally, until the cabbage is browned. Add the broth and simmer, partly covered, for 15 to 20 minutes, until the cabbage is tender. Serve over mashed potatoes.

SAUTÉED "PORK CHOPS" WITH TOMATO AND EGGPLANT SAUCE

Sure to please!

4	Gluten "pork chops" cut 1-inch thick
4 c.	Eggplant, peeled and cubed
2 T.	Olive oil
1 c.	Onion, chopped
1 1/2 tsp.	Garlic, minced
2 c.	Canned tomatoes, chopped, with the juice
1/3 c.	Water
1/2 tsp.	Sea salt
1/4 tsp.	Black pepper
1/3 c.	Parsley, chopped

Deep-fry the gluten and set aside. Deep-fry the eggplant and set it aside. In the oil sauté the onion and garlic for 9 minutes. Stir in the tomatoes, water, salt, pepper, and parsley. Bring to a boil and add the eggplant. Cook for about 20 minutes. Cover the bottom of a casserole with half of the sauce. Put the gluten over that. Cover with the rest of the sauce. Cover the casserole tightly and bake at 400° for 20 minutes.

SIMPLE "SAUSAGE"

Cook 2 cups of raw gluten according to Method 1, 2, or 3 in a broth made by combining and simmering together for 5 minutes:

2 T.	Low sodium soy sauce
1 tsp.	Kitchen Bouquet
1 T.	Nutritional Yeast
1/4 c.	Onions, chopped
1/8 tsp.	Sage, rubbed
1/4 tsp.	Black pepper
1/4 tsp.	Oregano
1/2 tsp.	Garlic powder
1 tsp.	Liquid smoke
2 T.	Sausage seasoning
2 T.	Corn oil
2 c.	Water

SOY GRITS "HAM"

1/2 c.	Soy grits
1 c.	Boiling Ham-like Broth

Stir grits into the broth and cook for 5 minutes.

SOY GRITS "SAUSAGE"

1/2 c.	Soy grits
1 c.	Boiling flavoring broth of sausage type desired

Stir grits into the broth and cook for 5 minutes.

WATKINS "SAUSAGE"

Cook 2 cups of raw gluten according to Method 1, 2, or 3 in a broth made by combining and simmering together for 5 minutes:

1/4 c.	Low sodium soy sauce
2 tsp.	Kitchen Bouquet
2 T.	Nutritional Yeast
1/2 c.	Onions, chopped
1/4 tsp.	Sage, rubbed
1/2 tsp.	Black pepper
1/2 tsp.	Oregano
1 tsp.	Garlic powder
2 tsp.	Liquid smoke
4 T.	Watkins Sausage Seasoning
2 T.	Corn oil
2 c.	Water

Poultry Substitutes and Dishes

For other "poultry" dishes, look in the "Gluten–For Goodness' Sake" section and use chicken gluten in those recipes.

Once flavored gluten is prepared, any that is not going to be used right away should be frozen. It will keep indefinitely. Gluten can also be refrozen.

"CHICKEN" GLUTEN

Cook 2 cups of raw gluten according to Method 1, 2, or 3 in a broth made by combining and simmering together for 5 minutes:

1/2 c.	Onions, chopped
4 1/2 tsp.	Monosodium glutamate
1 tsp.	Sea salt
1 tsp.	Poultry seasoning
1/3 c.	Nutritional Yeast
1 T.	Corn oil
2 c.	Water

"TURKEY" GLUTEN

Cook 2 cups of raw gluten according to Method 1, 2, or 3 in a broth made by combining and simmering together for 5 minutes:

2 T.	Low sodium soy sauce
1 tsp.	Kitchen Bouquet
1/8 tsp.	Sage, rubbed
1/2 c.	Onions, chopped
2 1/4 tsp.	Monosodium glutamate
1/2 tsp.	Sea salt
1/2 tsp.	Poultry seasoning
3 T. & 2 tsp.	Nutritional Yeast
1 T.	Corn oil
2 c.	Water

BRAISED "CHICKEN" AND "CHORIZO"

1/4 c.	Corn oil
3 c.	Chicken Gluten, cubed
1 T.	Curry powder
1 c.	Onion, chopped
1 T.	Garlic, minced
2 1/2 c.	Potatoes, cubed
1 1/4 c.	Tomatoes, minced
1/4 c.	Unbleached white flour
2 T.	Lea& Perrins Steak Sauce
2 T.	Tomato paste
3 1/2 c.	Chicken-like broth
1/4 c.	Ham Gluten, cubed
1/2 c.	Mexican Chorizo Sausage Gluten, cubed
1/2 c.	Green olives, chopped
1/2 c.	Thick coconut milk
1/4 tsp.	Cayenne pepper

In the oil brown the "chicken" gluten, transferring it to a bowl as it is browned. To the remaining oil add the curry powder and stir for about 30 seconds. Then add the onion, garlic, potatoes, and tomatoes, and cook, stirring, until the vegetables are softened. Stir in the flour and cook, stirring for 3 more minutes. Stir in the steak sauce, tomato paste, broth, "ham," "chorizo," olives, coconut milk, and pepper. Add the "chicken," and simmer, stirring occasionally, for 45 to 60 minutes.

CAJUN "CHICKEN" BAKE

	Sea salt
	Cayenne pepper
	Black pepper
6 c.	Chicken gluten, sliced 1/4-inch thick
	Corn oil
3 c.	Onions, chopped
1/2 c.	Green onions, chopped
1/2 c.	Bell pepper, chopped
1/2 c.	Celery, chopped
1 c.	Parsley, chopped
1/4 c.	Pimentos, cut in strips
4 c.	Water
4 T.	Lea & Perrins Steak Sauce
2 tsp.	Louisiana Hot Sauce

Sprinkle the salt and peppers on the gluten slices–both sides. Fry the gluten in the oil until it begins to brown. Pour a small amount of oil into the bottom of a baking pan. Put the gluten in the pan in a layer. On top of the gluten put the onions (both types), bell pepper, celery, and parsley. Put the pimento strips over that. Mix the water, steak sauce, and hot sauce together and pour over all. Bake, covered, at 375° for 1 hour. Just before serving, take off the cover and broil for a few minutes.

"CHICKEN" A LA KING

Truly worthy of a king!

4 c.	Chicken Gluten, cubed
5 T.	Non-dairy margarine
2 c.	Onions, chopped
4 c.	Mushrooms, sliced thick
4 1/2 tsp.	Garlic, crushed
1 T.	Unbleached white flour
2 T.	Pimentos, chopped
3/4 c.	Carrots, sliced thin and steamed
4 c.	Chicken-like Broth made with Cashew Milk
1/8 tsp.	Coarse black pepper
1/8 tsp.	Cayenne pepper

Deep-fry the gluten and set it aside. In the margarine sauté the onions, and mushrooms until they are soft. Add the garlic and cook 2 more minutes. Add the flour, and stir it in well. Add the rest of the ingredients and simmer for 10 minutes, adding more broth if it gets too thick. Serve on toast points or biscuits–rice, too.

"CHICKEN" AND "SAUSAGE" GUMBO

This is Haut Cuisine, I garontee!

	Sea salt
	Black pepper
	Cayenne pepper
6	Chicken Gluten slices, cut 1-inch thick
2 c.	Sausage Gluten, sliced 1/4-inch thick
1 c.	Corn oil
3/4 c.	Unbleached white flour
5 c.	Onions, chopped
1/2	Bell pepper, chopped
1 T.	Celery, chopped
5 c.	Canned tomatoes, crushed and drained
3 c.	Water
3 c.	Tomato juice
1 tsp.	Garlic clove, minced
1 T.	Parsley, chopped fine
3/4 c.	Green onions, chopped fine
1/2 tsp.	Cayenne pepper
1/2 tsp.	Sea salt
2 c.	Okra, chopped

Sprinkle the salt and both types of pepper on the gluten slices–both sides. Fry the gluten in 1/4 cup of the oil until brown, remove, and set aside. Pour the remaining oil into a large heavy pot, stir in the flour and cook, stirring constantly, until the flour is very dark brown but not burned. Lower the heat and add the onion, bell pepper, and celery. Cover and simmer until the onions are transparent, stirring occasionally. Add all the gluten, the tomatoes, water, tomato juice, garlic, parsley, green onions, pepper, and salt. Cover, and simmer stirring frequently. While that is cooking, sauté the okra in a skillet until soft, then add it to the rest of ingredients. Bring to a boil, reduce the heat, and simmer, covered, 30 to 40 minutes until most of the water is evaporated. Serve on rice.

"CHICKEN" CASSEROLE WITH MUSHROOMS, TOMATOES, AND RICE

2 c.	Onions, chopped
2 tsp.	Garlic, mashed
5 T.	Corn oil margarine
2 1/3 c	Mushrooms
1 c.	Rice
2 c.	Tomatoes, coarsely chopped
2 c.	Chicken broth
1/4 c.	Pimento strips
1 tsp.	Sea salt
1/2 tsp.	Cayenne pepper
3 c.	Chicken Gluten
1 1/4 c.	Frozen green peas

Sauté onions and garlic in margarine until onions are transparent. Add mushrooms and continue sautéeing until the mushrooms are tender. (Add a little more margarine, if necessary.) Add the rice and sauté for 5 minutes, tossing and turning. Now add the remaining ingredients and stir until blended. Simmer mixture until rice is cooked and liquid is absorbed. Stir and serve hot.

"CHICKEN" GUMBO

Wonderful flavor!

4 c.	Chicken Gluten, cubed
2 c.	Sausage or Ham Gluten, cubed
2/3 c.	Corn oil
2/3 c.	Unbleached white flour
1 1/2 c.	Onion, chopped fine
3/4 tsp.	Garlic, chopped fine
4 c.	Chicken-like broth
1/4 c.	Lea & Perrins Steak Sauce
1 tsp.	Louisiana Hot Sauce or 1/2 tsp. Tabasco

Sauté all the gluten in some corn oil until browned and set aside. Heat the 2/3 cup of oil in a skillet, stir in the flour and cook until it is dark brown but not burned. Add all the ingredients and simmer for 30 minutes.

"CHICKEN" PAELLA

5 c.	Chicken Gluten, cubed
3 T.	Olive oil
1 1/2 c.	Onion, chopped
3/4 tsp.	Garlic, minced
1/2 c.	Bell pepper, cut in strips
1 1/2 c.	Tomatoes, chopped
2 T.	Tomato paste
1	Bay leaf
1 tsp.	Thyme
1 tsp.	Paprika
2 c.	Uncooked rice
4 c.	Chicken-like broth, boiling

Lightly brown the gluten in the oil and transfer it to a warm plate. In the same oil sauté the onion, garlic, and bell pepper until the onion is transparent. Add the tomatoes, tomato paste, bay leaf, thyme and paprika. Cook 10 minutes. Stir in the rice. Add the broth and cook for 5 or 6 minutes, stirring occasionally. Mix in the gluten. Put in a casserole and bake at 325° for 20 to 25 minutes until the broth is absorbed.

"CHICKEN" TETRAZZINI

Something to sing–or crow–*about!*

1/2 lb.	Spaghetti
1/4 c.	Non-dairy margarine
1/4 c.	Unbleached white flour
2 c.	Mushrooms, sliced
1/2 c.	Bell pepper (red or green)
3/4 tsp.	Garlic, minced
3 1/2 c.	Chicken-like Broth made with Cashew Milk
1/8 tsp.	Tabasco sauce
1/2 tsp.	Black pepper
1/2 c.	Parsley, chopped fine
2 c.	Chicken Gluten (made by Method 3 is best), cubed and browned in oil
1 c.	"Parmesan 'Cheese'"

Cook the spaghetti, drain and blanch it. Set aside. Melt the margarine in a skillet, add in the flour and cook it, stirring, until it is dark brown but not burned. Add the mushrooms and bell pepper and sauté for 5 minutes. Add the garlic and sauté 2 more minutes. Add the broth, Tabasco, pepper, parsley, gluten, and 1/2 cup of the "parmesan." Cook until the mixture begins to thicken. Mix in the pasta, put in a casserole, sprinkle the rest of the "parmesan" on top, patting lightly to press it in. Cover and bake at 350° for 20 minutes. Uncover and broil until the top is brown.

CREAMED "CHICKEN" WITH MUSHROOMS AND HERBS

Amazingly flavorful!

1 c.	Mushrooms, cleaned and sliced
2 T.	Minced onion
1/8 tsp.	Thyme leaves
2 c.	Chicken Gluten
2 T.	Corn oil margarine
1/3 c.	Ritz-style cracker crumbs (Hi-Hos are best–they do not contain animal fat)
1 c.	Tofu Sour Cream
1/2 c.	Cashew Cream
Pinch	Sea salt
Pinch	Cayenne pepper

Sauté the mushrooms, onion, thyme, and gluten in the margarine until the mushrooms are tender. Stir in the remaining ingredients until blended.

JAMBALAYA

2 c.	Chicken Gluten, cut into pieces
2 c.	Rice, cooked
3 c.	Tomatoes, canned

1 1/2 c.	Onion, chopped
1/3 c.	Green pepper, chopped
2/3 c.	Celery, chopped
1/2 c.	Non-dairy margarine
1/2 tsp.	Sea salt
1/2 tsp.	Basil
1 1/2 c.	Bread crumbs

Mix the gluten, rice and tomatoes. Sauté the onion, green pepper and celery in 1/4 cup of the margarine. Add to the gluten mixture along with the salt and basil. Pour into an oiled 2-quart casserole. Melt the rest of the margarine and toss with the bread crumbs. Spread the crumbs on top and bake, uncovered, for 1 hour at 350°.

NOTE: Other flavors of gluten may also be used in this dish.

OMELETS

2 1/2 c.	Unbleached white flour
2 T.	Baking powder
2 T.	Sucanat
1 tsp.	Sea salt
2 3/4 c.	Nutritional yeast
1	N'egg
3 T.	Corn oil
2 c.	Cashew Milk
1/2 c.	Onions, chopped
1/2 tsp.	Garlic, minced
1/2 c.	Bell pepper, chopped
3/4 c.	Pimento "Cheese"
1/4 c.	Bacon Gluten, chopped fine

Mix the flour, baking powder, Sucanat, salt, and yeast. Add the n'egg, oil, and "milk" to that. This should be the consistency of pancake batter. Add water if needed to obtain this. Add onions, garlic, bell pepper, "cheese," and gluten and mix well. Using 1/3 cup of mixture for each omelet, cook on an oiled griddle at about 350°, turning once, until golden brown on both sides. Serve with salsa, tomato sauce, mushroom sauce, or onion sauce.

OVEN-FRIED GLUTEN

Good the first day but better the next. Cold it is very much like cold fried chicken.

1 c.	Onion, chopped fine
1 1/2 tsp.	Garlic, crushed
1/4 c.	Non-dairy margarine, melted
4 c.	Raw gluten, made from all white flour
1/2 tsp.	Sage
1 c.	Nutritional Yeast
4 1/2 tsp.	Sea salt
1 tsp.	Black pepper
1 tsp.	Paprika
1/4 c.	Tahini
	Non-dairy margarine for rolling up

Sauté the onions and garlic in the margarine. Add all the other ingredients along with the hot sautéed onion and garlic to the raw gluten and work them through with your fingers. Take about 1/3 cup piece of gluten and pull and flatten it out until it is about 1/4 inch thick and 3 to 4 inches long. Spread about 1 1/2 teaspoons of margarine on this stretched piece and roll it up like a jelly roll, then flatten it out with your fingers. Next, roll it in a mixture made of:

1 3/4 c. Cracker crumbs
1 tsp. Garlic powder
1/2 tsp. Sea salt
1/4 tsp. Black pepper

Pour 2 tablespoons of corn oil on a baking sheet or in a baking pan. Put the gluten pieces rolled in the crumbs on it. Bake at 375° for about 45 minutes, turning once when golden brown on the bottom. Be sure not to overcook.

ROASTED "CHICKEN" WITH POTATOES AND "CHORIZO"

1/2 c. Olive oil
4 c. Potatoes, peeled and halved (or quartered, if large)
1 T. Olive oil
2 c. Onions, coarsely chopped
1 c. Bell pepper (red preferred), cut into 1-inch squares
2 c. Mexican Chorizo Sausage Gluten, or other spiced sausage-type gluten, chopped fine
1 T. Garlic, minced
4 c. Chicken-like Broth
1/2 tsp. Black pepper
3 c. Chicken Gluten slices, coated with oil and broiled until brown

Heat the oil in a skillet and cook the potatoes until golden brown all over–about 20 minutes. Pour off the oil and set the potatoes aside in the skillet. Heat the tablespoon of oil in another skillet and sauté the onions and bell pepper until soft and starting to brown–about 12 or 15 minutes. Add the "sausage" and garlic and cook 5 more minutes. Add this to the potatoes. Add the broth and pepper and bring to a simmer. Cook, uncovered, until the potatoes are tender and the broth has reduced by half–about 10 minutes. Arrange the gluten slices in a baking dish, pour the potato mixture over them, and bake at 400° for 10 to 15 minutes to heat through.

SOY GRITS "CHICKEN"

1/2 c. Soy grits
1 c. Boiling Chicken-like Broth

Stir grits into the broth and cook for 5 minutes.

SPANISH "CHICKEN" AU GRATIN

3 T. Corn oil
4 c. Chicken gluten, sliced
2 c. Fresh mushrooms, sliced
1 1/2 c. Onions, chopped
1 T. Garlic, minced
3 c. Cream of Mushroom Soup
1/4 tsp. Cayenne pepper
2 T. "Parmesan Cheese"

Heat the oil in a skillet and fry the gluten until brown. Set aside. In the same skillet sauté the mushrooms, onions and garlic until the onions are soft. Put the gluten back in the skillet and cook 5 more minutes. Add the mushroom soup and cayenne and cook for another 5 minutes. Put in a casserole pan and sprinkle with the "parmesan." Bake at 400° for 20 minutes.

SPANISH "CHICKEN" WITH RICE

1 1/2 c.	Onion, chopped fine
3/4 tsp.	Garlic clove, crushed
1/2 c.	Bell pepper, chopped fine
1/2 c.	Olive oil
4 c.	Tomatoes, canned
1/2 tsp.	Sucanat
1 T.	Sea salt
2 T.	Paprika
1/2	Bay leaf
1/4 tsp.	Basil (ground)
3 c.	Water
2 c.	Rice, uncooked
3 c.	Chicken Gluten cut in pieces

Sauté the onion, garlic and bell pepper in the oil until soft. Add the tomatoes and seasonings and cook for 15 minutes. Add the water, rice and gluten. Cook or bake for 40 minutes, or until the rice is done.

"TURKEY" CUTLETS PICCATA

Something different.

1	N'egg
1 T.	Cashew Milk
1/4 c.	Non-dairy margarine
4	Turkey Gluten "cutlets" 1/4-inch thick
2 c.	Fresh bread crumbs
1 tsp.	Lemon juice
1/2 c.	Turkey Broth
Dash	Black pepper

Combine the n'egg and "milk." Melt the margarine in a skillet. Dip each cutlet into the n'egg mixture and then into the bread crumbs. Fry the cutlets, 2 at a time, until lightly browned on both sides, adding more margarine if needed. Set the cutlets aside. Put the lemon juice into the skillet. Add the broth, and pepper. Return the cutlets to the skillet, cover, and simmer 10 to 15 minutes.

"TURKEY" HOLIDAY CASSEROLE

You can't do without it!

2	Times the Turkey Gluten recipe
1	Times the Bread Dressing recipe
3	Times the Mushroom Gravy recipe–made with Turkey Gluten Broth

Slice the gluten thin. Spray both sides of the slices lightly with oil and broil lightly–not letting it get crisp. Set aside. Put the dressing ingredients in a large casserole and cook according to the instructions given in the Bread Dressing recipe. When the dressing is done, cover it with 1/3 of the gravy. Put 1/2 of the gluten slices over that. Cover that with another 1/3 of the gravy. Cover with the rest of the gluten slices. Pour the rest of the gravy over all. Bake at 400° for 30 minutes.

"TURKEY" SALAD BURRITOS

A masterpiece!

2 c.	Turkey Gluten, chopped
2 T.	Celery, chopped fine
1/2 c.	Onion, chopped fine
1/4 c.	Black olives, sliced (add up to 1/4 cup more if you like)
1 c.	Yeast, Pimento, or Mozzarella "Cheese"
1/2 c.	"Miraculous Whip"
1/3 c.	Salsa
1/8 tsp.	Sea salt
6	Flour tortillas–7-8 inches in diameter

Combine the gluten, celery, onion, olives, and "cheese." Whisk together the "Miraculous Whip," salsa, and salt. Pour this sauce over the gluten mixture and blend well. Spoon this filling onto the tortillas and wrap them burrito-style. Put in a baking dish or pan and bake at 350° for 20 minutes, until thoroughly warmed. Serve with extra salsa and olives.

Members of the Nebraska Vegetarian Society visiting the Monastery.

Seafood Substitutes and Dishes

GLUTEN FISH

These are the Gluten Scallops in a different shape.
Feed them to fish lovers and turn them into gluten lovers!

Make Basic Gluten using all unbleached white flour. Use Cooking Method 2, and slice the gluten 1/4 to 1/2-inch thick.

Make a broth by combining and simmering together for 5 minutes:

4 c. Water
2 T. MSG
1 T. Sea salt
2 T. Corn oil

Boil the gluten in the broth for 30 minutes. Then let it soak overnight in the broth. Drain well. Dip each piece in a mixture of:

2 c. Cashew milk
1/4 tsp. Cayenne pepper
1/4 tsp. Sea salt

Roll in a mixture of:

2 c. Corn flour, corn meal, Cream of Wheat (Farina), Malto-Meal, or powdered cracker crumbs
1/4 tsp. Cayenne pepper
1/4 tsp. Sea salt

Deep fry at 350° until light brown.

VARIATION: Coat in Deep-Frying Batter (see Etc. section) and deep-fry at 400°.

DEEP-FRIED "FISH"

DRENCH:

2 c. Cashew milk
1/4 tsp. Cayenne pepper

1/4 tsp. Sea salt

DREDGE:

2 c. Cracker crumbs OR corn flour
1/4 tsp. Cayenne pepper
1/4 tsp. Sea salt

Take slices of fish-flavored gluten cooked by Method 2. Dip each slice in the drench and then in the dredge, coating well, but gently shaking off excess crumbs or flour. Deep fry.

"FISH" SOUP

1 c. Green onions, chopped fine
1/3 c. Celery, chopped fine
2 T. Corn oil
1 c. Unbleached white flour
3 qt. Chicken-like Broth
1 c. Canned tomato sauce
1 T. Lemon juice
2 c. Fish Gluten, cut in 1-inch cubes
1 bag Zatarain's Crab Boil
1/2 tsp. Cayenne pepper

Sauté the onions and celery in the oil. Brown the flour and add it to the onions and celery. Combine everything and cook for 20-30 minutes. Remove the bag of crab boil before serving.

GLUTEN SCALLOPS

Because these are so much better than either the real thing, or the dreary canned imitations, words fail me. But your appetite won't!

Make Basic Gluten using all unbleached white flour. Use Cooking Method 1, tearing the gluten into 3/4-inch chunks. Make a broth by combining and simmering together for 5 minutes:

4 c. Water
2 T. MSG
1 T. Sea salt
1 tsp. Corn oil

Boil the gluten in the broth for 30 minutes. Then let it soak overnight in the broth. Drain well. Dip each piece in a mixture of:

4 c. Cashew milk
1/4 tsp. Cayenne pepper
1 tsp. Sea salt

Roll in a mixture of:

4 c. Powdered cracker crumbs, corn flour, corn meal, Cream of Wheat (Farina) or Malto-Meal
1/2 tsp. Cayenne pepper
1/2 tsp. Sea salt

Deep fry at 350° until light brown.
VARIATION: Coat in Deep-Frying Batter (see Etc. section) and deep-fry at 400°.

GLUTEN SHRIMP

When I became a vegetarian thirty years ago the only thing I missed was shrimp, which I loved heartily. Now after thirty years I can enjoy it again–and so can you. This makes a lot of "shrimp," but you can freeze it and it keeps just fine. Be sure you use the Zatarain's Crab Boil which is whole spices in a bag.

Make Basic Gluten and cook by Method 2. Slice the cooked gluten 1/4-inch thick and then cut into 1x2-inch pieces (or into shrimp-like shapes). Boil in a broth made by combining and simmering together for 5 minutes:

1 gal. Water
1/2 c. MSG
1/4 c. Sea salt
1 bag Zatarain's Crab Boil
2 T. Corn oil

(If you want to make less broth, break open the crab boil bag and use the quantity of spices proportionate to the amount of water you are using, tying them in a piece of cheesecloth. *Or:* If you do not have Zatarain's Crab Boil, use the broth given above for Scallops and Fish.)

Boil the gluten in the broth for 30 minutes. Then let it soak overnight in the broth–keeping the crab boil bag in the broth as well. Drain before using.

BROILED "SHRIMP"

3 T. Olive oil
3 T. Non-dairy margarine
4 tsp. Lea & Perrins Steak Sauce
1 tsp. Louisiana Hot Sauce
6 c. Gluten Shrimp
Cayenne pepper
1 c. Water

Put the oil in a baking pan, slice the margarine into it, and heat it in an oven until the margarine is melted. Take the pan from the oven and add the steak sauce and hot sauce, mixing well. Put the gluten in a single layer into the mixture and sprinkle them generously with cayenne pepper. Pour the water into the pan, using just as much as is needed to half-cover the gluten. Bake at 350° for 20 minutes, then place in a broiler, basting frequently and turning, until the gluten is well browned and dark around the edges.

FRENCH FRIED "SHRIMP"

Oh me, oh my, oh!
You won't believe how wonderful these are!

6 c. Gluten Shrimp
3 c. Cashew Milk
1/2 c. "Parmesan Cheese"
2 c. Onion, sliced
1 tsp. Garlic, sliced
1/2 c. Bell pepper, sliced

2 T. Lea & Perrins Steak Sauce
2 tsp. Louisiana Hot Sauce

Place the gluten in a large bowl. Combine the milk, "parmesan," onion, garlic, bell pepper, steak sauce, and hot sauce, and blend in a blender. Pour this over the gluten, adding more milk if needed to cover it. Stir a bit to mix everything evenly, and marinate overnight or at least 12 hours. When ready to fry the gluten, combine:

2c. Powdered cracker crumbs, corn flour, corn meal, Cream of Wheat (Farina) or Malto-Meal
1/4 tsp. Cayenne pepper
1/4 tsp. Sea salt

Put the "flour" mixture in a brown paper bag.

Drain the "shrimp" a bit at a time, shake in the bag, and deep fry at 400°. (Or coat in Deep-Frying Batter–see Etc. section–and fry.)

MARINATED "SHRIMP"

This is delicious breaded and deep-fried, too.

6 c. Gluten Shrimp
3 c. Gluten Shrimp Broth
3 c. Water
2 tsp. Tabasco Sauce or 4 tsp. of Louisiana Hot Sauce
2 T. Dry mustard
1/4 c. Vinegar
2 c. Onion, sliced
3 T. Sucanat
1/2 tsp. Angostura Bitters

Combine everything, bring to a boil, let cool, and marinate for several hours.

MEXICAN "SHRIMP"

This is quite similar to "Shrimp" Creole, but distinctive enough for me to include here for you to try. But be warned: this dish is HOT.

3/4 c. Onion, chopped
1/2 c. Bell pepper, chopped
1/2 c. Celery, chopped
2 T. Corn oil
3/4 c. Canned tomatoes
2 tsp. Garlic, minced
1/2 tsp. Cayenne pepper
Sea salt
1 tsp. Paprika
1/2 c. Water
1 T. Unbleached white flour
2 c. Gluten Shrimp

Sauté the onion, bell pepper, and celery in the oil. Add the tomatoes, garlic, pepper, salt, paprika, water, and flour. Blend well and simmer for 45 minutes. Add the shrimp and simmer 15 more minutes. Serve over rice and top with yeast cheese if desired.

"SHRIMP" AND CORN SOUP

3 1/2 c.	Water
3 1/2 c.	Gluten Shrimp Broth
1/2 tsp.	Cayenne pepper
1 c.	Onion, finely chopped
1/2 c.	Parsley, finely chopped
1 1/2 tsp.	Garlic, minced
3 T.	Non-dairy margarine
2 c.	Tomatoes, chopped or mashed
2 c.	Corn
4 c.	Gluten Shrimp

Combine the water, broth, and pepper in a pot and bring it to a boil. Sauté the onions, parsley, and garlic in the margarine until the onions are soft. Add this along with the tomatoes and corn to the broth and bring it back to a boil. Lower heat to a simmer and add the gluten. Cook on low heat for 30 to 40 minutes, stirring occasionally.

"SHRIMP" CREOLE

You can't eat this just once!

1/2 c.	Onion, chopped
1/2 c.	Celery, chopped
1/2 c.	Parsley, chopped
1/3 c.	Bell pepper, chopped
2 T.	Olive oil
2 c.	Water
2 c.	Okra, sliced
2 c.	Tomatoes, chopped
1 c.	Tomato puree or sauce
3/4 tsp.	Garlic, minced
1 tsp.	Lea & Perrins Steak Sauce
1/2 tsp.	Louisiana Hot Sauce
1/3 tsp.	Sea salt
2 c.	Gluten Shrimp
3 c.	Cooked rice

Sauté the onion, celery, parsley, and bell pepper in the oil until they are tender. Add the water, okra, tomatoes, tomato puree (or sauce), and garlic. Simmer for 5 minutes. Add the steak sauce, hot sauce, and salt. Cook for 30 minutes. Add the gluten and cook 30 more minutes until the mixture is thick. Serve over the rice.

"SHRIMP" CURRY

1 1/2 c.	Unsweetened shredded coconut
1 1/2 tsp.	Powdered coriander
1 1/4 c.	Warm water
3 T.	Corn oil
3/4 c.	Onions, chopped fine
1 T.	Garlic, minced
3/4 tsp.	Ginger, powdered
1 tsp.	Tumeric
1/2 tsp.	Cumin, ground

1/4 tsp.	Cayenne pepper
1/4 tsp.	Black pepper
2 1/2 c.	Gluten Shrimp

Put the coconut, coriander, and water in a blender and puree on high. Sauté the onions and garlic until the onions are soft. Add the ginger, tumeric, cumin, cayenne, and black pepper, and sauté for 30 seconds. Add the gluten, stirring to coat well with the oil and spices. Add the coriander-coconut milk, bring to a simmer and cook for 10 minutes. Serve over rice.

"SHRIMP" GUMBO

1 c.	Olive oil
1 1/2 c.	Unbleached white flour
3 c.	Onions
1 1/2 c.	Bell pepper, chopped
1 c.	Canned tomato sauce
3 T.	Garlic, minced
1 c.	Green onion, chopped
3/4 c.	Parsley, chopped fine
10 c.	Water
4 T.	Lea & Perrins Steak Sauce
1 tsp.	Sea salt
1 tsp.	Cayenne pepper
1 c.	Shrimp Broth
6 c.	Gluten Shrimp

Heat the oil in a skillet, stir in the flour and cook until it is dark brown but not burned. Add the onions and bell pepper and sauté until the onions are transparent. Add the tomato sauce, garlic, and green onion and cook until the mixture is back to its original dark brown color. Add the parsley, water, steak sauce, salt, pepper, and broth. Cook for 45 minutes. Add gluten and cook for 30 minutes. Serve over rice.

"SHRIMP" IMPERIAL

2 T.	Green onion, chopped fine
2 T.	Celery, chopped fine
2 T.	Carrot, chopped fine
6 T.	Non-dairy margarine
2 T.	Unbleached white flour
1 c.	Cashew Cream
1/4 tsp.	White pepper
1/4 c.	Fish-like Broth
Dash	Tabasco Sauce
1	N'egg
1/4 c.	Cashew Cream
2 c.	Shrimp Gluten, chopped or ground
2 T.	Parsley, chopped fine (leaves only)
1/2 c.	Bell pepper (red preferred), chopped fine
1/4 tsp.	Grated orange peel
1 c.	Fine bread crumbs
1/2 tsp.	Paprika

Sauté the onion, celery, and carrot in 4 tablespoons of the margarine for 1 minute. Stir in the flour and cook, stirring, for 3 minutes. Whisk in the 1 cup of "cream" in a stream, add the pepper, and simmer, whisking, for 5 minutes. Take off the heat and stir in the broth and Tabasco. Separately, whisk together the n'egg and 1/4 cup of "cream." Stir this into the vegetable mixture and combine well. Fold in the gluten, parsley, bell pepper, and orange peel. Put into a well-"buttered" baking dish. Sprinkle with the bread crumbs and paprika, drizzle the remaining 2 tablespoons of margarine, melted, over the top. Bake at 425° for 12 to 15 minutes, or until the bread crumbs are golden and heated clear through.

"SHRIMP" MOLD

1 can	Campbell's Tomato Soup
1 1/2 c.	Tofu Cream Cheese
2 pkg.	Unflavored KOSHER (non-animal) gelatin
1/2 c.	Water
1 c.	"Mayonnaise"
4 or 5	Green onions
1/4 tsp.	Sea salt
1/2 tsp.	Cayenne pepper
1/2 tsp.	Tabasco sauce
2 c.	Gluten Shrimp

Heat the soup–direct from the can without adding milk or water– to a boil. Stir in the "cream cheese." Dissolve the gelatin in the water and add it to the soup mix. Let it cool. Add all other ingredients except the gluten. In a mold place alternating layers of sauce and gluten. Chill until the mold is set.

"SHRIMP" PIE

Remember the song about "Crawfish Pie"? Shrimp Pie works just as well–maybe better.

1/4 c.	Unbleached white flour
4 tsp.	Corn oil
4 tsp.	Olive oil
1/2 c.	Onions, chopped
1/2 c.	Mushrooms, chopped
1/2 c.	Green onions, chopped
1 tsp.	Garlic, minced
1 c.	Water
1/2 c.	Peas, cooked and drained
1/2 c.	Carrots, diced and cooked
1/4 tsp.	Sea salt
1 1/2 tsp.	Louisiana Hot Sauce
2 c.	Gluten Shrimp

Combine the flour and oils in a skillet and cook, stirring, until the flour is dark brown but not burned. Add the onions, mushrooms, green onions, and garlic, stirring. Add the water and bring to a boil. Add the peas, carrots, salt, hot sauce, and gluten. Cook for 5 more minutes until it thickens. Put everything in a pie pan with crust and top it with more crust, cutting holes to let out the steam. Bake at 350° for 45 minutes until the crust is golden brown.

"SHRIMP" SALAD

3 c.	Macaroni
5 c.	Gluten Shrimp
2 c.	Onion, chopped fine

1 c. Celery, chopped fine
2 c. Black olives, chopped fine
2 c. Dill pickles, chopped
1 qt. Miraculous Whip
2 T. Olive oil
2 tsp. Louisiana Hot Sauce OR 1/2 tsp. cayenne pepper
2 T. Lemon juice
2 T. Lea & Perrins Steak Sauce
1 T. Mustard
2 T. Seafood Cocktail Sauce

Cook the macaroni, drain it and let it cool. In a large bowl combine the macaroni, gluten, onions, celery, olives, and pickles, and toss well. Combine the mayonnaise, oil, hot sauce, lemon juice, steak sauce, mustard and cocktail sauce. Pour this over the macaroni mixture and mix well. If the salad seems too dry, make some more sauce and mix it in. Refrigerate for 1 hour before serving.

"SHRIMP" SOUP

2 qt. Chicken-like Broth
1 c. Green onions, chopped
1/2 c. Celery, chopped
1 T. Garlic, diced
1 c. Parsley, chopped
2 c. Water
2 tsp. Louisiana Hot Sauce OR 1/2 tsp. cayenne pepper
2 T. Lea & Perrins Steak Sauce
3 c. Gluten Shrimp

Put the ingredients–except for the shrimp–in a pot. Bring to a boil and lower the heat. Cover and simmer for 45 minutes. Add the shrimp and simmer for 30 more minutes.

"SHRIMP" STEW

Eat it up and call for more!

3 T. Olive oil
1/4 c. Unbleached white flour
3 c. Onion, chopped
1/2 c. Bell pepper, chopped
1/2 c. Celery, chopped
1/2 tsp. Garlic, minced
1 c. Parsley, chopped OR 1/2 c. dried parsley
4 c. Water
4 c. Gluten Shrimp
1/4 tsp. Sea salt
1/4 tsp. Cayenne pepper

Heat the oil, add the flour, and cook to a dark brown over low heat, stirring constantly. Add the onion, bell pepper, celery, garlic, and parsley and cook for 10 minutes. Slowly add the water, stirring, and simmer over low heat for 30 minutes. Add the shrimp, salt, and pepper. Cover and simmer for 30 more minutes, keeping the heat low. Serve over rice or pasta.

VARIATION: Instead of the water, use 6 cups of canned tomatoes, crushed (without the liquid).

"SHRIMP" WITH CAPER SAUCE

"Memorable" is the word for this dish.
It is gourmet food, I garontee!

1 c.	Onion, chopped fine
1/2 c.	Parsley, chopped
3 T.	Olive oil
1 T.	Garlic, minced
1/2 tsp.	Dried mint, crumbled
1/4 c.	Lea & Perrins Steak Sauce
1 tsp.	Louisiana Hot Sauce or 1/4 tsp. cayenne pepper
1 c.	Water
4 c.	Gluten Shrimp
3/4 c.	Miraculous Whip
1 T.	Lemon juice
1 T.	Creole or poupon mustard
2 T.	Capers, drained

Sauté the onions and parsley in the oil until the onions are tender. Add garlic, mint, steak sauce, hot sauce, water, and gluten. Cook, stirring all the time, for 20 minutes. Combine the Miraculous Whip, lemon juice, mustard, and capers, and mix well. Serve shrimp over rice or spaghetti and top with the sauce. Do not mix the sauce with the shrimp before serving.

SALMON LOAF

Unlikely as this recipe looks, it works beautifully.

1 c.	Tomato juice
1 c.	Water
1 c.	Soy flour
1 1/2 tsp.	Onion salt
1 T.	Oil

Whirl everything in a blender until smooth and pour into an oiled baking dish. Bake at 400° about 40 minutes until a tan crust forms. Cool and turn onto a platter. Serve hot or cold.

Flavoring Broths

I think this is one of the most valuable sections in this cookbook. By using these formulas you can impart a richer taste to the food you cook.

These broths are also for flavoring the various dishes which need a meat-like taste without any actual gluten imitations. (They are not for flavoring the gluten substitutes. The recipes for those broths are given in the sections for those meat substitutes–some formulas are the same as these, however.)

Not only is the flavor given by these broths superior to any of the various powdered or cubed forms of "beef" or "chicken" flavoring, they are immensely more healthful.

CHICKEN-LIKE BROTH

Combine and simmer for 5 minutes:

1/4 c.	Onions, chopped
2 1/4 tsp.	MSG
1/2 tsp.	Sea salt
1/2 tsp.	Poultry seasoning
2 T. &	
2 1/2 tsp.	Nutritional Yeast
1 T.	Corn oil
2 c.	Water

BEEF-LIKE BROTH

Combine and simmer for 5 minutes:

2 T.	Low sodium soy sauce
1 tsp.	Kitchen Bouquet
1 T.	Nutritional Yeast
1/4 c.	Onions, chopped
1/8 tsp.	Sage, rubbed
1 T.	Corn oil
2 c.	Water

Flavoring Broths

FISH-LIKE BROTH

Combine and simmer for 5 minutes:

2 c.	Water
1 T.	MSG
1 1/2 tsp.	Sea salt
1 T.	Corn oil

VARIATION: Add 1/8 teaspoon of powdered kelp for 2 cups of broth and 1/4 teaspoon for 4 cups of broth.

HAM-LIKE BROTH

Combine and simmer for 5 minutes:

1/4 c.	Low sodium soy sauce
2 tsp.	Kitchen Bouquet
2 T.	Nutritional Yeast
1/2 c.	Onions, chopped
1/4 tsp.	Sage, rubbed
1/2 tsp.	Black pepper
1/2 tsp.	Oregano
1 tsp.	Garlic powder
1 1/4 tsp.	Liquid smoke
1 T.	Corn oil
1 tsp.	Sea salt
2 c.	Water

SAUSAGE-LIKE BROTH

Combine and simmer for 5 minutes:

2 T.	Low sodium soy sauce
1 tsp.	Kitchen Bouquet
1 T.	Nutritional Yeast
1/4 c.	Onions, chopped
1/8 tsp.	Sage, rubbed
1/4 tsp.	Black pepper
1/4 tsp.	Oregano
1/2 tsp.	Garlic powder
2 T.	Watkins Sausage Seasoning
1 tsp.	Liquid smoke
1 T.	Corn oil
2 c.	Water

VEGETABLES

ANANDAMAYI KITCHURI

This recipe was formulated by Sri Sri Anandamayi Ma, a leading religious teacher of India. She recommended it to all her students, saying that if a person ate this dish always, varying the vegetables, they would never be ill. I have personally known many people who ate this every day. The Ajwan–a small black seed with a slightly sour tang that is available in most Indian grocery stores–was not in the original recipe, but was recommended to me by one of those who cooked it daily. In the original there were no onions or garlic, either. This is very good served with Puris or Flat Bread (see Bread and Such section).

1 c.	Rice, uncooked
3 T.	Corn oil
1 c.	Onions, chopped
1 T.	Jalapeños, sliced or minced (in this dish sliced seems better)
1 1/2 tsp.	Tumeric, ground
1 tsp.	Powdered ginger or fresh ginger, grated
1 tsp.	Cumin, ground
1 tsp.	Fenugreek, ground
1 tsp.	Anise, ground
1/2 tsp.	Ajwan, ground
1 1/4 tsp.	Sea salt
1/4 tsp.	Garlic powder
1 qt.	Vegetables, chopped
2 1/2 c.	Tomatoes, fresh or canned (if canned drain well, and use the juice as part of the boiling water measure)
3 c.	Boiling water (and tomato juice if canned tomatoes are used)

Wash the rice over and over, changing the water, until there is no more starch in the water, and drain it well. Heat the oil until very hot. Sauté the onions and jalapeños, then add the spices and stir constantly as it all "fries" to a rich brown color of a heavenly fragrance. Add the vegetables, tomatoes, and rice and stir continually until all is covered with the hot oil/spice mixture. Add the boiling water and stir. Bring to a boil, cover and simmer until all vegetables are done.

VARIATIONS: Include 1 1/2 cups of cooked dal, garbanzos, or other beans. Leave out the tomatoes. Include 2 cups of chopped beef, chicken, or unflavored gluten. Fry the gluten in the spices until it browns before you add the vegetables and rice.

LAZY KITCHURI

1 c.	Rice, uncooked
3 T.	Corn oil
1 c.	Onions, chopped
1 T.	Jalapeños, sliced or minced (in this dish sliced seems better)
1/4 c.	Curry powder (madrasi style is best)
1 1/4 tsp.	Sea salt
1/4 tsp.	Garlic powder
1 qt.	Vegetables of choice, chopped
2 1/2 c.	Tomatoes, fresh or canned (drained well, using juice as part of the water measure)
3 c.	Boiling water (and tomato juice if canned tomatoes are used)

Prepare and cook just as in the above instructions for Anandamayi Kitchuri. The same variations apply.

BAKED MASHED POTATOES

6 c.	Potatoes, peeled and cut into 1-inch pieces
1 1/2 c.	Green onions, sliced thin
3/4 c.	Onion, chopped
1 1/4 tsp.	Garlic, minced
3 T.	Non-dairy margarine
2/3 c.	Cashew Milk
1 1/2 c.	Yeast, Pimento, or Mozzarella "Cheese"
1 tsp.	Chives, dried
1/2 tsp.	Sea salt
1/8 tsp.	Cayenne Pepper

Cook the potatoes. While the potatoes are cooking, sauté the onions and garlic in 2 tablespoons of the margarine until the onions are soft. Force the potatoes through a ricer or food mill, stir in the "milk," the rest of the margarine, the onion mixture, half the "cheese," the chives, salt, and pepper. Put this in a "buttered" baking dish, spread the rest of the "cheese" on top, and bake at 400° for 20 minutes.

BEANS WITH TOMATOES

3/4 c.	Onions, chopped
1 tsp.	Garlic, minced
2 T.	Corn oil
2 c.	Dried beans, cooked and drained, reserving the liquid
3 c.	Canned tomatoes, chopped
1 tsp.	Sea salt
Pinch	Cayenne pepper

Sauté the onions and garlic in the oil. Combine all ingredients and cook for one hour, adding bean water if it gets too dry.

BOILED CABBAGE

Take the outer leaves off a head of cabbage, cut it into sections and remove the core. Shred or chop it finely. Drop it into rapidly boiling Beef-like or Chicken-like Broth. Cook until it is barely tender (7 or 8 minutes).

BOILED CABBAGE DINNER

This is real frontier log cabin food not to be confused with the bland New England version.

3 T.	Olive oil
1	Medium cabbage, quartered
4	Large onions, quartered
4	Medium whole potatoes, peeled and quartered
4	Whole carrots, peeled and cut in large pieces
3 c.	Ham-like Broth
3 c.	Water
1 T.	Louisiana Hot Sauce
1 tsp.	Sea salt
4 c.	Ham or Sausage Gluten, cubed

In a pot large enough to hold all the ingredients put everything except the gluten and bring to a boil. After it boils add the gluten–and more water if necessary. Cook until the potatoes are done.

BOILED OKRA

Sounds dull, but is good!

4 c.	Okra, whole
4 1/2 tsp.	Corn oil
2 c.	Flavoring Broth of choice
1 c.	Water
2 tsp.	Louisiana Hot Sauce
2 tsp.	Sea salt

Wash the okra. Cut off most of the okra stems but keep a small bit on each one so the okra "glue" will not leak out and make the dish slimy. Combine everything in a pot, bring to a strong boil, turn down the heat and simmer slowly until the okra is tender.

BROCCOLI

1 T.	Non-dairy margarine
1 T.	Corn oil
2 c.	Onion, coarsely chopped
1 tsp.	Garlic, minced
1/4 tsp.	Red pepper flakes
3/4 c.	Celery, chopped
6 c.	Broccoli, the stems chopped and the tops broken into small flowerets
3/4 c.	Bell pepper, chopped
1 1/2 c.	Chicken-like Broth
1/2 tsp.	Sea salt

Melt the margarine in the olive oil. Sauté the onion, garlic, pepper flakes, and celery in the olive oil until transparent. Add the broccoli and bell pepper and sauté briefly. Then add the broth and stir well. Cover and cook until tender, but do not overcook.

VARIATION: Add 2 tablespoons of curry powder when sautéeing.

BROCCOLI, MUSHROOMS, AND TOMATOES

4 2/3 c.	Mushrooms, halved
1/4 tsp.	Sea salt
3 T.	Non-dairy margarine
5 c.	Bunch of broccoli, cut into 2 1/2x1-inch pieces and steamed
2 c.	Tomatoes, chopped
3/4 tsp.	Lemon-pepper seasoning salt

Sauté the mushrooms and salt in the margarine until tender and golden. Stir in the broccoli, tomatoes, lemon-pepper seasoning salt, and 1 more tablespoon of margarine. Heat through.

BROWNED POTATOES

Peel and boil potatoes in Beef-like or Chicken-like Broth until they are nearly tender. Drain. Melt 2 tablespoons of non-dairy margarine in a pan and cook and turn the potatoes until they are light brown. Season with salt and pepper. Bake them in a 400° oven until they are crisp and brown. Add more margarine if required. Turn the potatoes to brown them evenly.

CABBAGE, TOMATO AND "CHEESE"

3 c.	Cabbage, finely shredded, cooked and drained
3/4 tsp.	Sea salt
1/4 tsp.	Cayenne pepper
1 1/2 c.	Canned tomatoes, crushed or chopped
1 c.	Yeast or Pimento "Cheese"
2 c.	Bread crumbs
1 T.	Non-dairy margarine

Cook the cabbage with the salt and pepper. In an oiled baking dish put alternating layers of tomatoes and cabbage, beginning with tomatoes. Spread with the "cheese" and then with the bread crumbs. Dot the top with 1 tablespoon of margarine. Bake at 325° for about 30 minutes or until the crumbs are brown.

CAJUN PEAS OR FRESH BEANS

Without a doubt!

6 c.	Peas or fresh (not dried) beans
2 T.	Non-dairy margarine
1 c.	Ham gluten, chopped
2 c.	Ham-like Broth
1 1/2 c.	Onion, chopped
3/4 tsp.	Garlic, minced
1 tsp.	Louisiana Hot Sauce

Fry the gluten in the margarine for 5 minutes. Add everything else and cook until the peas are tender. Then salt to taste.

CARROTS AND PEAS

In salted water, cook carrots and peas separately–in any proportions desired. Drain well. Combine. Season with salt and pepper. Pour melted margarine (1 tablespoon to 1 cup of vegetables) over them, OR heat together in Thin or Medium White Sauce (one-half as much sauce as vegetables).

COPONATINI EGGPLANT

2	Medium eggplants, peeled and cubed
1 T.	Sea salt
3 T.	Olive oil
1 c.	Canned tomato sauce
3/4 c.	Onions, chopped
2/3 c.	Celery, chopped
1/2 tsp.	Garlic, minced
3 T. & 1 tsp.	Green olives, quartered
1 tsp.	Vinegar
1 tsp.	Sea salt

Sprinkle the tablespoon of salt over the cubed eggplant and let it sit for 30 minutes, then squeeze out the moisture lightly. Cook the eggplant in the oil until it is tender. Add the tomato sauce. Separately sauté the onion, celery, garlic, and olives in a little olive oil, then add the vinegar to the mixture. Combine all ingredients with the salt. Cook together until the flavors are blended. Serve with rice.

COPPER PENNIES

Unusual! Can be a salad, an appetizer, or a regular dish!

2 T.	Corn oil
1 c.	Sucanat
3/4 c.	Vinegar
1 1/2 c.	Tomato soup
1 T.	Powdered mustard
2 T.	Lea & Perrins Steak Sauce
4 c.	Carrots, sliced
1 c.	Onions, sliced
1	Small bell pepper, sliced

In a saucepan simmer the oil, Sucanat, vinegar, tomato soup, mustard, and steak sauce. Boil the carrots until they are tender. In a casserole alternately layer the carrots, onions, and pepper slices. Pour the sauce over all and refrigerate.

CORN A LA KING

3 T.	Onions, minced
1/2 c.	Bell pepper, chopped
2 T.	Pimento, chopped
1 T.	Non-dairy margarine
2 1/2 c.	Corn
1/2 c.	White sauce made with Chicken- like Broth
3/4 tsp.	Sea salt
1/8 tsp.	Cayenne pepper

Sauté the onions, bell pepper, and pimento in the margarine. Add the rest of ingredients and cook.

VARIATION: Use squash instead of corn.

CORN AND PEPPERS

3/4 c.	Bell Peppers
3 T.	Onions, chopped
1/8 tsp.	Cayenne pepper
2 T.	Non-dairy margarine
4 c.	Corn
1/2 tsp.	Sea salt

Sauté the bell peppers, onions, and cayenne in the margarine. Combine with rest of ingredients and cook.

CORN SPECIAL

2 tsp.	Non-dairy margarine
2 T.	Bell pepper, chopped
3 T.	Onions, chopped
2 c.	Corn
1/4 tsp.	Sea salt

Melt the margarine in a skillet. Sauté the bell peppers and onions in the margarine. Add the corn and salt and cook.

COTTAGE MASHED POTATOES

1/4 c.	Onions, chopped
4 1/2 tsp.	Margarine, melted
3 c.	Mashed potatoes
1 1/2 c.	"Cottage cheese"
1 1/2 c.	Peas
1/8 tsp.	Cayenne pepper
3/4 tsp.	Sea salt

Sauté the onions in margarine. Combine with rest of ingredients and serve.

COUNTRY CORN

Never ordinary!

1 1/2 c.	Sausage Gluten (any flavor), cubed small
2 T.	Non-dairy margarine
1/2 c.	Ham-like Broth
1/2 tsp.	Salt
6 c.	Corn

Fry the cubed gluten in a small amount of corn oil and set aside. Melt the margarine and add the broth and salt. Heat through. Add the corn and gluten. Cook for 5 minutes, stirring occasionally.

COUNTRY CORN AND OKRA

Even more so!

3 T.	Non-dairy margarine

1/2 c.	Onion, chopped
1 1/2 c.	Sausage Gluten (any flavor), cubed small
3 c.	Corn
3 c.	Okra
2 c.	Canned tomatoes, mashed
1/2 c.	Ham-like Broth
1/2 tsp.	Salt

Melt the margarine and sauté the onions and gluten until the onions are soft. Add the rest of the ingredients, bring to a boil, and cook until the okra is done, stirring occasionally.

COUNTRY CORN CREOLE-1

This has character!

1/2 c.	Bell pepper, diced
3 T.	Onions, minced
3 T.	Non-dairy margarine
2 1/2 c.	Tomatoes, chopped
3 c.	Okra, sliced
1 tsp.	Sea salt
1/2 tsp.	Oregano
3 c.	Corn
1/8 tsp.	Cayenne pepper

Sauté the bell peppers and onions in the margarine. Combine with rest of ingredients and cook.

COUNTRY CORN CREOLE-2

This, too!

2 c.	Onions, sliced
1/4 c.	Jalapeños, minced
1 1/2 c.	Bell pepper, diced
2 T.	Corn oil
2 1/2 c.	Tomatoes, chopped
3 c.	Sliced fresh okra
1 tsp.	Sea salt
1 tsp.	Oregano
1/2 tsp.	Cumin seed
1/8 tsp.	Cayenne pepper
3 c.	Corn

In the oil sauté the onion, jalapeños, and bell pepper until the onion is transparent. Add the rest of the vegetables and seasonings. Add just enough water to not quite cover the vegetables. Cook for 20 minutes over medium-low heat.

VARIATION: Instead of water, cook with Beef-like or Chicken-like Broth.

CREAM-STYLE CORN

Who can do without it?

4 1/2 tsp. Non-dairy margarine

5 c. Corn
1/4 tsp. Sea salt

Melt the margarine, put in a blender with the corn and salt, and blend–using two or three short spurts to get the corn to begin to break up. Be careful not to liquefy the corn. Heat and serve.

CREAMED CARROTS

3/4 c. Onions, chopped
1/2 tsp. Garlic, minced
4 1/2 tsp. Non-dairy margarine
4 c. Carrots, cooked and chopped
1 c. Cashew milk
1/2 tsp. Sea salt

Sauté the onions and garlic in the margarine. Place the carrots and "milk" in a blender and process. Add sautéed onions and salt to the blender and blend until smooth.

CREAMED GREEN PEAS

In a way, no big deal, but oh, so good!

3 T. Onions, chopped
1 T. Non-dairy margarine
2 c. Green peas, cooked
1/2 tsp. Sea salt
2/3 c. Thin White Sauce made with Chicken-like Broth

Sauté the onions in the margarine, then combine all ingredients and heat.

CREAMED POTATOES

3 T. Onions, chopped
1/2 tsp. Garlic, minced
4 1/2 tsp. Non-dairy margarine
3 c. Potatoes, boiled, cooled, and diced
1 1/2 c. Medium White Sauce
1 1/2 tsp. Dried parsley
1 c. Bread crumbs

Sauté the onions and garlic in the margarine. Combine the onions, potatoes, sauce, and parsley. Put in an oiled baking dish. Cover with bread crumbs. Dot with non-dairy margarine. Bake at 400° until the crumbs are brown.

VARIATION: Add 1/2 cup of Yeast or Pimento "Cheese" to the white sauce and stir in well.

CREAMY POTATOES AND PEAS

1/4 c. Onions, chopped
1/2 tsp. Garlic, minced
1 1/2 c. Peas
4 1/2 tsp. Non-dairy margarine
1 1/4 c. Thick White Sauce made with Chicken-like Broth
Pinch Cayenne pepper

1/4 tsp. Sea salt
3 c. Hot cooked potato slices

Sauté the onions, garlic, and peas in the margarine. Combine the white sauce, pepper, and salt, and cook over low heat, stirring until the sauce is smooth. Combine with the potatoes and peas.

CREOLE OKRA

Heaven on earth!

1/2 c. Bell pepper, diced
1 c. Onions, minced
2 T. Non-dairy margarine
4 c. Okra, sliced
1 tsp. Garlic, minced
1/8 tsp. Cayenne pepper
4 c. Tomatoes, diced
1 T. Parsley
1/4 tsp. Basil
1/4 tsp. Sea salt
3/4 c. Beef-like Broth
1 c. Cooked Tomato Salsa

Sauté the bell peppers and onions in the margarine. Combine with rest of ingredients–except the salsa–and cook until the okra is tender. Stir in the salsa.

CREOLE TOMATOES

1/3 c. Onions, finely chopped
1/2 c. Bell pepper, finely chopped
1/8 tsp. Garlic, minced
1/4 tsp. Jalapeños, minced
1 T. Non-dairy margarine
1 T. Fresh parsley, chopped
3 c. Tomatoes, chopped
1 1/2 tsp. Sea salt
1/8 tsp. White pepper
1 T. Non-dairy margarine
2 T. Unbleached white flour
1 c. Cashew Milk

Sauté the onions, bell pepper, garlic, and jalapeños in the margarine until the vegetables are soft but not brown. Add the parsley, tomatoes, salt, and pepper and cook for 10 minutes. In a separate pan melt the other tablespoon of margarine and stir in the flour. Stirring constantly with a whisk, pour in the "milk" in a slow, thin stream. Cook over high heat until the sauce comes to a boil, thickens slightly and is smooth. Reduce heat and simmer for 2 or 3 minutes to remove the raw taste of the flour. Stir into the tomato mixture.

CURRIED BROCCOLI

2 c. Onions, chopped
2/3 c. Bell pepper, chopped
2/3 c. Celery, chopped

1 tsp.	Garlic, minced
3 T.	Non-dairy margarine
2 T.	Curry powder
6 c.	Broccoli, the stems chopped and the tops broken into small flowerets
1 c.	Chicken-like Broth
3/4 tsp.	Sea salt

Sauté the onion, bell pepper, celery, and garlic in the margarine until the onions are transparent. Add the curry powder and sauté for 30 seconds, stirring constantly. Add the broccoli and stir until all is coated with the hot oil. Add the broth and the salt.

CURRIED GREEN BEANS

Everybody here calls for more!

2 c.	Onions, chopped
1 1/2 tsp.	Garlic, minced
1/4 tsp.	Red pepper flakes
2 T.	Corn oil
1 1/2 tsp.	Curry powder
1 T.	Lemon juice
1 1/2 c.	Water
3/4 tsp.	Sea salt
6 c.	Green beans

Sauté onions, garlic and pepper flakes in the oil until transparent. Add the curry powder and sauté 1 minute more, stirring constantly. Add the water, salt, and lemon juice and stir well. Stir in the beans. Cover and cook.

CURRIED PEAS

Whenever someone feels hungry around here, two times out of three they say: "How about some curried peas?"

1/2 c.	Onions, chopped
4 1/2 tsp.	Non-dairy margarine
1 T.	Curry powder
1 T.	Unbleached white flour
3 c.	Cashew Milk
1/8 tsp.	Cayenne pepper
1/2 tsp.	Sea salt
3 c.	Peas (if frozen, thawed; if fresh, lightly steamed)

Sauté the onions in margarine until transparent. Add the curry powder and sauté 30 seconds longer, stirring constantly. Add the flour and stir it in. Slowly add the "milk" as you stir continually. Add the cayenne and salt. Simmer for 10 minutes, stirring occasionally so it will not stick. Add the peas and cook for 5 more minutes. Serve with rice.

CURRIED PEAS, CARROTS AND POTATOES

1 c.	Onion, chopped
3/4 tsp.	Garlic, minced
1 1/2 tsp.	Curry powder
2 T.	Non-dairy margarine

3 c.	Potatoes, cooked and cubed
1 c.	Peas
1 c.	Carrots, cooked
1/2 c.	Boiling water
1/2 c.	Coconut milk

Sauté the onion, garlic, and curry powder in the margarine until the onions are transparent. Add the potatoes, peas, and carrots and stir until coated with the hot oil. Add the water and cook for 5 minutes. Add the coconut milk and cook for 5 more minutes.

CURRIED POTATOES AND PEAS

When I was starving in India nearly thirty years ago some Kashmiri friends made this for me and watched in awe as I ate their shares as well as mine!

1/4 c.	Non-dairy margarine
1/2 tsp.	Powdered ginger
1 tsp.	Garlic, minced
1/3 c.	Onions (red preferred), chopped
1 tsp.	Sea salt
1 tsp.	Cumin, ground
1/2 tsp.	Tumeric
1 tsp.	Coriander, powdered
1/4 tsp.	Garam Masala
1/4 tsp.	Cayenne
1 1/2 c.	Tomatoes, chopped
2 c.	Green peas
1 1/2 c.	Potatoes, peeled and cut into 1/2-inch cubes
1/2 c.	Water

Heat the margarine over high heat until a drop of water flicked into it splutters instantly. Stir in the ginger and garlic. Add the onions and salt. Lower the heat to moderate and, stirring constantly, sauté the onions for 7 or 8 minutes, until they are soft and golden brown. Add cumin, tumeric, coriander, garam masala, and cayenne. Stir in the tomatoes. Still stirring, cook briskly for 5 minutes, until most of the liquid in the pan evaporates and the mixture is thick enough to draw away from the sides and bottom of the pan in a dense mass. Drop in the peas and potatoes and turn them about with the spoon until they are evenly coated with the tomato mixture. Stir in the water, bring to a boil over high heat, cover tightly, and reduce the heat to low. Simmer for 10 minutes, or until the peas and potatoes are tender but still intact.

DEEP-FRIED OKRA

If your only acquaintance with okra is from those strange little "wheels" in Campbell's soup, or if you have only had okra cooked until it is gooshy, be sure to try this.

5 c.	Cashew Milk
1 T.	Louisiana Hot Sauce
1 T.	Low sodium soy sauce
3 c.	Corn flour
1 tsp.	Garlic powder
1 tsp.	Onion powder
1 tsp.	Sea salt
8 c.	Okra, cut into 1/2-inch pieces.

Combine the "milk," hot sauce, and soy sauce. Combine the corn flour, garlic and onion powders, and salt. Dip the okra in the cashew milk mixture, remove and roll it in the corn flour mixture. Deep fry at 350-365° until it is brown. Drain on paper towels and serve immediately.

DEEP-FRIED SQUASH

This tastes a goodly bit like fried oysters–but so much nicer to chew!

4-6 Yellow squash, cut into 1/4-inch slices

DRENCH:

1 c.	Water
1/2 tsp.	Garlic powder
1/2 tsp.	Onion powder
1/2 tsp.	Cayenne pepper
1 tsp.	Sea salt

DREDGE:

2 c.	Corn flour
1/4 tsp.	Sea salt
1/4 tsp.	Cayenne pepper

Combine the drench ingredients. Dip the squash in the drench and then in the dredge. Deep fry for 1 minute at 350°. Sprinkle with "Parmesan 'Cheese'" after frying. Serve immediately.

DUTCH SUCCOTASH

1/2 c.	Bell pepper, diced
1/3 c.	Onions, chopped
2 T.	Non-dairy margarine
3 c.	Potatoes, cubed and cooked
2 c.	Corn, cooked
1 1/2 c.	Lima beans, cooked
2 1/4 c.	Chopped tomatoes
1/4 tsp.	Cayenne pepper
1/2 tsp.	Basil
1 tsp.	Sea salt

Sauté the bell peppers and onions in the margarine. Combine with rest of ingredients and cook.

EGGPLANT AND TOMATOES

Tastes like more!

4 c.	Eggplant, sliced 1/8 to 1/4-inch thick
1/4 c.	Olive oil
1 1/2 c.	Onions, chopped
1 1/2 tsp.	Jalapeños, minced
1 1/2 tsp.	Garlic, minced
3 c.	Tomatoes, chopped

1 1/2 tsp. Sea salt
1/8 tsp. Cayenne pepper

Sauté the eggplant in half the oil until it becomes soft. Set aside on paper towels to drain. In the rest of the oil sauté the onions and jalapeños until the onions are soft. Add the garlic and tomatoes and cook for 2 minutes. Add the eggplant, salt, and cayenne. Cook until most of the liquid is evaporated.

EGGPLANT BURGERS

This will surprise you! We know how to make a lot of "burgers," but this is far and away my favorite!

1 Eggplant, peeled and cut into 1/2-inch slices
Sea salt
4 c. Unbleached white flour
1/4 tsp. Garlic powder
1/4 tsp. Onion powder
1/4 tsp. Basil
1/4 tsp. Black pepper
Corn oil

Sprinkle a layer of sea salt on a counter top or other large surface, and lay the eggplant slices out on that. Sprinkle sea salt over the top of the slices. Let them sit for twenty minutes to draw out the moisture. Take each slice and pat it dry with paper towels and set aside. Mix the flour with the garlic powder, onion powder, basil, and black pepper. Lightly dust each slice of eggplant in the flour mixture, shaking off any excess. Deep fry in a skillet that has 3/4-inch of hot corn oil until golden brown. Drain on paper towels. Put in buns just as you would "burgers."

FRENCH FRIED POTATOES

What I have said about potato chips applies to these, too.
This recipe is based on the McDonald's method of making french fries, and although it is somewhat tedious I think you will find the results worth the extra trouble.
The best type of potatoes for french fries are Russet Burbanks from Idaho.

1 qt. Cold water
1/2 c. White vinegar
4 c. Potatoes, sliced into 1/4-inch thick sticks
2 qt. Water
1 T. Sea salt
Ice water
Corn oil
Onion salt

Combine the quart of cold water and the vinegar. Put the potatoes in this, cover, and refrigerate for 2 hours. Drain in a colander. Bring the 2 quarts of water and salt to a boil. When the water is boiling hard, drop the potatoes into the water and cook for 1 minute. Put into the colander again and drain and IMMEDIATELY plunge them into ice water. Drain them on paper toweling as best you can to remove as much water as possible. Put corn oil in a heavy 2-to-3-quart saucepan to a depth of 4 inches. Using a french-frying basket, fry the potatoes at 400° for only 1 minute. Remove and turn into a paper towel lined bowl or basket. Repeat until all the potatoes have been fried, making sure the oil temperature never goes below 375° and can quickly come back up to 400°. Now start all over again and re-fry the potatoes till they are crisp and golden brown. Sprinkle with onion salt while they are hot and serve before they get cold. If you are frying a goodly number of potatoes and do not want the first ones to get cold, after salting a batch of fries transfer them to a pan lined with a double thickness of paper towels and put them in a 250° oven to keep them warm while you proceed with the remaining batches.

NOTE: Use only long white potatoes. The thicker the skin of the potato, the better the quality for frying.

FRIED MASHED POTATO BALLS

3 T.	Cornstarch
1/4 c.	Water
2 c.	Mashed potatoes, hot
1/4 tsp.	Onion powder
1/4 tsp.	Garlic powder
1 tsp.	Baking powder
1/4 tsp.	Sea salt
1/8 tsp.	Cayenne pepper

Dissolve the cornstarch in the (cold) water. Add the other ingredients and mix well. Form into balls and fry in oil until brown. Place them to drain on paper in a colander. If needed, keep them hot in a 425° oven.

FRIED 'TATERS 'N ONIONS

Just what it is. Yum!

3 T.	Corn oil
2 c.	Onions, sliced thin
1 qt.	Potatoes, sliced medium thick
	Garlic salt
	Pepper (black or cayenne), or curry powder

Heat oil, put in onions and potatoes and fry, turning regularly, until the potatoes brown. Toward the end of the frying, sprinkle with garlic salt and black or cayenne pepper as you fry, OR sprinkle with curry powder and salt as you fry.

GOLDEN VEGETABLE LAYER

2 c.	Potatoes, chopped
2 c.	Carrots, chopped
2 T.	Non-dairy margarine
1/2 tsp.	Sea salt
1/4 tsp.	Cayenne pepper
2 c.	Tomato Sauce (see recipes in Sauces and Gravies), cooked down into a thick purée and kept warm

Steam or boil the potatoes and carrots until they are just tender. Mash them coarsely–not letting them become smooth as in mashed potatoes–with the margarine, salt and pepper. Put the mixture into a serving dish, top with the tomato sauce, and serve at once.

GREEK POTATOES

Distinctive!

3 T.	Onions, chopped
4 1/2 tsp.	Corn oil
1	Bay leaf
1/2 tsp.	Oregano
1/4 tsp.	Thyme
1/2 tsp.	Basil
2 T.	Parsley, chopped
1 1/2 c.	Tomatoes, fresh or canned
1/2 c.	Tomato paste
1/2 c.	Water or Beef-like Broth
1/4 tsp.	Sea salt
1 tsp.	Garlic, minced
3 c.	Potatoes, cut in 1-inch chunks

Sauté the onions in the oil. Put all the ingredients–except for the potatoes–in a pot, stir and simmer for 15 minutes. Place the potatoes in an oiled baking dish or pan. Pour the sauce over the potatoes and toss until well covered. Bake at 375° for at least 1 hour, or until the potatoes test done when pierced with a fork. Check the potatoes near the end of the cooking time for moistness–the potatoes should soak up most of the sauce and be rather dry but not blackened. Add a little water if necessary.

GREEN BEAN, POTATO, AND TOMATO COMBO

This is always welcome!
Try olive oil as a variation!

3 T.	Onions, chopped
1/2 tsp.	Garlic, minced
2 T.	Corn oil
1 1/4 c.	Green beans (if fresh, stem and cut them into 1-inch sections)
1 1/4 c.	Potatoes, cut in 1-inch chunks and cooked
2 1/2 c.	Tomatoes, pureed in blender
1/8 tsp.	Basil
1/8 tsp.	Oregano
1/8 tsp.	Cayenne pepper
3/4 tsp.	Sea salt
1/2 c.	Beef-like Broth (omit if you are using canned tomatoes)

Sauté the onions and garlic in the oil. Combine with rest of ingredients and cook until the beans are done–about 25 minutes. During the cooking time, you may have to add additional water to keep the combo at a consistency of thick stew.

GREEN BEANS

String and shred green beans lengthwise. Drop the beans into boiling water to which onion salt (1 1/2 teaspoon per quart) has been added. Cook the beans until they are barely tender–no longer– about 20 minutes. Drain the beans. Return to the pot and reheat them in melted non-dairy margarine OR thin white sauce (half as much sauce as there are beans) to which yeast or pimento cheese may be added.

GREEN BEANS AND "HAM"

2 T.	Olive oil
1 c.	Baked Gluten Ham, cubed
4 c.	Green beans
1 1/2 c.	Onions, chopped
3/4 tsp.	Garlic, chopped
2 1/2 c.	Water
2 T.	Lea & Perrins Steak Sauce
2 tsp.	Louisiana Hot Sauce
1 tsp.	Sea salt

In the pot you are going to use for cooking, sauté the ham in the oil. Add the beans, onions, garlic, water, steak sauce, hot sauce, and salt. Cook until the beans are tender.

VARIATION: Use bacon or sausage gluten instead of the ham gluten.

GREEN BEANS AND MUSHROOMS

1 c.	Mushrooms, sliced
1/4 c.	Green onions, sliced
1 T.	Corn oil
2 c.	Green beans, cut in 2-inch pieces
3/4 c.	Beef-like or Chicken-like Broth, or water
1/4 tsp.	Sea salt
1/8 tsp.	Pepper
1/8 tsp.	Dried basil

Sauté the mushrooms and onions in the oil a few minutes, add the rest of the ingredients and cook 10 to 15 minutes until the beans are done.

GREEN BEANS STIR FRY

1 c.	Green beans, cut into 1-inch pieces
3/4 c.	Onions, chopped
1/2 tsp.	Garlic, minced
2 T.	Corn oil
1 c.	Beef-like or Chicken-like Broth
1 tsp.	Basil
1/4 tsp.	Sea salt
1 1/2 c.	Tomatoes, chopped
1	N'egg

Sauté the beans, onions, and garlic in the oil for 1 minute. Add the broth, basil and salt. Cover and simmer for 15 minutes, or until the beans are tender. Add the tomatoes, and n'egg. Cook, stirring constantly, until the mixture boils and thickens.

GREEN BEANS SUPREME

3 T.	Onions, chopped
1/2 tsp.	Garlic, minced
4 1/2 tsp.	Non-dairy margarine
4 c.	Green beans
1/2 c.	Beef-like or Chicken-like Broth
1/4 tsp.	Lemon peel

1/8 tsp.	Cayenne pepper
1/8 tsp.	Dill weed
1/4 tsp.	Sea salt
1 c.	Tofu Sour Cream or Cashew Sour Cream

Sauté the onions and garlic in the margarine. Combine all ingredients–except the sour cream–and cook until beans are cooked but not too soft. Mix in the "sour cream."

GREEN BEANS WITH BACON

1 T.	Non-dairy margarine
1 T.	Corn oil
2 c.	Onions, chopped
1 1/2 tsp.	Garlic, minced
1/4 tsp.	Red pepper flakes
6 c.	Green beans
1/3 c.	Gluten bacon, chopped fine
1 qt.	Chicken-like or Beef-like Broth

Put the margarine and olive oil together and melt the margarine. Sauté the onions, garlic, and pepper flakes until the onions are transparent. Add the green beans and stir well until they are coated with the hot oil. Add the gluten. Add the broth and cook until the beans are done.

GREEN BEANS WITH GARLIC

1 T.	Olive oil
2 c.	Green beans, trimmed and broken in half
2 T.	Garlic, minced
1/2 tsp.	Sea salt
1 T.	Low sodium soy sauce

Sauté the beans and garlic for 5 minutes. Keep heat high to singe the beans. Add the salt and soy sauce. Cover, lower heat, and stew for 5 minutes.

VARIATION: Use broccoli instead of beans, the broccoli having been pared and sliced into thin sticks.

GREEN BEANS WITH TOMATOES

2 c.	Onions, chopped
1 1/2 c.	Bell pepper, chopped
1 1/2 c.	Celery, chopped
1 1/2 tsp.	Garlic, minced
1/4 tsp.	Red pepper flakes
2 T.	Olive oil
6 c.	Green beans
3 c.	Canned tomatoes, drained (save the juice) and chopped
2 T.	Low sodium soy sauce
	Tomato juice as needed

Sauté the onions, bell pepper, celery, garlic and pepper flakes in the olive oil until the onions are transparent. Add the green beans and stir until they are coated well with the hot oil. Add the tomatoes and soy sauce. Cook until the beans are done, adding tomato juice if it seems to be getting too dry.

GREEN LIMA BEANS WITH FINES HERBS

2 1/2 c.	Lima beans, cooked in a little Chicken-like Broth until tender
4 1/2 tsp.	Non-dairy margarine
1 tsp.	Lemon juice
3 T.	Onions, chopped
1 T.	Minced parsley
1/2 tsp.	Fines Herbs
1/2 tsp.	Sea salt

Combine everything and cook together for 5 minutes.

GREEN PEAS AND ONIONS

3 T.	Onions, chopped
2 tsp.	Non-dairy margarine
2 c.	Green peas, cooked
1/8 tsp.	Garlic powder
1/2 tsp.	Sea salt

Sauté the onions in the margarine, then combine all ingredients and heat.

HASHBROWN WAFFLES

4 c.	Raw potatoes, shredded
2 T.	Corn oil
3 tsp.	Onion powder
1/2 tsp.	Garlic powder
1 tsp.	Sea salt
4 tsp.	Nutritional yeast
2 T.	Dried parsley
1	N'egg
1 T.	Unbleached white flour

Combine everything well. Press into a preheated and oiled waffle iron. Close and bake 12 to 15 minutes until browned.

VARIATION: Use crumbled or chopped cooked potatoes.

JAMAICA RICE AND "PEAS"

3 c.	Onions, chopped
1 1/2 tsp.	Garlic, minced
2 T.	Corn oil
3 c.	Red kidney beans, cooked and drained
1 T.	Sea salt
1 T.	Lemon juice
1 tsp.	Basil
1 tsp.	Oregano
2 1/3 c.	Rice, cooked
2 c.	Chicken-like Broth

Sauté the onions and garlic in the oil. Combine all ingredients, turn into a large casserole, and bake slowly for 1 hour, adding a little more broth if necessary.

"KENTUCKY FRIED" GREEN BEANS

My Kentucky grandmother Burge used to make these in a non-vegetarian version. The memory clung to me through the years until one day I went in the kitchen determined to duplicate them. I did!

1 qt.	Green beans, steamed
3/4 c.	Onions, chopped
1 T.	Gluten bacon, chopped fine
1/8 tsp.	Black pepper
1/4 tsp.	Garlic powder
1/2 tsp.	Sea salt (or 1/2 tsp. salt and 1/2 tsp. Monosodium Glutamate)
2 T.	Corn oil

Sauté the beans in the oil until nearly cooked. Add the rest of the ingredients and sauté until the beans are completely cooked.

LIMA BEANS

Cover 1 quart of lima beans with boiling Beef-like or Chicken-like Broth. Add 1 tablespoon of non-dairy margarine. Simmer for 15 minutes. Add 1 teaspoon of sea salt. Cook the beans over a good flame until the water evaporates. Add:

1 1/2 T.	Lemon juice
1 T.	Parsley, chopped

VARIATION: Instead of the last three ingredients, add 1/2 cup of cashew milk and heat thoroughly, but do not boil.

LIMA BEANS AND TOMATOES

3/4 c.	Onions, chopped
1/4 c.	Bell pepper, chopped
1/2 tsp.	Garlic, minced
2 T.	Corn oil
2 c.	Lima beans, dried-cooked, fresh, or frozen and thawed
1/4 tsp.	Cayenne pepper
2 tsp.	Sea salt
1 1/2 c.	Tomatoes, chopped
1/4 c.	Celery, chopped

Sauté the onions, bell pepper, and garlic in the oil. Add the rest of the ingredients and cook gently until all are well done.

LIMA BEANS IN "CHEESE" SAUCE

Add to cooked lima beans one-half as much "cheese" sauce.

LIMA BEANS IN PIQUANTE SAUCE

1/4 c.	Onions, chopped
1/4 c.	Celery, chopped
1/2 tsp.	Garlic, minced
2 T.	Non-dairy margarine

2 1/2 T.	Unbleached white flour
2 1/2 c.	Lima beans, cooked and drained
1 1/2 c.	Beef-like or Chicken-like Broth made with Cashew Milk
1/2 c.	Yeast, Pimento, or Mozzarella "Cheese"
1/4 tsp.	Sea salt
1/8 tsp.	Cayenne pepper
1/4 tsp.	Dry mustard
1/8 tsp.	Basil

Sauté the onions, celery, and garlic in the margarine until the onions are light brown. Stir in the flour until it bubbles. Slowly stir in the broth. Reduce the heat and stir in the "cheese." Add the rest of the ingredients and stir.

LIMA BEANS WITH "CHEESE"

More than a touch of class!

1/3 c.	Onions, chopped
1/2 tsp.	Garlic, minced
4 1/2 tsp.	Non-dairy margarine
1 c.	Yeast, Pimento, or Mozzarella "Cheese"
4 c.	Lima Beans, cooked
1 tsp.	Low sodium soy sauce
1/2 tsp.	Sea salt
1/4 tsp.	Cayenne pepper

Sauté the onions and garlic in the margarine. Stir in the "cheese" and stir over low heat until it melts. Add the rest of the ingredients. Put in a baking dish, cover with bread crumbs, dot with margarine, and bake at 350° for 1/2 hour or until crumbs are brown.

LIMA-CORN SUCCOTASH

The ultimate succotash, I guarantee!

1 1/2 c.	Onions, chopped
1/2 c.	Bell pepper, chopped
1 1/2 tsp.	Garlic, minced
1/4 tsp.	Red pepper flakes
3 T.	Non-dairy margarine
3 c.	Corn (if fresh, cooked, if frozen, thawed)
3 c.	Green lima beans, cooked
3/4 tsp.	Sea salt

Sauté the onions, bell pepper, garlic and pepper flakes in the margarine until the onion is transparent. Then add the corn, limas, and salt, and cook 5 minutes more.

VARIATION: Add 1/2 cup Gluten Bacon, chopped fine, and cut the salt in half.

LOUISIANA CORN AND TOMATOES

1 1/4 c.	Onions, coarsely chopped
1/8 tsp.	Garlic, minced
2 T.	Corn oil
4 c.	Corn
1/2 c.	Bell pepper, coarsely chopped

3 c.	Tomatoes, coarsely chopped
1 1/2 c.	Water
1/2 tsp.	Cayenne pepper
1 1/2 tsp.	Sea salt

Sauté the onions and garlic in the oil until the onions are soft and translucent but not brown. Stir in the corn, bell pepper, tomatoes, water, cayenne and salt. Bring to a boil over high heat. Reduce heat to low, cover partially, and simmer about 10 minutes, or until the corn is tender.

MASHED CARROTS

A worthy change from mashed potatoes.

Cook carrots, drain and mash. Add non-dairy margarine, salt, and pepper to taste.

MASHED POTATOES

Peel potatoes and cut them in large chunks. Boil in salted water until they can be broken apart with a fork but have not started to fall apart. Mash the potatoes with enough potato water to give a good consistency. For each gallon of potatoes, mash in 1 stick of non-dairy margarine and 2 teaspoons of salt.

VARIATIONS: Use Cashew Milk instead of the potato water in the mashing. Use Beef-like or Chicken-like Broth as the mashing liquid. Cook the potatoes in Beef-like or Chicken-like Broth.

MUSHROOMS IN CREAM SAUCE

Marvelous on toast, biscuits, or rice!

1 c.	Onions, chopped
6 c.	Mushrooms, cleaned, stemmed and sliced (save stems to use later in soup)
2 T.	Non-dairy margarine
3/4 tsp.	Sea salt
1/8 tsp.	Black pepper
1/8 tsp.	Nutmeg
Pinch	Paprika
2 1/2 c.	Thin White Sauce
1/2 c.	Fresh dill weed, chopped
1/2 c.	Fresh parsley, chopped

Sauté the onions and mushrooms in the margarine until the onions are soft. Add the salt, pepper, nutmeg, paprika and white sauce, and cook together for 10 minutes. Add dill and parsley and cook for 2 more minutes.

VARIATIONS: Add 1 tablespoon of garlic. Add 1 tablespoon of jalapeños.

OKRA AND TOMATOES

1 T.	Olive oil
2 c.	Bacon Gluten, cubed
2c	Onions, chopped fine
3/4 tsp.	Garlic, minced
6 c.	Okra, sliced
3 c.	Tomatoes, diced
1 c.	Water or tomato juice

2 tsp. Louisiana Hot Sauce
2 T. Lea & Perrins Steak Sauce
1/2 tsp. Sea salt

In the oil sauté the gluten, onions, and garlic for 10 minutes. Add the okra and tomatoes. Pour water or juice over all. Add the hot sauce, steak sauce, and salt. Cook until the okra is tender and no longer tastes "green."

OKRA WITH CUMIN

Tastes like you are in India!

3 c. Okra
3 T. Corn oil
1/3 c. Onions (red preferred), sliced lengthwise into paper-thin slivers
1 tsp. Sea salt
2 tsp. Cumin
1/4 tsp. White pepper

Wash the okra under cold running water. With a small, sharp knife scrape the skin lightly to remove any surface fuzz. Pat dry with paper towels. In a heavy skillet heat the oil over moderate heat until a drop of water flicked into it splutters instantly. Add the onions and salt and stir for 7 to 8 minutes, or until they are golden brown. Add the okra, cumin and pepper, and continue to fry, lifting and turning the vegetables constantly, for 25 minutes, or until the okra is tender and most of the liquid in the pan has evaporated (frozen okra will still be somewhat sticky).

ORIENTAL EGGPLANT AND MUSHROOMS IN GARLIC SAUCE

4 c. Eggplant, peeled and cut into small cubes
3 c. Mushrooms, sliced thick
2 c. Onions, chopped coarsely
3 T. Garlic, crushed
1/4 tsp. Garlic powder
3 T. Olive oil
1 1/4 c. Canned tomato sauce
4 1/2 tsp. Low sodium soy sauce or Maggi
4 1/2 tsp. Red chili paste with garlic
1/4 tsp. Sea salt

Deep-fry the eggplant and set aside. Sauté the mushrooms, onions, garlic and garlic powder in the oil until soft. Add the rest of the ingredients–including the eggplant. Cook until most of the liquid is evaporated–about 15 minutes. Serve with rice.

OVEN FRIED POTATOES

These are superb!

2/3 c. Corn oil
8 c. Potatoes, cut into 1-inch chunks
1 1/2 tsp. Dill weed
1 1/2 tsp. Oregano
1 1/2 tsp. Onion salt

Pre-heat oven to 450°. Put the oil in a baking pan. Put the potato chunks in the pan and roll them around to coat them with the oil. Sprinkle generously with dill, oregano, and onion salt. Bake for 1 hour or until done, basting and turning every 10 minutes. Drain in a colander.

VARIATIONS: Stir in 1/4 cup of Bacon Gluten, chopped fine, after 45 minutes. Use sea salt instead of onion salt with the dill and oregano, and stir in 1 cup of chopped onions after 45 minutes.

OVEN-ROASTED OKRA

At first this seems simple and bland–but then it reveals itself!

4 T.	Olive oil
1/2 tsp.	Cumin, ground
1/2 tsp.	Oregano, crumbled
1/4 tsp.	Sea salt
1/4 tsp.	White pepper
6 c.	Small whole okra, rinsed and patted dry

Combine oil and seasonings in a mixing bowl. Add the okra and toss to coat. Place okra in a heavy pan and roast at 500°, stirring occasionally, for 8 to 10 minutes, or until tender and evenly browned. May be served with lemon wedges.

PAELLA-LIMAS

1 c.	Green limas, frozen
2 c.	Rice, uncooked
1 c.	Carrots, sliced thin
1 c.	Onions, minced
1 tsp.	Garlic, minced
3 T.	Corn oil
4 1/2 c.	Boiling water
1 3/4 tsp.	Sea salt

Steam the lima beans and set aside. Sauté the rice, carrots, onions, and garlic in the oil until the vegetables are soft. Spoon into the boiling water, being careful not to get burned when the rice "explodes." (If it does not explode, something is wrong.) Put the rest of the ingredients into the water and boil for 30 minutes. Pour the paella into a casserole, cover and bake at 350 degrees for 1 hour, uncovering it for the last 5 minutes.

PEAS AND CARROTS

1 1/4 c.	Onions, chopped
1/2 tsp.	Garlic, minced
1/3 tsp.	Hot pepper flakes
1 T.	Corn oil
1 1/2 c.	Peas
1 c.	Carrots, sliced or diced
2/3 c.	Chicken-like Broth
1/4 tsp.	Sea salt
1 T.	Nutritional yeast
1 T.	Non-dairy margarine
2 c.	Rice, cooked

Sauté the onions, garlic and pepper flakes in the oil until onions are transparent. Add the peas and carrots and stir well until coated with the hot oil. Add the broth, salt, yeast, and margarine. Cover and cook. When done, add the rice and mix well.

VARIATION: Add 1/2 cup of Bacon Gluten, chopped fine.

PEPERONATA–1

1 1/2 c.	Bell peppers, cut in strips
1 c.	Onions, sliced
2 T.	Corn oil
4 c.	Potatoes, cubed and cooked
3 c.	Tomatoes, chopped
1 tsp.	Garlic, minced
1/3 tsp.	Sea salt
1/2 tsp.	Basil
1 c.	Beef-like Broth
1/8 tsp.	Cayenne pepper

Sauté the bell peppers and onions in the oil. Combine with rest of ingredients and cook.

PEPERONATA–2

Simple and heavenly!

1 T.	Non-dairy margarine
2 T.	Olive oil
6 c.	Onions, sliced 1/8 inch thick
6 c.	Bell pepper, cut in 1x1/2-inch strips
3 c.	Tomatoes, coarsely chopped
1 tsp.	Red wine vinegar
1 tsp.	Sea salt
1/4 tsp.	White pepper

Melt the margarine in a skillet along with the olive oil. Sauté the onions for 10 minutes, or until they are soft and lightly browned. Stir in the peppers, reduce the heat, cover the skillet and cook for 10 minutes. Add the tomatoes, vinegar, salt and white pepper. Cover and cook for another 10 minutes. Cook the vegetables uncovered over high heat stirring gently, until almost all the liquid has boiled away. May be served hot or cold.

POTATO CHIPS

These are not particularly healthy, yet sometimes we (or children) get a yen for "junk" food, and it is better to make our own not-so-junk versions.

Take Idaho potatoes, slice them paper-thin, and put them directly into salted (1 teaspoon of sea salt per quart) cold water to remove the starch and prevent discoloration. Heat oil to 400°. When ready to fry them, take the potato slices, a batch at a time, drain them in a colander, spread them out in a single layer on paper towels, and pat them thoroughly dry with more towels. Then fry them in the hot oil, turning them about with a slotted spoon, for 2 or 3 minutes, or until they are crisp and golden brown. Remove the chips from the oil, drain them in a colander, then transfer them to paper towels and sprinkle them, turning gently, with onion salt. Repeat until all the chips have been fried, making sure the oil temperature never goes below 375° and can quickly come back up to 400°. If you are frying a goodly number of chips and do not want the first ones to get cold, after salting a batch of chips transfer them to a pan lined with a double thickness of paper towels and put them in a 250° oven to keep them warm while you proceed with the remaining batches. To serve, put the chips in a heated bowl.

POTATO CHIPS–SPICED

1 T.	Chili powder
3/4 tsp.	Sea salt
Pinch	Cayenne pepper

Combine these ingredients. Make potato chips as above, and sprinkle them with this instead of onion salt, or use onion salt instead of sea salt in this combination.

POTATO CURRY

1/2 c.	Onions, chopped
1/4 c.	Bell pepper, chopped
1/2 tsp.	Red pepper flakes
1/2 tsp.	Sea salt
1/2 tsp.	Garlic salt
2 T.	Corn oil
1 T.	Curry Powder
4 c.	Potatoes, cubed and boiled

Sauté the onion, pepper, pepper flakes, and salts in the oil. Add the curry powder and sauté for 30 seconds more. Add the potatoes. Simmer 10 minutes.

POTATO PANCAKES

Although these are good plain, with Tofu Sour Cream or Cashew Sour Cream, salsa, Yeast, Pimento, or Mozzarella "Cheese," Tofu Ricotta Cheese, or a gravy or sauce from the Gravies and Sauces section they are outstanding.

2 c.	Potatoes, peeled and put in cold water to prevent discoloration.
1/2 c.	Unbleached white flour
1/2 tsp.	Sea salt
1/4 c.	Cashew Milk
3 T.	Non-dairy margarine, melted
1/2 tsp.	Dill weed
1/8 tsp.	Cayenne pepper

Stir together the flour, salt, "milk," melted margarine, dill weed, and pepper. Pat one of the potatoes dry and grate it coarsely into a sieve or colander. Press the grated potato firmly down into the sieve with the back of a large spoon to remove its moisture, then immediately stir the gratings into the flour and cashew milk mixture. Repeat this process with each potato until all have been grated and stirred into the cashew milk and flour. Heat a heavy skillet that has been lightly oiled. (After this initial oiling, the margarine in the pancake mixture will be sufficient for frying.) For each pancake drop about 1/3 cup of mixture into the skillet. Let it fry for about a minute until a skin forms on the bottom. Then turn over and press flat–not before. Cook 3 or 4 pancakes at a time, leaving enough space between them so that they can spread into 3 1/2 to 4-inch cakes. Fry them about 3 minutes on each side, or until they are golden brown and crisp around the edges. Transfer the finished pancakes to a heated plate and cover them with foil to keep them warm while the rest are being cooked. Add more margarine whenever you need it.

POTATO POT PIE

1/3 c. Onions, chopped
1 tsp. Garlic, minced
1/3 c. Celery, diced and steamed
1 T. Corn oil
1/4 c. Mushrooms, sliced
1 T. Unbleached white flour
1/2 c. Chicken-like Broth
2 c. Potatoes, diced and steamed
2 c. Carrots, diced and steamed

Sauté the onions, garlic, and celery in the oil until transparent. Add the mushrooms and sauté 2 to 3 more minutes. Add the flour. Slowly add the broth, letting the mixture cook and thicken. Stir in the potatoes and carrots, and heat through. Serve over biscuits.

POTATOES–BAKED

These are unparalleled in the baked potato world!
I like baked potatoes before eating these, but now I love them!
The boiling enables you to bake them for the shortest time possible so the nutrients will not be destroyed by long baking. I think it markedly affects the flavor and texture, too, making them so good that you need not bother putting anything on them at all for flavoring.

Scrub the potatoes, but do not peel them. Put in water, bring to a boil and simmer *lightly* for 30 minutes. Take out of the water and bake in a 350° oven for 30 more minutes.

POTATOES–BOILED

6 c. Potatoes, cubed
6 c. Beef-like or Chicken-like Broth
1/2 c. Onion, chopped
1 tsp. Garlic, minced or sliced
1 tsp. Jalapeño peppers, minced or sliced
2 T. Non-dairy margarine
1/2 tsp. Sea salt

Boil the potatoes in the broth and drain them, keeping the broth. Sauté the onion, garlic, and jalapeños in the margarine. Add this and the salt to the drained potatoes, plus 1 cup of the broth.

POTATOES IN BROTH

4 Large potatoes, peeled and cut in pieces
1/3 c. Onions, minced
3 c. Beef-like or Chicken-like Broth
1 T. Non-dairy margarine
1 T. Flour
1/2 tsp. Sea salt
1/4 tsp. Cayenne pepper

Simmer the potatoes with the onions in the broth until nearly tender. Drain, keeping the liquid. Make a sauce of the liquid with the margarine and flour. Add seasonings. Combine potatoes and the sauce and simmer until tender.

VARIATION: Add chopped chives to the sauce when it is finished.

POTATOES IN THEIR OWN GRAVY

Nothing special–and yet...

5 c.	Potatoes, diced
2 1/2 c.	Flavoring Broth of choice
1/4 tsp.	Sea salt
1/2 c.	Onion, chopped
1/2 c.	Mushrooms, sliced
2 T.	Non-dairy margarine
2 T.	Unbleached white flour
1 1/2 tsp.	Nutritional yeast flakes
1/2 tsp.	Garlic powder
2 tsp.	Low sodium soy sauce
1/8 tsp.	Black pepper

Cook the potatoes in the broth and salt until they are tender and drain them, retaining the liquid. Sauté the onions and mushrooms in the margarine until the onions are transparent. Stir in the flour, yeast, and garlic powder. Whisk in the potato liquid until all is smooth. Add the soy sauce and pepper and cook until thickened. Combine with the potatoes and serve.

POTATOES O'BRIEN

1/2 c.	Bell pepper, chopped
1 tsp.	Garlic, minced
3/4 c.	Onions, chopped
2 T.	Non-dairy margarine
1 T.	Unbleached white flour
1 c.	Cashew milk
1/2 tsp.	Sea salt
1/4 tsp.	Cayenne pepper
3/4 c.	Yeast or Pimento "Cheese"
4 c.	Potatoes, boiled, chilled, and diced
	Bread crumbs

Sauté the bell pepper, garlic, and onions in the margarine. Blend in the flour. Add the "milk" and bring to a boil. Add the salt, pepper, and cheese. Add the potatoes. Place in an oiled baking dish. Cover with bread crumbs. Dot with non-dairy margarine. Bake at 350° for 15 minutes, or until the crumbs are brown.

POTATOES PAPRIKA

1 c.	Onion, chopped
3/4 tsp.	Garlic, minced
3 T.	Corn oil
1 T.	Paprika
3	Medium-sized potatoes, peeled and cut into "French fries" 2 inches long
1 1/2 tsp.	Sea salt
2 c.	Water
1/2 c.	Bell pepper, cut in strips
1 1/4 c.	Tomatoes, chopped

Saute the onion and garlic in the oil until the onion is transparent. Stir in the paprika, add the potatoes and salt, and cook for a few seconds, stirring. Add the water, cover, and simmer for 10 minutes. Add the pepper strips and tomatoes. Cover and simmer until the potatoes are just tender–about 10 or 15 minutes.

QUICK SAUCY VEGETABLES

4 c.	Raw or frozen vegetables, cooked
2 c.	Beef-like or Chicken-like Broth
3 T.	Onions, minced
1 tsp.	Garlic, minced
2 T.	Non-dairy margarine
1/4 tsp.	Basil (if using Beef-like Broth)
1/4 tsp.	Dill weed (if using Chicken-like Broth)
1/4 tsp.	Cayenne pepper
2 T.	Cornstarch or arrowroot
1/4 c.	Water

Cook the vegetables in the broth until tender–about 15 minutes–and drain. Sauté the onions and garlic in the margarine. Add the vegetables. Add the seasonings. Mix the cornstarch or arrowroot in the water and add to the vegetable mixture while stirring. Cook and stir until thickened. Serve over grains or pasta.

QUICK SAUERKRAUT

I have a suspicion that this is a lot better for us than the canned stuff.

2 c.	Cabbage, coarsely shredded
1/3 c.	Wine vinegar
1 tsp.	Sea salt
2 c.	Water
1 1/2 tsp.	Unbleached white flour
1 T.	Water

Combine the cabbage, vinegar, salt, and 2 cups of water in a 2-quart pot. Bring to a boil and cook, partially covered, for 20 minutes. Mix the flour into a paste with tablespoon of water. Stir into the hot cabbage and cook, stirring constantly, until thickened.

RATATOUILE

Better than just good!

1	Small eggplant, peeled and cubed
2 T.	Olive oil
1 1/2 c.	Italian tomatoes, cubed
3/4 c.	Zucchini, chopped
1/2 c.	Bell pepper, chopped
2/3 c.	Onion, chopped
2 12 tsp.	Garlic, minced
1/2 tsp.	Sea salt
1/8 tsp.	Cayenne pepper

Sauté the eggplant in the oil until it is soft, then add all the ingredients, and cook on low heat for 10 to 20 minutes.

RED CABBAGE

This is an adaptation of the recipe hoarded by a famous Austrian resort hotel. Now it's yours!

2 T.	Non-dairy margarine
3 T.	Onions, chopped
6 T.	Barbados molasses
3 T.	Wine vinegar
1/4 tsp.	Sea salt
12 c.	Red cabbage, shredded

Melt the margarine and sauté the onions lightly. Add the molasses, vinegar, and salt. Add the cabbage and cook for 25 minutes, stirring frequently.

ROASTED POTATOES AND ONIONS

3 c.	Potatoes, peeled and cut into chunks
3 c.	Onions (red preferred), chopped
1/2 c.	Olive oil
3 T.	Cider vinegar
1/8 tsp.	Dried thyme
1 T.	Garlic, minced
1 1/2 tsp.	Sea salt
3/4 tsp.	Black pepper

Combine everything and mix well. Put on a baking sheet and bake at 450°, turning occasionally, until the potatoes are soft and brown on the edges. Put in a colander and drain the excess oil.

SAUTÉED VEGETABLES

2 T.	Corn oil
6 c.	Vegetables, sliced
1 1/2 c.	Onions, chopped
1 tsp.	Garlic, minced
1/4 tsp.	Cayenne pepper
1/3 c.	Low sodium soy sauce

Heat the oil in a pan or skillet, add the rest of the ingredients, stir and cook.

SCALLOPED CABBAGE

4 c.	Cabbage, chopped, cooked, and drained
2 T.	Bell pepper, chopped
2 T.	Pimento, chopped
1 c.	Yeast or Pimento "Cheese"
1 1/2 c.	White sauce
1 c.	Bread crumbs, tossed in 2 tablespoons of melted non-dairy margarine

Place the cabbage in an oiled baking dish. Sprinkle the bell pepper and pimento over the cabbage. Spread the "cheese" over that. Cover with the white sauce. Top with the bread crumbs. Bake at 365° for 40 minutes, or until the crumbs are browned.

SLUMGULLIAN

This is real "down home food" and I have adored it since the first time I ate it as a child!

1/3 c. Onions, chopped
2 tsp. Garlic, minced
1/2 c. Bell pepper, chopped
1/8 tsp. Cayenne pepper
4 1/2 tsp. Non-dairy margarine
1 1/2 c. Canned tomatoes, drained and chopped
1 c. Beef-like Broth
1 1/2 c. Corn

Sauté the onions, garlic, bell pepper, and cayenne in the margarine. Add the tomatoes and broth and continue to cook until the tomatoes break up. Add the corn and cook 5 minutes more.

VARIATION: Use water instead of broth, but in that case add 1/2 tsp. of sea salt.

SPANISH VEGETABLES

2 tsp. Corn oil
1/2 tsp. Garlic, minced
2 c. Tomatoes, chopped
1/4 tsp. Sucanat
1 tsp. Sea salt

Sauté the garlic in the oil until it browns. Add the rest of the ingredients and cook until done.

3 T. Corn oil
1/2 c. Bell pepper, chopped
3/4 c. Onions, chopped

Sauté the bell pepper and onions in the corn oil until tender. Add to the tomato sauce.

2 tsp. Corn oil
1 c. Vegetable(s), chopped or sliced
1/8 tsp. Cayenne pepper

Sauté the vegetables and pepper until all are tender. Add to the tomato sauce. Stir well.

SPINACH AU GRATIN

Put a thin layer of cooked and drained spinach in a baking dish. Cover it with a layer of Yeast, Pimento, or Mozzarella "Cheese." Season with pepper and salt. Pour 3 tablespoons of Cashew Milk over it. Broil until the "cheese" is spotted brown.

SPINACH, TOMATOES, AND RICE

This is a real staple. A Greek dish adapted by me. In my much younger days I used to cook up a huge pot of this and eat on it the rest of the week. It was never boring!

1 1/2 c. Onions, chopped
1 T. Garlic, minced
1/3 c. Bell pepper, chopped
3 T. Olive oil

2 T.	Corn oil
2 c.	Spinach
4 c.	Tomatoes, chopped
2 c.	Rice, uncooked
4 c.	Water
3/4 c.	Tomato paste
2 tsp.	Sea salt

Sauté the onions, garlic, and bell pepper in the oils. Add the remaining ingredients and simmer till cooked and of the proper consistency.

SPINACH WITH TOMATOES

1/4 c.	Onions, chopped
1 1/2 tsp.	Garlic, minced
2 T.	Corn oil
4 c.	Spinach, cooked, drained, chopped, or puréed
1 c.	Tomato paste or puree
1/2 tsp.	Sea salt
1/4 tsp.	Cayenne pepper

Sauté the onions and garlic in the corn oil. Add the rest of the ingredients and mix.

SQUASH AU GRATIN

4 1/2 tsp.	Non-dairy margarine
4 c.	Squash, thinly sliced
1/4 c.	Onions, chopped
1 tsp.	Sea salt
1/8 tsp.	Cayenne pepper
1 c.	Tomatoes, sliced
1/4 c.	Yeast or Pimento "Cheese"

Melt the margarine. Add the squash, onions, salt, pepper, and tomatoes. Cover and cook for 15 minutes or until tender, stirring occasionally. Add the "cheese" and heat through. Serve with rice.

SQUASH, BEANS, AND CORN

Just plain goodness!

3 c.	Squash, cubed
1 c.	Onion, chopped
3/4 tsp.	Garlic, minced
2	Jalapeño peppers, minced
2 1/2 c.	Tomatoes, chopped, or 1/2 c. canned tomatoes
2 c.	Lima beans, fresh or frozen
2 c.	Green beans, sliced
2 T.	Corn oil
1 c.	Water
3 c.	Corn
1 tsp.	Sea salt
1/4 tsp.	Black pepper

Sauté the squash, onion, garlic, jalapeños, tomatoes, and beans in the oil until the onions are transparent. Add the water and simmer until the beans are done, stirring frequently. Add the corn, salt, and pepper, and cook more 10 minutes.

SQUASH, GREEN BEANS, AND TOMATOES

1/3 c.	Onions, chopped
1 tsp.	Garlic, minced
2 T.	Non-dairy margarine
2 c.	Squash, sliced and chopped
2 c.	Green beans
2 c.	Tomatoes, blended
1/2 tsp.	Sea salt
Pinch	Cayenne pepper
1/4 tsp.	Basil
1/4 tsp.	Savory
1 c.	Beef-like Broth

Sauté the onions and garlic in the margarine. Combine with rest of ingredients and cook.

SQUASH AND PEAS

3 c.	Squash, sliced and chopped
3 c.	Peas
2 T.	Non-dairy margarine
1/4 tsp.	Sea salt
3 T.	Onions, minced
1/2 tsp.	Garlic, minced
Pinch	Cayenne pepper
1/4 tsp.	Basil
1 c.	Chicken-like Broth

Cook over medium heat until the squash is done.

SQUASH, MUSHROOM, AND PASTA PIE

1/3 c.	Non-dairy margarine
3 T.	Unbleached white flour
2 T.	Onion, minced
4 c.	Mushrooms, sliced
1 1/2 tsp.	Garlic, minced
2 c.	Cashew Milk
1/2 tsp.	Sea salt
1/4 tsp.	Black pepper
2 T.	Ham-like Broth
1 3/4 c.	Ham Gluten, in 1/2-inch cubes
1/4 c.	Parsley, minced
1/4 tsp.	Thyme
1/2 tsp.	Basil
1/2 tsp.	Dried mint leaves
4 c.	Squash, sliced or chopped
10 oz.	Spinach pasta
2 c.	"Mozzarella 'Cheese'"
1	Pie Crust recipe for 2 crusts

In a heavy saucepan melt the margarine, add the flour, and cook, whisking, for 3 minutes. Add the onions, mushrooms, and garlic and cook until they are soft. Add the "milk" and bring to a boil, whisking, and simmer it–still whisking–for 5 minutes, or until it is of the consistency of a sauce. Add the salt, pepper, broth, gluten, parsley, thyme, basil, and mint. Cook for 5 more minutes, adding more broth if it becomes too dry. Cut the squash lengthwise into 1/4-inch-thick slices. Deep-fry the squash at 380° until golden, transferring the fried slices to paper towels to drain. Cook the spinach pasta according to the maker's instructions, drain it in a colander, and briefly rinse it with cold water.

Combine the mushroom sauce, squash, and "cheese," and mix well. Put half of this into the unbaked pie shell. Over that make a layer of all the pasta. Put the rest of the sauce-filling on top of the pasta. Put on the top crust and seal it all around. Mist the dough with oil and prick it with a fork. Bake at 425° for 20 to 30 minutes, or until the top is golden.

SQUASH WITH TOMATOES

3/4 c.	Bell pepper, chopped
1/4 c.	Onions, chopped
1 tsp.	Garlic, minced
2 T.	Corn oil
3 c.	Squash, cut in half lengthwise and then cut into 1-inch chunks
1/8 tsp.	Cayenne pepper
3 c.	Tomatoes, chopped
4 1/2 tsp.	Low sodium soy sauce
1/4 tsp.	Basil
1/4 tsp.	Sea salt

Sauté the bell peppers, onions, and garlic in the oil. Combine with rest of ingredients and cook.

STEWED SQUASH

1/2 c.	Ham Gluten, cut in 1/2-inch cubes
3 T.	Corn oil
8 c.	Squash, chopped
2 tsp.	Louisiana Hot Sauce
3 c.	Onions, chopped coarsely
2 c.	Chicken-like Broth
1 c.	Water
2 tsp.	Garlic, minced

Sauté the gluten in the oil, but do not brown. Put in everything else, and bring to a vigorous boil. Lower the heat and simmer slowly until the squash is well cooked.

SUPER OKRA

1 c.	Onion, sliced thin
2 T.	Corn oil
2 1/2 tsp.	Garlic, minced
1/4 tsp.	Powdered ginger
1 tsp.	Jalapeños, minced
1/4 tsp.	Tumeric
2 T.	Almonds, ground
1 c.	Tomatoes, chopped
10	Okra "fingers" cut into 3/4-inch thick rounds

1/4 tsp. Sea salt
1 T. Parsley, chopped

Sauté the onion in the oil until it turns reddish brown–10 to 12 minutes. Stir in the garlic, ginger, jalapeños, tumeric, and almonds. Add the tomatoes and cook for 1 minute. Add the okra, mix well, and simmer, covered, for 6 to 7 minutes, until the okra is barely tender. Stir in the salt. Sprinkle with the parsley just before serving.

SWEET AND SOUR CABBAGE

As a cooked-cabbage hater I recommend this wholeheartedly. It is simply delicious and demands seconds!

1/4 c. Thinly sliced onions
3 T. Olive oil
8 c. Cabbage, cut into 1/4-inch strips
2 c. Italian tomatoes, coarsely chopped
2 T. Wine vinegar
1 1/2 tsp. Sea salt
1/4 tsp. Cayenne pepper
1 T. Sucanat

Sauté the onions in the oil for 2 or 3 minutes until they are transparent but not brown. Stir in the cabbage, tomatoes, vinegar, salt and pepper. Simmer uncovered, stirring frequently, for 20 minutes or until the cabbage is tender. Stir the Sucanat into the cabbage and cook 1 or 2 minutes more.

SZECHWAN BRAISED EGGPLANT

This is the breath of the dragon!

3 T. Corn oil
4 c. Eggplant, peeled and chopped into bite-size pieces
3 tsp. Garlic, minced
1/4 tsp. Ginger, powdered
2/3 c. Green onions, minced
2 T. Chili paste with garlic (from an Oriental grocery store)
1/3 c. Chicken-like Broth
2 T. Low sodium soy sauce
1/2 tsp. Sucanat
1 tsp. Red wine vinegar

Heat the oil to very hot, and saute the eggplant, coating thoroughly with the oil. Add the garlic, ginger, and onions, and stir in well. Add all the rest of the ingredients, mix well, and cook for 3 minutes, stirring occasionally. Cover and let simmer 10 to 15 minutes until tender.

THAI STYLE VEGETABLES

This is not for the faint-hearted. It was cooked for me by two friends from Thailand. I ate it up and demanded more. So they made me more. I ate that and demanded even more. So they gave me this recipe–and I went into their kitchen and made my own "more"!

1/4 c. Garlic, sliced
1/3 c. Jalapeño peppers, sliced

4 T. Corn oil
6 c. Vegetables, sliced thin (if the type to be sliced)
2 c. Onions, sliced
1/3 c. Low sodium soy sauce

Sauté the garlic and jalapeños in the oil, but do not let the garlic brown except slightly–if at all. Add the soy sauce and vegetables and cook.

NOTE: Frying the jalapeños takes away some of the "bite." So for full effect, do not sauté them, but add them along with the rest of the vegetables.

TOMATOES AND OKRA

3/4 c. Onions, finely chopped
2 T. Non-dairy margarine
1 1/2 tsp. Garlic, minced
4 c. Okra, sliced
2 1/2 c. Canned tomatoes, chopped
1 1/4 tsp. Sea salt
1/4 tsp. Cayenne pepper

Sauté the onions in the margarine until brown. Add and sauté the garlic and okra for 5 minutes. Add the rest of the ingredients and simmer, covered, until the okra is tender.

VARIATION: Add 1/2 cup of chopped bell pepper and/or 2 cups of corn.

TOMATOES AND VEGETABLES

1 c. Bell peppers, chopped
3 T. Onions, chopped
2 T. Non-dairy margarine
4 c. Tomatoes, chopped
2 c. Vegetables, chopped if need be
1/4 tsp. Cayenne pepper
1 tsp. Sea salt
1/3 tsp. Basil
1/3 tsp. Oregano

Sauté the bell peppers and onions in the margarine. Combine with rest of ingredients and cook.

TOMATOES, CORN AND "CHEESE"

1 Bell pepper, chopped
1/3 c. Onions, chopped
1 T. Non-dairy margarine
1 c. Canned tomatoes, chopped
2/3 c. Corn
1/8 tsp. Cayenne pepper
1/2 tsp. Sea salt
1 1/3 c. Yeast, Pimento, or Mozzarella "Cheese"

Sauté the bell pepper and onions in the margarine until they are browned. In a pan, heat the tomatoes and corn. Add the sautéed vegetables and the rest of the ingredients except the "cheese." Cook for 7 minutes, stirring frequently. Add the "cheese," stir in well, and heat through.

TOMATOES CREOLE

Perfect on rice!

1 c.	Bell pepper, chopped
1 1/2 c.	Onions, chopped
2 T.	Non-dairy margarine
3 c.	Canned tomatoes, chopped (or 4 large tomatoes, sliced)
3/4 tsp.	Sea salt
1/4 tsp.	Cayenne pepper
2 T.	Barbados molasses

Sauté the bell pepper and onions in the margarine. Add the remaining ingredients and cook until all is tender.

VEGETABLE CURRY

1/2 c.	Onions, chopped
1 1/4 c.	Beef, chicken, or unflavored gluten, chopped
1 tsp.	Curry powder
2 T.	Corn oil
2 1/2 c.	Cashew Milk
1/2 c.	Coconut milk
1 T.	Cornstarch
1/4 c.	Water
1 1/3 c.	Potatoes, diced
1 1/2 c.	Carrots, diced
2/3 c.	Green beans or green peas
1 tsp.	Sea salt

Sauté the onion, gluten, and curry powder in the oil until the onions are soft and the gluten is browned. Add the cashew milk and coconut milk. Dissolve the cornstarch in the water and add. Cook until slightly thickened. Cook the vegetables in water with the salt until tender. Drain them and add to the curry powder sauce. Serve over rice.

VEGETABLE FRIED RICE

This is as delicious as it is simple and quick.
Although it is worthy of serving at any time it is great as "emergency rations"!

2 T.	Corn oil
1/4 c.	Non-dairy margarine
2 c.	Onion, coarsely chopped
1 c.	Bell pepper, coarsely chopped
1/2 c.	Celery, chopped
3 c.	Mushrooms, sliced thick
1 1/2 tsp.	Garlic, minced
1 1/2 tsp.	Hot pepper flakes
4 c.	Fresh tomatoes, chopped coarse
1/2 tsp.	Sea salt
5 c.	Cooked rice

Combine the oil and margarine. Sauté the onion, bell pepper, celery, mushrooms, garlic, and pepper flakes until the bell pepper is soft. Add the tomatoes and salt. Cook for 5 more minutes.

Add the rice and continue to stir until most of the moisture is evaporated and the rice starts to brown.

YELLOW SQUASH CREOLE

1 c.	Onions, chopped
1 1/2 tsp.	Garlic, minced
1/4 tsp.	Hot pepper flakes
4 1/2 tsp.	Corn oil
3 c.	Yellow squash, sliced
1 c.	Creole Sauce
1/2 c.	Water

Sauté the onion, garlic, and pepper flakes in the oil until onion is transparent. Add the squash and stir well until all is coated with the hot oil. Stir in the creole sauce and water. Cover and cook until the squash is tender.

ZUCCHINI PLAIN

1 T.	Non-dairy margarine
1 T.	Olive oil
2 c.	Onions, coarsely chopped
1 tsp.	Garlic, minced
1/4 tsp.	Red pepper flakes
3/4 c.	Celery, chopped
3 c.	Zucchini, cut in half lengthwise and then cut into 1-inch chunks
3/4 c.	Bell pepper, chopped
1 1/2 c.	Chicken-like Broth
1/4 tsp.	Sea salt

Melt the margarine in the olive oil. Sauté the onion, garlic, pepper flakes, and celery until transparent. Add the zucchini and bell pepper and sauté briefly. Then add the broth and salt and stir well. Cover and cook until tender, but do not overcook.

VARIATION: Use other kinds of squash.

ZUCCHINI WITH TOMATOES

2 c.	Onions, coarsely chopped
1/2 tsp.	Garlic, minced
1/2 tsp.	Jalapeños, minced, or 1/2 tsp. red pepper flakes
3/4 c.	Celery, chopped
2 T.	Olive oil
3 c.	Zucchini, cut in half lengthwise and then cut into 1-inch chunks
3/4 c.	Bell pepper, chopped
3 c.	Tomatoes, chopped
1 T.	Low sodium soy sauce

Sauté the onion, garlic, jalapeños, and celery in the oil until transparent. Add the zucchini and bell pepper and sauté briefly. Then add the tomatoes and soy sauce and stir well. Cover and cook until tender, but do not overcook.

VARIATION: Use other kinds of squash.

CASSEROLES

BAKED CURRY

Don't judge by appearances!
This is one of those recipes that looks stupid on paper but cooks up a genius!

1 1/2 c.	Gluten, any flavor, cubed
1/4 c.	Onion, chopped
3 T.	Corn oil
2 tsp.	Curry powder
2 T.	Unbleached white flour
1 1/2 c.	Water
2 c.	Broccoli–cut into flowerets, along with the stem that has been peeled and sliced–and steamed
2 c.	Head of cauliflower cut into flowerets
1 c.	Potato, cubed
1 1/2 tsp.	Lemon juice
1 T.	Soy sauce
1/4 tsp.	Sea salt
1 c.	Dry bread crumbs, tossed in 1 1/2 tablespoons of melted non-dairy margarine
1/4 tsp.	Paprika

Sauté the gluten and onions in the oil until the onions are soft. Add the curry powder and stir for 1 minute over medium heat. Add the flour and stir for 1 more minute over medium heat. Stir in the water and cook until thickened, about 5 minutes. Add the rest of the ingredients except for the crumbs. Heat through. Put in a casserole and sprinkle the bread crumbs over all. Bake, covered, at 350° for 10 to 15 minutes. Uncover and bake until the crumbs begin to brown.

BROCCOLI AND CORN SCALLOP

2 T.	Non-dairy margarine
2/3 c.	Onions, chopped
1/2 tsp.	Garlic, minced
2 T.	Flour
3/4 c.	Water
2 c.	Yeast , Pimento, or Mozzarella "Cheese"
1 c.	Corn
1 c.	Cracker crumbs
5 c.	Broccoli, cooked and drained

Melt the margarine, sauté the onions and garlic, and blend in the flour. Gradually add the water and cook until thickened. Add the "cheese" and stir till it melts. Stir in the corn and 1/2 cup of the cracker crumbs. Arrange the broccoli in a baking dish and pour the "cheese" sauce over it. Toss the remaining crumbs with 2 T. of melted margarine and sprinkle them over the casserole. Bake at 350° for 30 minutes.

VARIATION: Omit the broccoli and add 5 cups more corn. OR omit the corn and add 1 cup more broccoli.

BROCCOLI AND POTATO CASSEROLE WITH CHIVES AND "CHEESE"

1 1/2 c.	Broccoli, chopped
2 c.	Potatoes, cubed and boiled
3/4 c.	Cashew milk
1 c.	Yeast or pimento "cheese"
1/2 c.	"Parmesan Cheese"
3 T.	Chives, chopped
1/2 tsp.	Garlic, minced
2 T.	Parsley, chopped
1 c.	Tofu, crumbled
1/2 c.	Fresh bread crumbs
1/2 tsp.	Sea salt
1/8 tsp.	Cayenne pepper

Combine all the ingredients in a bowl and stir until thoroughly mixed. Place the mixture into a heavily buttered 9x13-inch pan and spread evenly. Drizzle the top with a little melted margarine. Bake in a 350° oven for about 50 minutes or until the top is golden brown. Cut into squares and serve warm.

BREAD DRESSING

There's always room for this–forget Jello!

1 c.	Carrots, grated
1/2 c.	Fresh parsley, chopped
3/4 c.	Onions, chopped
1 1/2 lb.	Bread cut in 1/2 inch cubes
1 c.	Celery, chopped
1/4 c.	Bell pepper, chopped fine
1/2 c.	Mushrooms or black olives, sliced
1/4 tsp.	Black pepper
1/3 c.	Non-dairy margarine, melted
5 1/2 c.	Beef-like Broth

Mix the dry ingredients together. Combine the melted margarine and broth and pour over the dry ingredients gradually, stirring well. Pack into a casserole dish. Cover with aluminum foil and bake at 350° for 45 minutes. Uncover and bake for 15 minutes more to brown the top.

CABBAGE UN-ROLLS CASSEROLE

1	Cabbage head
4 c.	Ground flavored gluten
3 T.	Corn oil
2 c.	Onion, chopped
2 tsp.	Garlic, minced

1/4 tsp.	Cayenne pepper
1 c.	Broth of the flavor of gluten used
2 c.	Cooked rice
2 c.	Yeast or Pimento "Cheese"
2 1/2 c.	Canned tomato sauce

Separate the cabbage into leaves, trimming away the tough part of the stem on each leaf. Put the leaves in a pan of salted boiling water and boil them until they are slightly soft. Drain and set aside. Sauté the gluten in the oil until it just begins to brown. Add the onions, garlic, pepper, and broth, and continue cooking until the onions are soft and the liquid has been absorbed or evaporated–so the mixture is not mushy. Add the rice to the gluten mixture and cook for 2 more minutes. In a casserole put a layer of cabbage leaves. Spread the gluten mixture over the leaves. Cover with the remaining cabbage. Cover that with a layer of "cheese." Pour the tomato sauce over the "cheese." Bake at 375° for 30 minutes.

CARROT ROAST

4 c.	Carrots, grated
4 c.	Cooked rice, or cooked garbanzos
1 c.	Bread crumbs
1/2 c.	Water
1/3 c.	Onions, chopped
1/4 tsp.	Thyme
1/2 tsp.	Sea salt

Mix all together and bake, covered, at 350° for 45 minutes, and uncovered for 15 minutes. Serve with gravy.

CAJUN EGGPLANT

This was originally a recipe for an appetizer. Ha! It was so good everybody demanded more, so it became a main dish as it deserves to be.

3	Small eggplants, peeled and sliced 1/4-inch thick, and put in salted water.
6 T.	Olive oil
3 T.	Unbleached white flour, sifted
1 1/2 T.	Tomato paste
1 1/4 c.	Canned tomato sauce
1/4 c.	Celery, chopped fine
2 T.	Chopped parsley
1 c.	Onions, chopped fine
1/3 c.	Small bell pepper, chopped fine
1 tsp.	Garlic clove, minced
1 1/2 c.	Water
1 T.	Lea & Perrins Steak Sauce
1 tsp.	Louisiana Hot Sauce
1 1/4 tsp.	Sea salt
2-2 1/2 c.	Pimento "Cheese"
	"Parmesan Cheese"

Let the eggplant slices marinate in the salted water for 2 hours. Meanwhile, put 3 tablespoons of the olive oil in a skillet or heavy pot, heat it well, and stir in the flour. Cook the flour, stirring frequently, until it is browned to a very dark brown, but not burned. (This can take some time.) Add the tomato *paste* to the flour and, stirring constantly, cook it until all is the dark color it was before the sauce was added. Then add the tomato *sauce* to the flour and, stirring constantly, cook it until all is the dark color it was before the sauce was added. Add the celery, parsley, onions, bell pepper, and garlic, and cook over a very low flame for 20 to 30 minutes, stirring constantly. Add the water, Lea & Perrins, hot sauce, and salt. Add more water if the mixture is too thick. Cook on a low flame for 1 hour. When the sauce is nearly done, rinse the eggplant and drain it in a colander. Put the remaining 3 tablespoons of olive oil in a skillet and fry the drained eggplant slices to a deep brown. Place the slices in a casserole and spread some pimento cheese over them. Sprinkle some "Parmesan Cheese" over that. Spread some of the sauce liberally over all. Add another layer of eggplant and repeat. Do this until all the eggplant is used up, finishing with a layer of sauce. Bake at 375° for 20 minutes. Serve hot over rice or chill it in the refrigerator, cut it into squares, and serve.

CAULIFLOWER AU GRATIN

6 c.	Cauliflower flowerets
1/4 c.	Non-dairy margarine
1/2 c.	Onion, diced
1 1/2 c.	Yeast, Pimento, or Mozzarella "Cheese"
1 c.	Tofu Sour Cream or Cashew Sour Cream
1/4 tsp.	Sea salt
1/2 c.	Dried bread crumbs

Cook the cauliflower flowerets in boiling salted water for 10 minutes. Drain well. Combine the cauliflower with 2 tablespoons of the margarine, the onion, "cheese," "sour cream," and salt. Put into a casserole. Melt the rest of the margarine and toss with the crumbs. Sprinkle the crumbs over the cauliflower mixture. Bake at 350° for 30 minutes.

"CHEESE" AND POTATO BAKE

1/2 c.	Onions, sliced or chopped
1 tsp.	Garlic, minced
2 T.	Corn oil
4 c.	Potatoes, peeled, sliced, and boiled in salted water
1 tsp.	Celery salt
1/4 tsp.	Cayenne pepper
1/4 tsp.	Dill weed
2 1/2 c.	Thin White Sauce made with Chicken-like Broth
1 c.	Yeast, Pimento, or Mozzarella "Cheese"

Sauté the onions and garlic in the oil until the onions are soft. In an oiled casserole pan put a layer of onions. Add a layer of potatoes. Add another layer of onion. Mix the seasonings with the white sauce and add it to the casserole. Top with the "cheese." Cover and bake at 400° for 30 minutes, removing the cover for the last 10 minutes.

"CHEESE" ENCHILADAS-1

Plenty good and good and plenty!

4 T.	Corn oil
3 T.	Onion, minced
3 T.	Bell pepper, minced
3 T.	Celery, minced
2 tsp.	Garlic, minced
3 c.	Canned tomatoes, drained and crushed

1/2 tsp.	Cumin, ground
1/2 tsp.	Sucanat
1 1/2 tsp.	Paprika
3/4 tsp.	Oregano, dried and crumbled
1/2	Bay leaf
1/2 tsp.	Sea salt
1/4 tsp.	Cayenne pepper
1/2 c.	Onion, sliced thin
1/2 c.	Bell pepper (red preferred), sliced thin
8	Corn tortillas
2 1/2 c.	Yeast, Pimento, or Mozzarella "Cheese"

In 2 tablespoons of the oil sauté the onion, bell pepper, celery, and garlic until all is softened. Add the tomatoes, cumin, Sucanat, paprika, oregano, bay leaf, salt and pepper. Bring to a boil, reduce the heat, and simmer, stirring occasionally, for 20 minutes. Discard the bay leaf. In the other 2 tablespoons of the oil sauté the onion and bell pepper until they are softened, and transfer them with a slotted spoon to paper towels to drain. Dip the tortillas in the tomato sauce and set aside. To assemble the enchiladas, on each one put some of vegetables on the bottom third, top with 3 tablespoons of of the "cheese," and roll up. As each tortilla is done, put it in a baking dish. When all are in the dish, spoon the sauce over them and spread the remaining "cheese" over all. Bake at 400° for 20 minutes.

"CHEESE" ENCHILADAS-2

2 T.	Cornstarch
3 c.	Chicken-like Broth
3 T.	Chili powder
1/4 tsp.	Garlic powder
1/8 tsp.	Cumin, ground
1/8 tsp.	Cayenne pepper
1/2 tsp.	Sea salt
1/4 tsp.	Onion powder
3 T.	Corn oil
3/4 c.	Onions, chopped
4 c.	Pimento "Cheese"
1/4 c.	Black olives, chopped
12	Corn tortillas

Dissolve the cornstarch in the broth. Add the chili powder, garlic powder, cumin, pepper, salt, onion powder, and 1 tablespoon of the oil, and simmer together for 10 minutes. This is the "sauce." Sauté the onions in the 2 remaining tablespoons of oil. Add the "cheese" and olives to the onions. This is the filling. Put a small amount of the sauce in the bottom of a casserole pan or dish. Put a small amount of the filling in a tortilla, roll it up, and put it in the casserole. Do the same with the rest of the tortillas. 15 minutes before serving, put the rest of the sauce on the tortillas and heat in a 350° oven for 15 minutes.

"CHEESE" PIE

1 c.	Onions, chopped fine
1 tsp.	Garlic, minced
1/2 c.	Bell pepper, chopped fine
2 T.	Non-dairy margarine
3 T.	Cornstarch
2 c.	Cashew Milk

4 c. Pimento or yeast cheese
4 c. "Cottage cheese"
4 c. Canned tomatoes, drained and chopped
1 Pie crust recipe for two crusts

Sauté the onions, garlic, and bell pepper in the margarine. Mix the cornstarch with the "milk." Combine all ingredients. Put in unbaked pie shell and cover with top crust, perforating it with a fork or making cuts with a knife for steam to escape. Bake at 425° for 1 hour.

VARIATION: Use other vegetables.

COMPANY CASSEROLE

1 1/2 c. Baked Gluten Chicken, cubed
1 c. Baked Gluten Ham, cubed
2 1/2 c. Cooked rice
1 1/4 c. Broccoli, chopped
1 1/4 c. Yeast Cheese
1/2 c. Mushrooms, sliced
1 1/4 c. "Mayonnaise"
1 1/4 tsp. Prepared mustard
2 c. Curried Mushroom Soup
2 T. "Parmesan Cheese"

Fry the gluten (both kinds together) in a small amount of oil until browned. In an oiled casserole, spread the rice over the bottom. Over the rice spread the broccoli. Over the broccoli spread the gluten. Over the gluten spread the cheese. Over the cheese spread the mushrooms. Combine the mayonnaise, mustard, and soup, and spread over the mushroom layer. Sprinkle with the parmesan cheese. Bake at 350° for 45 to 60 minutes or until the top is light golden brown.

VARIATION: If you don't care for the taste of curry powder, just substitute a plain cream of mushroom soup by making some from the Basic "Cream Of" Soup recipe.

CORN AND SPINACH CASSEROLE

1/4 c. Onions, minced
1/2 tsp. Garlic, minced
2 T. Non-dairy margarine
2 c. Cream-style corn
1 1/2 c. Frozen spinach, chopped
1 tsp. Vinegar
1/2 tsp. Sea salt
1/4 tsp. Black or cayenne pepper
1/4 c. Fine dry bread crumbs
2 T. "Parmesan cheese"

Sauté the onions and garlic in half of the margarine. Add the corn, spinach, vinegar, salt, and pepper. Put in an oiled baking dish. Blend the crumbs, cheese, and remaining margarine. Spread over the vegetables. Bake at 400° for 20 minutes.

CORN BAKE

3 c. Corn, cooked and drained
1/4 c. Cashew milk

2 T.	Onions, finely chopped
1/2 tsp.	Sea salt
1/2 tsp.	Paprika
3/4 c.	Yeast or pimento cheese
1/2 c.	Bread crumbs
2 T.	Non-dairy margarine, melted

Combine the corn, cashew milk, onions, salt, paprika and cheese. Turn into a baking dish. Toss the bread crumbs with the melted margarine and sprinkle over the top. Bake at 350° for 25 minutes.

CORN TAMALE PIE

More than worth the trying!

1/2 c.	Bell pepper, chopped
3 T.	Onions, chopped
2 T.	Corn oil
3/4 c.	Corn meal
2 c.	Whole kernel corn
3 c.	Canned tomatoes
1/2 c.	Ripe olives, chopped
1/4 tsp.	Cayenne pepper
1/2 c.	Tomato sauce
1 tsp.	Sea salt
3 c.	Yeast or pimento cheese

Sauté the bell pepper and onions in the corn oil. Add the rest of the ingredients and simmer, covered, for 5 minutes, stirring occasionally and adding a little water (up to 3/4 cup) if it gets too thick. Put in a baking dish. Bake at 350° for 45 minutes. Within the last 10 minutes put the cheese on the top and let it brown slightly.

CORN-BEAN PIE

Simple goodness!

CRUST:

2 T.	Corn oil
2 c.	Cornmeal
1/2 c.	Beef-like Broth

In a small mixing bowl, stir the oil into the cornmeal with a fork. Add enough broth to make a stiff batter. Pat into an oiled baking dish or pie plate.

FILLING:

1/2 c.	Bell peppers, chopped
1/3 c.	Onions, chopped
1 tsp.	Garlic, minced
2 T.	Corn oil
2 c.	Potatoes, cooked and cubed
3 c.	Dried beans, cooked
1 c.	Tomatoes, chopped

Pinch	Cayenne pepper
1 c.	Beef-like Broth
1/4 tsp.	Sea salt
	Yeast or Pimento "Cheese"

Sauté the bell peppers, onions, and garlic in the oil. Combine with the rest of the ingredients–except for the "cheese"–in a pot. Cook for 2 minutes. Pour the filling into the prepared crust and bake at 350° about 30 minutes. Remove the pie and cover with the "cheese." Bake 10 more minutes.

VARIATION: Use squash instead of potatoes.

CREAMED BROCCOLI

2 T.	Non-dairy margarine
1/4 c.	Unbleached white flour
1 c.	Cashew Milk made with Chicken-like Broth
1/4 tsp.	Sea salt
Pinch	Cayenne pepper
1/2 tsp.	Paprika
1/2 c.	Onions, minced
1/2 tsp.	Garlic, minced
4 c.	Broccoli, cooked, drained, and chopped very fine
1 c.	Bread crumbs tossed in 2 tablespoons of non-dairy margarine

Melt the margarine and stir in the flour until well blended. Slowly stir in the cashew milk and add the salt, pepper, paprika, onions, and garlic. Add the broccoli, and beat the mixture until it is light. Put in a baking dish. Sprinkle with bread crumbs. Bake at 425° for 15 to 20 minutes.

CREAMED CABBAGE CASSEROLE

8 c.	Cabbage, shredded
1 1/2 c.	Onions, sliced
1/2 tsp.	Garlic, minced
2 T.	Non-dairy margarine
1/8 tsp.	Black pepper
2 c.	Yeast, Pimento, or Mozzarella "Cheese"
1 1/2 c.	Thin White Sauce made with Chicken-like Broth, boiling
2 c.	Bread crumbs

Boil cabbage in salted water. Sauté the onions and garlic in the margarine and mix with the cabbage and pepper. In a small oiled baking dish put a layer of half the cabbage. Spread 1 cup of "cheese" over that. Layer rest of cabbage. Rest of "cheese" over that. Pour the white sauce over all. Top with bread crumbs and dot liberally with non-dairy margarine. Bake at 400° until the crumbs are brown.

CREAMED POTATOES WITH "CHEESE"

6 c.	Potatoes, diced and boiled
3 c.	Thin White Sauce, made with Chicken-like Broth
3/4 c.	Onions, chopped
1 tsp.	Garlic, minced
2 T.	Non-dairy margarine
3 T.	Parsley, chopped

3 c.	Yeast or pimento cheese
3/4 tsp.	Sea salt
1 1/2 c.	Bread crumbs

Combine the potatoes and sauce. Sauté the onions and garlic in the margarine. Combine all ingredients. Put in an oiled baking dish. Cover with bread crumbs. Dot with non-dairy margarine. Bake at 400° until the crumbs are brown.

CREAMED SPINACH, MUSHROOMS, AND ONIONS IN "CHEESE" SAUCE

1 c.	Onions, chopped
1 T.	Garlic, minced
1 c.	Mushrooms, sliced
2 T.	Non-dairy margarine
3 c.	Cheese Sauce–1
3 1/2 c.	Frozen spinach, defrosted, drained, and chopped
1/4 tsp.	Sea salt
1/8 tsp.	Black pepper

Combine everything in a casserole, top with bread crumbs tossed in melted margarine, and bake at 350° for 20 minutes or until the crumbs have browned.

CREOLE RICE CASSEROLE

1 c.	Onions, chopped
2 tsp.	Garlic, minced
2 T.	Corn oil
6 c.	Rice, cooked in Chicken-like Broth
3 c.	Okra, sliced
1/4 tsp.	Cayenne pepper
4 c.	Creole Sauce
1/2 tsp.	Sea salt
	Yeast or pimento cheese

Sauté the onions and garlic in the corn oil. Combine with all other ingredients, put in a casserole, and bake for 25 minutes at 350°. Top with cheese and bake for 5 more minutes.

CRUNCH-TOP POTATOES

Try this!

3 T.	Non-dairy margarine
3 c.	Potatoes, peeled, cut in 1/2-inch slices, and boiled in Beef-like Broth
3/4 c.	Corn flakes, crushed
1 1/2 c.	Yeast or pimento cheese
1/2 tsp.	Sea salt
1 1/2 tsp.	Paprika

Melt the margarine in a pan in a 375° oven. Add a single layer of potatoes, turning them once in the margarine. Mix the remaining ingredients and sprinkle over the potatoes. Bake for 1/2 hour or until done and the tops are crisp.

EGGPLANT AND "CHEESE"

This can be either a main dish (good on rice) warm, or an appetizer, cold.

2 c.	Bacon or Ham Gluten, cubed
1/4 tsp.	Sea salt
1/8 tsp.	Cayenne pepper
1 c.	Unbleached white flour
6 c.	Eggplant, sliced
	Oil for deep frying
2 tsp.	Low sodium soy sauce
1 1/2 c.	Mozzarella "Cheese"
2 T.	"Parmesan 'Cheese'"

Deep fry the gluten in the oil and drain on paper towels. Salt, pepper, and flour the eggplant, then deep fry it and drain well on paper towels. Put a layer of eggplant in a casserole dish or pan. Sprinkle soy sauce over the eggplant. Spread the "mozzarella" over the eggplant. Sprinkle a layer of gluten over the eggplant. Sprinkle "parmesan" over that. Keep repeating this layering until all the eggplant is used up, finishing with a layer of "cheese," gluten, and "parmesan." Bake at 350° for 20 minutes.

EGGPLANT CASSEROLE WITH TOMATOES, GARLIC, AND RICE

1	Small eggplant, peeled and cut into 1/4-inch slices
4 c.	Zucchini, unpeeled and cut into 1/2-inch slices
2 c.	Onions, chopped
4 tsp.	Garlic, crushed
1 1/4 c.	Bell pepper, cut into strips
2 T.	Olive oil
6 c.	Canned tomatoes, drained and chopped
1/4 c.	Parsley, chopped
1/4 tsp.	Basil
1/4 tsp.	Thyme
1/2 tsp.	Sea salt
1/4 tsp.	Cayenne pepper
3 c.	Cooked rice–cooked in Chicken-like Broth
	Yeast , Pimento, or Mozzarella "Cheese" to cover
1/4 c.	"Parmesan 'Cheese'"

Deep fry the eggplant and set aside. Steam the zucchini. Sauté the onions, garlic, and bell pepper in the oil until the onions are soft. Add the tomatoes, herbs, and seasonings and simmer the mixture for 25 minutes, adding water if the sauce gets too thick. Stir in the cooked rice and vegetables. Place the mixture in a casserole and top with the "cheeses." Bake at 350° for 20 minutes.

EGGPLANT LASAGNE

A good idea and even better eating!

3 c.	Eggplant, peeled and sliced 1/3-inch thick
4 c.	Spanish Tomato Sauce
2 c.	Canned tomatoes, chopped
1/2 tsp.	Sucanat
1 tsp.	Garlic salt

1/2 tsp.	Basil
1/4 tsp.	Oregano
1 c.	Frozen tofu, thawed and crumbled
1 1/4 c.	Mushrooms, chopped
3/4 c.	Onions, chopped
3 T.	Olive oil
1/2 c.	Tofu Sour Cream or Cashew Sour Cream

Fry eggplant slices in a small amount of corn oil. Drain well on paper towels. Simmer the tomato sauce, canned tomatoes, and seasonings for about 5 minutes. Sauté the tofu, mushrooms, and onions in the oil. Add the "sour cream" and 1 cup of the tomato sauce. Layer ingredients in an 11x7x2-inch baking dish in this order:

Tomato sauce
Eggplant slices
Tofu mixture

Repeat, ending with tomato sauce. Bake at 350° for 30 minutes.

EGGPLANT PARMESAN

A specialty of the house!

3 c.	Eggplant, peeled and cut in 1/2-inch slices
	Sea salt
	Unbleached white flour
	Corn oil
2 c.	Italian Tomato Sauce (Gravies and Sauces section)
	Mozzarella, Pimento, or Yeast "Cheese"
	"Parmesan cheese"

Sprinkle both sides of the eggplant slices with salt to draw out their moisture and spread them out in a single layer on a platter or board. After 20 to 30 minutes, pat the eggplant dry with paper towels. Dip each slice in flour, shaking or brushing off any excess. Heat the oil in a skillet and brown the eggplant a few slices at a time, working quickly to prevent them from soaking up too much oil. (If the oil cooks away, add more.) As the eggplant browns, transfer the slices to fresh paper towels to drain. Pour 1/2 cup of the tomato sauce into an oiled casserole pan. Layer the eggplant slices over the sauce. Cover with "cheese," and sprinkle the "parmesan" over that. Repeat 1 or 2 more layers, finishing with a layer of tomato sauce, "cheese" and "parmesan." Cover with foil and bake at 400° on the middle shelf for 30 minutes. Remove the foil and bake, uncovered, for 10 minutes. Watch closely to avoid over-cooking.

FRESH CORN AND TOMATO CASSEROLE

This has endured the test of years to still be a favorite!

1 c.	Corn
1	N'egg
2 T.	Corn oil
1 c.	Water
4 c.	Corn
1 c.	Bread crumbs
3/4 tsp.	Sea salt
1/4 tsp.	Cayenne pepper
3 T.	Onions, chopped
	Sliced tomatoes

Blend together the corn, n'egg, corn oil, and water to make "corn milk." Combine all the ingredients except the tomatoes and cook until it begins to bubble. Turn out into a casserole and bake at 350° for about an hour or until firm. Place the sliced tomatoes on top and sprinkle lightly with salt. Bake an additional 15 minutes.

GOLDEN VEGETABLE BAKE

2 T.	Non-dairy margarine, melted
2 T.	Unbleached white flour
1 c.	Cashew milk, scalded
1 tsp.	Sea salt
1/8 tsp.	Black or cayenne pepper
3/4 tsp.	Paprika
1 1/2 c.	Carrots, shredded
2 c.	Cream style corn
2 T.	Onions, chopped
1/3 c.	Bell pepper, chopped

Blend the melted margarine and flour. Gradually add the cashew milk. Cook, stirring constantly, until thickened. Add seasonings. Cool slightly. Stir in rest of ingredients. Pour into an oiled casserole dish or pan. Bake at 350° 50 to 55 minutes.

GREEN BEAN CASSEROLE

2 c.	Green beans
1 c.	Bell pepper, chopped
1 1/2 c.	Onions, chopped
1 tsp.	Garlic, minced
3 T.	Non-dairy margarine
1/4 tsp.	Paprika
2 T.	Low sodium soy sauce

Cook the green beans in salted water and drain. Sauté the bell pepper, onions and garlic in the margarine. Mix with the beans, paprika, and soy sauce and put in a baking dish "buttered" with margarine. Cover and bake at 350° for about 30 minutes.

GREEN BEANS IN TOMATO SAUCE

2 c.	Green beans
2 T.	Non-dairy margarine
2 T.	Unbleached white flour
2 c.	Tomato juice
2 T.	Low sodium soy sauce
1/4 tsp.	Sea salt
1/4 tsp.	Paprika
1/2 c.	Bread crumbs tossed in margarine

Cook the green beans in salted water. While the beans are cooking melt the margarine and stir in the flour. Gradually add the tomato juice, stirring constantly. Add the soy sauce, salt, and paprika, and cook for 5 more minutes. Drain the beans and place them in an oiled baking dish. Pour the sauce over the beans. Bake at 350° for about 20 minutes. Cover the top with the crumbs. Bake at 450° until the crumbs are brown–about 10 more minutes.

VARIATIONS: Instead of the crumbs tossed in margarine, use Yeast or Pimento cheese and dry crumbs, dotted with margarine. Good over rice or toast.

GREEN BEANS SUPREME-1

Just what the name says!

3/4 c.	Onions, sliced
1/2 tsp.	Garlic, minced
1 T.	Parsley, minced
2 T.	Non-dairy margarine, melted
2 T.	Unbleached white flour
1/2 tsp.	Sea salt
1/4 tsp.	Paprika
4 c.	Green beans, julienne, steamed
1 c.	Tofu Sour Cream or Cashew Sour Cream
1/2 c.	Yeast or Pimento "Cheese"
1/2 c.	Dry bread crumbs

Sauté the onions, garlic, and parsley in half of the margarine. Add flour, salt, and paprika and mix well. Stir in the beans and heat. Take off the heat and mix in the "sour cream." Put all into a baking dish. Top with "cheese." Toss the crumbs in the remaining margarine and sprinkle them over the "cheese." Bake in a 325° oven until the crumbs brown.

GREEN BEANS SUPREME–2

Ditto!

3 T.	Onions, chopped
3/4 c.	Mushrooms, chopped
1/2 tsp.	Garlic, minced
2 T.	Non-dairy margarine
6 c.	Green beans, cooked
1/4 tsp.	Lemon peel
1/4 tsp.	Cayenne pepper
1/8 tsp.	Dill weed
1/2 tsp.	Sea salt
1 1/2 c.	Bread crumbs, tossed in an additional 2 tablespoons of melted non-dairy margarine
1 1/2 c.	Yeast , Pimento, or Mozzarella "Cheese"

Sauté the onions, mushrooms, and garlic in the margarine. Combine everything except the crumbs and the "cheese." Put in casserole pan and cover with "cheese." Top with bread crumbs. Bake at 400° until the bread crumbs brown.

GREEN CHILI CORN CASSEROLE

12 Tortillas

FILLING:

3 c.	Onions, diced
3 T.	Corn oil
3 c.	Rice, cooked
2 1/4 c.	Corn kernels (thawed, if frozen)
2/3 c.	Red bell pepper, diced
2/3 c.	Green bell pepper, diced
1/2 tsp.	Oregano

1 tsp.	Coriander
1 tsp.	Salt
3 tsp.	Chili powder
2 T.	Low sodium soy sauce
1/2 tsp.	Curry powder
1/2 tsp.	Cumin, ground

SAUCE:

4 c.	Potatoes, steamed
1 1/2 c.	Green Chilies (mild), diced
1/2 T.	Salt
3 c.	Water

Sauté the onion in the oil until transparent. Mix the onion and all the filling ingredients together and set aside. Blend together all the sauce ingredients and set aside. To assemble, dip 4 corn tortillas into the sauce and layer them on the bottom of a 9x12 inch pan. Spread 4 cups of filling over the tortillas. Spread 1 cup of sauce over the filling. Repeat this assembly procedure, ending with 4 tortillas. Pour 2 cups of sauce over the top. Cover the pan and bake at 350° for 50 minutes.

"HAM" AND POTATO CASSEROLE

Fundamentally good!

2 c.	Onions, chopped
1 T.	Garlic, minced
1/2 tsp.	Red pepper flakes
1/4 c.	Non-dairy margarine
2 T.	Unbleached white flour
4 c.	Pork-like Broth make with Cashew Milk
3 c.	Ham gluten, sliced and broiled on both sides
2 c.	Pimento "Cheese"
6 c.	Potatoes, sliced 1/4-inch thick and boiled

Saute the onions, garlic, and pepper flakes in the margarine. Add the flour and stir in well. Slowly add the broth and let it simmer for 15 minutes. Put a thin layer of this broth in a casserole pan, a layer of gluten, a layer of "cheese," and a layer of potatoes. Repeat the layering once more. Put any remaining broth over the top to cover the potatoes. Bake at 400° for 30 minutes. Just before serving, broil for a few minutes to lightly brown the top.

ITALIAN EGGPLANT CASSEROLE

3 c.	Eggplant, sliced thin
1 1/2 c.	Onions, chopped
1/2 tsp.	Garlic, chopped
2 T.	Olive oil
1 c.	Black olives, chopped
1 c.	Tofu, crumbled
1 1/2 c.	Canned tomato sauce
1 c.	Golden Sauce (see Gravies and Sauces section)

Fry the eggplant in a small amount of olive oil. Drain well on paper towels. Sauté the onions and garlic in the 2 tablespoons of olive oil. Mix the onions with the olives and tofu. In an oiled

casserole, alternate layers of:
eggplant
tofu mixture
tomato sauce
Golden Sauce
Ending with Golden Sauce. Bake for 30-45 minutes at 350°.

LAYERED CASSEROLE

Plain goodness!

3 c.	Green beans, cooked in Chicken-like or Beef-like Broth
4 c.	Potatoes, cooked with salt and sliced
1/4 c.	Onions, chopped
1/2 tsp.	Garlic, minced
1 T.	Corn oil
3 c.	Corn
1 c.	Water
2 T.	Non-dairy margarine
	Cracker crumbs for topping, tossed in some melted margarine

In an oiled casserole pan place the cooked green beans. Cover with the potato slices. Sauté the onions and garlic in the oil. Blend with the corn, water and margarine together and pour over all. Top with cracker crumbs. Bake at 350° until the cracker crumbs brown.

VARIATIONS: Instead of green beans use green peas, squash, pumpkin, or cooked dried beans. Put a layer of Yeast or Pimento "Cheese" on top of the corn and top with the cracker crumbs.

LEFT-OVER VEGETABLES WITH "CHEESE"

Always the same but different!

Moisten the vegetables with one of the Flavoring Broths, soups, or tomato juice. Place them in an oiled baking dish. Cover them with Mozzarella, Pimento, or Yeast "Cheese." Top with bread crumbs tossed in melted non-dairy margarine. Bake at 375° until well heated.

LIMA BEANS WITH "CHEESE"

1/2 tsp.	Paprika
3/4 c.	Beef-like Broth
1 T.	Non-dairy margarine
2 1/2 c.	Lima beans, fresh, cooked (or frozen, thawed, and cooked)
1/2 c.	Yeast or Pimento "Cheese"
1/2 c.	Bread crumbs

Heat the paprika, broth, and margarine together until the margarine is melted. Mix in the lima beans. Oil a baking dish. Place alternating layers of beans and "cheese" in the dish. Cover the top with bread crumbs and dot with margarine. Bake at 350° for 30 minutes.

MEXICAN LASAGNA

Si! Si!

1 c.	Onions, chopped

1 tsp.	Garlic, minced
2 T.	Corn oil
2 c.	Pinto, red, pink, or kidney beans, cooked
2 c.	Corn
4 c.	Canned tomato sauce
1/4 c.	Cooked Tomato Salsa
1/2 tsp.	Oregano
1 tsp.	Sea salt
20	Corn tortillas
3 c.	Yeast or Pimento "Cheese"

Sauté the onions and garlic in the oil. Combine all the ingredients except the tortillas and "cheese." In an oiled casserole pan, place a layer of tortillas. Over that put a layer of the filling. Over that spread 1 cup of the "cheese." Repeat one more time. Cover with another layer of tortillas. Top with the third cup of "cheese." Bake at 350° for 20 minutes.

MEXICAN LIMA BEAN CASSEROLE

1/3 c.	Onions, chopped
1/4 c.	Bell pepper, chopped
Pinch	Cayenne pepper
2 T.	Non-dairy margarine
1/2 tsp.	Garlic, minced
2 T.	Barbados molasses
2 c.	Canned tomatoes
1 tsp.	Sea salt
2 c.	Lima beans, cooked

Sauté the onions, bell pepper, and cayenne pepper in the margarine. Combine all ingredients and bake in an oiled casserole dish at 375° for 45 minutes.

VARIATION: Add Yeast or Pimento "Cheese."

NOODLE CASSEROLE WITH ZUCCHINI, TOMATOES, AND "CHEESE"

2 c.	Zucchini, grated and sprinkled with 1/2 teaspoon of salt and allowed to drain in a strainer and pressed dry
3/4 c.	Onions, chopped
1 1/2 tsp.	Garlic, minced
3 T.	Olive oil
3 c.	Canned tomatoes, drained and finely chopped
1/2 tsp.	Sea salt
1/8 tsp.	Cayenne pepper
1	8 oz. package of noodles, cooked, drained and tossed in 4 tablespoons of melted non-dairy margarine
1 c.	Yeast or Pimento "Cheese"
1/2 c.	"Parmesan 'Cheese'"

Sauté the zucchini, onion, and garlic in the oil until the zucchini and onions are tender. Add the tomatoes, salt, and pepper and simmer for 10 minutes or until the sauce is thick. Toss the cooked noodles with the "cheeses" until blended. Toss the noodles with the sauce. Place in a casserole and heat in a 350° oven until heated through.

ONIONS IN TOMATO SAUCE

2 T.	Non-dairy margarine
2 T.	Unbleached white flour
2 c.	Tomato juice
2 T.	Low sodium soy sauce
1/4 tsp.	Sea salt
1/4 tsp.	Paprika
2 c.	Sliced onions
1/2 c.	Bread crumbs tossed in margarine

Melt the margarine and stir in the flour. Gradually add the tomato juice, stirring constantly. Add the soy sauce, salt, and paprika, and cook for 5 more minutes. Put the sliced onions in an oiled baking dish. Pour the sauce over the onions. Bake at 350° for about 20 minutes. Cover the top with the crumbs. Bake at 450° until the crumbs are brown–about 10 more minutes.

VARIATIONS: Instead of the crumbs tossed in margarine, use Yeast or Pimento cheese and dry crumbs, dotted with Non-dairy margarine. Good over rice or toast.

PAELLA-LIMAS

1 c.	Green limas, frozen
1/4 c.	Non-dairy margarine
2 c.	Rice, uncooked
1 c.	Onion, minced
1 c.	Carrot, sliced thin
4 1/2 c.	Boiling water
1 tsp.	Sea salt

Steam the lima beans and set aside. Melt 2 tablespoons of the margarine in a heavy skillet, and stir in the rice. Continue stirring until the rice is slightly brown and popping (some rice does not pop). Sauté the onions and carrots together in the other 2 tablespoons of margarine for 3 minutes. Pour all the ingredients into the boiling water with the salt and boil for 30 minutes. Pour the paella into a casserole, cover and bake at 350° for 1 hour. Leave uncovered the last 5 minutes.

PIFFEL

I made this up, but couldn't think of a name for it. In disgust I said: "Piffel"–and it had a name!

3/4 c.	Onions, chopped
1/2 c.	Bell pepper, chopped
2 T.	Corn oil
6 c.	Vegetables, chopped or sliced–fresh or frozen (thawed well)
1 1/2 c.	Tomatoes, chopped
1/2 tsp.	Oregano
1/2 tsp.	Basil
3 c.	Yeast or pimento cheese
1/4 tsp.	Garlic powder
1 1/2 c.	Chicken-like Broth

Sauté the onions and bell pepper in the oil. Combine all ingredients in a casserole dish and bake at 400° for 45 minutes.

CREAM OF PIFFEL

I wanted a variation on Piffel–and succeeded!

3/4 c.	Onions, chopped
1/4 c.	Bell pepper, chopped
2 T.	Corn oil
4 c.	Thick White Sauce made with Chicken-like Broth
6 c.	Vegetables, chopped or sliced–fresh or frozen (thawed well)
1/2 tsp.	Italian Herb Seasoning
1/4 tsp.	Garlic powder
1/2 tsp.	Cayenne pepper
3 c.	Yeast or Pimento "Cheese"
2 c.	Bread crumbs tossed in margarine

Sauté the onions and bell pepper in the oil. Combine with the sauce, vegetables, herb seasoning, garlic powder and pepper, and pour into a casserole dish. Cover with the "cheese." Top with bread crumbs. Bake at 400° for 30 minutes.

"PIMENTO CHEESE" LOAF

1 c.	Pimento "Cheese"
1 tsp.	Corn starch or arrowroot flour
2 c.	Cooked lima beans, mashed
1/4 c.	Onions, chopped
2 T.	Parsley, chopped
1/2 tsp.	Sea salt
3/4 c.	Bread crumbs tossed in melted non-dairy margarine

Mix all ingredients except the crumbs and shape into a loaf, adding a little water if needed. Put in a pan and sprinkle with the crumbs. Bake at 325° for 1 hour.

VARIATION: Instead of the pimento cheese, use 1 cup of Tofu Cream Cheese and 3 tablespoons of chopped pimentos.

POLENTA CASSEROLE

1 c.	Cornmeal
4 c.	Beef-like Broth
1/2 tsp.	Sea salt
3 T.	Onions, chopped
1 tsp.	Garlic, minced
2 c.	Vegetable(s), cooked
1/2 c.	Yeast or Pimento "Cheese"
2 T.	Non-dairy margarine
2 c.	Tomato Sauce (one of the recipes from Gravies and Sauces)

Mix the cornmeal with 1 cup of the broth until blended. Bring the remaining 3 cups of broth to a boil in a heavy saucepan. Add salt, then stir in the cornmeal paste and return to a boil, stirring continuously. Reduce heat to low and simmer, stirring occasionally with a wooden spoon, until the mixture is very thick. Add a little water if needed. Cook 15-20 minutes, depending on how fine or coarse the cornmeal is. Sauté the onions and garlic in a little corn oil and add them to the cooked vegetables. Add the vegetables to the cooked cornmeal. Stir in the "cheese" and the margarine. Put the cornmeal mixture into a well-oiled casserole pan. Top with the tomato sauce. Bake at 375° for about an hour.

POTATOES AU GRATIN

2 c.	Onions, sliced thin
1 tsp.	Garlic, minced
3 T.	Non-dairy margarine
1/8 tsp.	Cayenne pepper
1/8 tsp.	Black pepper
1/4 tsp.	Sea salt
6 c.	Potatoes, sliced 1/2-inch thick and boiled in salted water
3 c.	Yeast, Pimento, or Mozzarella "Cheese"
	"Parmesan Cheese" for sprinkling on top
2/3 c.	Chicken-like, Beef-like, or Ham- like Broth

Sauté the onions and garlic in the margarine until the onions are soft. Stir in the peppers and salt. Oil a casserole very well with the corn oil, including the sides. Layer half of the boiled potato slices in the casserole, then a layer of one half of the onion-garlic mixture, and a layer of one half of the "cheese." Repeat the layering as above. Sprinkle some "parmesan" over that. Pour the broth over that. Bake at 375° for 45 minutes or until brown on top.

VARIATION: Use cauliflower or broccoli instead of potatoes.

POTATOES SCALLOPED IN MARGARINE

Wash and peel the potatoes, and cut them in slices 1/8-inch thick. Place them in cold water to cover for 15 minutes. Drain them and dry between towels. Generously "butter" a baking dish with non-dairy margarine. Sprinkle it with fine dry bread or cracker crumbs. Cover the bottom carefully with the potato slices. Dot them generously with margarine and sprinkle them lightly with salt and paprika. Repeat this process until the dish is filled. Cover the dish and bake at 375° for about 1 hour or until they are tender.

RICE DRESSING

1/4 c.	Onions, chopped
1/3 c.	Bell pepper, chopped
2 T.	Non-dairy margarine
4 c.	Rice cooked in Chicken-like Broth
1 c.	Dry bread crumbs
2/3 c.	Black olives, chopped
3/4 tsp.	Sea salt
1 c.	Thin White Sauce made with Chicken-like Broth

Sauté the onions and bell pepper in the margarine. Combine all ingredients. Bake, uncovered, at 350° for 30 minutes.

RUMBLEDETHUMPS

A pity someone does not write a fairy story with this as a title!
It is actually colcannon, a Scottish dish, adapted from an American version given in Gourmet *magazine.*

6 c.	Potatoes, peeled, diced, and cooked
1/2 c.	Non-dairy margarine, cut into bits
2 T.	Fresh chives or green onions, minced
1/2 c.	Cashew Milk
4 c.	Cabbage, diced and cooked

1 tsp.	Sea salt
1/4 tsp.	Black pepper
1 1/2 c.	Yeast, Pimento, or Mozzarella "Cheese"

Mash the potatoes, stir in the margarine, chives (or green onions), "milk," cabbage, salt, and pepper. Put into a baking dish, spread the "cheese" over the top, and bake at 400° for 30 minutes, or until heated through. Just before serving broil until the top browns lightly.

SCALLOPED BROCCOLI

3 c.	Cashew Milk
2 T.	Non-dairy margarine
1/2 c.	Onions, chopped
1 tsp.	Garlic, minced
2 T.	Unbleached white flour
1 1/2 tsp.	Sea salt
1/8 tsp.	Black or cayenne pepper
1 1/2 c.	Pimento or Yeast "Cheese"
6 c.	Broccoli, steamed and chopped

Preheat the "milk." Melt the margarine in a saucepan over low heat and sauté the onion and garlic. Blend in the flour, salt, and pepper. Add the "milk" slowly. Cook quickly, stirring constantly, until the mixture thickens and bubbles. Add the "cheese" and stir it in well. Put half the broccoli in an oiled casserole. Cover with half of the sauce. Repeat this layering. Cover and bake at 350° for 1 hour. Uncover and bake 30 minutes longer.

SCALLOPED CARROTS AND POTATOES

1 c.	Onions, sliced
1 tsp.	Garlic, minced
2 T.	Non-dairy margarine, melted
4 c.	Potatoes, peeled, sliced, and boiled in salted water
2 c.	Carrots, peeled, sliced, and boiled in salted water
2 T.	Bacon Gluten, minced
1/2 tsp.	Sea salt
1/8 tsp.	Black pepper
1/8 tsp.	Rosemary leaf, crumbled
1/4 c.	Parsley, minced
2 c.	Thin white sauce

Sauté the onions and garlic in the margarine and mix with the cooked potatoes. Oil the bottom of a small casserole pan and put in a layer of the potato-onion mixture. Put in a layer of carrots. Combine the gluten, salt, pepper, rosemary, and parsley, and sprinkle 1/2 of that over the carrots. Pour 1/2 the white sauce over all. Repeat. Bake at 350° for 20 minutes.

SCALLOPED EGGPLANT

3 c.	Eggplant, peeled and cubed
2 T.	Bell pepper, chopped
2 T.	Onions, chopped
1/2 tsp.	Garlic, minced
3 T.	Non-dairy margarine
2 c.	Tomatoes, cooked or canned
1 tsp.	Sea salt

3/4 c. Bread crumbs

Peel the eggplant and cut it into small pieces. Sauté the bell pepper, onion, garlic, and eggplant in one half of the margarine, adding some corn oil if needed. Add the tomatoes and salt. Simmer 20 to 30 minutes or until tender. Pour into an oiled baking dish. Melt the remaining margarine, mix with bread crumbs, and spread over the top of the eggplant mixture. Bake at 350° for 20 minutes, or until the eggplant is tender and the bread crumbs are brown.

SCALLOPED PEAS AND SQUASH

1/3 c. Onions, chopped
2 T. Non-dairy margarine
2 c. Squash, sliced or cubed
2 c. Peas (if frozen, partially thawed)
3 c. Medium white sauce
1 c. Yeast or Pimento "Cheese"

Sauté the onions in the margarine. Combine the squash and peas. Place in an oiled baking dish. Pour the sauce over the vegetables. Top with the "cheese." Bake at 375° for 45 minutes.
VARIATION: Use pumpkin instead of squash.

SCALLOPED POTATOES-1

Oil a baking dish. Fill it with layers of peeled and very thinly sliced raw potatoes, sprinkling each layer generously with unbleached white flour, salt, and low sodium soy sauce and dotting it with non-dairy margarine. Heat cashew milk that has been seasoned with salt and paprika. Pour it over the potatoes until it can be seen through the top layer. Bake at 350° for 75 minutes. (You may turn the potatoes with a spoon while cooking to ensure even baking.)

SCALLOPED POTATOES-2

3 c. Cashew Milk
2 T. Non-dairy margarine
1/2 c. Onions, chopped
1 tsp. Garlic, minced
2 T. Unbleached white flour
1 1/2 tsp. Sea salt
1/8 tsp. Black or cayenne pepper
1 1/2 c. Pimento or Yeast "Cheese"
6 c. Potatoes, peeled and thinly sliced

Preheat the "milk." Melt the margarine in a saucepan over low heat. Sauté the onion and garlic. Blend in the flour, salt, and pepper. Add the "milk" slowly. Cook quickly, stirring constantly, until the mixture thickens and bubbles. Add the "cheese" and stir it in well. Put half the potatoes in an oiled casserole. Cover with half of the sauce. Repeat this layering. Cover and bake at 350° for 1 hour. Uncover and bake 30 minutes longer.

SCALLOPED POTATOES AND MUSHROOMS

1 1/2 c. Onions, chopped
2 1/2 c. Mushrooms, stemmed and chopped coarsely
1 T. &
1 1/2 tsp. Jalapeños, chopped fine

2 tsp.	Garlic, minced
2 T.	Non-dairy margarine
4 c.	Medium White Sauce made with Chicken-like Broth
6 c.	Potatoes, peeled, sliced 1-inch thick, and boiled in salted water

Sauté the onions, mushrooms, jalapeños, and garlic in the margarine. Add to the white sauce and cook for 5 minutes. Add the sauce to the potatoes and stir well. Place in a casserole pan and bake at 375° for 45 minutes.

SHEPHERD'S PIE–1

I never tire of this.

2 c.	Peas or dried beans, cooked
2 c.	Corn
2 c.	Green beans, cooked
1/4 c.	Non-dairy margarine
1/2 tsp.	Sea salt
2 c.	Beef-like Gravy 1 or 2
2 1/2 c.	Mashed potatoes

Combine the peas, corn, beans, and margarine together in a deep casserole. Sprinkle them with the salt. Pour the gravy over the vegetables. Spread the mashed potatoes on top. Heat in oven about 30 minutes before serving until the peaks of the mashed potatoes are light brown.

SHEPHERD'S PIE–2

This merits a blue ribbon!

2 c.	Potatoes, cubed
	Just enough Beef-like Broth to cover the potatoes
1/3 c.	Onions, chopped
2 T.	Corn oil
1 c.	Tomatoes, chopped
1 c.	Vegetable(s) of choice, chopped
2 T.	Parsley, chopped
1 tsp.	Arrowroot
1/4 tsp.	Sea salt
1/2 c.	Beef-like Broth
1 c.	Pizza "Cheese"
1	Pie Crust recipe for 2 crusts

Boil the potatoes in the broth for 5 to 10 minutes. Sauté the onions in the corn oil. Add the potatoes, tomatoes, vegetables, and parsley. Cover and cook 5 more minutes. Dissolve the arrowroot and salt in the half cup of broth, then add it and the "cheese" to the vegetables. Cook for 10 minutes, stirring occasionally. Oil a pie pan and put one of the unbaked crusts in it. Pour in the filling. Lay the other crust over the vegetable mixture. Seal the top. Cut steam holes or slits and brush the top with oil. Bake at 350° for 30 minutes or until the pastry is lightly browned.

SOY GRITS CASSEROLE

1 c.	Rice
1 1/2 c.	Beef-like Broth

1/4 c.	Bell pepper
2 T.	Non-dairy margarine
2 c.	Soy grits, soaked in 4 c. of Beef-like Broth
2 1/2 c.	Tomatoes, chopped
1/4 c.	Tomato paste
4 c.	Yeast or pimento cheese
1/4 tsp.	Sea salt

Cook rice in the broth. Sauté the bell pepper in margarine. Combine all ingredients and put in baking dish. Bake at 350° for 20 minutes or until brown.

SOY GRITS ENCHILADA CASSEROLE

Hold on to your sombrero–this is GOOD!

1 c.	Soy grits
2 c.	Beef-like Broth, boiling hot
1/3 c.	Onions, chopped
2 T.	Bell pepper, chopped
1/2 tsp.	Garlic, minced
4 tsp.	Corn oil
1/8 tsp.	Cayenne pepper
3 c.	Tomato sauce
6 T.	Cooked Salsa
1 c.	Yeast, Pimento, or Mozzarella "Cheese"
8	Corn tortillas

Soak the grits in the broth for at least 10 minutes, making sure the broth is enough for the grits to absorb, adding more if needed. Sauté the onions, bell pepper, and garlic in the oil. Add the grits and pepper and fry a few minutes more. Add the salsa. Dip the tortillas in hot oil to make them limp. Layer in a casserole pan as follows:

Tomato sauce
Tortillas
"Cheese"
Grits Filling
Tomato sauce
Tortillas
"Cheese"
Grits Filling
Tomato sauce
Tortillas

Spread a thin layer of "cheese," salsa, and chopped onions on top. Bake for 15 minutes at 400°.

SPICY POTATOES

2 c.	Potatoes, thinly sliced
2 T.	Olive oil
1/2 tsp.	Garlic, minced
1 T.	Red Onions, chopped
1/4 c.	Parsley, chopped (2 T. dried)
1 tsp.	Unbleached white flour
1/4 tsp.	Cayenne pepper
1/2 c.	Tomatoes, chopped
1/2	Bay leaf

1/4 tsp. Sucanat
1/4 tsp. Sea salt

Brush the potato slices with 1 tablespoon of the olive oil. Place on a lightly oiled baking sheet and bake for 20 minutes, or until lightly browned and tender. Set aside. Heat the remaining tablespoon of oil in a heavy skillet. Add garlic, onion and parsley. Cook until the onion is transparent but not browned. Whisk in the flour and cayenne. Add the rest of the ingredients. Cook over low heat for 10 minutes, stirring occasionally. Remove bay leaf. Pour sauce over potatoes, and bake, uncovered, at 350° for 15 minutes.

SPINACH AND HERB POTATO CASSEROLE

I call this a "politician dish"–it stands on its record!

6 Large potatoes, peeled and boiled
1 c. Tofu Cream Cheese
1 c. Tofu Sour Cream or Cashew Sour Cream
1/2 c. Non-dairy margarine
2 tsp. Sea salt
1 1/2 tsp. Dill weed
1/4 tsp. Black pepper
1 10-oz. pkg., frozen chopped spinach, cooked and well drained

Whip the potatoes, cream cheese, sour cream, and margarine together until smooth. Add all the rest and beat until well mixed. Put into an oiled casserole and bake at 375° for 20 minutes.

SQUASH AND MACARONI BAKE

2 c. Squash, chopped fine
1/2 c. Onions, chopped
1/2 tsp. Garlic, minced
3 T. Non-dairy margarine
1/4 c. Unbleached white flour
1/4 tsp. Sea salt
1/2 tsp. Oregano
1 3/4 c. Water
3 c. Yeast Cheese or Pimento Cheese
2 c. Macaroni, cooked and drained
1 c. Tomatoes, chopped

Sauté the squash, onions, and garlic in the margarine. Blend in the flour and seasonings. Gradually add the water. Cook, stirring, until thickened. Stir in 1 1/2 cups of the "cheese." Stir in the macaroni and tomatoes. Pour into a casserole. Top with remaining "cheese" and bake at 350° for 25 minutes.

VARIATION: Use pumpkin instead of squash.

SQUASH CASSEROLE WITH TOMATOES, "CHEESE" AND RICE

1/4 c. Onions, chopped
2 T. Non-dairy margarine
2 c. Squash, sliced
2 c. Tomatoes, chopped
1/8 tsp. Cayenne pepper

1 1/2 c.	Yeast or pimento cheese
1/2 tsp.	Sea salt
2 1/2 c.	Cooked rice

Sauté the onions in the margarine. Combine all the ingredients and stir until nicely blended. Place the mixture in a casserole and bake at 350° for 45 minutes.

SQUASH CREOLE

You can rely on this!

2 1/2 c.	Squash, sliced
2 T.	Corn oil
1/4 c.	Bell pepper, chopped
1/3 c.	Onions, chopped
1 tsp.	Garlic, minced
3 T.	Unbleached white flour
1 c.	Beef-like Broth
2 c.	Canned tomatoes, chopped
1 T.	Barbados molasses
1/4 tsp.	Cayenne pepper
1 tsp.	Sea salt
1/2	Bay leaf
3/4 c.	Yeast, Pimento, or Mozzarella "Cheese"
1 1/2 c.	Bread crumbs
1/4 c.	Margarine, melted

Steam the sliced squash until tender and put in an oiled baking dish. Heat the oil; add bell pepper, onions, and garlic and sauté. Add flour and stir until blended. Add broth, tomatoes, molasses, and spices to this mixture. Cook these ingredients for 5 minutes, or until the peppers are tender. Pour this sauce over the squash. Cover with the "cheese." Mix the bread crumbs with 1/4 cup melted margarine and put on top of the "cheese." Bake at 350° for 30 minutes or until crumbs are well browned.

SQUASH TAMALE BAKE

So easy and so good!

1/2 c.	Bell pepper, chopped
1 tsp.	Garlic, minced
1/3 c.	Onions, chopped
4 tsp.	Corn oil
2/3 c.	Corn meal
3 c.	Canned tomatoes
2 c.	Squash, cubed
1/4 tsp.	Cayenne pepper
1/2 tsp.	Sea salt
2 c.	Water

Sauté the bell pepper, garlic, and onions in the oil. Place all the ingredients together in a saucepan and stir until the squash has released its juice well, and the corn meal has thickened. After partly cooking, turn out into a baking dish. Bake at 350° for about 1 hour.

TOMATO AND CORN SCALLOP

1 c.	Yeast or Pimento "Cheese"
1 1/2 c.	Corn
3/4 c.	Bread crumbs
	Sliced tomatoes–enough to make two layers in the casserole
1 T.	Non-dairy margarine, melted

Combine the "cheese," corn, and 1/2 cup of the crumbs. In a casserole place half the corn mixture and cover with tomato slices. Repeat. Toss the remaining crumbs with the margarine and sprinkle over the top. Bake at 350° for 30 minutes.

TOMATO EGGPLANT BAKE

As delicious as it is simple!

3 c.	Eggplant, cubed
1 c.	Onions, chopped
1/2 c.	Bell pepper, chopped fine
1 tsp.	Garlic, minced
2 T.	Olive oil
2 c.	Stewed Italian tomatoes
1/8 tsp.	Cayenne pepper
1/4 tsp.	Sea salt

Deep fry the eggplant until it begins to brown and transfer it to paper towels to drain. Sauté the onions, bell pepper, and garlic in the olive oil. When the onions are soft, add the tomatoes, pepper, and salt and cook for 15 minutes. Mix in the eggplant. Transfer to a casserole and bake at 350° for 20 minutes.

TOMATO RICE WITH "CHEESE"

2 T.	Bell pepper, chopped well
3 T.	Onions, chopped
2 T.	Non-dairy margarine
1 1/2 c.	Rice, cooked in Beef-like Broth
1 c.	Tomatoes, chopped
1/2 tsp.	Barbados molasses
1/2 tsp.	Sea salt
1/4 tsp.	Paprika
1 c.	Yeast or Pimento "Cheese"
1/4 c.	Dry bread crumbs

Sauté the bell pepper and onions in the margarine. Mix everything together–except the crumbs–and put in an oiled casserole dish. Cover with the crumbs. Dot with 1 tablespoon of margarine. Bake at 350° for about 40 minutes.

TRIPLE LAYER CASSEROLE

A pot-luck staple!

3 c.	Beef or Chicken Gluten, ground, or Baked Cubed Steak
1/4 c.	Corn oil
2 c.	Onions, chopped

2 tsp.	Garlic, minced
1 1/2 tsp.	Jalapeños, minced
3 c.	Potatoes, peeled, sliced, and boiled
3/4 c.	Cashew Milk
Pinch	Black pepper
5 c.	Cream-style corn
1 c.	"Cheese" Cracker crumbs tossed in 1 tablespoon of melted corn oil margarine

Brown the gluten in 2 tablespoons of the oil. Set aside. Sauté the onions, garlic, and jalapeños in the remaining oil. When the onions are soft, add the gluten and cook for 5 more minutes. Lightly oil a casserole pan and place the gluten on the bottom. On top of that put the cooked potatoes. Stir the "milk" and pepper into the corn and pour that over the potatoes. Sprinkle the cracker crumbs on top. Bake at 375° until the crumbs start to brown.

VEGETABLE CASSEROLE WITH TOMATOES AND RICE

1/2 c.	Bell pepper, chopped
1/4 c.	Onions, chopped
1 tsp.	Garlic, minced
2 T.	Corn oil
4 c.	Vegetables, cut in pieces and cooked
3 c.	Canned tomatoes, drained and chopped
1 T.	Parsley, chopped
1/4 tsp.	Basil
2 1/2 c.	Cooked rice
1 tsp.	Sea salt
1 c.	Yeast or Pimento "Cheese"

Sauté the bell pepper, onions, and garlic in the oil. Combine all ingredients in a casserole pan. Top with the "cheese" and bake for 20 minutes at 400°.

VEGETABLE CRUMBLE

CRUMBLE:

2 T.	Non-dairy margarine
2 c.	Unbleached white flour
1 c.	Yeast or Pimento Cheese

Rub the margarine into the flour until the mixture resembles fine crumbs. Add the "cheese."

BASE:

1/3 c.	Onions, chopped
1/2 tsp.	Garlic, minced
1/4 c.	Non-dairy margarine
3 c.	Mixed vegetables, chopped if need be
1/4 c.	Unbleached white flour
1 1/2 c.	Tomatoes, chopped
1 c.	Beef-like Broth
1/2 c.	Cashew milk
3 T.	Parsley, chopped
1/2 tsp.	Sea salt
1/4 tsp.	Paprika

Sauté the onions and garlic in the margarine until the onions are transparent. Add the vegetables and cook over gentle heat, stirring occasionally, for 10 minutes. Stir in the flour, then add the rest of the ingredients. Bring to a boil, reduce the heat, cover, and simmer about 15 minutes, or until the vegetables are just tender. Put in a casserole dish. Press the crumble topping over the vegetables. Bake at 375° about 30 minutes, or until golden brown.

VEGETABLES PARMESAN–1

Excellent at all times!

1/3 c.	Onions, chopped
1 tsp.	Garlic, minced
3 c.	Vegetables, in 1/2-inch slices
4 tsp.	Corn oil
2 c.	Canned tomato sauce
1 1/2 c.	Yeast or Pimento Cheese
1/2 c.	"Parmesan 'Cheese'"

Sauté the onions, garlic, and vegetables in the oil. Oil a casserole dish. In the dish, pour 1/4-inch of the tomato sauce. Over that put a layer of vegetables. Over that put a layer of "cheeses." Repeat, ending with a layer *each* of tomato sauce, vegetables, and "cheeses." Cover with foil and bake at 400° for 30 minutes. Remove foil and bake uncovered for 10 minutes. Watch closely to avoid over-cooking.

VEGETABLES PARMESAN–2

Fancier than Number 1, but worth all the making!

2 c.	Potatoes, cut into pieces
2 T.	Corn oil
2 c.	Vegetables, cut into pieces if needed
2 T.	Non-dairy margarine
1/3 c.	Onions, chopped
1 tsp.	Garlic, minced
1 c.	Tomatoes, chopped
2 T.	Unbleached white flour
1/2 c.	Cashew Milk
1/2 tsp.	Sage
1/2 tsp.	Basil
1/2 tsp.	Oregano
1/2 tsp.	Sea salt
1/4 tsp.	Paprika
1 c.	"Parmesan Cheese"
1 c.	Bread crumbs

Boil the potatoes for about 10 minutes, or until just tender. Drain, keeping back 1 cup of liquid. Heat the oil and sauté the vegetables until they are tender. Melt half of the margarine and sauté the onions and garlic until the onions are transparent. Add tomatoes to onions, stir in the flour and cook 1 minute. Add the potato liquid, "milk," herbs and seasonings to this. Bring to a boil, reduce heat, and simmer 15 to 20 minutes. Put the potatoes and vegetables in a casserole dish. Pour the tomato sauce over that. Sprinkle the "parmesan" and then the bread crumbs over all. Dot with the remaining margarine. Put in the oven at 400° about 20 minutes, or until heated through.

VARIATION: Instead of using 2 cups of potatoes plus 2 cups of vegetables, use 4 cups of vegetables, including or excluding potatoes as one of the vegetables.

ZUCCHINI CASSEROLE

6 c.	Zucchini, sliced
2 c.	Beef gluten, chopped or cubed
1/2 c.	Onions, chopped
1 tsp.	Garlic, minced
2 T.	Corn oil
1 c.	Rice, cooked
1 tsp.	Garlic salt
1 tsp.	Oregano
2 c.	Tofu Cottage Cheese
2 c.	White Sauce to which 3 T. low sodium soy sauce has been added
1 c.	Pimento or Yeast "Cheese"

Cook the sliced zucchini in salted water for 2 to 3 minutes and drain well. Place half the zucchini in an oiled baking dish. Sauté the gluten, onions, and garlic in the oil until the onions are transparent. Pour over the zucchini in the baking dish. Sprinkle the cooked rice and seasonings over the gluten layer. Spoon the "cottage cheese" over the rice layer, and cover with the remaining zucchini. Spread white sauce over all. Spread the "cheese" over that. Bake at 300° for 35 to 40 minutes.

ZUCCHINI CASSEROLE WITH TOMATOES, CHEESE, AND RICE

1 c.	Mushrooms, sliced
1/2 c.	Onions, chopped
1 tsp.	Garlic, crushed
2 c.	Zucchini, unpeeled, thinly sliced
2 T.	Non-dairy margarine
1 1/2 c.	Tomatoes, chopped
1/2 c.	Tofu Sour Cream or Cashew Sour Cream
1 c.	Yeast or Pimento "Cheese"
1/4 tsp.	Sea salt
1/8 tsp.	Cayenne pepper
3 c.	Cooked rice

Sauté the mushrooms, onions, garlic, and zucchini in the margarine until the zucchini is soft. Place in a large bowl and add the tomatoes. Beat together the "sour cream," "cheese," salt, and pepper. Combine all the ingredients and stir until nicely blended. Place the mixture in a casserole and bake at 350° for 45 minutes.

VARIATION: Cook the rice in Beef-like or Chicken-like Broth.

ZUCCHINI CREOLE

Always welcome!

3 T.	Non-dairy margarine
3 T.	Unbleached white flour
1 1/2 c.	Tomatoes, chopped
1/4 c.	Bell pepper, chopped
1/4 c.	Onions, chopped
1/2 tsp.	Sea salt
1/2 tsp.	Sucanat

1/2	Bay leaf
Pinch	Powdered cloves
2 1/2 c.	Zucchini, sliced but not peeled, and steamed
1 c.	Bread crumbs
3/4 c.	Yeast "Cheese"

Melt the margarine and stir in the flour until blended. Add the tomatoes, bell pepper, onion, and spices and cook for 5 minutes (if larger quantities are used, cook until the onion and pepper are tender). Place zucchini in an oiled baking dish and pour the tomato mixture over it. Cover with "cheese." Top with bread crumbs and dot with margarine. Bake at 350° until the crumbs turn light brown.

ZUCCHINI PARMIGIANA

4 1/2 c.	Tomatoes, chopped
1/2 c.	Onion, minced
1/4 c.	Parsley, minced
1 tsp.	Basil
1/2 c.	Olive oil
1/2 tsp.	Sea salt
1/4 tsp.	Cayenne pepper
5 c.	Zucchini, sliced lengthwise into 1/4-inch-thick slices
	Unbleached white flour
5	All-purpose N'eggs
2 1/2 c.	Mozzarella "Cheese"

Cook the tomatoes over medium heat for 15 to 25 minutes–until they are falling apart. Put them through a food mill (medium disk) into a bowl. Cook the onion, parsley, and basil in the oil over medium heat, stirring occasionally, for 15 minutes. Add the tomatoes, salt, and pepper, and simmer, stirring occasionally, for 20 to 30 minutes–until it is thickened slightly. Put the flour and n'eggs in two separate bowls. Dip the zucchini slices in the n'eggs, letting any excess drip off, and then dip them in the flour, shaking off any excess. Deep fry the zucchini at 380°, turning, for 2 minutes–until they are golden. When done, transfer them to paper towels to drain. Spread a thin layer of the tomato sauce in a baking dish. Over that put half of the zucchini in a layer. Over the zucchini pour half of the remaining tomato sauce. Over that spread a layer of half of the "cheese." Repeat this layering once more. Bake at 350° for 20 to 30 minutes. Put under a broiler, about 6 inches from the heat, for 2 to 4 minutes–until the top is slightly browned.

Dried Beans and Lentils

Dried beans are essential to a balanced and healthy vegetarian diet–in fact, they are virtually indispensable. However, when legumes dry, the nutrients are locked in, and it takes a great deal of breaking down through cooking to release them. *Dried beans cause gas only because they are undercooked.* To unlock the nutrients of beans it is best to pressure cook them thoroughly. This applies to all dried beans, including lentils (whose "skins" will *not* clog the pressure cooker vent if enough water is used–as in the following instructions), soy beans, and whole dried peas. Cooking dried beans by boiling them the time required to fully release the nutrients is a tremendous waste of fuel-energy. Even cooking them for twelve to fourteen hours in a crock pot has not always proven to be sufficient, whereas pressure cooking has proven completely effective.

Do not soak dried beans overnight before cooking as they will tend to ferment, especially in warm weather.

To cook beans/lentils in a pressure cooker use the following procedure.

1) Put the beans in the pressure cooker along with salt (1 tsp. per quart of dried beans) and enough water to cover the beans with water at least 2 inches deep.
2) Add 1 tablespoon of corn oil (this is so the skins will not clog the pressure cooker vent).
3) Cover–WITHOUT the weight– and bring them to the boil.
4) Continue to boil for 5 minutes.
5) Turn off the heat and let them rest for 1 hour.
6) Turn on the heat, put on the weight, and cook at 15 pounds of pressure.

Here is a list of times (minutes) recommended for pressure cooking dried beans:

Black–35
Black-eyed peas-20
Garbanzos-25
Great Northern (White)-25
Kidney–20
Lentils–5
Lima–25
Navy–25
Peas, whole–25
Pinto–25
Soy–45

Dal and split peas are cooked in water on the stove rather than pressure cooked, as they foam up and tend to clog the cooker vent.

The amount that dried beans yield when cooked varies. Here is a listing of how much ONE CUP of dried beans will yield according to type.

Black–2 cups
Black-eyed peas-2 cups
Garbanzos-2 1/2 cups
Great Northern (White)-2 1/2 cups
Kidney–2 1/2 cups
Lentils–2 cups
Lima–2 1/2 cups
Navy–2 1/2 cups
Peas, whole–2 cups
Pinto–2 1/2 cups
Soy–2 1/2 cups

BAKED BEANS–1

2 c.	Dried beans
3 T.	Onions, minced
1 tsp.	Garlic, minced
2 T.	Corn oil
1/8 tsp.	Cayenne pepper
3/4 c.	Barbados molasses
2 c.	Canned tomato sauce
1/2 c.	Beef-like Broth
1/2 tsp.	Savory
1/2 tsp.	Sea salt

Pressure cook and drain the beans. Sauté the onions and garlic in the oil. Combine all ingredients and simmer for 10 minutes, uncovered. Place in baking dish, cover with Yeast or Pimento Cheese. Bake at 400° 15 to 20 minutes.

BAKED BEANS–2

2 c.	Dry beans
3/4 c.	Onions, chopped
2 T.	Corn oil
1/4 c.	Bacon Gluten, minced
1/2 c.	Sucanat
1/4 c. & 2 T.	Barbados molasses
1 T.	Dry mustard
1 tsp.	Salt
2 c.	Canned tomato sauce

Pressure cook the beans and drain them. Sauté the onions in the oil. Combine everything in a covered casserole dish and bake, covered, at 350° for *at least* 90 minutes–the longer the better.
VARIATION: Cut some Loma Linda Big Franks into pieces, and sauté with the onions.

BAKED LENTILS

3 c.	Dried lentils
1/3 c.	Onions, chopped
1/2 tsp.	Garlic, minced
4 tsp.	Corn oil

2 tsp.	Sea salt
2 c.	Tomatoes, blended until smooth
1/2 c.	Bread crumbs tossed in melted non-dairy margarine

Pressure cook the lentils. Sauté the onions and garlic in the oil. Combine all the ingredients except the bread crumbs and place in a baking dish. Top with the crumbs. Bake until the crumbs are golden brown.

BARBECUE BAKED BEANS

1/2 c.	Bell peppers, chopped
1/2 c.	Onions, chopped
2 tsp.	Garlic, minced
2 T.	Corn oil
4 c.	Dried beans, pressure cooked and drained
1/2 tsp.	Cayenne pepper
3 c.	Tomato Sauce (one of the recipes from Gravies and Sauces)
1/4 c.	Barbados Molasses
1/4 c.	Wine vinegar
1 T.	Sovex or Vegex (dissolve in the vinegar)
1 tsp.	Sea salt
	Yeast or Pimento "Cheese"

Sauté the bell pepper, onions, and garlic in the corn oil. Combine all ingredients. Pour into a large oiled casserole. Add more tomato sauce if it is needed to cover the beans. Bake 30 minutes at 400°, then cover with Yeast or Pimento "Cheese" and bake 10 more minutes.

BARBECUE BEANS

Soybeans work well in this.

2 1/4 c.	Onions, chopped
2 tsp.	Garlic, minced
2 T.	Corn oil
1 c.	Tomato paste
3 c.	Water
1/2 c.	Sucanat
1 T.	Barbados molasses
2 T.	Low sodium soy sauce
1/2 tsp.	Allspice
1 tsp.	Sea salt
1 1/2 tsp.	Red pepper flakes
1/4 c.	Vinegar OR 1/2 c. Lemon juice
4 c.	Beans, cooked and drained

Sauté the onions and garlic in the oil. Add the tomato paste and stir in well. Add the rest of the ingredients–except the beans–bring to a boil, and simmer for 15 minutes. Stir in the beans and cook for 15 to 20 more minutes.

BEAN BURGERS

6 c.	Pressure-cooked dried beans
3 c.	Rice cooked in Beef-like Broth
2 c.	Tomatoes

1 c.	Tomato sauce
1 c.	Bell pepper
1/3 c.	Onions, chopped
1 tsp.	Minced garlic
3 T.	Low sodium soy sauce
1 1/2 tsp.	Sea salt
1/2 tsp.	Basil
1/4 tsp.	Oregano
1 T.	Parsley
1/4 c.	Corn oil

Mash the cooked beans. Mix all ingredients together. Form into patties and place on oiled sheet pan. Bake at 400° until light brown, turning once, or cook on a griddle.

BEAN ENCHILADAS

8 6-inch corn tortillas made according to the recipe given in the Bread and Such section

TOPPING:

Pimento or Yeast "Cheese"
Onions, chopped
Black olives, chopped

SAUCE:

1 c.	Onions, chopped
1 1/2 T.	Garlic, minced
2 T.	Corn oil
6 c.	Canned tomatoes, crushed
5 T.	Chili powder
1 1/2 tsp.	Sea salt
1 1/2 tsp.	Sucanat

Sauté the onions and garlic in the oil until the onions are soft, then add the rest of the ingredients and simmer for 45 minutes.

FILLING:

4 c.	Cooked pinto beans, drained
2 tsp.	Onion salt
3/4 tsp.	Garlic powder
1/2 tsp.	Cumin, ground
2/3 c.	Canned tomato sauce

Partially mash the beans in a bowl. Mix the rest of filling ingredients together and add to the beans. Mix well.

ASSEMBLY:

Cover the bottom of a casserole with some of the sauce. Put some of the filling in each tortilla, roll it up, and put in the casserole with the seam side down. Cover with the rest of the sauce. Spread the "cheese" over all. Sprinkle the onions and olives over that. Bake, uncovered, at 350° for 25 minutes.

BEAN LOAF

2 1/2 c.	Dried beans, cooked and mashed
1 tsp.	Sea salt
1/2 c.	Bell pepper, chopped well
1/2 c.	Tomato pulp
1/2 c.	Corn flakes
1/3 c.	Onions, chopped
1/2 tsp.	Paprika
1 tsp.	Low sodium soy sauce
1 T.	Corn oil

Combine all ingredients in an oiled loaf pan. Bake at 350° for about 1 hour. Serve with Yeast or Pimento "Cheese" or tomato sauce.

BEAN POT

2 c.	Dry beans
3/4 c.	Onions, chopped
2 T.	Non-dairy margarine
1 1/2 tsp.	Sea salt
1/2 tsp.	Minced garlic
1/2 c.	Pimento
1/2 tsp.	Paprika

Pressure cook the beans. Sauté the onions in the melted margarine for 5 minutes. Combine all ingredients and cook for 20-30 minutes

BEANS BOURGIGNONNE

3/4 c.	Onions, chopped
2 T.	Corn oil margarine
1/2 c.	Carrot, sliced in half-rounds
1 1/4 c.	Potato, cubed
1 c.	Chicken-like Broth
3 T.	Italian tomato paste
1/8 tsp.	Thyme
1	Bay leaf
2 c.	Mushrooms, sliced
4 c.	Pinto beans, cooked
2	Garlic cloves, crushed
1 tsp.	Sea salt

In a soup pot, sauté the onion in 1 tablespoon of the margarine. Add the carrot and potato. Stir in the broth, tomato paste, thyme, and bay leaf. Bring to a boil and simmer briskly until the potatoes and carrots are cooked–about 20 minutes–adding extra broth to keep the vegetables covered if necessary. Toward the end of the cooking time, sauté the mushrooms in the other tablespoon of margarine over low heat, then add them to vegetables along with the beans, garlic, and salt. Return to a boil, lower the heat, and simmer, uncovered, for another 10 minutes. Remove and discard the bay leaf.

BLACK BEAN CHILI-1

2 c.	Dry black beans

2 c.	Onions, chopped
2 tsp.	Garlic, minced
3 T.	Corn oil
1 T.	Jalapeños, minced
1 tsp.	Cumin seeds
1/2 tsp.	Cayenne pepper
1/2 tsp.	Paprika
1 tsp.	Oregano
1 tsp.	Sea salt
4 c.	Canned tomatoes, chopped

Pressure cook and drain the beans, reserving the cooking water. Sauté the onions and garlic in the oil until onions are transparent. Add the jalapeños and spices and sauté for 1 more minute. Add rest of ingredients and simmer for 1 hour–adding bean water if more liquid is needed. Serve with vinegar on the side to be added to taste.

BLACK BEAN CHILI-2

2 c.	Black beans
1 1/2 tsp.	Cumin seed
1 1/2 tsp.	Oregano
1 tsp.	Paprika
1/2 tsp.	Cayenne pepper
1 1/2 c.	Onion, chopped
2 tsp.	Corn oil
1/2 c.	Bell pepper, diced
1 1/2 tsp.	Garlic, minced
1 1/2 c.	Italian tomatoes, chopped
1 c.	Tomato juice
1/2 tsp.	Sea salt
1/4 c.	Green onion (including the tops), chopped

Wash the beans thoroughly and pressure cook them. In a small dry skillet, heat the herbs, and toss them until they are fragrant. Sauté the onion in the oil for 2 to 3 minutes. Stir in the bell pepper, garlic, and herbs until the onion is soft and golden. Add to the cooked beans, along with the tomatoes, juice, and salt. Simmer for 30 or more minutes. Serve with the green onion on the top.

BLACK BEAN SOUP-1

2 1/2 c.	Dry black beans
1 c.	Bell pepper, chopped
3 T.	Onions, chopped
3 T.	Corn oil
6 c.	Beef-like or Chicken-like Broth
3/4 tsp.	Sea salt
1/8 tsp.	Cayenne pepper
2 c.	Tomatoes, chopped
1/4 tsp.	Summer savory

Pressure cook the beans. Sauté the bell peppers and onions in the oil. Combine with rest of ingredients and cook about 30 minutes more. If needed, add more broth or water to keep a soup consistency.

BLACK BEAN SOUP–2

2 c.	Dry black beans
1/3 c.	Onions, chopped
1/2 c.	Celery, chopped
1/2 tsp.	Garlic, minced
1/4 c.	Corn oil
1/8 tsp.	Italian Herb Seasoning
1/4 tsp.	Sage
1	Bay leaf
1/4 tsp.	Cayenne pepper
2 c.	Potatoes, cooked and diced
1 c.	Carrots, cooked and sliced into rounds
1 c.	Bacon Gluten, chopped fine
4 c.	Chicken-like Broth

Pressure cook the beans. Sauté the onions, celery, and garlic in the corn oil. Combine all ingredients and cook for 30 minutes.

VARIATIONS: Omit the gluten and use Beef-like Broth instead.

BLACK BEAN SOUP–3

1 c.	Dry black beans
3/4 c.	Onions, chopped
2 T.	Non-dairy margarine
2 c.	Beef-like or Chicken-like Broth
1/4 tsp.	Cayenne pepper

Pressure cook the beans. Sauté the onions in the margarine. Combine all ingredients and simmer for 1 hour.

BLACK BEANS WITH TOMATOES

2 c.	Dry black beans
2 c.	Tomatoes, canned
1 c.	Onions, chopped
1 c.	Celery, chopped
2 T.	Corn oil
1/2 tsp.	Garlic powder
2 tsp.	Sea salt
1/2 tsp.	Black pepper

Pressure cook the beans. Blend the tomatoes in a blender. Sauté the onion and celery in the oil. Combine everything and cook 20 to 30 minutes.

BUDAPEST BEAN SOUP

Every spoonful of this is a delight!

1 lb.	Dried white beans
9 c.	Chicken-like Broth
1	Bay leaf
1/2 tsp.	Oregano
1 c.	Onion, chopped

1/2 c.	Celery, chopped
3 T.	Olive oil
2 T.	Paprika (or 1/2 tsp. hot paprika)
1/4 tsp.	Cayenne pepper
4 c.	Zucchini, cubed
1/2 tsp.	Black pepper

Pressure cook the beans in 6 cups of the chicken-like broth with the bay leaf and oregano. Put half the beans through a food mill or purée them in a food processor and mix back in with the rest of the beans. Sauté the onion and celery in the oil until the onion is translucent. Stir in the paprika, cayenne, zucchini, and rest of broth. Cook for 5 minutes. Combine with the beans and add the black pepper. Cook 5 more minutes, adding more broth or water if it gets too thick.

BUCKAROO BEANS

I can't describe these–but I sure can eat them!

2 c.	Pinto beans, dry
1/2 c.	Onions, chopped
1 tsp.	Garlic, minced
1/2 c.	Bell pepper, chopped
2 T.	Corn oil
1	Bay leaf (whole)
1/2 c.	Imitation bacon bits
2 c.	Tomatoes, canned
2 tsp.	Chili powder
1/2 tsp.	Dry mustard
1/4 tsp.	Oregano
1 tsp.	Sea salt

Pressure cook the beans. Sauté the onions, garlic, and bell pepper in the oil. Combine everything and cook until well done. Add more water if necessary.

CAMPFIRE RED BEANS

These taste more like they were cooked over a smokey hickory campfire than if they really were.
Mexican Chorizo Sausage is especially good in this dish.

4 c.	Dry kidney beans
2 c.	Ham or Sausage Gluten, cubed
2 T.	Corn oil
1 c.	Onion, chopped
1 T.	Garlic, chopped
1 tsp.	Liquid smoke
1 T.	Louisiana Hot Sauce
2 T.	Lea & Perrins Steak Sauce
2 T.	Parsley flakes (dried)
1 T.	Bell pepper flakes (dried)
3 c.	Ham-like or Sausage-like Broth
3 c.	Water

Pressure cook the beans according to the directions given in the Dried Beans section. Sauté the gluten in the oil. Add the onions and garlic and sauté until the onions are soft. Put everything together and cook for 15 minutes.

CHILI BEANS-1

Good by themselves or with "cheese" and tortillas.

3/4 c.	Onions, chopped
1 c.	Bell pepper, chopped
2 T.	Corn oil
4 c.	Pressure-cooked dried beans
1 tsp.	Minced garlic
2 1/2 c.	Tomatoes
1/4 tsp.	Cayenne pepper
1 tsp.	Sea salt

Sauté the onions and bell pepper in the oil. Combine all ingredients with sufficient water and simmer together slowly for 45 minutes.

CHILI BEANS-2

Good by themselves or with "cheese" and tortillas.

2 c.	Dried Pinto or kidney beans
1 1/2 c.	Onions, chopped
1 tsp.	Garlic, minced
2 T.	Corn oil
2 tsp.	Sea salt
2 T.	Chili powder
2 tsp.	Cumin

Pressure cook the beans. Sauté the onions and garlic in the oil. Combine everything and cook 10 to 15 minutes, adding any needed water.

CHIMICHUNGAS

Never fails!

5 c.	Refried Beans (the recipe is given later in this section)
1	Time the recipe for Flat Bread (see Bread and Such section), uncooked

Put 1/2 cup of beans on an uncooked "bread." Fold in the two sides and then the top and bottom. Deep fry at 375° until light brown, being careful to prevent them from unfolding. If not served immediately, refry *quickly* to reheat and recrisp the chimichungas shortly before serving. Serve with Tofu Sour Cream, Cashew Sour Cream, or Miraculous Whip, or some other type of vegan "mayonnaise," chopped tomatoes and chopped lettuce.

VARIATION: Use Flour Tortillas instead of Flat Bread

COWBOY BEANS

These are addicting!

2 c.	Pinto or pink beans, DRY
2 tsp.	Sea salt
3/4 tsp.	Crushed red pepper

1/2 c.	Onions, chopped
2 tsp.	Garlic, minced
2/3 c.	Bacon Gluten, minced
3 T.	Corn oil

Pressure cook the beans with the salt. Drain. Cover with water. Add rest of ingredients and bring to a boil. Simmer for 30 minutes.

CREAM OF PINTO BEAN AND TOMATO SOUP

1/4 c.	Onions, sliced
1 T.	Corn oil
1 c.	Pinto beans, cooked
1 c.	Canned tomatoes, chopped
3 c.	Thin white sauce

Sauté the onions in the oil. Combine with beans and tomatoes and heat together. Put through a sieve or blender. Combine with the white sauce just before serving.

DAL SOUP

1/4 c.	Bell pepper, chopped well
3 T.	Onions, chopped
2 T.	Corn oil
2 c.	Dal, dry
3/4 tsp.	Sea salt
1/8 tsp.	Crushed red pepper
1 c.	Tomatoes
4 1/2 c.	Chicken-like Broth

Sauté the bell peppers and onions in the oil. Combine with rest of ingredients and cook.

DRIED BEAN PATTIES

2 c.	Cooked dried beans of choice, mashed
1/2 c.	Tomatoes, chopped
3/4 c.	Onions, chopped
1/2 c.	Bell peppers, chopped
1/8 tsp.	Cayenne pepper
2 c.	Bread crumbs
2 tsp.	Sea salt
1 T.	Low sodium soy sauce
1/2 tsp.	Sage

Combine ingredients. Shape into balls and flatten. Dip them in flour. Chill the patties for one hour or more. Fry them slowly until brown on both sides.

GARBANZO CREOLE

3/4 c.	Onions, chopped
1 tsp.	Minced garlic
1/2 c.	Bell peppers, chopped
2 T.	Corn oil
3 c.	Pressure-cooked garbanzos

Pinch	Cayenne pepper
2 c.	Canned tomatoes
1/2 tsp.	Sea salt
1	Bay leaf
1/2 c.	Tomato Sauce
1/2 c.	Chicken-like Broth

Sauté the onions, garlic, and bell pepper in the oil. Combine everything and cook for 30 minutes.

VARIATION: Use another type of dried bean.

GARBANZOS BOMBAY
(Kabuli Channa)

4 c.	Dry garbanzos
4 c.	Onions, chopped
4 tsp.	Garlic, minced
2 T.	Jalapeños, minced
4 tsp.	Tumeric
2 T.	Coriander, powdered
3/4 tsp.	Ginger, powdered
1 T.	Garam masala
1/4 c.	Non-dairy margarine
6 c.	Tomatoes
1/4 c.	Lemon juice
1 T.	Sea salt

Pressure cook the garbanzos, keeping back the water in which they are cooked. Sauté the onions, garlic, jalapeños, tumeric, coriander, ginger, and garam masala in the melted margarine. Add the cooked garbanzos and stir well until coated with the hot oil. Add the tomatoes, lemon juice and salt, stirring well. Add 1 quart of the garbanzo water (adding some plain water if there is less than a quart). Cover and cook for about one hour. You may want to add some more (garbanzo) water if it seems to be getting too dry.

GARBANZOS

2 c.	Garbanzos, dry
2 tsp.	Sea salt
1 1/2 c.	Onions, chopped
1/2 c.	Corn oil
1 tsp.	Powdered ginger root
1/2 tsp.	Ground cumin
1 tsp.	Tumeric
1 tsp.	Ground coriander
1/4 tsp.	Garam masala
1/2 tsp.	Chili powder
1/8 tsp.	Cayenne pepper
3 c.	Canned tomatoes, crushed, with juice

Cook the garbanzos in 1 teaspoon of the salt and reserve the liquid. Sauté the onions in the oil until they are tender. Add the ginger and cumin, and sauté for 2-3 minutes more. Add the rest of the spices and stir to blend together. Combine everything, including the garbanzo liquid, and simmer for 30 minutes.

HERBED BEANS

3/4 c.	Onions, chopped
2 T.	Corn oil
2 c.	Dried beans, pressure cooked
2 tsp.	Sea salt
1/4 tsp.	Fines Herbes
Pinch	Cayenne pepper

Sauté the onions in the oil. Combine everything and cook for 1 hour.

HUMMUS

1 1/3 c.	Dry garbanzos
2 T.	Olive oil
1 T.	Sea salt
1 T.	Garlic, minced
1/4 c.	Lemon juice
1 c.	Tahini
1/4 tsp.	Cayenne pepper
	Water from cooking the garbanzos

Pressure cook the garbanzos, drain, and mash them. Add the remaining ingredients except the garbanzo water. Using the garbanzo water, blend all in a blender until smooth and of the consistency of a medium-thick sauce.

KERALA DAL

Kerala is the state at the southernmost tip of India where Saint Thomas the Apostle established the Indian Orthodox Church in 54 A.D. I expect he ate this very dish. If so, I hope he liked it as much as I do!

1 c.	Orange dal (the tiny kind that turns yellow when cooked)
3 c.	Water
1/2 tsp.	Sea salt
2 T.	Corn oil
1 T.	Black mustard seeds
1/2 tsp.	Cumin seeds
1 T.	Garlic, minced
1 tsp.	Tumeric
3 c.	Tomatoes, chopped
1/4 tsp.	Hing (asafoetida), optional
1/4 tsp.	Ground cumin
1/4 tsp.	Cayenne pepper
1/2 tsp.	Sea salt

Cook the dal in the water and salt until it just begins to fall apart. Remove from heat and drain. Heat the oil in a very heavy, small pan. Add the mustard seeds, spreading them over the bottom of the pan evenly, and cook, stirring, until they turn black(er) and start to pop. Add the cumin and garlic and cook just one minute more. Stir in the tumeric and immediately remove pan from the heat. In a large saucepan, combine tomatoes, hing, cumin, cayenne pepper, salt, and the fried seed mixture. Bring to a boil and cook for 15 minutes. Add the dal and cook until it falls apart.

LENTIL AND TOMATO SOUP

1/2 c.	Lentils, dry
3/4 c.	Onions, chopped
1 tsp.	Garlic, minced
2 T.	Corn oil
4 c.	Tomatoes, chopped
1 c.	Tomato juice
3 3/4 c.	Beef-like Broth
1/4 tsp.	Sea salt
1/4 tsp.	Cayenne pepper

Pressure cook the lentils. Sauté the onions and garlic in the oil until the onions are transparent. Add the rest of ingredients, cover, and simmer for 30 minutes.

LENTIL PATTIES

These are really distinctive. Many who do not usually like lentils love these.

2 c.	Lentils cooked in Beef-like Broth, drained, and mashed
3 c.	Fine bread crumbs
3/4 c.	Onions, minced
1 tsp.	Garlic, minced
1 tsp.	Sea salt
1/4 c.	Beef-like Broth (can be that left over from cooking the lentils)
2 T.	Parsley, chopped

Mix the ingredients thoroughly and let sit for 15 minutes. Form into patties. Place on floured cookie sheet and bake at 350° for 20 to 30 minutes or until browned. Or dip the patties into flour and sauté in corn oil until brown. Good with Lentil Patty Sauce following.

LENTIL PATTY SAUCE

1/3 c.	Onions, chopped
2 T.	Corn oil
2 1/2 c.	Cooked tomatoes
1/2 tsp.	Sea salt
3 T.	Cornstarch
3 T.	Water

Sauté the onions in the oil. Add to tomatoes and salt. Bring to a boil. Blend the cornstarch with the water and stir into the tomatoes. Bring to a boil again and remove from heat.

LENTIL POT

2 c.	Lentils
3/4 c.	Onions, chopped
1 tsp.	Minced garlic
1 1/2 tsp.	Wine vinegar
1 c.	Tomatoes
3/4 c.	Bell pepper, chopped
2 T.	Corn oil
1 1/2 tsp.	Low sodium soy sauce
1	Bay leaf

1/2 tsp. Sea salt

Pressure cook the lentils. Add the rest of the ingredients–including sufficient water–and cook 30 more minutes.

LENTIL SOUP-1

2 1/2 c. Dry lentils
Enough Beef-like or Chicken-like Broth to cover the lentils with 2 inches of broth.
1 c. Bell pepper, chopped
3 T. Onions, chopped
3 T. Corn oil
3/4 tsp. Sea salt
1/8 tsp. Cayenne pepper
2 c. Tomatoes, chopped
1/4 tsp. Summer savory

Cook the lentils in the broth for about 30 minutes until they are soft. Sauté the bell peppers and onions in the oil. Combine with rest of ingredients and cook about 30 minutes more. If needed, add more broth or water to keep a soup consistency.

LENTIL SOUP-2

2 c. Dry lentils
1/3 c. Onions, chopped
1/2 c. Celery, chopped
1/2 tsp. Garlic, minced
1/4 c. Corn oil
1/8 tsp. Italian Herb Seasoning
1/4 tsp. Sage
1 Bay leaf
1/4 tsp. Cayenne pepper
2 c. Potatoes, cooked and diced
1 c. Carrots, cooked and sliced into rounds
1 c. Bacon Gluten, chopped fine
4 c. Chicken-like Broth

Pressure cook the lentils. Sauté the onions, celery, and garlic in the corn oil. Combine all ingredients and cook for 30 minutes.

VARIATIONS: Omit the gluten and use Beef-like Broth instead.

LENTIL SOUP-3

1 c. Dry lentils
3/4 c. Onions, chopped
2 T. Non-dairy margarine
2 c. Beef-like or Chicken-like Broth
1/4 tsp. Cayenne pepper

Pressure cook the lentils. Sauté the onions in the margarine. Combine all ingredients and simmer for 1 hour.

LENTIL SOUP–4

1 c.	Lentils, dry
3/4 c.	Onions, chopped
3/4 c.	Celery, chopped
1/4 tsp.	Garlic, minced
2 T.	Corn oil
3/4 c.	Carrots, chopped
1 c.	Tomatoes, chopped
1/8 tsp.	Basil
1/8 tsp.	Oregano
1	Bay leaf
1 tsp.	Sea salt
3/4 c.	Potatoes, diced
3 c.	Beef-like or Chicken-like Broth

Pressure cook the lentils for 5 minutes. Sauté the onion, celery, and garlic in the oil. Put everything together and cook for 30 minutes.

MEXICAN BEAN POT

2 c.	Dry pinto beans
2 c.	Sausage Gluten of choice (Mexican Chorizo is obvious)
1 1/2 c.	Onions, chopped
1 tsp.	Minced garlic
1/4 c.	Bell pepper
2 T.	Corn oil
2 c.	Tomatoes, chopped
1 tsp.	Sea salt
1 tsp.	Oregano
1/2 tsp.	Ground cumin
1/2 tsp.	Black pepper

Pressure cook the beans and retain the cooking water. Sauté the gluten, onions, garlic, and bell pepper in the oil. Combine everything and cook for 60 minutes, using the bean water and any extra water (or tomato juice) if it gets too dry.

MEXICAN GARBANZOS

3/4 c.	Onions, chopped
1 tsp.	Minced garlic
2 T.	Corn oil
4 c.	Garbanzos, pressure cooked
1/2 c.	Bell pepper, chopped
1 T.	Barbados molasses
1/2 c.	Tomato paste
1 tsp.	Sea salt

Sauté the onions and garlic in the oil. Combine all ingredients and cook slowly for 30 to 60 minutes.

PEASE PORRIDGE

Remember the nursery rhyme? Well, here it is!

2 c.	Dry green split peas
2 c.	Water
1 tsp.	Sea salt
2 T.	Non-dairy margarine
1/4 tsp.	Paprika

Pick over the split peas and discard any discolored ones. Wash them thoroughly under cold running water and continue to wash until the draining water runs clear. In a heavy 3 to 4-quart saucepan, bring the water to a boil. Drop in the peas slowly so the water continues to boil. Reduce the heat and simmer, partially covered, for 1 1/2 hours, or until the peas can be easily mashed against the side of the pan with a spoon. Drain the peas in a colander and purée them in a food mill or force them through a fine sieve set over a large bowl. Return the peas to the pan, stir in salt, margarine and paprika, and cook over low heat, stirring constantly, until the purée is heated through. Serve at once from a heated dish.

REFRIED BEANS

Cannot be equaled much less surpassed by the canned stuff!

3 c.	Dry pinto beans
3 c.	Onions, chopped
4 tsp.	Garlic, minced
1/4 c.	Jalapeños, chopped
3 T.	Corn oil
1 c.	Tomato paste
1/2 tsp.	Sea salt
	Bean water

Cook the beans and drain them, saving the water. Sauté the onions and jalapeños in the oil until the onions are transparent. While the onions are sautéing, put the beans through a food processor or mill and purée them, adding the tomato paste, salt, and enough bean water to get a smooth texture. Add the garlic to the onion and jalapeños and cook for 2 more minutes. Add the bean mixture and combine everything thoroughly. Continue cooking on high heat, stirring frequently for 10 minutes. You may need to add more bean water if this gets too dry.

SIMPLE CASSOULET

1/2 c.	Onions, diced
1 c.	Carrots, diced
1 c.	Potatoes, diced
1 T.	Garlic, minced
2 T.	Olive oil
1 c.	Chicken, Ham, or Sausage Gluten, cubed
1/4 tsp.	Thyme
1/4 tsp.	Basil
1/4 tsp.	Marjoram
1/4 tsp.	Rosemary
1/2 tsp.	White pepper
1 T.	Prepared mustard
1/2 tsp.	Sea salt

2 c. White beans, cooked
2 c. Water or broth of the type of gluten being used

Sauté the vegetables and garlic in the oil for about 5 minutes in a heavy ovenproof pot or casserole dish. Add the gluten, the seasonings, and the beans. Add enough of the water or broth to barely cover the mixture. Cover and bake at 350° for 45 minutes. Stir before serving.

SOUTHERN PINTO BEANS

This is what it's all about!

4 c. Pinto beans, pressure cooked and drained
1 1/2 c. Yeast or Pimento "Cheese"
2 c. Corn
2 c. Tomatoes, sliced (more, if needed for complete layer)
1 1/2 tsp. Sea salt
1/2 c. Bread crumbs
2 T. Non-dairy margarine

In a casserole pan layer: beans, "cheese," corn, "cheese," tomatoes, salt, and bread crumbs mixed with the melted margarine. Bake at 350° for 30 minutes until heated through and brown on top.

SOY FRITTERS

4 c. Soybeans, cooked and drained
1 1/2 c. Water from cooking the beans
2 c. Unbleached white flour
1 1/2 T. Baking powder
1 tsp. Sea salt
1 1/2 tsp. Garlic powder
1 1/2 c. Onions, chopped

Mash 3 cups of the soybeans. Combine everything to make a thick paste-batter. Drop into hot oil from a spoon and fry, turning them so they will brown all over. (Add more flour if the batter does not hold together in the frying.) Serve with a sauce such as Tartar Sauce, Tomato Sauce, "Cheese" Sauce, Tofu Sour Cream, or Cashew Sour Cream.

VARIATION: Use some other type of beans.

SOYBURGERS

1 1/2 c. Onions, chopped
1 c. Carrot, grated
1 1/4 c. Celery, chopped fine
3/4 c. Bell pepper, chopped fine
1 1/2 tsp. Garlic, minced
3 T. Corn oil
6 c. Cooked soybeans (save the cooking water)
3 c. Cooked rice
1 1/2 tsp. Sea salt
3/4 tsp. Basil
3/4 tsp. Parsley
1/2 tsp. Garlic powder
1/2 c. Low sodium soy sauce

1/3 c. Tahini

Sauté onions, carrot, celery, bell pepper, and garlic in the oil. Mash beans, combine everything, and mix well. If too dry, add bean water or tomato juice. Form into patties and place on an oiled sheet pan. Bake at 400° until light brown, turning once, or fry on a griddle.

SOYTEENA

This is very much like some of the canned meat substitute commercially available, but I think it is better. It is very good fried–especially the next day.

1 c. Dry soy beans
2 c. Water
1 c. Tomato juice
1/2 c. Peanut butter
2 tsp. Sea salt
1/3 c. Celery, chopped fine
1/4 c. Nutritional Yeast flakes
1/2 c. Onions, chopped fine
4 T. Low sodium soy sauce
1/2 tsp. Garlic powder
1 c. Cornmeal

Combine all the ingredients, except the cornmeal, and process them in a blender until smooth. Remove from the blender and mix in the cornmeal well. Pour into oiled Number 2 cans. Cover cans with metal foil and secure it with rubber bands. Steam for 2 hours or longer in a large kettle that is about 1/3 full of water when the cans are set in it. Keep the water simmering in the kettle with the lid on. When cooled, remove the cans.

SPECIAL GARBANZOS

3/4 c. Onions, chopped
2 tsp. Garlic, minced
2 T. Corn oil
3 c. Garbanzos, cooked
2/3 c. Carrots or squash, sliced
1 c. Bell peppers, chopped
1 tsp. Sage, dried
2 T. Parsley, chopped
1/2 tsp. Louisiana Hot Sauce
1 1/2 tsp. Sea salt
1/4 tsp. Cayenne pepper

Sauté onion and garlic in the oil until soft. Combine everything and cook 10 minutes over low heat, stirring occasionally.

VARIATION: Use other types of beans.

SPLIT PEA SOUP–1

Now this does what it is supposed to!

2 1/2 c. Dry split peas
Enough Beef-like or Chicken-like Broth to cover the peas with 2 inches of broth.
1 c. Bell peppers, chopped

3 T.	Onions, chopped
2 T.	Corn oil
3/4 tsp.	Sea salt
1/8 tsp.	Cayenne pepper
2 c.	Tomatoes, chopped
1/4 tsp.	Summer savory

Cook the peas in the broth for about 30 minutes until they are soft. Sauté the bell peppers and onions in the oil. Combine with rest of ingredients and cook about 30 minutes more. When done the peas will be "dissolved." If needed, add more broth or water to keep a soup consistency.

SPLIT PEA SOUP-2

2 c.	Split peas
1/3 c.	Onions, chopped
1/2 c.	Celery, chopped
1/2 tsp.	Garlic, minced
2 T.	Corn oil
1/8 tsp.	Italian Herb Seasoning
1/4 tsp.	Sage
1	Bay leaf
1/4 tsp.	Cayenne pepper
2 c.	Potatoes, diced and cooked in water
1 c.	Carrots, sliced into rounds and cooked in water
1 c.	Imitation bacon bits
4 c.	Chicken-like Broth

Pressure cook the split peas. Sauté the onions, celery, and garlic in the corn oil. Combine all ingredients and cook for 30 minutes.

VARIATIONS: Omit the bacon bits and use beef-like broth instead. Use lentils instead of split peas.

SPLIT PEA SOUP-3

1 c.	Green split peas, dry
3/4 c.	Onions, chopped
2 T.	Non-dairy margarine
2 c.	Beef-like or Chicken-like Broth
1/4 tsp.	Cayenne pepper

Pressure cook the split peas. Sauté the onions in the margarine. Combine all ingredients and simmer for 1 hour.

SWEDISH BROWN BEANS

The only Swedish Brown Bean recipe I like–and love!

4 2/3 c.	Pinto beans, DRY
3/4 c.	Onions, chopped
1/2 tsp.	Garlic, sliced
2 T.	Corn oil
2 c.	Beef-like Broth
1/2 tsp.	Sea salt
1/4 c.	Imitation bacon bits

1/4 tsp.	Black or cayenne pepper
1/4 c.	Barbados molasses
1 c.	Catsup or tomato sauce
1 tsp.	Louisiana Hot Sauce
1/2 c.	Wine vinegar
1/4 tsp.	Dry mustard

Pressure cook the beans and drain. Sauté the onions and garlic in the oil. Combine all ingredients and cook together for 30 minutes.

TORTILLA AND TOSTADO FILLING–1

4 c.	Pressure cooked dried beans, drained
2 c.	Salsa
2 c.	Tofu sour cream
1 1/3 c.	Tomatoes, chopped
1/3 c.	Onions, chopped
2 c.	Yeast or pimento cheese

Combine. Good rolled up in tortillas or spread on them. Add shredded lettuce if desired.

TORTILLA AND TOSTADO FILLING–2

1/3 c.	Onions, chopped
1 tsp.	Garlic, minced
2 T.	Corn oil
1 tsp.	Sea salt
1/4 tsp.	Cayenne pepper
1 c.	Tomatoes
4 c.	Pressure cooked dried beans, drained

Sauté the onions and garlic in the oil. Combine with the salt, pepper, and tomatoes and cook well. Blend with the beans.

TUSCAN WHITE BEAN CASSEROLE–1

1 c.	Dry white beans
1/2 c.	Onion, chopped
2 T.	Olive oil
2 c.	Tomatoes, chopped
3 T.	Tomato paste
1/2 tsp.	Sage (dried)
1	Bay leaf
3 T.	Parsley, chopped
1/2 tsp.	Sea salt
1/8 tsp.	Pepper

Pressure cook the beans. Sauté the onion in the olive oil until transparent. Add the tomatoes, tomato paste, sage, bay leaf, salt, pepper, and parsley. Simmer for 15 minutes. Put the beans in a casserole. Stir in the tomato mixture. Cover and bake in a moderate oven for 20 to 25 minutes.

TUSCAN WHITE BEAN CASSEROLE–2

1 c.	Ham, Sausage, or Bacon Gluten, cut into strips
1 c.	Onion, chopped
2 1/2 tsp.	Garlic, minced
1/4 tsp.	Black pepper
2 T.	Olive oil
3 c.	Cooked white beans
	Chicken-like Broth
1 c.	Gluten Sausage–any flavor–sliced
4	Tomatoes, peeled, sliced, and soaked in olive oil and pepper
1/8 tsp.	Sage
1/8 tsp.	Black pepper
	Bread Crumb Topping (see Etc.)

Sauté the gluten strips with the onions, garlic, and pepper in the oil until the gluten is browned. Put all this into a saucepan with the cooked beans and enough broth to cover everything. Simmer for 20 minutes. Oil a casserole with garlic oil (plain olive oil if you have none). Put half of the beans in a layer in the casserole. Put the gluten slices on top of the beans. Put a layer of tomato slices and sage on top of the sausages. Sprinkle with the pepper. Put the other half of the beans on top in a layer. Cover the beans with Bread Crumb Topping. Bake at 350° for 20 minutes in the upper half of the oven.

VEGEBURGERS

2 c.	Cooked (save the cooking water) soybeans, ground
1 c.	Cooked (save the cooking water) garbanzos, ground
1 1/2 c.	Rice, cooked in Chicken-like Broth
1 1/2 c.	Onions, chopped
1 1/2 tsp.	Sage
3/4 tsp.	Celery salt
1/2 tsp.	Garlic powder
2 T.	Corn oil

Combine all ingredients, adding bean water if too dry, or crumbs or oatmeal if too wet. Form patties and bake, covered with foil, for 25 minutes at 350° then turn and bake 10 minutes or more.

WHITE BEANS WITH "BACON"

2 c.	Dry white beans
1 c.	Onions, chopped
1/2 tsp.	Garlic, minced
2 T.	Corn oil
1/2 tsp.	Sea salt
1 c.	Imitation bacon bits, or Bacon Gluten, chopped fine or ground
1/4 tsp.	Black or cayenne pepper

Pressure cook the beans. Sauté the onions and garlic in the oil. Combine everything and cook together 20 to 30 minutes, adding any water that might be needed.

WHITE BEANS WITH TOMATOES–1

1/3 c.	Onions, chopped
1 1/2 tsp.	Garlic, minced
2 T.	Corn oil
3 c.	Cooked white beans
2 c.	Tomatoes
1/2 tsp.	Sea salt
1/8 tsp.	Cayenne pepper
1 T.	Wine vinegar

Sauté the onions and garlic in the oil. Stir in the rest of the ingredients. Cover and simmer over low heat for 10 minutes.

WHITE BEANS WITH TOMATOES–2

2 c.	Dry white beans
1 c.	Onions, chopped
1 tsp.	Garlic, minced
1/2 c.	Celery, chopped
1/4 c.	Bell pepper, chopped
2 T.	Corn oil
2 tsp.	Sea salt
1/4 tsp.	Basil, dried
1/4 tsp.	Black or cayenne pepper
1 c.	Tomatoes, chopped
1 c.	Carrots, chopped or sliced

Pressure cook the beans. Sauté the onions, garlic, celery, and bell pepper in the oil. Combine everything and cook together 20 to 30 minutes, adding any water as needed.

GRAINS

BARLEY

Basic proportions for cooking barley are:

1 c.	Barley
2 c.	Water
3/4 tsp.	Sea salt

Wash the barley well under cold running water while the cooking water is coming to a boil. Add the salt and the barley to the water and stir. Turn the flame down very low. Cover and cook for about 45 minutes–poor quality barley will cook faster than good quality.

BASIC RICE

Basic proportions for cooking Jasmine or Basmati Rice are:

1 c.	Rice
1 1/2 c.	Water
1 tsp.	Sea salt

Wash the rice well under cold running water while the cooking water is coming to a boil. Add the salt and the rice to the water and stir. Turn the flame down very low. Cover and cook for about fifteen minutes.

This makes 2 1/2 cups of cooked rice.

"CHEESE" RICE

1 c.	Rice that was cooked in Beef-like or Chicken-like Broth
1/2 c.	Yeast or pimento cheese
1/4 tsp.	Paprika

Cook the rice, and while it is still hot and in the pot, stir in the other ingredients.

VARIATION: Add 1 cup of Tomato juice. Add 1/2 cup of Tofu Sour Cream or Cashew Sour Cream.

CRACKED WHEAT

Cracked wheat should not be confused with Tabouli Wheat which needs no cooking.

Basic proportions for cooking Cracked Wheat are:

1 1/2 tsp.	Corn oil
1 c.	Cracked Wheat
3/4 tsp.	Sea salt
1 1/2 c.	Boiling water

Heat the oil until it begins to smoke. Add the cracked wheat and stir rapidly and continuously to avoid burning and coat all the wheat with oil. Fry on high heat about 5 minutes until it starts to brown. Add the salt, then the wheat, to the boiling water and stir. Bring back to boil. Turn the flame down very low. Cover and cook for about fifteen minutes.

VARIATION: Use Beef-like or Chicken-like Broth instead of water, and use only 1/3 teaspoon of salt.

CREOLE RICE

1 c.	Onions, chopped
2 tsp.	Garlic, minced
2 T.	Corn oil
3 c.	Okra, sliced
1/4 tsp.	Cayenne pepper
4 c.	Creole Sauce
1/2 tsp.	Sea salt
6 c.	Rice, cooked in Chicken-like Broth

Sauté the onions and garlic in the corn oil. Combine with all other ingredients except the rice. Cook over medium heat for 20 minutes. Add the rice and cook for 10 minutes more, adding more Creole sauce if it becomes too dry.

DIRTY RICE

5 c.	Beef, Pork, Sausage, Ham, or Chicken Gluten–or a combination
3 T.	Olive oil
1 c.	Onion, chopped fine
1 c.	Green onions, chopped fine
1/2 c.	Bell pepper, chopped fine
1/2 c.	Parsley, chopped fine
1/2 c.	Celery, chopped fine
2 T.	Garlic, chopped fine
1/2 tsp.	Dry mint, crushed
1/2 tsp.	Cayenne pepper
1 tsp.	Louisiana Hot Sauce
4 1/2 tsp.	Lea & Perrins Steak Sauce
1 c.	Flavoring Broth of the type of gluten used
3 c.	Cooked rice

Combine everything except the rice and cook together for 20 minutes, covered, stirring occasionally. Add the cooked rice and mix thoroughly. Cook over low heat for another 20 minutes.

FLAVORED RICE

1 c. Rice
1 1/2 c. Flavoring Broth of choice
1/2 tsp. Sea salt

Wash the rice well under cold running water while the broth is coming to a boil. Add the salt and the rice to the water and stir. Turn the flame down very low. Cover and cook for about fifteen minutes.

FRIED RICE

3 c. Rice, uncooked
4 tsp. Non-dairy margarine
4 tsp. Corn oil
4 1/2 c. Beef-like or Chicken-like Broth
1/2 tsp. Sea salt

Wash rice thoroughly and drain. Combine the margarine and oil in a skillet and melt the margarine. Add the washed rice and stir frequently until the rice becomes light brown–this takes quite a while, so don't give up. (Some of the rice kernels may even "pop" like popcorn.) If the rice becomes too dry add more margarine or oil to keep it shiny as it fries. Bring broth to a boil. Add the salt. Then add the rice–which must be coming directly from the skillet and be hot and frying– to the boiling water a little bit at a time, taking care because it will "explode." Cover the pot and turn the flame down. Simmer for 10 minutes.

GREEN RICE–1

1 c. Rice that was cooked in Chicken-like Broth
1/2 c. Yeast or pimento cheese
1/2 c. Parsley, finely chopped
1 c. Tomato juice
Pinch Cayenne pepper
1/3 c. Onions, minced

Cook the rice, and while it is still hot and in the pot, stir in the other ingredients.
VARIATION: Add Tofu Sour Cream or Cashew Sour Cream.

GREEN RICE–2

3/4 c. Mushrooms, sliced
3/4 c. Celery, chopped
3/4 c. Onions, chopped
1/2 tsp. Garlic, minced
2 T. Non-dairy margarine
2 c. Broccoli, chopped and steamed
1 1/2 c. Rice, cooked

Sauté the mushrooms, celery, onions, and garlic in the margarine until the onions and celery are transparent. Carefully stir in the broccoli and rice until all is heated through.

RICE JAMBALAYA

1/2 c. Bell pepper, chopped

3/4 c.	Onions, chopped
1 tsp.	Minced garlic
1 c.	Squash or pumpkin, sliced
2 T.	Pimentos, chopped
1 c.	Tomatoes, cubed
2 T.	Corn oil
1 c.	Rice, uncooked
2 c.	Chicken-like Broth
1/4 tsp.	Cayenne pepper
1 tsp.	Sea salt

Sauté the vegetables in the oil until just tender. Add rice, broth, pepper, and salt. Cook until rice is tender.

MILLET

Basic proportions for cooking millet are:

1 c.	Millet
1 1/2 c.	Water
3/4 tsp.	Sea salt

Wash the millet well under cold running water while the cooking water is coming to a boil. Add the salt and the millet to the water and stir. Turn the flame down very low. Cover and cook for about 30 minutes–poor quality millet will cook faster than good quality.

VARIATION: Use Beef-like or Chicken-like Broth instead of water, and use only 1/3 teaspoon of salt.

PILAF IMPERIAL

3 c.	Cracked wheat
4 1/2 c.	Beef-like or Chicken-like Broth, boiling
1/4 c.	Low sodium soy sauce
1 tsp.	Paprika
1 1/2 c.	Onions, chopped
1 tsp.	Minced garlic
1 1/2 c.	Celery, chopped
1 1/2 c.	Water chestnuts, sliced
1/3 c.	Bell pepper, chopped
3 T.	Non-dairy margarine

Combine the wheat, broth, soy sauce, and paprika and bake in a covered casserole at 350° for 45 minutes. Sauté the onions, garlic, celery, chestnuts, and bell pepper in the margarine until tender. Combine all and serve with Tofu Sour Cream or Cashew Sour Cream.

SIMPLE RISOTTO

1/3 c.	Onions, chopped
1 tsp.	Garlic, minced
1/4 c.	Bell pepper, chopped
1/2 c.	Mushrooms or black olives, chopped
1 T.	Non-dairy margarine
1 T.	Corn oil
1 c.	Tomatoes, chopped

1 1/3 c.	Rice that was cooked in Chicken-like Broth
1/4 tsp.	Sea salt
1/4 tsp.	Paprika

Sauté the onions, garlic, bell pepper, and mushrooms (or olives) in the margarine and oil until the bell pepper is just tender. Add the tomatoes, rice, salt, and paprika. Continue stirring until the rice is heated through.

SPANISH RICE–1

1/2 c.	Bell peppers
3/4 c.	Onions, chopped
1 T.	Garlic, minced
2 T.	Corn oil
5 c.	Tomatoes, chopped
1/4 tsp.	Cayenne pepper
1 tsp.	Sea salt
1/2 tsp.	Basil
Pinch	Dill weed, dried
1 1/4 c.	Beef-like Broth
3 1/2 c.	Rice that was cooked in Beef-like Broth

Sauté the bell peppers, onions, and garlic in the corn oil. Combine with the rest of the ingredients except for the rice and cook for 20 to 30 minutes, until it gets thick. Add the cooked rice and cook for 5 more minutes.

VARIATION: Include 4 cups of eggplant, cubed, and sauté it along with the bell peppers and onions.

SPANISH RICE–2

1 c.	Onion, chopped
1 tsp.	Garlic, minced
2 T.	Jalapeños, minced
1/2 c.	Bell pepper, chopped small
2 T.	Olive oil
3/4 c.	Tomato paste
2 c.	Chicken-like Broth
2 T.	Unbleached white flour
1/4 tsp.	Sea salt
3 c.	Rice that was cooked in Chicken-like Broth
1 c.	Garbanzos, cooked

Sauté the onion, garlic, jalapeños, and bell pepper in the oil. Mix the tomato paste and the broth. Add the flour and salt to the sautéed vegetables. Add the tomato-broth mixture. Simmer gently until thickened, about 3-5 minutes. Add the rice and garbanzos. Bake in an oiled casserole 25 minutes at 350°.

VARIATION: Substitute other dried beans or dried green peas for the garbanzos.

SPANISH RICE–3

2 c.	Beef Gluten or Soy Grits Beef
1 1/2 c.	Onions, chopped
1/2 tsp.	Garlic, minced
1/4 c.	Bell pepper, chopped fine

3 T.	Corn oil
1 c.	Rice, cooked
4 1/2 c.	Canned tomatoes
1 1/2 tsp.	Sea salt
2 tsp.	Chili powder
1/2 c.	Salsa
1/2 c.	Black olives, sliced
1/2 c.	Mushrooms, sliced
1 c.	Pimento or Yeast "Cheese"

Sauté the gluten (or grits), onions, garlic, and bell pepper in the oil until tender. Add the rice, tomatoes, salt, chili powder, and salsa. Simmer at least 10 minutes. Stir in the rest of the ingredients, cover and bake 75 minutes at 350°.

SPICY BULGHUR PILAF

2 T.	Non-dairy margarine
3/4 c.	Onion, chopped
1 1/2 tsp.	Garlic, crushed
1 c.	Bulghur wheat
1/4 tsp.	Cayenne pepper
1/4 tsp.	Ground cumin
1/4 tsp.	Celery seed
1/2 c.	Bell pepper, finely diced
1/4 tsp.	Sea salt
2 1/4 c.	Chicken-like or Beef-like Broth, boiling

Melt the margarine. Add the onion, garlic, and bulghur and cook 2 to 3 minutes, stirring occasionally. Stir in the cayenne pepper, cumin, and celery seed, and continue cooking for 3 to 5 more minutes. Add the bell pepper and salt. Pour in the boiling broth. Reduce to a simmer, cover, and cook until all liquid is absorbed.

SPINACH RISOTTO

2 c.	Rice, uncooked
2 T.	Non-dairy margarine
10 oz.	Frozen spinach, thawed and drained
3 1/2 c.	Chicken-like Broth
1/4 tsp.	Black pepper

Sauté the uncooked rice in the margarine. Combine the other ingredients and bring them to a boil. Add the rice, lower the heat, and simmer, covered, until the rice is done–about 15 minutes.

TABOULI WHEAT

Put the wheat in a bowl and cover with warm water—about two inches above the top of the wheat. Spring water takes fifteen minutes, distilled water takes about twice as long. Drain in a colander, pressing lightly to press out excess water.

VEGETABLE FRIED RICE–1

3 c.	Rice, uncooked
4 tsp.	Non-dairy margarine
4 tsp.	Corn oil

4 1/2 c. Beef-like or Chicken-like Broth
1/2 tsp. Sea salt
1 1/2 c. Onions, chopped
3 c. Vegetables of choice, chopped if need be
2 T. Corn oil

Wash rice thoroughly and drain. Combine the margarine and oil in a skillet and melt the margarine. Add the washed rice and stir frequently until the rice becomes light brown–this takes quite a while, so don't give up. (Some of the rice kernels may even "pop" like popcorn.) If the rice becomes too dry add more margarine or oil to keep it shiny as it fries. Bring broth to a boil. Add the salt. Then add the rice–which must be coming directly from the skillet and be hot and frying– to the boiling water a little bit at a time, taking care because it will "explode." Cover the pot and turn the flame down. Simmer for 10 minutes. While the rice is cooking, sauté the onions and vegetables until softened. When the rice is done, add the rice into the vegetables and continue to sauté until all excess water is evaporated.

VEGETABLE FRIED RICE–2

1/2 c. Onion, chopped
2 T. Corn oil
1/2 c. Bell pepper, chopped
1/3 c. Celery, chopped
1 c. Mushrooms, chopped
1/2 c. Squash, chopped
3 T. Soy sauce
1 c. Rice, cooked

Sauté the onions in the oil until transparent, then sauté the rest of the ingredients for 15 minutes.

Tofu Dishes

Tofu–especially when it is frozen, thawed, and pressed–can be used in many of the recipes that call for gluten, and can be flavored by simmering or soaking the tofu in the same broths as are used to flavor the gluten.

TOFU

5 c. Dry soybeans
2 1/2 gal. Boiling water

ONE OF THE FOLLOWING:

2 T. Nigari
2 T. Epsom Salts
1 c. Vinegar (any kind)
1 c. Lemon juice

Wash the soybeans well and drain them.

Put them in a bowl, cover them with 12 cups of *cold* water, and let them soak 8 to 12 hours. (If the room temperature is below 65° then let them soak 16 to 20 hours.)

Drain off the water and wash again.

Put 1/3 of the beans in a blender or food processor, add 5 cups of the boiling water, and grind into a puree. Set aside.

Repeat this twice more.

Put the water-bean mixture into a large pot on the stove, add 15 more cups of boiling water, bring to a boil, and boil slowly for 10 minutes, stirring constantly.

Remove from the stove and strain through cheesecloth in a colander or large strainer, pressing hard to squeeze out all excess milk. (Use a rubber glove on your hand or the back of a large spoon for the pressing.)

Set the soy milk aside and return the soybean pulp to the pot. Add 10 cups of boiling water, put back on the stove and bring to a boil again.

As soon as it comes to a boil, remove from the heat and press out as before, adding the milk to the first batch.

Let the milk cool to 185°. *This is important. A higher temperature will not work, and a cooler temperature will cause the tofu to be too soft.*

Dissolve the 2 tablespoons of nigari in 2 1/2 cups of hot water.

Take 1/3 of the nigari mixture, hold it high above the surface of the soy milk, and while constantly stirring rapidly, add it all at once and continue stirring only 3 to 5 seconds more.

Take the second 1/3 of the nigari mixture and sprinkle it over the top of the soy milk.

Let it sit for 5 minutes.

Take the last 1/3 of the nigari mixture and sprinkle it over the top of the soy milk.

Let it sit for 5 minutes, then as gently and slowly as possible stir the mixture once to circulate the milk.

Let it sit for 5 more minutes, then a second time as gently and slowly as possible stir the mixture once to circulate the milk.

Let it sit for 5 more minutes, then a third time as gently and slowly as possible stir the mixture once to circulate the milk.

Let it sit for 5 minutes more.

The mixture should by now have turned into curds and whey. (If this is not the case, then something has gone wrong, and you should mix up 1 tablespoon of nigari in 1 cup of hot water and sprinkle it on the top of the soy milk, stirring very slowly for 3 seconds and then let it sit for 10 to 15 minutes, stirring every 5 minutes as previously described. But if the directions are followed correctly this should not be necessary.)

Pour or ladle the curds and whey slowly into a colander or large strainer lined with cheesecloth.

Transfer the curds in the cheesecloth to a tofu press and press lightly with a weight for 5 minutes.

Remove the weight and lift up the curds in the cheesecloth, and shake around gently to remove any folds that may have formed in the cheesecloth.

Put all back into the tofu press and press with heavy weights for 15 minutes for soft tofu and 30 minutes for firm tofu.

Cut into convenient size blocks.

For storage in the refrigerator, cover with cold water and put in an airtight container. Change the water every 24 hours. The tofu will keep for 7 to 10 days.

NOTES: Nigari (bittern) is the best coagulant to use in making your own tofu–both for flavor and for efficiency (amount of curds obtained). It is extracted from sea water.

Nigari and Epsom Salts make firm tofu. Vinegar and lemon juice make soft tofu.

If you want to use vinegar or lemon juice and yet get firm(er) tofu, then you must stir the curds for a few minutes longer.

OVEN METHOD TOFU

This recipe looks pretty silly, but it really works quite well. As you can see, the advantage of this method is the ability to add flavorings to the tofu beforehand. You can add other flavorings not given in this recipe, but some flavorings may keep the tofu from solidifying very well. So you must be willing to experiment.

4 c.	Water
2 1/4 c.	Soy flour
2/3 c.	Pimentos
2 1/2 tsp.	Salt
2 1/2 T.	Nutritional yeast
1/2 c.	Flour
1/3 c.	Lemon juice
1/4 t.	Garlic salt
3 T.	Corn oil

Place everything in a blender and whirl until smooth. Pour into a small, greased loaf pan. Bake 2 hours at 275°. Turn off the oven, but keep it in the oven for one more hour. Chill before turning out of the pan. Peel off the brown skin on the top and trim the loaf to shape. Slice or cube for serving.

"BEEF" ENCHILADAS

4 c.	Tofu, frozen, thawed, pressed and crumbled (or cut in small pieces)
4 T.	Corn oil
2 tsp.	Garlic, minced
2 c.	Onions, chopped
2 tsp.	Jalapeños, minced
3 T.	Chili powder
3/4 c.	Black olives, chopped
1/4 tsp.	Sea salt
10 c.	Spanish Tomato Sauce
1	Recipe of Corn Tortillas or Flour Tortillas
	Yeast or Pimento "Cheese" to cover

Sauté the tofu in 2 tablespoons of the oil until the edges begin to brown. Set aside. In the other 2 tablespoons of oil, sauté the garlic, onions, and jalapeños until the onions are transparent. Add the chili powder and sauté for 2 more minutes, stirring constantly. Add olives, salt, tofu, and 3 cups of the tomato sauce and cook for another 5 minutes. Dip a tortilla in the tomato sauce, put some of the filling on it and roll it up and put it in a casserole pan. Do this with all the tortillas until the filling is used up. Cover the enchiladas with the remaining sauce. Spread a layer of "cheese" over that. Bake at 350° for 30 minutes.

BEEF-LIKE TOFU

Magnificently simple!
This sauce can be used to flavor 4 cups of gluten as well.

2 c.	Onions, coarsely chopped
1 tsp.	Garlic, minced
2 tsp.	Jalapeños, chopped
3 T.	Corn oil
3 T.	Cornstarch
1 1/2 c.	Cold (not warm) water
1/4 c.	Low sodium soy sauce
1 tsp.	Kitchen Bouquet
1 tsp.	MSG
1 1/2 c.	Water
4 c.	Frozen tofu that has been thawed and pressed

Sauté the onions, garlic, and jalapeños in the oil. Mix the cornstarch and water together and add it, stirring constantly. Add the rest of the ingredients–except the tofu–and simmer until it starts to thicken. While this sauce is cooking, cut or slice the tofu into pieces about 1/2-inch thick. Deep fry the tofu in corn oil–making sure the oil is very hot–until the tofu is brown. Drain in a colander and put on paper towels to absorb excess oil. When the sauce is done, add the tofu to it and cook for five minutes.

CHICKEN-LIKE TOFU

What I have said about the recipe above applies to this one, too.

2 c.	Onions, coarsely chopped
2 tsp.	Jalapeños, chopped
3 T.	Corn oil
3 T.	Cornstarch

1 1/2 c.	Cold (not warm) water
1/4 tsp.	Poultry seasoning
1 1/2 T.	Nutritional Yeast
1/2 tsp.	Salt
1 tsp.	MSG
1 1/2 c.	Water
4 c.	Firm tofu, or frozen tofu that has been thawed and pressed

Sauté the onions and jalapeños in the oil. Mix the cornstarch and water together and add it, stirring constantly. Add the rest of the ingredients–except the tofu–and simmer until it starts to thicken. While this sauce is cooking, cut or slice the tofu into pieces about 1/2-inch thick. Deep fry the tofu in corn oil–making sure the oil is very hot–until the tofu is brown. Drain in a colander and put on paper towels to absorb excess oil. When the sauce is done, add the tofu to it and cook for five minutes.

STIR-FRY TOFU AND VEGETABLES

A standby you can count on!

2 c.	Tofu, cut in 1-inch cubes
1 1/2 c.	Onions, cut in wedges
2 T.	Corn oil
1 c.	Carrots, sliced thin
1/2 c.	Green beans, cut in 1-inch pieces
1/2 c.	Mushrooms, sliced
1/2 c.	Chicken-like Broth
3/4 tsp.	Garlic, minced
1/2 tsp.	Dried basil
1/8 tsp.	Pepper

Deep-fry the tofu in corn oil and put on paper towels to drain. Sauté the onions in the 2 tablespoon of oil for 1 minute. Add the carrots and sauté for 1 more minute. Add the green beans and sauté for 1 more minute. Add the mushrooms and sauté for 1 more minute. Add the tofu and the rest of the ingredients and sauté 5 minutes, or until the vegetables are soft.

TOFU HUMMUS

Just as good as the chick pea type!

4 c.	Tofu
2/3 c.	Lemon juice
1/3 c.	Olive oil
1 1/3 tsp.	Sea salt
1/3 c.	Low sodium soy sauce
2/3 c.	Tahini
2 T.	Garlic, minced

Blend all in a blender or food processor.

TOFU "SCRAMBLED EGGS"

Extraordinary!

1 T.	Corn oil

1/2 c.	Onions, chopped
1 T.	Low sodium soy sauce
1/2 tsp.	Sea salt
1/4 tsp.	Garlic powder
1/4 tsp.	Tumeric powder
1 drop	Liquid smoke
2 T.	"Bacon," chopped fine
1 T.	Nutritional yeast flakes
2 tsp.	Jalapeños, chopped
2 c.	Soft tofu, crumbled

Put everything but the tofu in a skillet and stir well. Add the tofu and mix well with a fork until the seasonings are evenly distributed. Cook together until the water in the tofu evaporates and the mixture resembles scrambled eggs.

VARIATIONS: Add 1/4 cup chopped bell pepper. Add 1/2 cup sliced mushrooms or other vegetables. Try green onions instead of regular ones. Serve with salsa or some kind of tomato sauce.

TOFU "SCRAMBLED EGGS"
BREAKFAST CASSEROLE

1	Recipe of Tofu Scrambled Eggs made with bell pepper and mushrooms
1 c.	Ham or Sausage Gluten, ground and browned in corn oil
1 c.	Yeast or Pimento "Cheese"

Put the Tofu Scrambled Eggs in a casserole dish or a loaf pan, spread the gluten over that, spread the "cheese" over the gluten. Bake at 350° for 10 minutes.

Gravies and Sauces

Get creative with these sauces! Use them in many ways: over bread, biscuits, grains, pasta, vegetables, as dips–whatever!

BARBECUE SAUCE–1

1 c.	Onions, chopped
2 T.	Corn oil
6 T.	Tomato paste
1 1/4 c.	Water
1/4 c.	Sucanat
1 T.	Barbados molasses
1/4 c.	Lemon juice
2 T.	Prepared mustard
2 tsp.	Sea salt
1/4 tsp.	Cayenne pepper

Put all together and cook for 1 hour.

BARBECUE SAUCE–2

4 T.	Corn oil
2 c.	Onions
2	Garlic cloves
1/2 c.	Parsley
3/4 tsp.	Louisiana Hot Sauce
1 c.	Water
1 T.	Lemon juice
4 T.	Lea & Perrins Steak Sauce
1 1/2 tsp.	Sea salt
1 1/2 c.	Canned tomato sauce
1 tsp.	Liquid smoke

Heat the oil in a large saucepan. Blend the onions, garlic, parsley, and hot sauce in a blender with just enough water so it will blend. Pour this into the saucepan and simmer for 30 minutes. Add the rest of the ingredients and simmer for 30 more minutes, covered, adding more water if it is needed.

SPICY BARBECUE SAUCE–1

4 1/2 c.	Tomato sauce
3/4 c.	Tomato paste
1/3 c.	Barbados molasses
1/2 c.	Water
1/3 c.	White wine vinegar
2 T.	Lemon juice
2 T.	Prepared mustard
2 T.	Lea & Perrins Steak Sauce
2 tsp.	Hot pepper sauce
1/2 c.	Onions, finely chopped
1 tsp.	Garlic, minced
1/2 tsp.	Ground black pepper
1/2 tsp.	Ground cloves
1/2 tsp.	Allspice
1/4 tsp.	Ground ginger
2 T.	Corn oil

Combine all the ingredients in a large saucepan. Cook over medium heat for about 30 minutes, stirring frequently to prevent sticking.

SPICY BARBECUE SAUCE–2

This is the sauce given for Barbecue Ribs, but it is good for everything.

1/2 c.	Onion, chopped
1 tsp.	Garlic, minced
2 T.	Corn oil
2 1/2 c.	Tomato sauce
1/4 c.	Water
1 c.	Sucanat
2 T.	Barbados molasses
1/2 c.	Prepared mustard
1 T. & 1 tsp.	Sea salt
1 tsp.	Allspice
1 1/2 tsp.	Red pepper, crushed
1 1/2 tsp.	Dried parsley or 1 sprig of fresh parsley
1/4 c.	Water
2 T.	Lemon juice
1 tsp.	Liquid smoke
1 T.	Low sodium soy sauce

Sauté the onion and garlic in oil or margarine until the onions become clear and golden. Add tomato sauce, water, Sucanat, molasses, mustard, salt, allspice, pepper and parsley. Bring to a boil, reduce heat and let simmer for about an hour. Add water, lemon juice, liquid smoke and soy sauce. Cook 10-15 minutes longer.

"BEEF" AND TOMATO SAUCE

1 1/2 tsp.	Garlic, minced
1 c.	Onions, chopped
2 T.	Corn oil

2 c.	Beef-flavored gluten
3 c.	Tomatoes, finely chopped
2/3 c.	Tomato paste
2 T.	Sucanat
1 tsp.	Italian Herb Seasoning
1	Bay leaf
1/2 tsp.	Salt
1/8 tsp.	Black or cayenne pepper

Sauté the garlic and onion in the oil until the onions are soft. Add the gluten and sauté it well. Add the remaining ingredients. Simmer the sauce uncovered for about 20 to 30 minutes.

BEEF-LIKE GRAVY–1

1/4 c.	Unbleached white flour
2 T.	Corn oil
2 c.	Beef-like Broth

In a skillet blend the flour in the heated oil. Slowly add the broth. Cook for 10 minutes.
NOTE: If potatoes have been boiled, use the potato water in making the broth.

BEEF-LIKE GRAVY–2

2 T.	Corn oil
4 T.	Unbleached white flour
1 tsp.	Kitchen Bouquet
1 1/2 c.	Onions, chopped
1 1/2 tsp.	Garlic, minced
3 c.	Beef-like Broth
1/2 tsp.	Sea salt
2 T.	Lea and Perrins Steak Sauce
1 T.	Louisiana Hot Sauce

Heat the oil in a skillet and stir in the flour. Turn the fire down so it will cook slowly. Add the Kitchen Bouquet and keep stirring the flour constantly, adding more oil if the mixture is too dry, until it is a rich brown. Add the onions and garlic, stirring constantly. Add the broth and keep stirring until it starts to form a thick gravy. Add the salt, steak sauce, and hot sauce. Add more water if you need to, and bring all to a boil and simmer for 10 minutes.

BROWN SAUCE

2 T.	Non-dairy margarine
3 T.	Onions, sliced
1/2 tsp.	Garlic, minced
2 T.	Unbleached white flour
1 c.	Tomato, pureed
3/4 c.	Beef-like Broth
1/4 tsp.	Sea salt
1/4 tsp.	Paprika

Melt the margarine and sauté the onions and garlic until the onions are light brown. Remove the onions and stir in the flour and cook until it turns brown, as well. Slowly stir in the puréed tomatoes. Add the onions, broth, salt and paprika. Stir and cook until the sauce is smooth and boiling.

"BUTTER" SAUCE WITH HERBS

1 T.	Unbleached white flour
1/4 c.	Non-dairy margarine
2 T.	Cashew milk
2 T.	Onions, minced
1/2 tsp.	Garlic, minced
1 1/2 tsp.	Basil
1 1/2 tsp.	Parsley
1/8 tsp.	Sea salt

Place all ingredients in a double boiler, cook and stir until smooth.

CAJUN CATSUP

This am delighteous, I garontee!

4 c.	Onion, chopped
1 c.	Celery, chopped
1 c.	Bell pepper, chopped
1 c.	Parsley, chopped
1/4 c.	Corn oil
2 T.	Garlic, chopped
3 c.	Lea & Perrins Steak Sauce
1/2 c.	Louisiana Hot Sauce
3 c.	Tomato sauce
3 tsp.	Sea salt

In a large skillet, sauté the onions, celery, bell pepper, and parsley in the oil until the onions are soft and transparent. Add the garlic and cook a little longer. Add the steak sauce, hot sauce, tomato sauce, and salt, and bring to a boil. Lower the heat and cover, and cook for 2 to 3 hours. This can be kept refrigerated for a few weeks.

CAJUN "BEEF" GRAVY

Get adventurous!

4 T.	Corn oil
1 c.	Beef gluten, ground
1/4 c.	Corn oil
1/4 c.	Unbleached white flour
1 1/4 tsp.	Kitchen Bouquet
3 c.	Mushrooms (fresh preferred), stemmed and halved
1 c.	Onion, chopped
2 tsp.	Garlic, minced
4 c.	Beef-like Broth
3 T.	Lea and Perrins Steak Sauce
4 tsp.	Louisiana Hot Sauce

In a skillet heat 2 tablespoons of the oil and fry the gluten until it is browned on all sides. Remove the gluten and set aside. Put the other 2 tablespoons of oil in the skillet and heat. Stir the flour into the oil and turn the fire down so it will cook slowly. Add the Kitchen Bouquet and keep stirring the flour constantly–adding more oil if the mixture is too dry–until the mixture is a rich brown. Add the mushrooms, onions, and garlic, stirring constantly. Continue to cook for 10 minutes, adding up to 1/2 cup of the broth if needed to keep it from sticking. Add the rest of the broth, steak sauce, and hot sauce, turn the heat down and continue cooking until it starts to thicken–about 20 minutes–stirring occasionally.

CATSUP

1 c.	Tomato purée
4 tsp.	Corn oil
2 tsp.	Molasses
1 tsp.	Sea salt
2 T.	Wine vinegar
3 T.	Onions, chopped

Combine all the ingredients and cook for 15-30 minutes. While still warm, pour into a blender and blend until smooth as possible.

"CHEESE" SAUCE–1

2 T.	Corn oil
1/2 c.	Flour
3 c.	Water
1 1/2 tsp.	Sea salt
1/8 tsp.	Cayenne pepper
3 c.	Yeast or Pimento "Cheese"

Heat the oil. Slowly add the flour, blending it with a whisk. Slowly add the water, continuously blending with the whip. Cook until bubbly and thick. Add the salt, pepper, and "cheese."

VARIATION: Use Beef-like Broth or Chicken-like Broth instead of water, and cut the salt in half.

"CHEESE" SAUCE–2

2 T.	Non-dairy margarine
2 T.	Unbleached white flour
1 1/2 c.	Cashew Milk
1 c.	Yeast or pimento cheese
1/2 tsp.	Sea salt
1/8 tsp.	Paprika
Dash	Cayenne pepper
1/2 tsp.	Dry mustard

Melt the margarine in a saucepan. Stir in the flour until it is blended. Slowly stir in the "milk." When the sauce is smooth and boiling, reduce the heat and add the rest of the ingredients, stirring in well.

VARIATION: Make the "milk" with Chicken-like Broth, and cut the salt in half.

"CHEESE" SAUCE–3

1 c.	Tofu Sour Cream or Cashew Sour Cream
2/3 c.	Yeast or Pimento "Cheese"
2 T.	Onions, chopped
2 T.	Lemon juice
1/4 tsp.	Sea salt

Combine everything well. Use over broccoli, brussels sprouts, spaghetti, etc.

"CHEESE" SAUCE–4

1/2 c. Yeast or Pimento "Cheese"
1/4 c. Miraculous Whip
1/2 c. Tofu Sour Cream or Cashew Sour Cream
1/4 tsp. Paprika

Combine everything well. Use over broccoli, brussels sprouts, spaghetti, etc.

"CHEESE" AND ONION SAUCE

1 1/2 c. Onions, chopped
1 tsp. Garlic, minced
2 T. Non-dairy margarine
2 T. Unbleached white flour
2 c. Cashew Milk, warm
1 tsp. Sea salt
1/4 tsp. Paprika
1/2 c. Yeast or Pimento "Cheese"

Sauté the onions and garlic in the margarine. Add the flour and blend. Add the "milk" slowly while stirring. Stir in the salt, paprika, and "cheese."

CHICKEN-LIKE GRAVY

1/4 c. Unbleached white flour
2 T. Corn oil
2 c. Chicken-like Broth

In a skillet blend the flour in the heated oil. Slowly add the broth. Cook for 10 minutes.
NOTE: If potatoes have been boiled, use the potato water in making the broth.

CHILI SAUCE

1 c. Catsup
2 T. Prepared horseradish
2 T. Lemon juice
1 tsp. Chopped parsley
1 tsp. Chopped chives

Combine all the ingredients and stir to blend. Put in a container and refrigerate.

COCKTAIL SAUCE–1

1 1/2 c. Catsup
2 1/2 T. Lemon juice
1 T. &
1 1/2 tsp. Horseradish
2 T. Lea & Perrins Steak Sauce
1 tsp. Onions, grated
2 dashes Louisiana Hot Sauce

Combine all the ingredients and stir to blend. Put in a container and refrigerate.

COCKTAIL SAUCE–2

1/2 c. Miraculous Whip
2 T. Olive oil
2 tsp. Louisiana Hot Sauce
2 c. Catsup
1 tsp. Sea salt
2 T. Lea & Perrins Steak Sauce
3 T. Lemon juice
1 T. Creamed style horseradish

Put the Miraculous Whip in a bowl, and while beating constantly with a fork, add the oil. Continuing to beat, add the hot sauce and then the catsup. Add the salt, steak sauce, lemon juice, and horseradish, mixing well. Cover and chill for at least 30 minutes. Beat just before serving.

CREOLE SAUCE

2 T. Non-dairy margarine
1/3 c. Onions, chopped
1/2 c. Bell pepper, chopped
1/3 c. Mushrooms, chopped
1 tsp. Jalapeños, minced
1 1/2 c. Tomatoes, chopped
1/3 tsp. Sea salt
1 tsp. Barbados molasses
1 T. Unbleached white flour
1/3 c. Water

Melt the margarine, and sauté the onions, bell peppers, mushrooms, and jalapeños for 2 minutes. Add the rest of the ingredients and cook until the sauce is thick. Good over rice.

GOLDEN SAUCE

1/2 c. Onion, chopped
1/2 tsp. Garlic, minced
2 T. Corn oil
3/4 c. Water
1/2 c. Potatoes, cooked
1/4 c. Carrots, cooked
3 T. Nutritional Yeast
1/2 tsp. Sea salt
1 T. Lemon juice

Sauté the onion and garlic in the oil. Liquefy all the ingredients together in a blender until smooth. Heat to serving temperature.

HAM GRAVY

1 1/3 c. Gluten Ham or Gluten Bacon, ground
1 1/3 c. Onions, chopped
3 T. Corn oil

1/3 c. Unbleached white flour
1 qt. Cashew milk
1/4 tsp. Black pepper

Sauté the onions and "ham" in the oil. Add the flour and blend well. Gradually add the cashew milk, and then the rest of the ingredients. Cook for 10 minutes.

HAM-LIKE GRAVY

2 T. Corn oil
1/4 c. Unbleached white flour
2 c. Ham-like Broth

In a skillet blend the flour in the heated oil. Slowly add the broth. Cook for 10 minutes.
NOTE: If potatoes have been boiled, use the potato water in making the broth.

HAMBURGER GRAVY

We like this on mashed potatoes, though it goes just as well on bread and biscuits–even rice!

2 c. Beef gluten, ground or chopped small, or soy grits soaked in Beef-like Broth
1/4 c. Onions, chopped
1/2 tsp. Garlic, minced
2 T. Corn oil
6 T. Unbleached white flour
4 c. Cashew milk made with Beef-like Broth

Sauté the gluten (or grits), onions, and garlic in the oil until it is lightly browned. Add the flour and mix well. Gradually add the "milk," stirring constantly. Cook and stir over medium heat until thickened.

ITALIAN PASTA SAUCE

1 c. Bell peppers, chopped
1 1/2 c. Onions, chopped
3 T. Corn oil
6 c. Tomatoes, chopped
1/2 tsp. Sea salt
3 c. Squash, chopped
1/2 tsp. Basil
1/2 tsp. Oregano
1/2 tsp. Cayenne pepper
2 tsp. Garlic, minced
3 c. Beef-like Broth

Sauté the bell peppers and onions in the oil. Combine all ingredients and cook.

MAITRE D'HOTEL BUTTER SAUCE

1/4 c. Non-dairy margarine
1/2 tsp. Sea salt
1/8 tsp. Paprika
1/2 T. Parsley, chopped
1 1/2 tsp. Lemon juice

Cream the margarine until it is very soft. Add the salt, paprika, and parsley. Very slowly add the lemon juice, stirring the sauce constantly.

MUSHROOM GRAVY

Don't pass this by!

2 c.	Mushrooms, sliced
1 tsp.	Garlic, crushed
2 T.	Corn oil
1/4 c.	Unbleached white flour
4 c.	Beef-like or Chicken-like Broth

Sauté the mushrooms and garlic in the oil. Blend in the flour. Slowly add the broth. Cook for 15 minutes.

OLIVE SAUCE–1

2 T.	Non-dairy margarine
3 T.	Onions, sliced
1/2 tsp.	Garlic, minced
2 T.	Unbleached white flour
1 c.	Tomato, pureed
12	Black olives, sliced
3/4 c.	Beef-like Broth
1/4 tsp.	Sea salt
1/4 tsp.	Paprika

Melt the margarine and sauté the onions and garlic until the onions are light brown. Remove the onions and stir in the flour and cook until it turns brown, as well. Slowly stir in the puréed tomatoes. Add the onions, olives, broth, salt and paprika. Stir and cook until the sauce is smooth and boiling.

OLIVE SAUCE–2

1/4 c.	Green onions, sliced
1/4 c.	Mushrooms, sliced
1 T.	Non-dairy margarine
1 c.	Black olives, sliced
2 T.	Liquid from the olives
1 c.	"Sour cream"
1/2 tsp.	Garlic powder
1/2 tsp.	Low sodium soy sauce

Sauté the onions and mushrooms in the margarine for 1 minute. Stir in the rest of the ingredients and heat just until hot–but not boiling.

ONION SAUCE–1

3/4 c.	Onions, chopped
2 T.	Non-dairy margarine
1 tsp.	Low sodium soy sauce
1/2 tsp.	Sea salt
1/2 tsp.	Paprika

Sauté onions for 5 minutes in margarine. Add rest of ingredients.
VARIATION: Use chives instead of onions.

ONION SAUCE–2

3 c. Onions, chopped
Boiling water
2 c. Boiling water
Beef-like Broth
2 T. Non-dairy margarine
3 T. Unbleached white flour

Cover the onions with boiling water and cook for 5 minutes. Drain and cover with 2 more cups of boiling water. Boil them until they are soft. Rub through a sieve. Add enough broth to make 2 1/2 cupfuls. Melt the margarine and stir in the flour until blended. Stir in the onion purée.

PIQUANTE SAUCE

2 T. Non-dairy margarine
5 T. Onions, sliced
1/2 tsp. Garlic, minced
2 T. Unbleached white flour
1 c. Tomato, pureed
1 T. Lemon juice
1 T. Bell pepper, minced
1/8 tsp. Cayenne pepper
1/4 tsp. Sea salt
1/4 tsp. Paprika
3/4 c. Beef-like Broth

Melt the margarine and sauté the onions and garlic until the onions are light brown. Remove the onions and stir in the flour and cook until it turns brown, as well. Slowly stir in the puréed tomatoes. Add the onions, lemon juice, bell pepper, cayenne, salt, paprika, and broth. Stir and cook until the sauce is smooth and boiling.

PIZZA SAUCE–1

1 c. Onions, chopped
1 T. Garlic, minced
3 T. Olive oil
6 c. Tomatoes, chopped
1 tsp. Sea salt
1/2 tsp. Basil
1/2 tsp. Oregano
1/2 tsp. Red pepper flakes
2 c. Mushrooms, chopped
1 c. Water

Sauté the onions and garlic in the oil. Combine with the rest of the ingredients and cook for 45 minutes, adding more water if it gets too thick.

PIZZA SAUCE-2

1 1/2 c.	Onion, chopped
1 1/2 c.	Mushrooms, thickly sliced
1 1/2 tsp.	Garlic, minced or sliced
1 1/2 tsp.	Jalapeños, minced or sliced
3 T.	Corn oil
4 c.	Canned tomatoes with juice
1/2 tsp.	Sea salt
1/2 tsp.	Basil
1/4 tsp.	Oregano
1/4 tsp.	Fennel seed

Sauté the onion, mushrooms, garlic, and jalapeños in the oil. Combine everything in a pot, bring to a boil, lower the heat, and simmer, uncovered, for 1 hour, adding more tomato juice if it gets too thick. Nutritional yeast may be stirred in at the end for added flavor and nutrition.

BLENDER PIZZA SAUCE

I made this up in a pinch, and it was so good it became a permanent item in our cooking!

7 1/2 c.	Canned tomatoes
1/2 c.	Tomato paste
2 tsp.	Onion powder
1/2 tsp.	Garlic powder
1 tsp.	Oregano
1 tsp.	Sea salt
1/2 tsp.	Cayenne pepper
3 T.	Olive oil

Drain the tomatoes well in a colander, shaking them to drain fully. Put tomatoes into a blender and blend just until they are barely "scrambled." Pour them back into the colander and drain again, shaking to drain fully. Put the drained tomato pulp back into the blender and add the rest of the ingredients. Blend to mix everything well, but make sure the sauce does not become too liquid but remains thick and substantial.

SOUR CREAM AND CHIVE SAUCE

1 c.	Tofu Sour Cream or Cashew Sour Cream
4 tsp.	Chives
1/4 tsp.	Louisiana Hot Sauce

Combine well.

SPAGHETTI SAUCE

This never fails to please!

1 c.	Onions, coarsely chopped
3/4 c.	Celery, chopped
3/4 tsp.	Garlic, minced
2 T.	Olive oil
6 c.	Tomatoes, chopped
1 1/2 c.	Beef-flavored gluten or Soy Grits Beef

1/2 tsp. Red pepper flakes
1 1/2 tsp. Sea salt
1 1/2 tsp. Italian seasoning
1/4 c. Beef-like Broth
1/2 c. Tomato paste

Sauté the onion, celery, and garlic in the olive oil. Combine everything and cook for 1 hour or more.

"CREAM CHEESE" SPAGHETTI SAUCE

Forget modesty–this is another wonderful "invention" of mine!

4 c. Tofu Cottage Cheese blended smooth
4 c. Cashew Milk made with Chicken-like Broth
2 T. Non-dairy margarine
1/4 tsp. Garlic powder
1/4 tsp. Black pepper
1/4 c. "Parmesan cheese"

Combine the "cottage cheese" and "milk" and heat in a double boiler. Combine the other ingredients and stir into the "milk" mixture. Cook for 30 minutes.

MARY KRIEGER'S SURE-TO-PLEASE SPAGHETTI SAUCE

This is heavenly simple and simply heavenly. It never fails.
Thanks, Mary!

2 qts. Canned tomato Sauce
1 T. Dried minced onion
1/2 tsp. Dried minced garlic
1 1/2 tsp. Italian Seasoning
1 c. Mushrooms, sliced or chopped

Combine everything. Bring to a low boil, reduce the heat, and simmer 1 to 1 1/2 hours, cooking until thickened, stirring occasionally.

ONION SAUCE FOR SPAGHETTI

Reliable!

2 c. Onions, chopped
1 tsp. Garlic, minced
1 T. Non-dairy margarine
1 T. Olive oil
1/2 tsp. Sea salt
1/2 tsp. Black or cayenne pepper
1 tsp. Sucanat
2 c. Tomato sauce
1 c. Beef-like Broth

Sauté the onions and garlic in the margarine and oil until soft. Mix and simmer all ingredients for 30 minutes.

ZUCCHINI SPAGHETTI SAUCE

3/4 c.	Onions, chopped
1 tsp.	Garlic, minced
2 c.	Zucchini, thinly sliced
1 1/2 c.	Bell peppers, cut in julienne strips
2 T.	Corn oil
3 c.	Tomatoes, chopped
1/3 c.	Chicken-like Broth
2 tsp.	Sea salt
1/8 tsp.	Paprika

Sauté the onions, garlic, squash, and bell pepper in the corn oil. Add rest of ingredients and cook for 15 minutes.

VARIATION: Use another type of squash–or even another type of vegetable.

TACO SAUCE

5 c.	Tomatoes, chopped
2 1/2 tsp.	Garlic, minced
1 tsp.	Crushed red pepper flakes
2 tsp.	Sea salt
1 T.	Bell pepper, minced
1 1/2 c.	Onion, chopped fine
1 tsp.	Chili powder
1 tsp.	Oregano
1 tsp.	Thyme
1 T.	Sucanat
1 T.	Unbleached white flour
2 T.	Corn oil
1 T.	Wine vinegar

Blend in blender or food processor and cook for 1 hour.

TARTAR SAUCE

Never make "fish" without making some of this, too!

1 c.	Tofu Mayonnaise, Cashew Mayonnaise, or Miraculous Whip
1 T.	Onions, minced
1 1/2 tsp.	Prepared mustard
1 T.	Horseradish
1/4 c.	Dill pickles (or sweet pickles, if you prefer)

Combine well and refrigerate for a while to let the flavor develop.

TOMATO SAUCE–1

1/3 c.	Onions, chopped
1 tsp.	Garlic, minced
2 T.	Corn oil
6 c.	Tomatoes, coarsely chopped
1/2 c. & 1 T.	Tomato paste

1 T.	Dried Basil
1 1/4 tsp.	Sea salt
1/8tsp.	Cayenne pepper
1 T.	Barbados molasses

Sauté the onions and garlic in the oil. Combine with rest of ingredients and cook.

TOMATO SAUCE–2

1/3 c.	Onions, chopped
1 tsp.	Garlic, minced
2 T.	Corn oil
6 c.	Tomatoes, coarsely chopped
1/2 c. & 1 T.	Tomato paste
1 1/2 tsp.	Italian seasoning
1 1/2 tsp.	Fennel seed
1 1/4 tsp.	Sea salt
1/8 tsp.	Cayenne pepper
1 T.	Barbados molasses

Sauté the onions and garlic in the oil. Combine with rest of ingredients and cook.

TOMATO SAUCE–3

1/2 tsp.	Garlic, minced
2 T.	Olive oil
1 qt.	Tomatoes, chopped
3/4 c.	Tomato paste
1	Bay leaf
2 tsp.	Sea salt
1/2 tsp.	Oregano
1/2 tsp.	Basil
1 tsp.	Sucanat (optional)

Sauté the garlic in the olive oil. Purée the tomatoes in a blender and add to the oil. Put all together, adding water if needed, and simmer until thick.

TOMATO AND "CHEESE" SAUCE

2 T.	Non-dairy margarine
3/4 c.	Onions, chopped
3 c.	Tomatoes, chopped
1/2 c.	Cashew milk
1/4 tsp.	Basil (or 1 tsp. fresh Basil, finely chopped)
1/4 tsp.	Oregano
Pinch	Cumin, ground
1/2 tsp.	Sea salt
1/4 tsp.	Paprika
1 c.	Yeast, Pimento, or Mozzarella "Cheese"

In a skillet heat the margarine over moderate heat. Sauté the onions until transparent, but not brown. Add everything else but the "cheese" and cook, stirring, for 5 minutes. Then, stirring constantly, add the "cheese."

TOMATO AND ONION SAUCE

Once when there was a tremendous thunderstorm punctuated with hurricane-strength winds which kept me from going out to get anything to cook for several guests, I had to use what was at hand. That turned out to be tomatoes, onions, and rice. So this dish was born–to stay. This is excellent over rice or pasta.

4 c.	Onions, chopped
1 T.	Garlic, minced
1 c.	Bell pepper, chopped
1 c.	Celery, chopped
1 T.	Jalapeño pepper, minced
1/4 c.	Corn oil
4 c.	Tomatoes, chopped
1 tsp.	Sea salt
1/2 tsp.	Cayenne pepper
3 T.	Low sodium soy sauce
1 c.	Water

Sauté the onions, garlic, bell pepper, celery, and jalapeños in the oil until the onions are soft and transparent, but not brown. Add the rest of the ingredients and cook with the onions thoroughly until the consistency is thick, but not dry.

VARIATION: Sauté 2 tablespoons of curry powder along with the onions, etc.

SPANISH TOMATO SAUCE

Truly special!

1/2 tsp.	Garlic, minced
2 T.	Olive oil
1 qt.	Tomatoes, chopped
3/4 c.	Tomato paste
1	Bay leaf
2 tsp.	Sea salt
1/2 tsp.	Oregano
1/2 tsp.	Basil
1 c.	Onions, chopped
1/2 c.	Bell pepper, chopped
1/2 tsp.	Cumin, ground

Sauté the garlic in the oil. Purée the tomatoes in a blender and add to the oil. Put all together, adding water if needed, and simmer until thick.

YEAST GRAVY

1/3 c.	Unbleached white flour
1/3 c.	Nutritional Yeast
2 T.	Non-dairy margarine or corn oil
2 c.	Water
1 T.	Low sodium soy sauce
1/4 tsp.	Sea salt
1/8 tsp.	Black or cayenne pepper

Toast the flour over medium low heat until it starts to smell "toasty." Stir in the yeast. Add the margarine or oil and cook for a few minutes until it is bubbly. Add the water and cook, whisking until it thickens and bubbles. Add the soy sauce, salt, and pepper.

WHITE SAUCE

THIN:

1 T.	Non-dairy margarine
2 tsp.	Unbleached white flour
1/4 tsp.	Sea salt
1 1/2 c.	Cashew Milk

MEDIUM:

2 T.	Non-dairy margarine
1 T.	Unbleached white flour
1/4 tsp.	Sea salt
1 c.	Cashew Milk

THICK:

3 T.	Non-dairy margarine
2 T.	Unbleached white flour
1/4 tsp.	Sea salt
1 c.	Cashew Milk

Melt the margarine in a saucepan over low heat. Blend in the flour and salt. Add the "milk" all at once. Cook quickly, stirring constantly, till the mixture thickens and bubbles. Remove the sauce from the heat when it bubbles. Add other flavorings–if any–at this point, stirring until smooth.

IF SAUCE COOKS TOO LONG, it becomes too thick and the margarine separates out. To correct this, stir in a little more "milk" and cook quickly, stirring constantly, until the sauce bubbles again.

PASTA

A NOTE ON MAKING AND COOKING PASTA

Although pasta can be made by simply mixing and rolling it out, a pasta machine is invaluable. If you have a hand operated machine, when ready for the "rolling out" step put the dough through the machine at the thickest setting. Then narrow it down one point and run the dough through again. Keep repeating this until you run it through at the desired thickness (thinness, actually).

Whether you have a hand operated or electric pasta maker, it will help keep your noodles from falling apart if you position an electric fan so it will blow on the noodles as they emerge from the machine.

If you will not be using the pasta completely, dry it out in a 200° oven. Then you can store it indefinitely in a sealed bag that is free from moisture.

Do not put oil in the water in which you cook pasta. It will make the pasta more likely to stick together and it will coat the pasta so seasonings and sauces will not adhere to it as they should.

BASIC PASTA

2 c.	Unbleached white flour
1/4 c.	Gluten flour
1/2 tsp.	Sea salt
2 T.	Corn oil
1/2 c.	Water
1/2 c.	Nutritional yeast

Mix all ingredients into a stiff dough, adding more water as needed. Knead briefly. Roll dough as thin as possible. Cut into size and shapes desired. Dry in the air overnight or in a 200° oven on cookie sheets until all moisture is gone.

BASIC N'EGG PASTA

Make the Simple Pasta recipe, but add 3 n'eggs to the ingredients if you find that the Simple Pasta tends to fall apart.

BASIC SEMOLINA PASTA

Make the Simple Pasta recipe, but in place of the 2 cups of unbleached white flour use 1 cup of flour and 1 cup of *white* semolina. And for any additional "flouring" use semolina instead of regular flour.

SIMPLE PASTA

1/2 c.	Onions, chopped
1 tsp.	Garlic, minced or sliced
1/4 c.	Olive oil
6 c.	Pasta, cooked
1 tsp.	Total of herbs of choice, such as basil, oregano, rosemary, thyme, savory, bay leaf, dill weed, or Italian Seasoning
1/4 tsp.	Cayenne pepper
1/2 tsp.	Paprika

Sauté the onion and garlic in the oil for 5 minutes. Combine all and heat through for 5 minutes, stirring occasionally. Nutritional yeast may be stirred in at the end for added flavor and nutrition.

BAKED MACARONI WITH TOMATOES

4 c.	Macaroni, cooked
3 c.	Yeast or Pimento "Cheese"
3 c.	Tomato juice
1 tsp.	Sea salt
1/4 c.	Parsley, chopped
2 tsp.	Basil or thyme
1/2 c.	Yeast or Pimento "Cheese"
1/2 tsp.	Paprika
1/4 tsp.	Onion powder
1/4 tsp.	Garlic powder
1 c.	Bread crumbs

Mix the macaroni, "cheese," tomato juice, salt, parsley, and basil in a casserole dish. Combine the 1/2 cup of cheese, paprika, onion powder, garlic powder, and bread crumbs. Spread this over all and bake at 350° for 30 minutes.

CALZONE

1 T.	Sucanat
1 c.	Water (lukewarm)
1 T.	Yeast (dry)
2 c.	Unbleached white flour
1 T.	Oil
1/2 tsp.	Sea salt
	Apple juice

Place the Sucanat, water, and yeast in a large bowl and stir until the yeast and Sucanat is dissolved. Let sit for 8 to 10 minutes or until it is foamy. Stir in 1 cup of flour and mix well. Let rise 20 minutes. Stir down and add remaining flour, oil and salt. Knead 5 to 10 minutes or until pliable and not sticky, adding more flour as needed. Place dough on a floured board, cover with a towel and let it rise for 1 1/2 hours. Divide the dough into 8 balls and roll each into an even circle. Place a filling–such as from the recipes found in the Casseroles, Dried Beans, Gravies and Sauces, Meat Substitutes, Pies, Square Meals, or Vegetables sections–in the center of each circle (if you like, include tomato sauce), spreading it to within 1 inch from the edge. Fold the circles into half-moon shapes and pinch the edges tightly closed. Pierce the tops three or four times with a fork to let out the steam. Brush the tops with apple juice. Place on an oiled baking sheet and bake at 400° for 25 minutes.

PIROSHKIS

Follow the above recipe for calzone, but roll out the entire dough as you would for a pie crust and then cut in rounds of the size you prefer. Bake at 400° until they start to brown.

VARIATION: Use pie crust dough instead of calzone dough.

CHILI-MAC

This is great "kid food"–and am I ever a kid!

1 c.	Onions, chopped
1 tsp.	Garlic, minced
1 tsp.	Jalapeños, minced
2 T.	Corn oil
1 lb.	Macaroni, cooked in salted water and drained
1/4 tsp.	Sea salt
6 c.	Chili (see Soups section)

Sauté the onions, garlic, and jalapeños in the oil. Toss the macaroni with this along with the salt. Put the macaroni in a casserole, top with the chili, and bake at 350° for 30 minutes. (If you are using leftover chili that has gotten thick overnight, dilute it with 1 cup of tomato juice and heat.)

VARIATION: Top with Yeast or Pimento "Cheese" before baking.

FETTUCINI WITH SPINACH PESTO

12 oz.	Fettucini, uncooked
3 T.	Corn oil
3/4 tsp.	Basil leaves
1/8 tsp.	Cayenne pepper
3 T.	Onions, chopped
1 tsp.	Garlic, minced
3 T.	Corn oil
2 c.	Fresh spinach
2/3 c.	Yeast , Pimento, or Mozzarella "Cheese"
1 c.	Tofu Sour Cream or Cashew Sour Cream

Cook the fettucini. Put the first 3 tablespoons of corn oil, basil, cayenne, onions, and garlic in a blender and blend until smooth. Add the additional 3 tablespoons of oil, then the spinach, "cheese," and "sour cream," blending well and scraping down the sides of the blender when needed. Let sit a few minutes for the flavors to blend. Toss with the drained fettucini.

FRIED NOODLES

Make the Simple Pasta recipe, and cut into 1x3/4-inch strips and deep fry. These can be used in various recipes, including Chinese dishes, and can also be a snack for hungry children. These may be lightly salted or sprinkled with garlic salt, onion salt, or low sodium soy sauce for more flavor.

GNOCCHI

	Beef-like Broth
2 c.	Unbleached white flour
1/4 tsp.	Sea salt

1 T.	Corn oil
4 c.	Potatoes, mashed with Chicken-like or Beef-like Broth
	Spaghetti sauce

Heat a large pot of Beef-like Broth. Meanwhile mix the flour and salt and shape into a mound in the center of a breadboard. Make a well in the center and pour in the oil and add the mashed potatoes. Knead the mixture with your hands (use extra flour if it gets sticky). Divide the dough into 4 balls and roll into long cylinders no more than an inch thick. Cut into 1-inch pieces. Rub fork tines over each piece of dough to make an impression. Drop the gnocchi into boiling broth. They will sink, then rise to the surface as they cook. Remove with a slotted spoon as soon as they rise. Toss with spaghetti sauce.

HERBED NOODLES

When you are in a hurry for something good–this is it!

12 oz.	Noodles of any type, cooked and tossed in 1/4 cup of melted corn oil margarine
2 c.	Tofu Cottage cheese
1 c.	Tofu Sour cream or Cashew Sour Cream
1/3 c.	Onions, finely chopped
1/4 tsp.	Garlic powder
1/4 c.	Chopped parsley
1/2 tsp.	Italian Herb Seasoning
1 T.	Lemon juice
1 tsp.	Sea salt
1/8 tsp.	Cayenne pepper

Combine and let sit for a while to exchange flavors.

HERBED NOODLES WITH CHEESE, LEMON, AND GREEN ONIONS

1/4 c.	Non-dairy margarine, melted
12 oz.	Noodles of any type, cooked
2 c.	Tofu, crumbled
3/4 c.	Yeast, Pimento, or Mozzarella "Cheese"
1 c.	"Parmesan Cheese"
1/2 c.	Green onion, finely chopped
1/4 c.	Chopped parsley
1 1/2 tsp.	Garlic, minced
1/2 tsp.	Italian Herb Seasoning
3 T.	Lemon juice
1/2 tsp.	Sea salt
1/8 tsp.	Cayenne pepper

In a 9x13-inch pan, toss the melted margarine with the cooked noodles. Beat together the remaining ingredients until thoroughly blended. Pour the mixture on the noodles and toss and turn until all is blended. Bake at 350° for about 20 minutes or until the top begins to brown.

VARIATION: Add 10 oz. of chopped frozen spinach to the cheese mixture.

HUNGARIAN NOODLE BAKE

1/4 lb.	Spaghetti, uncooked
1/4 c.	Onions, finely chopped
1/2 tsp.	Garlic, minced

1 T.	Non-dairy margarine
1 1/2 c.	Tofu Cottage cheese
1 c.	Tofu Sour cream or Cashew Sour Cream
Dash	Louisiana Hot Sauce
2 tsp.	Poppy seeds
1/2 tsp.	Sea salt
Dash	Paprika or cayenne pepper

Cook the spaghetti in boiling salted water till tender. Drain. Sauté onion and garlic in margarine till soft. Combine all together and put in an oiled baking dish. Bake at 350° for 25 minutes or until hot. Sprinkle with paprika. Serve with "Parmesan 'Cheese.'"

LASAGNA

A leading favorite!

1/2 lb.	Lasagne noodles, uncooked
3 c.	Beef gluten, ground
1/4 c.	Olive oil
1 1/2 c.	Mushrooms, sliced
1 1/2 c.	Onions, chopped
2 tsp.	Garlic, minced
4 tsp.	"Parmesan 'Cheese'"
1/8 tsp.	Cayenne pepper
9 c.	Tomato Sauce–1
2 c.	Tofu Cottage cheese
2-3 c.	Yeast, Pimento, or Mozzarella "Cheese"

Cook the noodles, drain, and set aside. Sauté the gluten in half the oil and set aside. Sauté the mushrooms, onions, and garlic in the rest of the oil until the onions are soft. Then add to the gluten along with the "parmesan," cayenne, and 2 cups of the tomato sauce and cook for 5 more minutes. Layer a casserole dish or pan as follows:

tomato sauce
noodles
"cottage cheese"
gluten mixture
a thin layer of the "cheese"
tomato sauce
noodles
"cottage cheese"
gluten mixture
a thin layer of the "cheese"
tomato sauce
noodles
"cottage cheese"
tomato sauce

Bake at 375° 30-40 minutes.

LASAGNA NOODLES

Use Basic Pasta recipe. Roll out to 1/8-inch thickness. Cut into 1 1/2-inch strips. Dry in the air overnight or in a 200° oven on cookie sheets until all moisture is gone.

MACARONI AND "CHEESE"

3 c.	Elbow macaroni, uncooked
1/4 c.	Non-dairy margarine
1/3 c.	Onions, chopped
1/3 c.	Unbleached white flour
3 c.	Cashew Milk
3/4 tsp.	Sea salt
1/4 tsp.	Cayenne pepper
3 c.	Pimento Cheese
	Sliced tomatoes

Cook the macaroni in boiling salted water as per package instructions. Drain and blanch. Set aside. In a saucepan melt the margarine and sauté the onions. Blend in the flour. While stirring, slowly add the "milk," salt, and pepper. Cook until thick and bubbly. Add the "cheese" and stir in well, being careful it does not burn. Pour this sauce into the macaroni and stir until all is well mixed. Put in a casserole and top with the tomatoes. Bake at 350° for about 30 minutes, until the top is slightly browned.

VARIATIONS: Use fettucini noodles instead of macaroni. Add 4 cups of a cooked vegetable, cut in small pieces, and 1 teaspoon of Basil to the sauce while it is cooking.

MACARONI AND YEAST "CHEESE" CASSEROLE

This is simple, but so flavorful that I could eat it just about every day.

1/4 c.	Onions, chopped
1/3 c.	Non-dairy margarine
1/2 c.	Unbleached white flour
5 1/4 c.	Water
3 T.	Low sodium soy sauce
2 1/4 tsp.	Garlic powder
1/4 tsp.	Tumeric
1 1/2 tsp.	Sea salt
1/3 c.	Corn oil
1 1/2 c.	Nutritional yeast flakes
8 1/2 c.	Cooked macaroni

Sauté the onions in the margarine. Beat in the flour with a whisk, and continue to beat until the mixture is smooth and bubbly. Then whip in the water, soy sauce, garlic powder, tumeric, and salt, beating well until all is well mixed and smooth. Cook this until it thickens and bubbles. Finally whip in the corn oil and yeast flakes. Mix 3/4 of the sauce with the macaroni and put in a casserole dish. Pour the rest of the sauce on top and sprinkle paprika over that. Bake at 350° for 15 minutes. Put under the broiler for a few minutes until the "cheese" is spotted brown.

VARIATIONS: Use fettucini noodles instead of macaroni. Add 4 cups of a cooked vegetable, cut in small pieces, and 1 teaspoon of Basil to the sauce while it is cooking.

MEXICAN BEAN AND PASTA DISH

1/3 c.	Bell pepper, chopped fine
1/3 c.	Onions, chopped
2 T.	Corn oil
6 c.	Tomatoes
1/2 tsp.	Cayenne pepper

1/2 tsp.	Oregano
1 tsp.	Sea salt
3 c.	Beef-like Broth
2 1/2 c.	Pasta broken in small pieces and cooked
1 1/2 c.	Corn
3 c.	Pinto or kidney beans–cooked

Sauté the bell pepper and onion in the corn oil. Add to the tomatoes, cayenne, oregano, salt, and broth in a pot and bring to a boil. Simmer for 15 minutes. Add the pasta, corn, and beans and simmer, uncovered, for 10 more minutes.

NOODLE BAKE

1/4 lb.	Spaghetti, uncooked
3/4 c.	Onions, chopped
1/2 tsp.	Garlic, minced
1 T.	Non-dairy margarine
2 c.	Yeast or Pimento Cheese
1/4 tsp.	Sea salt
1/2 tsp.	Paprika

Cook and drain the spaghetti. Sauté the onions and garlic in the margarine. Combine everything. Put into a greased baking dish. Bake at 350° for 25 minutes. Sprinkle with paprika.

NOODLES ROMANO

2 T.	Non-dairy margarine
2 T.	Dried parsley flakes
1 tsp.	Basil, dried
1 c.	Tofu Cottage Cheese, blended smooth
1/8 tsp.	Paprika
2/3 c.	Boiling water
8 oz.	Spaghetti, uncooked
1 tsp.	Garlic, minced
2 T.	Non-dairy margarine
1/2 c.	"Parmesan 'Cheese'" or Pimento, Mozzarella, or Yeast "Cheese"

Combine the first 2 tablespoons of margarine, parsley flakes, and basil. Blend in the "cottage cheese" and paprika. Stir in the boiling water. Blend the mixture well and keep warm over a pan of hot water or in a double boiler. Cook the spaghetti in salted water until just tender and drain. Sauté the garlic in the second 2 tablespoons of margarine for 1 to 2 minutes, then pour over the spaghetti and toss lightly and quickly to coat well. Sprinkle (or spread) the "cheese" over the spaghetti. Add the "cottage cheese" sauce and mix well.

PASTA SHELLS WITH BROCCOLI

3 T.	Onions
1 tsp.	Garlic, minced
2 T.	Olive oil
1 lb.	Small pasta shells, cooked and drained
1 head	Broccoli
1 c.	Tofu Cottage Cheese
1/8 tsp.	Cayenne pepper

1/2 tsp. Basil
1/2 tsp. Oregano
1/2 tsp. Sea salt

Sauté the onions and garlic in the oil. Add the shells and set aside and keep warm. Cut the stems off the broccoli head and set aside. Cut the head into tiny flowerets and steam until just tender. Keep warm. Chop the broccoli stems into tiny pieces and cook until very tender. Cool and blend in a food processor or blender until smooth. Add the "cottage cheese," cayenne, basil, oregano, onions, garlic, and salt. Combine well. Heat the cottage cheese mixture BUT DO NOT COOK OR BOIL. Pour over the warm pasta and toss till all is coated. Add the broccoli flowerets and toss lightly. Serve with "sour cream" on the side.

PASTA SNACKS

These can be made from leftover pasta, too.

After cooking the pasta, drain well, cool under cold running water, and pat dry. When pasta is dry, coat lightly with corn oil–1 tablespoon per 2 cups of pasta. Place on broiler trays and brown, turning a few times. These may be lightly salted or sprinkled with garlic salt, onion salt, or low sodium soy sauce for more flavor.

QUICK "CHEESE" DUMPLINGS IN TOMATO SAUCE

2 c. Biscuit Mix
2/3 c. Yeast or Pimento Cheese

Make biscuits with the mix, adding 2 tablespoons of the "cheese" to the biscuit dough. Pat or roll out the dough 1/8-inch thick. Cut into 3-inch rounds. Place 1 teaspoon of "cheese" in the center of each round. Wet the edges of the rounds with cold water. Gather up the edges to form a ball. Pinch them well. Drop the dumplings into thin tomato sauce, soup, or juice. Cover tightly and cook for 15 minutes. DO NOT LIFT THE LID UNTIL THE TIME IS UP!

SPAGHETTI BOLOGNESE

Top of the line!

2 1/2 c. Onions, chopped
2 1/2 c. Mushrooms, chopped
1/4 c. Olive oil
1 1/2 tsp. Low sodium soy sauce
1 1/2 tsp. Sucanat
1 T. Garlic, minced
1 1/2 c. Tomato paste
3 c. Water
1 1/2 tsp. Basil
1/4 tsp. Fennel seed
1/4 tsp. Oregano
1 1/2 tsp. Sea salt
3/4 tsp. Black or cayenne pepper
1/2 lb. Spaghetti, uncooked

Sauté the onions and mushrooms in the oil. Add the remaining ingredients–except the spaghetti–and cook for 30 minutes. Cook and drain the spaghetti. Combine with the sauce.

SPECIAL SPAGHETTI

6 oz.	Spaghetti, uncooked
1/2 c.	Yeast or Pimento Cheese
1/4 c.	Onions, chopped
1/2 tsp.	Garlic, minced
2 T.	Mushrooms or black olives, chopped
1 T.	Corn oil
1 c.	Tomatoes, chopped
1 T.	Non-dairy margarine
1/2 tsp.	Sea salt
1/4 tsp.	Paprika

Cook the spaghetti in salted water. Drain, blanch, then rinse with hot water. Add the "cheese" and mix. Sauté the onions, garlic, and mushrooms (or olives) in the oil. Add the tomatoes, margarine, salt, and paprika, and cook for 10 minutes. Add the sauce to the spaghetti.

THAI-STYLE PASTA

Sesame oil can be used in this instead of corn oil, if you like.

1 c.	Onions, chopped
2 T.	Corn oil
1 lb.	Pasta, cooked and drained
1 tsp.	Sucanat
1/4 c.	Low sodium soy sauce
3 T.	Fresh lemon juice
1/4 tsp.	Crushed red pepper
2/3 c.	Unsalted roasted peanuts, chopped
1/2 c.	Water

Sauté the onions in the oil until transparent. Add rest of ingredients and sauté for 5 more minutes.

WHITE LASAGNA

This is really special–I know you will agree!
It is also a gourmet's way to use up leftovers.

1/2 lb.	Lasagne noodles, uncooked
2 c.	Onions, chopped
2 c.	Mushrooms, sliced thick
1 T.	Garlic, minced
1 1/2 c.	Chicken Gluten, ground
2 c.	Broccoli, chopped fine, boiled, and drained
3 T.	Olive oil
2 c.	Chicken-like Broth made with Cashew Milk
2 c.	"Mozzarella 'Cheese'"
1/8 tsp.	Cayenne pepper
1/8 tsp.	Black pepper
	"Parmesan Cheese"

Cook the noodles in salted water and set aside. Sauté the onions, mushrooms, garlic, gluten, and broccoli in the oil until the onions are soft. Combine the broth, "cheese," and peppers, and heat until it becomes like a thick batter. In an oiled casserole put a layer of noodles. Spread half of the vegetable mixture over the noodles. Spread one third of the "cheese" sauce over the vegetables. Repeat these three layers. Make another layer of noodles. Spread the remaining third of the "cheese" sauce over the noodles. Sprinkle the "parmesan" over the sauce. Bake at 375° for 30 minutes or until light brown on top.

VARIATION: Instead of broccoli in the filling, use spinach or some other vegetables or beans (green or dried).

Father Philaret pours homemade pasta into the pot. Yum!

Pizza

QUICK PIZZA

(Makes two 14-inch pizzas)

Make three cups of Yeast, Pimento, or Mozzarella "Cheese." Make one time the Cracker recipe. Make one time the Blender Pizza Sauce recipe. Sprinkle 1 tablespoon of corn meal onto each pizza pan. Divide the dough into two equal parts. Roll out the dough and put it into the pizza pans, trimming off any excess. Bake at 550° for about 5 minutes. Spread the sauce on the crusts. Spread on the cheese. Sauté any topping such as ground gluten, onions, bell peppers, mushrooms, green olives, black olives, etc., in the smallest amount of oil and sprinkle over the pizzas. Bake until the crust lightly browns on the bottom–about 10 to 15 minutes.

"CHEESE"-ONLY PIZZA

Make Quick Pizza, but omit the tomato sauce. Omit the toppings, too, if you like.

EASY PIZZA CRUST

Make up the dough for the White Bread recipe, roll out, and use as crust for 2 pizzas.

"MEATZA" PIE

This is an adapted version of a Middle Eastern dish which does not have cheese–though it is good with cheese.

4 c.	Unbleached white flour
1 1/2 c.	Warm water
2 tsp.	Yeast
1 T.	Olive oil
1 tsp.	Sea salt
2 c.	Onions, chopped
1/2 c.	Bell pepper, chopped
1/4 c.	Olive oil
2 c.	Italian Sausage, ground with 2 1/2 tsp. of minced garlic
1 c.	Tomatoes, chopped
1/4 c.	Tomato paste
1/4 c.	Parsley, chopped
1 tsp.	Fresh mint or 1/4 tsp. of dry mint

	Garlic Oil (see Seasonings section)
1 1/2 c.	"Mozzarella Cheese"
	"Parmesan 'Cheese'"

Put the flour in a bowl and make a "well" in the center. Pour the water in the "well," spinkle the yeast on top of the water and stir it in lightly with your fingers. Let it rest for a few minutes until it becomes bubbly. Add the tablespoon of oil and the salt and mix it all together into a dough with your hands. Knead for a couple of minutes until you have a smooth dough. Let the dough rise for 1 to 1 1/2 hours in a warm place. Sauté the onion and bell pepper in the 1/4 cup of oil. When the onions become transparent, add the gluten and sauté until it starts to brown. Mix in the tomatoes, tomato paste, parsley, and mint and cook for 10 to 15 minutes. Roll out the dough to any shape you desire for the pizza, making sure it is thicker around the edges. Put the dough in a pan that has been dusted with corn meal. Wipe some garlic oil along the outer edges of the dough. Spread the "mozzarella" over the dough. Put on the gluten topping. Sprinkle "parmesan" over the topping. Bake at 450° until the crust begins to brown. Take the pizza from the oven and brush more garlic oil around the edges of the crust. Continue to bake until the dough is golden brown and the bottom is brown (at least in spots) as well.

VARIATIONS: Use other types of sausage gluten. Instead of gluten, use 4 cups of fresh mushrooms, and when sautéeing them, add 1/4 cup of low sodium soy sauce. Leave out the "cheeses."

ONION-GARLIC PIZZA

This is an adaptation of the famous "Great White Pizza" that used to be made at Sadie's Saloon in Lincoln, Nebraska. Makes two 14-inch pizzas.

CRUST:

3 T.	Yeast
1 3/4 c.	Water
1 1/2 tsp.	Sucanat
5 1/4 c.	Unbleached white flour
1 1/2 tsp.	Sea salt
2 T.	Oil

Dissolve yeast in the water with the Sucanat. Allow to froth. Sift the flour into a bowl, add the salt and oil and stir. Add yeast mixture and combine thoroughly. Knead until smooth and elastic. Sprinkle 1 tablespoon of corn meal onto each pizza pan. Divide the dough into two equal parts. Roll out the dough and put it into the pizza pans, trimming off any excess dough.

TOPPING:

6 c.	Onions, sliced by being put through a food processor
2 T.	Garlic, minced
1/4 c.	Non-dairy margarine
1 c.	Parsley, chopped
2 T.	Low sodium soy sauce

Sauté onions and garlic in melted margarine until soft. Add parsley and soy sauce and sauté 1-2 minutes. Spread evenly over two 14-inch pizzas. Bake at 350° for 15 minutes, then take out. Mix together:

2 tsp.	Rosemary, crushed
2 tsp.	Sage, rubbed
2 tsp.	Thyme, crushed

Sprinkle over the partially baked pizzas, along with salt and paprika. Top each pizza with Yeast, Pimento, or Mozzarella "Cheese." Lightly sprinkle some of the herb mixture over the "cheese." Return to the oven and continue to bake at 350° for fifteen minutes more.

PIZZA BREAD

2 1/2 c.	Water
2 T.	Yeast
3 T. & 1 1/2 tsp.	Sucanat
4 c.	Unbleached white flour
3 T.	Oil
1 T.	Sea salt

Make dough from the above ingredients. Spread out in a well-oiled casserole pan. Spread pizza sauce thickly over it. Bake at 500° until the sauce darkens.

TACO PIZZA

This makes 2 pizzas. Yum!
Since there are a lot of onions in the refried beans, none are put on the top, but if you are an onion lover, do so.

1	Times the Meatza Pie dough recipe
6 c.	Refried Beans (our recipe)
4 c.	Pizza "Cheese"
4 c.	Lettuce, finely chopped
8 c.	Tomatoes, finely chopped
	Garlic Oil (see Etc. section)

Divide the dough in half and press it out on 2 sheet pans oiled with garlic oil. Coat the tops of the dough with garlic oil. Spread the refried beans over the dough. Put the pizzas in the oven and bake at 450° until the crust just begins to show color. Remove the pizzas from the oven and spread the "cheese" over the beans. Brush garlic oil around the outer edges of the pizza dough. Return to the oven and bake until the crust is golden brown. Take out of the oven and put the lettuce and tomatoes on top.

VARIATION: Put chopped black olives, pickled green tomatoes, pickled jalapeño slices, or Tomato Salsa on top as well as lettuce and tomatoes.

TOMATO AND CHEESE PIZZA

This is our version of the "Garden Pizza" that used to be available from Sadie's Saloon in Lincoln, Nebraska.

1	White Bread dough recipe
1/4 c.	Mushrooms, chopped or sliced
1/4 c.	Onions, chopped
1 tsp.	Garlic, minced
2 T.	Corn oil
2 c.	Tomatoes, chopped
1/4 c.	Tomato paste
1/2 tsp.	Sage
1/2 tsp.	Basil
1/2 tsp.	Oregano

1/4 tsp.	Sea salt
1/4 tsp.	Paprika
12	Black olives, chopped
2 T.	Bell pepper, chopped
5	Tomatoes, in slices or wedges
2 c.	Yeast or pimento cheese

Knead the dough lightly, then–on a lightly floured surface–roll out to 12 inches in diameter, OR make 4 4-inch rounds. Place dough on an oiled baking sheet, cover with oiled plastic wrap, and leave in a warm place for 30 minutes to rise. Sauté the mushrooms, onions, and garlic in the oil until the onions are transparent. Add the chopped tomatoes, tomato paste, herbs and seasonings. Simmer gently, stirring occasionally, until the mixture is pulpy. Spread the tomato mixture over the dough. Put the olives, bell pepper and tomato slices (or wedges) over the top. Spread on the "cheese." Bake at 425° for about 25 minutes (small pizzas will take about 15).

The Nebraska Vegetarian Society potluck dinner at the Monastery.

Sandwiches and Spreads

BARBECUE BEAN SANDWICH SPREAD

Mix together 1 part of Barbecue Beans and 1 part of "Cheese" Spread.

BEAN SANDWICH SPREAD

4 c.	Dried beans, pressure cooked and mashed
1/2 c.	Bell pepper, chopped fine
2 c.	Tomatoes, chopped
1/2 c.	Onions, minced
2 T.	Lemon juice
2 T.	Corn oil
1 1/2 tsp.	Sea salt

"CHEESE" SPREAD–1

6 c.	Yeast or pimento cheese
1/3 c.	Onions, chopped
1 c.	Black olives, chopped
1 c.	Bell pepper, finely chopped
1 1/2 c.	Tofu Mayonnaise, Cashew Mayonnaise, or Miraculous Whip
1/4 tsp.	Cayenne pepper
1/2 tsp.	Basil
1/8 tsp.	Dill weed
1 1/2 tsp.	Sea salt

VARIATION: If this seems a bit too bland, put in a little wine vinegar or lemon juice.

"CHEESE" SPREAD–2

6 c.	Yeast or pimento cheese
1/2 c.	Onions, chopped
1 c.	Dill pickles or green olives, chopped fine
1/4 c.	Pimento, chopped fine
1 1/2 c.	Tofu Mayonnaise, Cashew Mayonnaise, or Miraculous Whip
1 T.	Prepared mustard
2 tsp.	Louisiana Hot Sauce
1/2 tsp.	Sea salt

"CHEESE" TOAST

Spread slices of bread with non-dairy margarine–better yet, with melted margarine that has been mixed with onion or garlic powder. Bake on high, or broil until toasted. Take from oven. Lightly sprinkle each slice with imitation bacon bits. Cover each slice with yeast or pimento "cheese." Replace in oven and broil or bake until brown spots appear.

"EGG" SALAD

1/2 c.	Onion, chopped fine
1/4 tsp.	Tumeric
1/4 tsp.	Dill weed
1/4 tsp.	Sea salt
1 1/2 tsp.	Olive oil
1 c.	Firm tofu, crushed
1/2 c.	Tofu Mayonnaise, Cashew Mayonnaise, or Miraculous Whip
2 T.	Green onion tops, chopped
1/2 tsp.	Louisiana Hot Sauce
1 tsp.	Nutritional yeast flakes

Sauté the onions, tumeric, dill, and salt in the oil till the onions are soft, and set aside. When cool, combine with the rest of the ingredients.

VARIATIONS: Add 1/4 tsp. garlic powder. Add 1 T. jalapeños, minced. Add sliced lettuce and tomatoes (in making the sandwiches).

EGGPLANT APPETIZER SPREAD

1/4 c.	Corn oil
6 c.	Eggplant, peeled and cut into 1/2-inch cubes
1 tsp.	Cornstarch
2/3 c.	Chicken-like broth
1 tsp.	Garlic, minced
1/2 tsp.	Powdered ginger
3 tsp.	Red chili paste
1 T.	White wine vinegar or rice vinegar
3	Green onions, sliced thin
2 T.	Low sodium soy sauce
2 tsp.	Sucanat
1	Bell pepper (red preferred), minced

In the corn oil sauté the eggplant until it is tender and browned. Transfer with a slotted spoon to paper towels to drain. Dissolve the cornstarch in the broth. In the oil sauté the garlic, ginger, chili paste, and vinegar for 30 seconds. Add the onions and sauté for 30 more seconds. Add the soy sauce, Sucanat, cornstarch mixture, bell pepper, and eggplant, and sauté for 1 minute, or until the eggplant has absorbed most of the liquid.

"GRILLED CHEESE" SANDWICHES

Not really the same, but plenty good!

2 1/2 c.	Tofu, lightly salted and crumbled
3 c.	Yeast or Pimento "Cheese"

Stir the crumbled tofu into the "cheese." Spread between two slices of bread. Put non-dairy margarine on the outsides of the bread and grill. Chopped onions, bell pepper bits, "bacon bits," or slices or pieces of tomato can also be added to the "cheese" before grilling.

FRUIT BUTTER

This makes about 6 cups of "butter"–which will go quickly once you taste it!

1 gal.	Pureed fruit
3 c.	Sucanat (4 cups for peach butter)
1	Orange, peeled and diced with all the juice
1 Pinch	Sea salt

Combine and cook on low heat (simmer) for six hours, or till it turns dark brown and is thick. This keeps very long in the refrigerator.

APPLE BUTTER: Add 2 Tablespoons of lemon or lime juice to the above.

PIMENTO "CHEESE" SPREAD

1/3 c.	Tofu Mayonnaise, Cashew Mayonnaise, or Miraculous Whip
1/4 c.	Pimentos, drained
1 tsp.	Prepared mustard
1 c.	Yeast Cheese or Pimento Cheese
1 tsp.	Low sodium soy sauce

Process in a blender until smooth and creamy. Or: Chop the pimentos and mix with the rest of the ingredients by hand.

REUBEN SANDWICHES

Reliable goodness!

In a wok put 1/2 c. water and bring it to a boil. Add:

4 c.	Cabbage, shredded
3/4 c.	Bell pepper, chopped

Stir well, cover and let steam until tender–about 1 or 2 minutes. Remove the cabbage and peppers from the wok and put in a bowl. Add:

1/2 tsp.	Dill weed
1/2 tsp.	Sea salt
3/4 c.	Tofu Sour Cream

Spread a slice of bread with Italian Dressing. Put 1/2 c. of cabbage mixture on the bread. Put tomato slices on the cabbage. Top with yeast or pimento cheese and broil until spotted brown.

VARIATION: Try Quick Sauerkraut instead of the cabbage-bell pepper mixture.

SATURDAY NIGHT SPECIALS

Special is the word!

2 c.	Pimento, Yeast, or Mozzarella "Cheese"
1/2 c.	Onions, finely chopped

1/4 c.	Bell pepper, finely chopped
1/2 c.	Green or black olives, sliced or chopped
1/8 tsp.	Cayenne pepper
1/8 tsp.	Garlic powder
1/4 c.	Catsup
1 T.	Prepared mustard
3 T.	Imitation bacon bits

Mix all ingredients. Spread 1/4-inch thick over bread. Broil until the "cheese" gets brown spots.

SLOPPY JOES

Not just for kids!

1 c.	Soy grits
2 c.	Beef-like Broth
1 1/2 c.	Onions, chopped
1/2 c.	Bell pepper, chopped fine
1/4 c.	Celery, chopped fine
3 T.	Corn oil
2 c.	Tomato sauce
1/4 tsp.	Cayenne pepper
1 1/2 tsp.	Chili powder
1/4 tsp.	Sea salt

Soak the grits in one cup of the broth. Sauté the onions, bell pepper, and celery in the oil until the onions are transparent. Add the grits and sauté for 10 minutes. Add the rest of the ingredients–including the second cup of broth–and stir around, sautéeing for another 10 minutes, adding more tomato sauce if needed.

VARIATION: Instead of the soy grits, use 2 cups of ground Beef Gluten, leaving out the second cup of the Beef-like Broth.

SUPER "CHEESE" SANDWICHES

Garlic "butter" made with corn oil margarine
"Parmesan Cheese"
"Pimento Cheese"
"Mozzarella Cheese"
Shredded lettuce
Chopped black olives
Sliced onions
Sliced tomatoes
Dill pickles, sliced
Pickled jalapeño slices
Prepared mustard
Hamburger buns (or something like)

Spread halves of the buns with garlic butter and sprinkle with "Parmesan Cheese." Spread 1/2 of the halves with Pimento Cheese. Spread the rest of the halves with Mozzarella. Bake at 550° until the cheese starts to brown in spots. Take out of oven and top with mustard, lettuce, onions, tomatoes, olives, pickles, and pickled jalapeños. Join together and serve.

VARIATION: Use a salad dressing, such as Thousand Island, instead of mustard. Use guacamole instead of mustard.

IT'S NOT OVER YET!

SUBSCRIBE TO THE

Simply Heavenly! Recipe Letter

As we continue to test and develop new recipes in our Monastery kitchen, they are made available to you through our *Simply Heavenly! Recipe Letter*.

Each issue of the newsletter is sent to you as soon as we have enough recipes to fill up a complete newsletter of ten pages.

The subscription fee for four issues is $16.00. Mail your check or money order to:

SAINT GEORGE PRESS
Rt. 1, Box 75 • Geneva, NE 68361

Square Meals

Really a variation on the piroshki (perogi) and calzone, these are marvellous. They are great to take along on trips or to "potluck." When we visit someone and want to bring along the food as well, these are the favorite for both ease and outright good eating.

Use other fillings than those given here, such as are in the Casseroles, Dried Beans, Sauces and Gravies, Meat Substitutes, or Vegetables sections. The possibilities for variety are limited only by your imagination.

Square meals freeze very well for future use.

HOW TO MAKE SQUARE MEALS

2 T.	Yeast
1 c.	Warm water
1 tsp.	Sucanat
3 T.	Corn oil
3 c.	Unbleached white flour
1 1/2 tsp.	Sea salt
1/4 c.	Nutritional Yeast
1/2 tsp.	Onion powder

Mix the yeast, water and Sucanat. Let stand in a warm place for 10-15 minutes until risen and foamy. Whisk in the oil. In another bowl sift together the flour, salt, nutritional yeast, and onion powder, and mix well. Add this, small amounts at a time, with a whisk, to the yeast mixture. Continue to mix it with a spoon till it is smooth. Knead it for a while, just until it is a nice soft ball. Roll it out to 1/8-inch thickness. Cut into 4-inch squares. Moisten all 4 edges with water. Put 1/3 cup of filling (see recipes following) in the center of each square. Bring the corners up over the filling and pinch together. Pinch the four seams closed as well. Put on a lightly oiled cookie sheet, seam side down. Poke holes in the top several times (at least 4) with a fork. Brush the tops with corn oil. Bake in a 400° oven for about 8 to 10 minutes, or until golden brown on top.

VARIATION: Add 1/4 tsp. of garlic powder to the dough.

BARBECUE FILLING–1

2 c.	Beef Gluten or Soy Grits Beef
3 T.	Corn oil
1 1/2 c.	Onions, chopped

2 tsp.	Garlic, minced
1/2 c.	Bell pepper, chopped
1/4 c.	Celery, chopped
2 c.	Tomato sauce
1/2 c.	Tomato paste
1/3 tsp.	Cayenne pepper
2 tsp.	Chili powder
1/2 tsp.	Sea salt

Sauté the gluten (or grits) in half of the oil until it browns and set it aside. Sauté the onions, garlic, bell pepper, and celery in the rest of the oil until soft. Add the tomato sauce, tomato paste, and spices, and cook for 5 minutes. Add the gluten and cook 5 more minutes.

BARBECUE FILLING–2

2 T.	Corn oil
3 c.	Beef Gluten, sliced and chopped
1 c.	Onions, chopped
1 tsp.	Garlic, minced
1/3 c.	Bell pepper
3 T.	Celery, chopped
1/4 tsp.	Hot pepper flakes
1 1/2 c.	Barbecue "Spare Rib" Sauce

In half the oil, sauté the gluten until it browns and set aside. In the rest of the oil, sauté the onion, garlic, bell pepper, celery, and pepper flakes until the bell pepper is soft. Add the gluten and barbecue sauce. Cook for 10 minutes. If it becomes too dry, add more barbecue sauce.

BROCCOLI & "CHEESE" FILLING

2	16 oz. pkgs. frozen cut broccoli
1 c.	Chicken-like Broth made with Cashew Milk
3 c.	Onions, chopped
3 T.	Corn oil
1/3 c.	Unbleached white flour
2 c.	Yeast or Pimento Cheese
1 tsp.	Sea salt
1/4 tsp.	Cayenne

Thaw broccoli. Cook until tender in the broth. Sauté the onions in oil until transparent. Add flour, stirring until blended. Gradually add the broccoli, stirring constantly. Add "cheese," salt, and cayenne and mix well.

HOT DOG AND BARBECUED BEAN FILLING

BARBECUED BEANS:

1/2 c.	Bell peppers, chopped
2 tsp.	Garlic, minced
1/2 c.	Onions, chopped
3 T.	Corn oil
4 c.	Cooked dried beans, drained
1/2 tsp.	Cayenne pepper
3 c.	Tomato Sauce (one of the recipes from Gravies and Sauces)

1/4 c. Barbados Molasses
1/4 c. Wine vinegar
1 T. Sovex or Vegex (dissolve in the vinegar)
1 tsp. Sea salt

Sauté the bell peppers, garlic, and onions in the corn oil. Combine all ingredients. Pour into a large oiled casserole. Add more tomato sauce if it is needed to cover the beans. Bake 40 minutes at 400°. *Refrigerate for one day before using. This is important.*

HOT DOGS:

4 c. Loma Linda "Big Franks," drained and ground

Sauté the Big Franks in a small amount of corn oil.

ASSEMBLY:

Mix the refrigerated beans and franks together.

VARIATION: Use 4 cups of ground Ham Gluten Sausage Gluten instead of Big Franks.

HOT DOG AND SAUERKRAUT FILLING

2 c. Loma Linda "Big Franks," ground
3 T. Corn oil
2 c. Onions, chopped
4 c. Sauerkraut, with juice *sqeezed* out (not just drained)
1/2 tsp. Caraway seeds
1/8 tsp. Cayenne pepper

In half the oil, sauté the hot dogs until slightly browned and set aside. In the rest of the oil sauté the onions until soft. Put everything together and cook for 10 minutes.
VARIATION: Use 4 cups of ground Sausage Gluten instead of Big Franks.

"MEAT PIE" FILLING

1 1/2 c. Beef, Chicken, Pork, Ham, or Sausage Gluten, ground or chopped
3 T. Non-dairy margarine
1/4 c. Bell peppers or pimentos, chopped
1/4 c. Onions, minced
1/8 tsp. Cayenne pepper
1 T. Unbleached white flour
3 c. Mixed vegetables, cooked
1 1/2 c. Medium White Sauce

Sauté the gluten in half the magarine until browned and set aside. Sauté the bell peppers (or pimentos), onions, and cayenne in the rest of the margarine. Stir in the the flour well. Add everything, including the gluten, and cook, stirring, until it is thick–about 10 minutes.
VARIATION: Make the white sauce with broth the flavor of the gluten.

MEXICAN FILLING

1/2 c. Onions, coarsely chopped
2 tsp. Garlic, minced

1/4 c.	Bell pepper, chopped
4 1/2 tsp.	Corn oil
3/4 c.	Tomatoes, coarsely chopped
1 1/2 c.	Cooked pinto beans, drained and partially mashed
1/4 tsp.	Cumin
1 1/2 tsp.	Chili powder
1/2 tsp.	Black pepper
1 tsp.	Sea salt

Sauté the onion, garlic, and bell pepper in the oil until they begin to brown–about 5 minutes. Add the tomatoes and cook another 2 minutes. Stir in the rest of the ingredients, lower the heat, and simmer for 20 minutes.

PIZZA FILLING

2 c.	Onions, chopped
2 c.	Mushrooms, chopped
2 tsp.	Garlic, minced
1 c.	Bell pepper, chopped
2 T.	Olive oil
2 c.	Tomato Sauce–2
1/4 tsp.	Red pepper flakes
3/4 c.	Yeast Cheese

Sauté the onions, mushrooms, garlic, and bell pepper in the oil until the onions and peppers are soft. Add the tomato sauce and pepper flakes and stir in the "cheese." If this seems too dry, add some more tomato sauce; if too wet, let it cool down.

SPANAKOPITA FILLING

1 1/2 c.	Onions, finely chopped
2 tsp.	Garlic powder
2 T.	Olive oil
1 1/2 lb.	Frozen spinach, thawed and squeezed free of liquid
2 tsp.	Sea salt
2 tsp.	Oregano
1 1/2 tsp.	Black pepper
2 1/2 c.	Tofu Cottage Cheese, crumbled

Sauté the onion and garlic in the olive oil for 5 minutes, or until the onion begins to brown. Add the spinach and the spices, and cook, stirring frequently, for 5 minutes. Let it cool and add the "cottage cheese."

SPICY GARBANZO FILLING

1/2 c.	Onions, finely chopped
1 tsp.	Garlic, minced
2 T.	Olive oil
3/4 c.	Tomatoes, chopped
1 1/3 c.	Cooked garbanzos
1/4 c.	Parsley, chopped
2 tsp.	Lemon juice
3/4 tsp.	Cumin, ground
3/4 tsp.	Coriander, ground

1 1/2 tsp. Tumeric
1/8 tsp. Cayenne pepper
1/2 tsp. Sea salt

Sauté the onions and garlic in the oil until the onion begins to brown. Add the tomatoes and sauté for 2 or 3 minutes more. Add the rest of the ingredients, and cook together for 20 minutes.

HOW TO MAKE SWEET SQUARE MEALS

2/3 c. Cashew Milk
1/2 c. Sucanat
1/3 c. Non-dairy margarine
2 T. Yeast
1/4 c. Lukewarm water
1 tsp. Sucanat
1 N'egg
4 1/2 c. Unbleached white flour
1 tsp. Lemon rind, grated
1/2 tsp. Mace

Heat the cashew milk with the Sucanat, and margarine until the margarine melts. Allow this mixture to cool to lukewarm. Combine the yeast, water, and 1 teaspoon of Sucanat until dissolved. Add the n'egg and the yeast mixture to the cashew milk mixture. Combine half the flour with lemon rind and mace, then add the liquid, beating until smooth. Mix in the remaining flour. Let it stand for 10 minutes. Knead for 5 minutes on a lightly-floured board. Place dough in a lightly-greased bowl, turning once to bring the greased side up. Cover with a damp cloth and let rise in a warm place until double. Punch down, turn over, cover, and let rise until double again. Punch down, shape into a ball, and put on a lightly-floured surface. Cover with a bowl and let it rest 10 minutes. Roll it out to 1/8-inch thickness. Cut into 4-inch squares. Put 1/3 cup of filling (see recipes following) in the center of each square. Bring the corners up over the filling and pinch together. Pinch the four seams closed as well. Put on a lightly oiled cookie sheet, seam side down. Poke holes in the top several times (at least 4) with a fork. Brush the tops with corn oil. Bake in a 400° oven for about 8 to 10 minutes, or until golden brown on top.

APPLE FILLING–1

2 1/2 c. Apples, peeled, cored, and sliced
1 T. Water
2 c. Sucanat
2 T. Barbados molasses
Half Lemon rind, grated
1/4 tsp. Cinnamon

Put the apples, water, Sucanat, molasses, lemon rind, and cinnamon in a saucepan. Simmer 10 minutes, stirring occasionally. Do not allow the apple to become mushy. Cool.

VARIATION: For a "Mincemeat" flavor, use ground cloves instead of cinnamon.

APPLE FILLING–2

6 c. Apples, peeled, cored, and cut up small
1 1/4 c. Sucanat
1/2 tsp. Cinnamon
Dash Nutmeg
2 T. Non-dairy margarine

2 T. Unbleached white flour

Mix all ingredients together and simmer for 10 to 15 minutes, or until the apples are soft.

BLUEBERRY FILLING

1 3/4 c. Canned blueberries
1/3 c. Sucanat
1/4 c. &
2 T. Unbleached white flour
3/4 tsp. Sea salt
3/4 tsp. Cinnamon
1/4 c. Non-dairy margarine

Drain berries and save liquid. Combine Sucanat, flour, salt and cinnamon, and stir into the liquid saved from the berries. Heat, stirring constantly, until thick and smooth. Add the margarine and berries.

CHERRY FILLING

1 1/3 c. Liquid from canned cherries, or water if they are fresh
1/2 c. Cornstarch
1 1/3 c. Sucanat
2 T. Non-dairy margarine
1/4 tsp. Sea salt
4 c. Cherries, pitted (if canned, save liquid and use in recipe)

Mix some of the liquid with the cornstarch. Heat rest of liquid to boiling. Add cornstarch mixture, stirring with a wire whisk. Cook until thick and clear. Stir in the Sucanat, margarine, and salt. Bring to a boil, stirring. Remove from heat. Add cherries and mix gently. Cool thoroughly.

DRIED FRUIT FILLING

1 c. Mixed dried fruit, coarsely chopped
1 c. Apple juice, unsweetened
1/4 c. Walnuts, chopped
1/2 c. Sucanat
1 1/4 tsp. Cinnamon
1/8 tsp. Brandy or rum extract

Put dried fruit and apple juice in a saucepan. Let it soak for 1 hour. Bring to a boil, partially covered, and simmer for 10 minutes or until the liquid is absorbed and the fruit is soft. Add the walnuts, Sucanat, cinnamon, and extract (if used). Combine.

PEACH FILLING

2 T. Non-dairy margarine
2 T. Unbleached white flour
4 c. Peaches, sliced
1 c. Sucanat
1/8 tsp. Cinnamon
1/8 tsp. Sea salt

Melt the margarine. Stir in the flour well. Add the rest of the ingredients and keep stirring until the Sucanat liquefies. Cook until the peaches turn darker.

STRAWBERRY FILLING

4 c.	Frozen strawberries
1 c.	Sucanat
3 T.	Unbleached white flour
1/2 tsp.	Sea salt

Thaw and drain the berries and save the liquid. Combine the Sucanat, flour and salt, and stir into the liquid. Heat, stirring constantly, until thick and smooth. Add berries.

Pickles, Relish, Salsa, Etc.

CAJUN CATSUP

This am delighteous, I garontee!

4 c.	Onion, chopped
1 c.	Celery, chopped
1 c.	Bell pepper, chopped
1 c.	Parsley, chopped
1/4 c.	Corn oil
2 T.	Garlic, chopped
3 c.	Lea & Perrins Steak Sauce
1/2 c.	Louisiana Hot Sauce
3 c.	Tomato sauce
3 tsp.	Sea salt

In a large skillet, sauté the onions, celery, bell pepper, and parsley in the oil until the onions are soft and transparent. Add the garlic and cook a little longer. Add the steak sauce, hot sauce, tomato sauce, and salt, and bring to a boil. Lower the heat and cover, and cook for 2 to 3 hours. This can be kept refrigerated for a few weeks.

CHILI MACHO

Go ahead–I dare you!

3 c.	Canned tomatoes
1 c.	Onions, chopped
1	Garlic clove, minced
1 c.	Jalapeño peppers
1 1/2 tsp.	Sea salt

Blend all in the blender, but only until coarsely chopped. Let sit until the flavors are well blended.

CHILIPETIN SAUCE

Whew!

1 c.	Green chili peppers, chopped

1 c.	Onions, chopped
1	Garlic clove
1	Green tomato
1 tsp.	Flour
1 c.	Vinegar
2 T.	Sucanat
1 tsp.	Sea salt

Grind fine or chop the peppers, onion, garlic and tomato. Put in a saucepan with the flour and stir well. Bring the vinegar, Sucanat and salt to a boil. Pour into the pepper mixture. Stirring occasionally, boil, uncovered, for about 30 minutes, or until it thickens slightly. Seal while hot in sterilized jars. The sauce will be thin, but it thickens with age.

DILL PICKLES

If the angels in heaven make dill pickles they use this recipe!

4 lb.	Cucumbers
3 c.	White vinegar
3 c.	Water
1/3 c.	Sea salt

For each pint jar:

2 T.	Dill seed
3	Peppercorns
1 or 2	Dried chili peppers
1	Garlic clove

Wash the cucumbers. Either leave them whole or cut them in half or into spears. Combine the vinegar, water, and salt, and heat to the boiling point. Pack the cucumbers into hot, sterilized jars. Add the dill seed, peppercorns, peppers, and garlic. Fill the jars up to the mark (molded in the glass) with the boiling hot vinegar mixture. Seal the jars and process in a boiling water bath for 10 minutes. Makes 6 to 8 pints.

DILLED GREEN BEANS

8 c. Whole green beans

For each pint jar:

1/4 tsp.	Crushed red pepper flakes
1/2 tsp.	Mustard seed
1/2 tsp.	Dill seed (or 1 dill head)
1	Garlic clove

5 c.	Vinegar
5 c.	Water
1/2 c.	Sea salt

Wash beans thoroughly. Drain and cut into lengths that will fit into pint jars. Pack the beans in sterilized, hot jars. Add the red pepper flakes, mustard seed, dill seed and garlic. Combine the vinegar, water and salt; heat to boiling. Pour boiling liquid over the beans. Seal and process in a boiling water bath for 5 minutes.

GREEN TOMATO PICKLES

Simply beyond description. The tomatoes are exquisitely flavorful with a texture like butter. This recipe can be used to pickle any vegetables you wish–alone or in combination–including cucumbers.
For a stronger dill taste, use fresh dill weed instead of seeds.

Wash the tomatoes well. Sterilize the quart jars and lids. Combine and bring to a boil:

9 c. Water
6 c. Cider vinegar
3/4 c. Sea salt

In each quart jar put enough green tomatoes cut in halves or quarters to fill the jar to its neck. As you are filling each jar with the tomatoes, intersperse among them:

3 Garlic cloves, peeled and cut in half
1 tsp. Dill seed
3 Red chili peppers, stemmed

Pour the boiling brine into the jars, making sure the tomatoes are completely covered. Seal and process in a boiling water bath for 20 minutes.

HOT HERBED CARROTS

4 Hot peppers
4 Garlic cloves
1 tsp. Rosemary
4 c. Baby carrots, or 2 lbs. larger carrots cut in 4-inch lengths
2 c. Water
2 c. White vinegar
3 T. Sucanat
3 T. Sea salt

Halve the peppers lengthwise. In each of 4 pint jars, put 1 pepper (2 halves), 1 garlic clove and 1/4 tsp. of rosemary. Pack the jars full of carrots. Combine the water, vinegar, Sucanat and salt, and bring to a boil. Reduce the heat and simmer for 5 minutes. Pour the liquid over the carrots. Seal and process in a boiling water bath for 10 minutes.

HOT STUFF

This is half-way between a simple salsa and a relish.
It brings out the flavor of dishes that are bland in both flavor and texture.

2 c. Onions, chopped fine
2 c. Hot peppers, stemmed, seeded, and chopped
Sea salt
3/4 c. White vinegar
1/4 c. Water

Combine the onions and peppers in a bowl. Spoon into sterilized canning jars and add the salt–1 teaspoon per quart jar, or 1/2 teaspoon per pint jar. In a small saucepan, heat the vinegar and water together, but do not bring it to a boil. When the liquid is too hot to stir with your finger, it is ready. Pour it into the jars, making sure to cover the peppers and onions. Seal, and let it sit for 3 to 4 days before using it.

LOUISIANA HOT SAUCE

This has the zing of the commercial version, yet is somehow milder. Because of the garlic it has more flavor, too.

3 c. Hot peppers, stemmed and finely chopped
1 c. White vinegar
1/2 c. Water
1 T. Garlic, chopped fine
1 T. Sea salt

Combine all the ingredients in a saucepan and simmer, covered, until the peppers are very soft, stirring occasionally. Take from the heat and mash with a potato masher. Press the mixture through a sieve so that only the skins and seeds remain in the sieve. Discard them. If the mixture is too thick to pour, add more salt and vinegar. Pour into sterilized jars and seal.

MARINATED TOMATOES

Taste-full!

3 c. Tomatoes, sliced thick
1/3 c. Olive oil
1/4 c. Red wine vinegar
1 tsp. Sea salt
1/4 tsp. Black pepper
1/2 tsp. Garlic, minced
2 T. Onion, chopped
1 T. Parsley, chopped
1 T. Fresh basil, chopped, or 1 tsp. dried

Put the tomato slices in a large shallow dish. Combine the rest of the ingredients in a blender and blend well. Pour over the tomato slices. Cover and refrigerate a few hours.

PICKLED BEANS AND ONIONS

6 c. Green beans
2 c. Vinegar
2 c. Sucanat
1 1/2 c. Water
1 T. Pickling spice
1 T. Mustard seed
2 c. Pearl onions, peeled

Wash beans and trim the ends. Parboil in salted water about 5 or 6 minutes and drain well. Combine vinegar, Sucanat, water, and spices in a large saucepan. Simmer about 15 minutes. Pack the beans and onions into sterilized hot jars, leaving 1/4-inch head space. Remove any air bubbles with a non-metallic spatula. Adjust the caps. Seal and process for 10 minutes in a boiling water bath canner. Makes four 1-pint jars.

PICKLED CALICO VEGETABLES

6 c. Cauliflower flowerets (1 large head)
1 c. Onions, cut in chunks
2 Bell peppers, chopped into 1/2-inch pieces

2 c.	Carrots, sliced
1/4 c.	Pickling salt
	Crushed ice
1 qt.	White Vinegar
1 1/2 c.	Sucanat
2 tsp.	Mustard seed
2 tsp.	Celery seed
2 tsp.	Louisiana Hot Sauce

Combine the vegetables and salt in a large mixing bowl. Cover with crushed ice and let it stand for 3 hours. Drain the vegetables. Rinse them well. Combine the vinegar, Sucanat, mustard seed, celery seed, and hot sauce in a large saucepan or pot. Bring to a boil. Add the vegetables and simmer 5 to 7 minutes. Carefully pack into sterilized hot jars, leaving 1/4-inch head space. Remove any air bubbles with a non-metallic spatula. Seal and process 10 minutes in a boiling water bath canner. Makes 5 1-pint jars.

QUICK TOMATO RELISH

3 c.	Tomatoes, diced
2 c.	Bell pepper, chopped
1/4 c.	Italian Dressing

Combine and refrigerate so flavor can develop.

TOMATO RELISH

Zesty!

1 qt.	Tomatoes, finely chopped
1/3 c.	Onions, finely chopped
1/2 c.	Celery, finely chopped
1/4 c.	Bell pepper, finely chopped
1 tsp.	Sea salt
1/3 c.	Lemon juice
2 T.	Olive oil

Combine and refrigerate so flavor can develop.

TOMATO SALSA

This is a staple for us. Unbeatable!

1 c.	Bell pepper, chopped
1/4 c.	Onions, chopped
2 T.	Corn oil
1 c.	Jalapeños, chopped, or 2 tsp. of hot pepper flakes
4 c.	Tomatoes, chopped
1 tsp.	Garlic powder
1 1/2 tsp.	Sea salt
1 T.	Vinegar

Sauté the bell peppers and onions in the corn oil. Combine with rest of ingredients and cook.
VARIATION: Instead of fresh tomatoes, use 2 cups of canned tomato sauce.
NOTE: When made with jalapeños, this gets hotter in a few days, so you might want to use

only 1/2 cup of jalapeños the first time around.

TOMATO SALSA CRUDA

Nothing crude about this sophisticated relish!

2 c.	Canned tomatoes
2 T.	Onions, minced
1 tsp.	Red pepper flakes
1 T.	Parsley, minced
1 tsp.	Lemon or lime juice
1 T.	Olive oil
1/4 tsp.	Sea salt

Purée the tomatoes in a blender or processor until fairly smooth. Combine the purée with the remaining ingredients and let them stand for at least 15 minutes to flavor. Use as soon as possible.

TOMATO SALSA FRESCA

2 c.	*Canned* tomatoes, chopped well
3 T.	Onions, minced
1/2 c.	Bell pepper, minced
1 tsp.	Red pepper flakes
1 T.	Lemon or lime juice
1 T.	Olive oil
1 tsp.	Sea salt

Combine and let stand for 30 minutes to blend.

BREAD AND BUTTER ZUCCHINI

12 c.	Zucchini, sliced 1/4-inch thick
1 1/2 c.	Onions, thinly sliced
2	Large garlic cloves
1/3 c.	Sea salt
2 qts.	Crushed ice
4 c.	Sucanat
1 1/2 tsp.	Tumeric
1 1/2 tsp.	Celery seed
2 T.	Mustard seed
3 c.	White vinegar

Combine the zucchini, onions, and garlic. Add the salt and mix thoroughly. Cover with crushed ice or ice cubes. Let stand for 3 hours. Drain thoroughly. Remove garlic cloves. Combine Sucanat, spices and vinegar. Heat just to boiling. Add the drained zucchini and onion slices and heat for 5 minutes. Pack hot pickles loosely into sterilized, hot pint jars to 1/2 inch of the top. Seal and process in a boiling water bath for 5 minutes.

ZUCCHINI PICKLES

Try it and like it!

8 c.	Zucchini, thinly sliced

2 c.	Onions, thinly sliced
1/2 c.	Coarse salt
	Water
1 qt.	White vinegar
2 c.	Sucanat
2 tsp.	Celery seeds
2 tsp.	Mustard seeds
2 tsp.	Dill seeds
1 tsp.	Dry mustard

In a large bowl, combine the zucchini, onions and salt with enough water to cover. Let it stand 1 hour. In a saucepan, combine the vinegar, Sucanat, celery seeds, mustard seeds, dill seeds and the dry mustard. Bring to a boil and boil for 3 minutes. Drain the zucchini and onions. Pour the hot vinegar mixture over the zucchini and onions. Let stand 1 hour. Transfer to the large saucepan, bring to a boil and boil for 3 minutes. Pack into sterilized jars, seal and process in boiling water, enough to cover the jars, from 10 to 15 minutes, according to the jar manufacturer's instructions. Cool and store in a cool, dry place.

ZUCCHINI-RED PEPPER RELISH

2 c.	Zucchini, cut in 1/2-inch cubes
2 c.	Sweet red pepper, cut in 1/4-inch squares
2 T.	Sea salt
2 1/2 c.	Water
1 1/2 c.	White vinegar
1 1/4 c.	Sucanat
2 T.	Instant minced onion
1 tsp.	Cumin seed
1 tsp.	Instant minced garlic
1/2 tsp.	Hot pepper flakes

In a large bowl, place zucchini, peppers, and salt. Mix well. Cover and refrigerate 12 to 15 hours. Take from the refrigerator, drain off liquid, rinse vegetables well, and drain thoroughly. In a large saucepan, place the water, vinegar, Sucanat, onion, cumin, garlic and pepper flakes. Bring to a boil. Reduce the heat and simmer, covered, for 10 minutes. Add the zucchini and peppers. Simmer, covered, stirring occasionally until the vegetables are tender, about 15 minutes. Ladle into 8 (1/2-pint) sterilized hot canning jars, leaving 1/4-inch head space. Cover, following manufacturer's directions. Process for 10 minutes in a boiling water bath according to the jar manufacturer's directions.

ZUCCHINI RELISH

This is worth its weight in gold!

5 c.	Zucchini, minced
1/2 c.	Sea salt
2 1/2 c.	Onions, minced
1/2 c.	Celery, diced
3/4 c.	Bell pepper, diced
1 tsp.	Tumeric
1 1/2 tsp.	Dry mustard
4 1/2 tsp.	Celery seed
3 c.	Sucanat
2 1/2 c.	White vinegar

1 1/2 T. Cornstarch

Combine the zucchini, salt, onions, celery, and bell pepper. Allow this to stand overnight to draw out the juices. Drain and rinse thoroughly. Drain again in a colander. While the vegetables are still in the colander, press out as much liquid as possible. Combine the pressed vegetables with the rest of the ingredients in a pot and bring it to a rolling boil. Reduce the heat and simmer for 20 minutes. Ladle the relish into hot sterilized jars and seal, or put in refrigerator and keep.

Father Arsenios prepares some gluten "meat."

N'EGGS

In many recipes from ordinary cookbooks, eggs are called for when the dish will come out just fine without them as you adapt them for vegetarian use. However this is not always so, therefore you will sometimes find that you need a "N'egg," the formulas for which are given in this section.

These two formulas–whose name is an abbreviation of "No egg"–can be used whenever an egg is called for in a recipe.

One is specifically for use in baked goods–pastries. The other is for everything else.

PASTRY N'EGG

1/3 cup of this formula equals one egg.

1/4 c. Flax seeds
3/4 c. Water

Grind the seeds to a powder. Mix in a blender with the water. As said above, 1/3 cup of this equals one egg. Refrigerate what you don't use, but use it within 24 hours, for it does not keep well.

ALL PURPOSE N'EGG

This formula equals one egg.

2 T. Gluten flour, or unbleached white flour
1 1/2 tsp. Corn oil
1/2 tsp. Baking powder
2 T. Water

Combine thoroughly. Use right away, because the baking powder loses its effectiveness within 2 hours.

SEASONINGS

ALL-PURPOSE SEASONING

Make this up, taste it, and decide in what ways you can use it.

1/4 tsp. Red pepper flakes
2 1/2 tsp. Sage, rubbed
1/2 tsp. Nutmeg, ground
1/2 tsp. Dry mustard
1/2 tsp. Black pepper
4 tsp. Paprika
1 1/2 tsp. Sea salt

Put everything in a blender and blend on high until all is ground fine. Do not take the mixture out of the blender but let it sit 3 minutes. Remove it and store it in a covered container.

FINES HERBES

1 part Rosemary
1 part Thyme
1/2 part Oregano or Summer Savory
3 parts Basil

Combine and store in an airtight container.

GARAM MASALA–1

This is one formula for the Garam Masala (Hot Mixture) that is used in Indian cooking. You might like to try it also in other dishes, as in Anandamayi Kitchuri, or try substituting it for curry powder or even for black or cayenne pepper.

3 T. Coriander seed
2 tsp. Cumin seed
8 Whole cloves
1 2-inch stick cinnamon
1/2 tsp. Black pepper
4 Bay leaves

Roast the coriander and cumin seeds in a dry frying pan over medium heat, shaking often, for 4 minutes or until they are lightly browned. In a blender or nut grinder grind all the ingredients together to a fine powder. Store in an airtight container.

GARAM MASALA-2

This is far more complex than the first formula, but well worth the making.

1 T. & 1 1/2 tsp.	Cayenne pepper
2 T.	Paprika
1 T.	Onion salt
1 tsp.	Garlic powder
1 tsp.	Basil, dried
1/2 tsp.	Ginger, powdered
1/4 tsp.	Black pepper
1/8 tsp.	Cloves, ground
1/8 tsp.	Cinnamon, ground
1/8 tsp.	Cardamon
1/8 tsp.	Nutmeg
1/8 tsp.	Allspice
1/8 tsp.	Cumin
1/8 tsp.	Fenugreek
1/8 tsp.	Tumeric

Grind everything together in a blender or nut grinder to a fine powder and store in an airtight container.

GARLIC OIL

Keep this always on hand. It has many uses, such as spreading on pizza or bread dough, sautéeing vegetables, or mixing in with other oils to give a subtle garlic taste to dishes.

4 1/2 tsp.	Garlic, crushed
1 c.	Olive oil

Stir the crushed garlic into the oil, and let it sit overnight in the refrigerator before using. Keep in refrigerator.

SPECIAL SEASONING

Make this up, taste it, and decide in what ways you can use it.

1 1/3 c.	Nutritional yeast flakes
1 T.	Onion powder
2 tsp.	Garlic powder
1 T.	Paprika
1/2 tsp.	Celery seed, ground
1/2 tsp.	Tumeric
1 tsp.	Dried parsley
1 T.	Barley malt powder
3 T.	Sea salt

Put everything in a blender and blend on high until all is ground fine. Do not take the mixture out of the blender but let it sit 3 minutes. Remove it and store it in a covered container.

DESSERTS

APPLE CRISP

Fit for a king!

8 c.	Apples, sliced
1/2 c.	Cashew Milk
1/2 c.	Non-dairy margarine
3/4 c.	Rolled oats
1/2 c.	Unbleached white flour
2 tsp.	Cinnamon
1/2 tsp.	Salt
2 1/2 c.	Sucanat

Grease a casserole dish with some non-dairy margarine. Put in the apples and pour in the "milk" on top. Melt the 1/2 cup of margarine. As margarine is melting, mix all the other ingredients together. Add margarine and stir with a fork until all is moistened. Spread (crumble) this mixture over the apples. Bake at 350° for about 45 minutes until the apples are done and topping is brown.

VARIATION: Use other kinds of fruit.

BLUEBERRY CHEESELESS CAKE

So virtuous it's positively sinful!

1 c.	Tofu Cream cheese
1 c.	Sucanat
1 tsp.	Vanilla
1 c.	Soy Whipped Cream or Tofu Whipped Cream
1	Recipe of Graham Cracker Crust
1	Recipe of Blueberry Pie Filling

Beat together the "cream cheese," Sucanat, and vanilla until smooth. Fold in "whipped cream." Spoon into graham cracker crust. Spoon blueberry filling on top. Chill to set.

CAROB CUSTARD

1/2 c.	Pecans
1/4 tsp.	Vanilla
3 1/4 c.	Water
1/2 tsp.	Salt
1/4 c.	Carob powder
1 1/2 c.	Sucanat
6 T.	Cornstarch
	Shredded dried coconut

Blend ingredients together in a blender until the nuts are smooth. Heat until thick, stirring constantly. Pour into custard cups. Sprinkle with the coconut.

CAROB PUDDING

3 T.	Cornstarch
2 T.	Soy flour
3 T.	Carob powder
1/4 tsp.	Salt
1/2 c.	Sucanat
2 c.	Cashew Milk
2 tsp.	Vanilla
1 c.	Whole, lightly toasted peanuts

Mix all ingredients except the vanilla and the peanuts. Cook for 5 minutes, stirring constantly. Add the vanilla and peanuts. Pour into molds to cool.

COCONUT RICE PUDDING

You will remember this long and lovingly!

2 c.	Cashew Milk
6	Sticks cinnamon
1 tsp.	Whole cloves
1/4 tsp.	Powdered ginger
1 qt.	Water
1 c.	Rice, uncooked
2 c.	Coconut milk
1 c.	Sucanat
1 tsp.	Sea salt
1/2 c.	Raisins

Put the "milk," cinnamon sticks, cloves and ginger in a saucepan. Bring to a boil over high heat, then lower the heat and simmer, uncovered, for 5 minutes. Remove from heat and set aside for at least 1 hour. Strain the "milk" through a fine sieve. Discard the cinnamon, cloves and ginger. If there is less than 2 cups of "milk," add more to make 2 cups. Bring the water to a boil and drop in the rice. Cook, uncovered, for 5 minutes, then drain the rice in a sieve and wash it under cold water. In a saucepan, combine the coconut milk, strained spiced "milk," Sucanat, and salt. Bring to a boil over high heat, then stir in the rice, cover the pan, and reduce the heat. Simmer for 30 minutes, then stir in the raisins, recover the pan, and cook for 10 minutes longer, or until the liquid is completely absorbed and the rice is tender. Sprinkle with cinnamon and serve at room temperature.

DATE AND APPLE SQUARES

2 c.	Apples, chopped
1 1/2 c.	Pitted dates, chopped
1 c.	Unbleached white flour
1 1/2 tsp.	Baking powder
1/2 c.	Sucanat
1/3 c.	Barbados molasses
2 T.	Non-dairy margarine, melted
1	N'egg
Pinch	Salt

Mix all together well to combine evenly. Spread mixture into a lightly oiled square cake pan. Bake at 400° about 30 minutes, or until golden brown and risen. Cut into squares.

FRUIT COCKTAIL BREAD PUDDING

When you've got to–you've got to!

10	Slices of stale bread
3	N'eggs
2 3/4 c.	Sucanat
1/3 c.	Non-dairy margarine
1 c.	Raisins
1 c.	Pecans, chopped
1	16-oz. can of low calorie fruit cocktail sweetened with fruit juice
2 1/2 c.	Cashew Milk
2 T.	Vanilla

Mix all ingredients together in a large bowl, blending well. Turn into an oiled 9x13-inch pan. Bake at 400° for 55 minutes or until it gets brown on top.

FRUIT SHORTCAKE

This gives a whole new meaning to "heavenly"!

FILLING:

1	3-inch cinnamon stick, crushed
4	Whole cloves
2 c.	Fruit, sliced
1 c.	Water
1 c.	Sucanat

Tie the cinnamon and cloves into a small piece of cheesecloth. Put the fruit, water, Sucanat, and spice bag into a saucepan and simmer 5 to 7 minutes–until the fruit is just tender. Transfer the fruit with a slotted spoon to a bowl. Boil the cooking liquid until it is reduced by half. Add any fruit juice that may have accumulated in the bowl. Let the syrup cool to room temperature and discard the spice bag. Add the syrup to the fruit and chill, covered, for at least 1 hour, or until it is cold.

SHORTCAKES:

2 c.	Unbleached white flour

2 T.	Sucanat
1 T.	Baking powder
1/2 tsp.	Sea salt
1/3 c.	Non-dairy margarine
1/2 c.	Cashew Cream
2	N'eggs
1 tsp.	Vanilla
	Apple juice
2 c.	Soy Whipped Cream or Tofu Whipped Cream, well chilled

Next make the shortcakes: Sift the flour, Sucanat, baking powder, and salt together into a bowl. Blend in the margarine until the mixture resembles coarse meal. Whisk together the "cream," n'eggs, and vanilla, and add this to the flour mixture, stirring with a fork just until a soft dough is formed. Turn the dough out onto a floured surface and knead it gently for 20 seconds. Pat the dough into an 8-inch round, transfer it to a "buttered" baking sheet, and cut it into 6 equal wedges without cutting all the way through. Brush the wedges with apple juice, and bake at 425° for 15 to 20 minutes, or until it is golden. Transfer to a rack, cool, and separate the wedges. Split each wedge horizontally with a fork, arrange the bottom halves on 6 plates, and spoon the filling over them. Top the filling with the "whipped cream" and then put on the top half of the wedge.

FRUIT SQUARES

CRUMBLE:

2 T.	Vegetable oil
1/2 c.	Sucanat
1/3 c.	Water
1 c.	Unbleached white flour
1 tsp.	Salt
1 1/2 c.	Quick oats
1/2 c.	Oat flour (make by grinding rolled oats in a blender)

FILLING:

1 c.	Dates or Raisins
1 c.	Water
1 tsp.	Lemon juice
1/2 tsp.	Vanilla
1/8 tsp.	Salt
2 T.	Cornstarch

In a bowl mix the oil, Sucanat, and water. In another bowl, mix the flour, salt, quick oats and oat flour. Combine both bowls, and crumble together. Prepare the filling by mixing the fruit, water, lemon juice, vanilla, salt and cornstarch, and boiling it until it is soft. Press half of the crumble on the bottom of a greased pan. Spread the filling over it. Cover with the rest of the crumble. Bake at 375° for 40 minutes, until browned. Cool. Wet the top layer by spooning 3/4 cup of pineapple juice over it. Cover the pan and keep in the refrigerator overnight. Cut into squares.

VARIATION: Instead of dates (or raisins) and water, prepare the filling from 2 cups of crushed, unsweetened pineapple, canned pears, or apples.

LEMON CHEESELESSCAKE

1 c.	Very fine graham cracker crumbs
3 T.	Non-dairy margarine
3 1/2 c.	Tofu Cottage Cheese, made without garlic power
2	Lemons–juice and grated rind
1 1/3 c.	Powdered Sucanat

Stir the crumbs into the margarine and press into the base of a round cake pan. Run the "cottage cheese" through blender until it is perfectly smooth. Beat the lemon juice and rind together with the Sucanat. Slowly add the blended cottage cheese, beating, until all is smooth. Spread the mixture in the cake pan and smooth surface. Cover and refrigerate for several hours.

LEMON CHEESELESSCAKE DELUXE

For the sophisticate in you!

2 1/2 c.	Graham cracker crumbs
1/4 c.	Sucanat
10 T.	Non-dairy margarine, melted
3 c.	Tofu Cream Cheese, made without onion powder
3	N'eggs
1 1/2 c.	Powdered Sucanat
3 T.	Lemon juice
1 tsp.	Vanilla
1 T.	Grated lemon peel
1	Lemon, sliced paper-thin
3 c.	Water
1 1/2 c.	Sucanat
2 T. & 2 tsp.	Cornstarch
1/3 c.	Lemon juice

Combine the graham cracker crumbs, Sucanat, and margarine, and press into the bottom and 2 inches up the sides of a 9-inch springform pan. Bake at 350° for 5 minutes and cool. Beat the "cream cheese" and n'eggs. Gradually add in the Sucanat, lemon juice, and vanilla, and mix well. Fold in the lemon peel. Pour into the crust. Bake at 350° for 40 minutes. Cool to room temperature and refrigerate at least 4 hours. Remove any seeds from the lemon slices, reserve 1 slice for garnish, and coarsely chop the rest of the slices. Place these in a saucepan with 2 cups of the water, bring to a boil, reduce the heat, and simmer, uncovered, for 15 minutes. Drain and discard the liquid. In a saucepan combine the Sucanant and cornstarch, stir in the remaining water, lemon juice, and cooked slices, bring to a boil, stirring constantly, and boil for 3 minutes. Chill until cool, stirring occasionally. Pour over the cheesecake and garnish with the lemon slice. Chill until ready to serve.

LEMON CUSTARD

1	Lemon, quartered, seeds removed
1/2 c.	Water
2 c.	Orange juice
2 T.	Oil
1 1/4 c.	Sucanat
1/4 c.	Cornstarch

Place the lemon in a blender–peel and all–with all the other ingredients and blend until it is finely ground. Place in a saucepan and bring to a boil. Simmer about 2 minutes, stirring constantly. Pour into serving dishes. Put a few pecans, a few raisins, or a date on top.

Use also as a pie filling.

VARIATION: Use 3 oranges, peeled and with seeds removed, instead of the orange juice. They should be blended with the lemon until fine.

MAPLE PECAN CHEESELESSCAKE

A triumph!

2 c.	Ginger Snaps (see Cookies section), crushed into fine crumbs
6 T.	Non-diary margarine, melted
4 c.	Tofu Cream Cheese, made without onion powder
1 c.	Powdered Sucanat
1/2 c.	Genuine maple syrup
3	N'eggs
1/2 c.	Tofu Sour Cream or Cashew Sour Cream
1/2 tsp.	Sea salt
1 tsp.	Vanilla
3/4 tsp.	Maple flavoring
1 c.	Pecans, toasted lightly and chopped fine

Make the crust by stirring together the gingersnap crumbs and margarine until well combined, and press this onto the bottom and halfway up the side of a 9-inch springform pan. With an electric mixer cream the "cream cheese" and Sucanat together until light and fluffy. Beat in the syrup, n'eggs, "sour cream," salt, vanilla, maple flavoring, and pecans. Put the filling into the crust, and bake at 350° for 1 hour. Turn off the heat and let the cake cool down thoroughly in the oven with the door slightly open, and then chill, covered, overnight.

PINEAPPLE PUDDING

4 c.	Unsweetened pineapple juice
1 1/2 c.	Sucanat
1/3 c.	Cornstarch
1/2 tsp.	Mint flavoring
1 c.	Crushed unsweetened pineapple, drained
1/2 tsp.	Salt

Bring 3 cups of the juice and Sucanat to a rolling boil. Mix the cornstarch with the other 1 cup of the juice and add gradually to the rest, stirring constantly. Add the remaining ingredients. Pour into dessert cups. Chill. May serve with "whipped cream," if desired.

SPICED BREAD PUDDING

8	Slices of bread
1 1/2 c.	Cashew Milk
2/3 c.	Raisins, soaked in 1 cup of hot water and drained
2 T.	Non-dairy margarine
1/3 c.	Sucanat
1/3 c.	Barbados molasses
1 T.	Allspice
1	N'egg
Pinch	Nutmeg

Break up the bread and place it in a mixing bowl with the "milk." Let soak. Add the raisins, margarine, Sucanat, molasses, allspice, and n'egg. Beat well. Put in an oiled casserole dish, level the surface, sprinkle with nutmeg, and bake at 350° about 45 minutes or until "set." Serve hot or cold.

STEAMED IRISH RAISIN PUDDING

1 3/4 c.	Cashew Milk
1/2 c.	Sucanat
1 1/2 c.	Plumped raisins
1 1/2 c.	Unbleached wheat flour
1/2 tsp.	Salt
1/4 tsp.	Coriander
1 T.	Lemon rind, grated
1 1/2 c.	Bread crumbs
1 c.	Apples–peeled and grated

"Plump" the raisins by putting them loosely in a container and covering them with hot water. Let them sit overnight or until soft as fresh prunes. (May be stored in the refrigerator until you need them.) Blend the "milk" and Sucanat together. Combine all the ingredients and turn into a well-greased 2 quart tube mold or large can. Steam for 2 hours. Cool and unmold. Slice and serve with a dessert sauce.

VANILLA PUDDING–1

2 1/4 c.	Cashew Milk
1/2 c.	Sucanat
1/8 tsp.	Salt
2 tsp.	Agar flakes
2 T.	Arrowroot powder
1 tsp.	Vanilla extract
1 T.	Non-dairy margarine

Combine 1 3/4 cup of the "milk" with the Sucanat and salt in a small saucepan. Sprinkle in the agar flakes and bring to a simmer over medium heat without stirring. Simmer for one minute. Thoroughly dissolve the arrowroot in the remaining 1/4 cup of cashew milk and add it to the pudding while stirring briskly. Return to a simmer and cook for 1 to 2 minutes. Remove from heat and mix in the vanilla and margarine. Chill.

VANILLA PUDDING–2

3 T.	Cornstarch
1/3 c.	Sucanat
1/4 tsp.	Salt
2 c.	Cashew Milk
2 tsp.	Vanilla

Mix cornstarch, Sucanat, and salt in top of a double boiler. Gradually add "milk" until smooth. Place over boiling water and cook, stirring constantly, until mixture thickens. Cover and continue cooking 10 minutes. Stir in vanilla and chill.

N'Ice Cream

From the health standpoint, the major reason we "went vegan" was our realization that every bout of 'flu that swept through the monastery occurred the day after a big ice cream bash. (I had once had a private 'flu epidemic on my own when travelling that was also preceded by an ice cream orgy.) What, then, to do? And here is the answer. Freeze and enjoy!

BANANA N'ICE CREAM

Simple and heavenly!

4	Large FROZEN bananas
1 tsp.	Sucanat

Cut the frozen bananas into chunks. Place them in a food processor fitted with a steel blade. Pulse until chopped. Add the Sucanat. Process until the bananas are smooth and creamy. Serve immediately.

VARIATION: Add one cup of frozen fruit when processing.

COCONUT N'ICE CREAM

Better than You-Know-Who's!

2 c.	Coconut, shredded
3 c.	Coconut milk
1 c.	Raw cashew pieces
2 tsp.	Vanilla
2 1/2 c.	Tofu
1 1/2 c.	Bananas
1 c.	Genuine maple syrup
2/3 c.	Coconut oil
1/4 tsp.	Sea salt

Put everything in a food processor in batches and purée until creamy and smooth. Freeze in an ice cream freezer.

TAHINI N'ICE CREAM

A character all its own!

1 1/3 c.	Fruit puree
2/3 c.	Tahini
2 T.	Sucanat
1/2 tsp.	Almond or vanilla extract

Mix fruit purée with tahini until smooth, stir in the remaining ingredients, and freeze.

TOFU N'ICE CREAM-1

You won't regret it!

2 1/4 c.	Tofu, well chilled
6 T.	Genuine maple syrup
1 T.	Corn oil
2 tsp.	Vanilla
1/8 tsp.	Salt

Combine 1 1/2 cups of the tofu with the syrup, oil, vanilla, and salt in a blender and puree for 1 minute. Put in a covered container and put in the freezer overnight. Purée the other 3/4 cup of tofu in a blender until smooth. Cut the frozen tofu into small chunks. While pureeing at high speed, add a few chunks of the frozen tofu at a time to the tofu in the blender until all has been added and the mixture is smooth and thick. Serve immediately.

VARIATIONS: Toward the end of the puréeing add 1/2 cup (well packed) of frozen fruit. Instead of 2 teaspoons of vanilla, use 1 teaspoon of vanilla and 1 teaspoon of almond extract. Instead of 2 teaspoons of vanilla, use 1 teaspoon of vanilla and 1 teaspoon of rum extract and at the end add 1/2 cup of chopped pecans. Add 2 teaspoons of peppermint or other extract.

TOFU N'ICE CREAM–2

This is the deluxe model!

4 c.	Fruit
1 c.	Pineapple juice
1 c.	Raw cashew pieces
2 tsp.	Vanilla
2 1/2 c.	Tofu
1 1/2 c.	Bananas
1 c.	Genuine maple syrup
2/3 c.	Corn oil
3 T.	Lemon juice
1/4 tsp.	Sea salt

Put everything in a food processor in batches and purée until creamy and smooth. Freeze in an ice cream freezer.

NOTE: When making peach or mango n'ice cream, use 2 teaspoons of almond extract instead of vanilla.

Cake

CAROB CAKE

1 1/2 c.	Unbleached white flour
3 T.	Carob powder
1/2 tsp.	Sea salt
2 tsp.	Baking powder
1/3 c.	Sucanat
1/3 c.	Barbados molasses
1 tsp.	Vanilla
6 T.	Non-dairy margarine, melted
3/4 c.	Water

Sift the dry ingredients into a bowl. Mix the liquid ingredients–including the melted margarine–in a separate bowl. Pour the liquid ingredients into the dry, and stir until the batter is smooth. Pour the batter into an oiled, floured pan. Bake in a preheated 350° oven for 35 to 45 minutes.

VARIATION: Leave out the carob powder for a white cake.

CHRISTMAS FRUITCAKE

1/3 c.	Crystallized ginger, coarsely chopped
1 c.	Walnuts, coarsely chopped
1/2 c.	Almonds, coarsely chopped
3/4 c.	Golden raisins
1/3 c.	Currants
1/2 c.	Dried prunes, quartered
3/4 c.	Dried apricots, quartered
1	Orange peel, grated
1	Lemon peel, grated
1 tsp.	Brandy extract in 1/3 c. water
1 1/4 c.	Sucanat
1/2 c.	Non-dairy margarine
2	N'eggs
1 c.	Flour
1 1/2 tsp.	Baking powder
1/4 tsp.	Baking soda
1 tsp.	Cinnamon
1/2 tsp.	Nutmeg

Combine the first 10 ingredients. Stir well. Cover and let rest for 30 to 60 minutes. Cream the Sucanat and margarine. Beat in the n'eggs. Sift the flour, baking powder, soda, cinnamon and nutmeg, and add to the margarine mixture and beat until smooth. Combine with the fruit. Mix thoroughly by hand. Spoon into an oiled 1/2 quart cake pan that has been lined with waxed paper. Bake at 275° for 2 hours. Remove and let rest for 5 minutes. Unmold. Decorate top with nuts and apricot halves. Cool.

COTTAGE PUDDING

Simply indescribable as a "shortcake."

1/4 c.	Corn oil
1 3/4 c.	Unbleached white flour
2 tsp.	Baking powder
1/2 tsp.	Sea salt
3/4 c.	Sucanat
3/4 c.	Cashew Milk
1	N'egg
1 tsp.	Vanilla

Mix the oil, flour, baking powder, salt, and Sucanat. Add the "milk," n'egg, and vanilla and beat until smooth. Pour into an oiled and floured baking pan, cover and bake at 350° for 45 to 60 minutes. Let stand 5 minutes before removing from pan.

CRAZY CAKE

3 c.	Unbleached white flour
2 c.	Sucanat
1/2 c.	Carob powder
1 tsp.	Sea salt
2 tsp.	Baking soda
2 T.	White vinegar
2 tsp.	Vanilla
2 c.	Water
3/4 c.	Corn oil

Sift the dry ingredients together. Add the vinegar, vanilla, water, and oil. Bake at 350° for 50 minutes, or until a toothpick inserted comes out "clean."

DATE-NUT CAKE

Quietly good.

2 3/4 c.	Sucanat
1 c.	Non-dairy margarine
2	N'eggs
1 c.	Walnuts, chopped
2 c.	Dates, chopped
1 tsp.	Cinnamon
1/2 tsp.	Allspice
1/2 tsp.	Cloves
3 c.	Unbleached white flour, sifted
2 tsp.	Baking soda
1/2 tsp.	Sea salt

1 1/2 c. Water
1/2 c. Liquid barley malt

Cream the Sucanat and margarine. Sir in the n'eggs, nuts, dates, and spices. In another bowl sift the flour, baking soda, and salt together and stir in the water and malt. Combine the mixture with the margarine-Sucanat and mix until well blended. Bake in a casserole pan at 350° for 1 hour and 15 minutes.

DEVON APPLE CAKE

2 c. Unbleached white flour
3 tsp. Baking powder
1/4 tsp. Sea salt
1/2 tsp. Cinnamon, ground
1/2 tsp. Allspice, ground
1/3 c. Sucanat
1/3 c. Molasses
1/2 c. Non-dairy margarine
2 c. Apples, peeled, cored, and coarsely chopped
1 N'egg

Oil and flour the base of a square cake pan. In a bowl combine the flour, baking powder, salt, cinnamon, allspice, Sucanat, and molasses. Rub in the margarine until the mixture resembles fine crumbs. Add apples and n'egg to mixture and stir quickly to combine. Spread evenly in the pan and bake at 375° about 30 minutes, or until risen and firm to the touch. Allow to cool in pan before cutting into squares.

FRUIT CAKE

1 1/2 c. Non-dairy margarine
3 c. Sucanat
6 N'eggs
1 c. Cashew Milk
1 tsp. Brandy extract
1 tsp. Vanilla
1/2 tsp. Sea salt
1/2 tsp. Cream of Tartar
1 c. Water
3 1/2 c. Unbleached white flour
1 c. Raisins
1 c. Dry apricots, chopped and soaked
1/2 c. Dried cherries, chopped and soaked
1/2 c. Dried orange, chopped (you may have to make this yourself by chopping up an orange and letting it dry)
1/2 c. Dried lemon, chopped (ditto)
1 c. Pecans, chopped

Cream the margarine and Sucanat together. Add the n'eggs, "milk," brandy extract, vanilla, salt, cream of tartar, and water. Add the flour slowly and mix while doing so. Fold in the fruits and nuts. The batter should be stiff but not dry. If needed, add more water. Divide in half and place in two oiled loaf pans. Bake at 275° for 2 to 2 1/2 hours. Use a toothpick to tell if the cake is done. Also, the sides of the cake should not adhere to the pan when it is done.

GINGERBREAD

If the old witch had known this recipe the kids would have truly eaten her out of house and home!

1/2 c.	Non-dairy margarine
1/2 c.	Sucanat
1 c.	Barbados molasses
2 1/2 c.	Unbleached white flour
2 1/2 tsp.	Baking soda
1 tsp.	Cinnamon
2 tsp.	Ginger, ground
1/2 tsp.	Cloves, ground
1/2 tsp.	Sea salt
1 c.	Boiling water

Cream margarine and Sucanat. Add molasses and dry ingredients. Blend well. Add boiling water and beat well. Pour batter into a well-greased and floured baking pan. Bake at 350° for one hour or until it passes the "toothpick test."

LEMON CAKE

8 T.	Non-dairy margarine
3/4 c.	Sucanat
1	Lemon–its juice and its rind, grated
1	N'egg
1 c.	Unbleached white flour
1 1/2 tsp.	Baking powder

Oil and flour a square cake pan. Heat margarine and 1/2 cup of the Sucanat over low heat until the margarine is melted. Take off the heat and stir in the lemon rind. Beat the n'egg into the Sucanat mixture. Fold in the flour and baking powder and turn the mixture into the pan. Bake at 350° about 30 minutes or until it is just firm to the touch. Warm the lemon juice and 1/4 c. of Sucanat and mix together. Prick the cake all over with a fork or toothpick, and spoon the syrup over it. Leave in the pan to cool.

VARIATION: Use a small orange–juice and rind–instead of lemon.

MEXICAN FRUITCAKE

2 c.	Unbleached white flour
2 c.	Sucanat
1	20-oz. can of unsweetened crushed pineapple with the juice
2	N'eggs
2 1/2 tsp.	Baking soda
2/3 c.	Shredded coconut
2/3 c.	Pecans, coarsely chopped

Mix all together. Put in an oiled 9x13 pan (or in two 8x8 pans). Bake at 350° for 40 minutes (if in the two pans–for 30 minutes). Top with "whipped cream."

MOLASSES CAKE

3/4 c.	Barbados Molasses
2 T.	Non-dairy margarine

1 1/2 c.	Unbleached white flour
Pinch	Sea salt
1/2 tsp.	Allspice, ground
1/4 tsp.	Nutmeg, ground
1/4 tsp.	Cinnamon, ground
1	N'egg
3/4 tsp.	Baking soda
3 T.	Cashew Milk

Heat the molasses and margarine together until the margarine has melted. Remove from heat and beat in the flour, salt, spices, and n'egg. Blend the baking soda and "milk" together and stir into mixture. Put in an oiled cake pan. Bake at 350° for 25 to 30 minutes, or until golden brown and firm to the touch. Cool slightly before turning out onto a wire rack.

ORANGE GINGERCAKE

2 c.	Unbleached white flour
1 1/2 tsp.	Ginger, ground
1 1/2 tsp.	Baking powder
1/2 tsp.	Baking soda
1/2 tsp.	Sea salt
1 1/3 c.	Sucanat
2 T.	Barbados molasses
6 T.	Non-dairy margarine
4 T.	Cashew Milk
1	N'egg
1	Orange–grated rind
2 T.	Orange juice

Oil and flour a cake pan. Put the flour, ginger, baking powder, baking soda, and salt in a mixing bowl. Heat together the Sucanat, molasses, and margarine until the margarine is melted. Combine all ingredients, beat well, and pour into the pan. Bake at 325° about 1/2 hour, or until just firm to the touch. Cool in the pan. Cut into squares.

PINEAPPLE UPSIDE-DOWN CAKE

This truly bears repeating!

2 T.	Non-dairy margarine
1 c.	Sucanat
2 1/2 c.	Crushed pineapple, drained well
1 1/2 c.	Unbleached white flour
2 tsp.	Baking powder
1/2 tsp.	Salt
3/4 c.	Sucanat
1	N'egg
1/2 c.	Water
1/2 c.	Non-dairy margarine

Melt the 2 tablespoons of margarine. Add the 1 cup of Sucanat and mix well. Put this in the bottom of a cake pan. Cover this with the pineapple and set aside. Sift the flour, baking powder, salt, and 3/4 cup of Sucanat together. Mix the n'egg, water and 1/2 cup of margarine together. Mix this into the flour mixture well until it is smooth. Spread this over the pineapple. Bake at 400° for about 35 minutes until brown and crusty. Let cool for 30 minutes and then turn out of the pan, fruit side up, onto a serving tray or platter.

VARIATION: At the beginning mix in 1 cup of pecan pieces with the margarine and Sucanat.

SHORTCAKE

2 1/3 c.	Biscuit Mix
1/2 c.	Cashew Milk or water
3 T.	Sucanat
3 T.	Non-dairy margarine, melted

Mix all together until a soft dough forms. Spread in an ungreased pan. Bake at 425° for 15 to 20 minutes until golden brown. Cool for 10 minutes, cut into pieces, and split each horizontally.

UNCOOKED FRUIT CAKE

1 c.	Raisins, ground
1 c.	Dates, chopped
2 c.	Dried fruit (any kind), chopped
3/4 c.	Water
1 c.	Fruit juice or nectar
1 c.	Bread crumbs
1 c.	Sunflower seeds, or other nuts broken small

Soak the dried fruits in the water and fruit juice for 2 hours. Add the crumbs and seeds, pack into an oiled mold and set for one or more days in the refrigerator. Unmold, slice, and serve.

VANILLA CAKE-1

1 3/4 c.	Unbleached white flour
1 tsp.	Baking powder
1/2 tsp.	Sea salt
3/4 c.	Sucanat
1/3 c.	Non-dairy margarine, melted
2/3 c.	Water
2 tsp.	Vanilla
1 T.	Wine vinegar

Sift the dry ingredients in a mixing bowl. Whip together the liquid ingredients and pour them into the dry. Stir with a wooden spoon until smooth, with no lumps remaining. Pour the batter into an oiled cake pan or muffin tin (for cupcakes). Bake at 375° for 30 to 40 minutes.

VANILLA CAKE-2

3 1/2 c.	Unbleached white flour
2 c.	Sucanat
1 tsp.	Sea salt
2 tsp.	Baking soda
2 T.	White vinegar
4 tsp.	Vanilla
2 c.	Water
3/4 c.	Corn oil

Sift the dry ingredients together. Add the vinegar, vanilla, water, and oil. Bake at 350° for 50 minutes, or until a toothpick inserted comes out "clean."

VELVET CRUMB CAKE

1 1/2 c.	Biscuit Mix
1/2 c.	Sucanat
1	N'egg
1/2 c.	Cashew milk or water
2 T.	Non-dairy margarine
1 tsp.	Vanilla
1/2 c.	Flaked coconut
1/3 c.	Powdered Sucanat (packed in well)
1/4 c.	Chopped nuts
3 T.	Non-dairy margarine, softened
2 T.	Cashew Milk or water

Beat the first six ingredients together, at low speed, stirring constantly, for 30 seconds, then beat at medium speed, scraping the bowl occasionally, for 4 minutes. Pour into a greased and floured baking pan and bake at 350° for 30 to 35 minutes until a wooden pick inserted in center comes out clean. Cool slightly and spread with topping made by combining the rest of the ingredients. Broil 3 inches from the heat for 3 minutes until the topping is golden brown.

The Ladies Club of Bruning, Nebraska get a taste of vegetarian "Swiss steak" at the Monastery.

Cookies

APPLE CAKES

A perfect soft cookie-cake.

2 c.	Unbleached white flour
Pinch	Sea salt
1/2 tsp.	Cinnamon, ground
1 tsp.	Baking powder
3/4 c.	Non-dairy margarine
2	Apples, peeled, cored, and diced
1 c.	Sucanat
1	N'egg

In a bowl combine flour, salt, cinnamon, and baking powder. Rub in the margarine until the mixture resembles fine crumbs. Add remaining ingredients and combine well together. Place heaped spoonfuls, on a lightly oiled baking sheet and bake at 375° for 20 to 25 minutes or until golden brown. Cool slightly before transferring to a wire rack.

CAROB CHIP COOKIES

Now THIS has enough chips to satisfy!

1/2 c.	Non-dairy margarine
3/4 c.	Sucanat
1	N'egg
1 tsp.	Vanilla
1 c.	Unbleached white flour
1/2 tsp.	Baking soda
1/4 tsp.	Sea salt
1 1/2 c.	Carob chips

Let margarine stand at room temperature until soft. In a bowl, cream together the softened margarine, Sucanat, n'egg, and vanilla. In a separate bowl stir the flour, baking soda and salt together. Add to creamed mixture and stir well. Stir in carob chips. Drop from a teaspoon 2 inches apart onto a greased cookie sheet. Bake at 375° for 10 to 12 minutes, or until golden brown.

Cookies

COCONUT COOKIES

These are excellent for those who do not like overly sweet goodies.
If Red Riding Hood had some of these in her basket the wolf might have taken them and been satisfied!

1/2 c.	Non-dairy margarine
1/2 c.	Corn oil
1/3 c.	Water
3/4 c.	Sucanat
1/4 tsp.	Sea salt
1/2 tsp.	Vanilla
2/3 c.	Coconut
1 tsp.	Baking powder
1 T.	Cornstarch
2 c.	Unbleached white flour

Whip together the margarine, oil, water and Sucanat until creamy. Beat in the salt, vanilla and coconut. Mix the baking powder, corn starch, and flour and add to the creamed mixture to make a smooth drop batter. Drop the batter by heaping teaspoonfuls on to an oiled baking sheet. Bake at 350° for 10 to 12 minutes, until set. Remove immediately from the sheet and cool on a rack.

COLOSSAL COOKIES

The name says it all!

2/3 c.	Non-dairy margarine
5 c.	Sucanat
2/3 c.	Tofu Mayonnaise, Cashew Mayonnaise, or Miraculous Whip
1 1/2 tsp.	Vanilla
2 1/2 c.	Chunky peanut butter
7 1/2 c.	Rolled oats
1 1/4 c.	Carob chips
1 T.	Baking soda

Cream the margarine and Sucanat. Add "mayonnaise" and vanilla. Add rest of ingredients. Drop by 2 tablespoonfuls on an oiled baking sheet. Bake at 375° in the middle of the oven until golden brown.

CRUNCHIES

8 T.	Non-dairy margarine
2/3 c.	Sucanat
1 1/2 c.	Unbleached white flour
1 3/4 tsp.	Baking powder
1/2 c.	Oatmeal
2 T.	Currants
1 T.	Barbados molasses
1/2 tsp.	Allspice, ground

Melt the margarine in a saucepan. Remove from heat and stir in all the ingredients until evenly blended. Roll mixture into balls about the size of a walnut. Place well apart on a lightly greased baking sheet. Bake at 350° 12 to 15 minutes. Allow to cool slightly on the baking sheet before transferring to a wire rack.

FIG BARS

FILLING:

2 c.	Dried figs
2 tsp.	Lemon peel, grated
Pinch	Sea salt
1 1/2 c.	Apple juice or cider

CRUST:

1/2 c.	Non-dairy margarine
2/3 c.	Sucanat
1 c.	Unbleached white flour
1 c.	Rolled oats
1 tsp.	Baking powder
1/4 tsp.	Sea salt

Bring figs, lemon peel, salt, and juice (or cider) to a boil. Simmer, covered, about 15 minutes, until the figs are fairly tender. Mash figs thoroughly with a potato masher. If necessary, simmer 10 more minutes and mash again until the mixture is smooth.

In a mixing bowl, combine the margarine and Sucanat. Add the flour, oats, baking powder, and salt, and mix well. Crust should be crumbly. Press half the crust in the bottom of an 8-inch square baking pan. Spread the fig mixture evenly over it. Press the remaining crust mixture evenly on top. Bake for 40 minutes or until the topping is lightly browned.

VARIATION: Use other kinds of dried fruit.

FROSTED APPLE-DATE BITS

COOKIES:

3/4 c.	Non-dairy margarine
1 c.	Sucanat
1 tsp.	Vanilla
2/3 c.	Cashew Milk
2 c.	Unbleached white flour
1/2 tsp.	Baking soda
1/2 tsp.	Sea salt
1 tsp.	Cinnamon
1/4 tsp.	Nutmeg
1 c.	Apples, very finely chopped
1 c.	Dates, finely chopped

In a large bowl, cream together margarine and Sucanat. Add vanilla and "milk" and mix well. Separately, mix the flour, baking soda, salt and spices. Add flour mixture to creamed mixture. Stir until well blended. Stir in chopped apples and dates. Drop by large tablespoonfuls onto greased cookie sheet. Bake at 375° for 8 to 10 minutes or until done. Cool.

FROSTING:

2 T.	Non-dairy margarine
1/4 c.	Water

1 tsp.	Cinnamon
1 1/2 c.	Powdered Sucanat

Heat together the margarine and water over low heat until the margarine melts. Transfer to a mixing bowl. Add cinnamon and Sucanat. Blend well. Let set until thickened, then spread on cooled cookies.

FRUIT BARS

Truly elegant.

3 T.	Corn oil
1 T.	Barbados molasses
2/3 c.	Sucanat
3/4 c.	Dates, chopped, or raisins
1	N'egg
2 tsp.	Vanilla
1 1/2 c.	Unbleached white flour
1/4 tsp.	Sea salt
1/2 tsp.	Baking powder
1/3 c.	Water

Beat together the first 8 ingredients. Stir in the baking powder and water. Beat well, then pour into a greased and floured cake pan. Bake at 350° for 25 to 30 minutes, or until just firm to the touch. Cut into bars while still warm.

GINGER SNAPS

Yes, they do!

3/4 c.	Non-dairy margarine
1 1/2 c.	Sucanat
1/4 c.	Barbados molasses
1	N'egg
2 1/4 c.	Unbleached white flour, sifted
2 tsp.	Baking soda
1/2 tsp.	Sea salt
1 tsp.	Ginger
1 tsp.	Cinnamon
1/2 tsp.	Cloves

Cream together the margarine, Sucanat, molasses, and n'egg till light and fluffy. Sift together the other ingredients and stir into the molasses mixture till blended. Form in small balls. Roll in Powdered Sucanat and place 2 inches apart on an oiled cookie sheet. Bake at 375° for about 10 minutes. Remove from the pan immediately. Makes about 5 dozen cookies.

GINGERNUTS

If you've read about these in Jane Eyre*–here they are. And if you haven't, cook a batch and read the book as you eat them!*

5 T.	Non-dairy margarine
1 1/2 c.	Unbleached white flour
1 3/4 tsp.	Baking powder

1/3 c.	Sucanat
4 T.	Barbados molasses
3/4 tsp.	Baking soda
2 tsp.	Ginger, ground

Rub margarine into flour and baking powder until mixture resembles fine crumbs. Stir in Sucanat. Warm molasses in a saucepan and stir in baking soda and ginger. Add ginger mixture to dry ingredients, and knead well to form a soft dough. Roll mixture into balls about the size of a walnut. Place well apart on oiled baking sheets and flatten slightly. Bake at 350° about 15 minutes. Allow to cool slightly on the baking sheet before transferring to a wire rack.

MAPLE NUT CHEWS

These have real style and rich flavor.

1/2 c.	Raisins
	Apple juice
1/3 c.	Non-dairy margarine
1/2 c.	Sucanat
1/2 tsp.	Maple flavoring
1	N'egg
1/2 c.	Unbleached white flour, sifted
1/4 tsp.	Sea salt
1/4 tsp.	Baking powder
1/2 c.	Pecans or walnuts, chopped

In a small saucepan, put the raisins and cover them with apple juice. Bring to a boil, turn off the heat, and let the raisins sit for 10 minutes. Drain the raisins and reserve the apple juice. In a saucepan, melt margarine and Sucanat, then cool slightly. Beat in the maple flavoring and n'egg. Sift flour, salt, and baking powder. Stir in the margarine mixture and 2 tablspoons of the reserved apple juice. Stir in the raisins and nuts. Spread 1/2 to 3/4-inch thick in a greased pan. Bake at 350° for 25 to 30 minutes. Cool slightly and cut in bars. (The flavor is markedly better the next day.)

MOLASSES COOKIES–1

A favorite cookie, one to which we often turn whenever the cookie hunger strikes.

3/4 c.	Non-dairy margarine
1 c.	Sucanat
1	N'egg
1/4 c.	Barbados molasses
2 1/4 c.	Unbleached white flour
2 tsp.	Baking soda
1/4 tsp.	Sea salt
1 tsp.	Ginger, ground
1 tsp.	Cinnamon, ground
1/2 tsp.	Cloves, ground
1/4 c.	Powdered Sucanat for rolling

Cream together the margarine and Sucanat. Add n'egg and molasses and mix well. Separately combine the flour, baking soda, salt and spices. Add flour mixture to creamed ingredients and blend well. Form dough into small or medium balls. Roll in Powdered Sucanat and place 2 inches apart on a greased cookie sheet. Bake at 375° for 6 to 8 minutes.

MOLASSES COOKIES-2

6 c.	Unbleached white flour
3/4 c.	Sucanat
1 1/2 tsp.	Sea salt
4 1/2 tsp.	Baking powder
3/4 tsp.	Baking soda
2 1/4 c.	Barbados molasses
1 1/2 tsp.	Wine vinegar
1 c.	Corn oil

Sift the dry ingredients together. Blend the liquid ingredients. Slowly add the dry into the wet ingredients while mixing with an electric hand mixer. Spoon out onto oiled cookie sheets. Bake at 350° for 10 minutes.

MOLASSES COOKIES-3

1 1/4 c.	Sucanat
1/4 c.	Water
1 tsp.	White vinegar
1 c.	Non-dairy margarine
1 3/4 c.	Barbados molasses
3 c.	Unbleached white flour
2 tsp.	Ginger
2 tsp.	Cinnamon
1 tsp.	Salt
1 T.	Baking powder
1/2 tsp.	Baking soda

Blend Sucanat, water, vinegar, margarine and molasses together. Sift together all remaining ingredients. Add blended and sifted ingredients, and mix together well. Roll into balls, each about 2 tablespoons. Place in greased cookie sheet. Bake at 350° for about 10 minutes.

OATMEAL CHEWIES

6 c.	Rolled oats
2 c.	Unbleached white flour
4 tsp.	Soy flour
1 tsp.	Baking soda
1/2 tsp.	Sea salt
2 dashes	Cinnamon
2/3 c.	Corn oil
2/3 c.	Water
2 c.	Barbados molasses
2 tsp.	Vanilla
1 c.	Raisins

Sift the dry ingredients together. Add rest of ingredients and mix together. Place on an oiled cookie sheet –2 tablespoons per cookie. Bake at 375° until light brown on the bottom.

OATMEAL-RAISIN COOKIES

If you missed these in childhood, then make up for it by eating plenty throughout your adulthood!

3/4 c. Non-dairy margarine
3/4 c. Sucanat
1/4 c. Barbados molasses
2 tsp. Vanilla
1 1/2 c. Unbleached white flour
1 tsp. Baking soda
1 1/2 c. Rolled oats
1 c. Raisins

Cream together the margarine, Sucanat, and molasses. Stir in vanilla. Separately, combine the flour and baking soda. Combine flour mixture and creamed mixture and blend thoroughly. Add oats and raisins and mix well. Drop by large spoonfuls unto greased cookie sheet. Bake at 375° for 10 to 12 minutes or until done.

PEANUT BUTTER COOKIES–1

I think that peanut butter cookies–not apple pie–have become the standard of Americanism! And these can set the standard!

1 1/4 c. Unbleached white flour
3/4 tsp. Baking soda
1/4 tsp. Sea salt
1/2 c. Non-dairy margarine
1 c. Sucanat
1/2 c. Peanut butter
1 N'egg
1/2 tsp. Vanilla
1/2 tsp. Water
Powdered Sucanat

Combine the flour, soda, and salt. Separately combine the margarine and Sucanat. Combine everything and mix thoroughly, adding more water if necessary to get a moist–but not sticky–consistency. Shape in 1-inch balls. Roll in Powdered Sucanat and place on a cookie sheet. Press on the tops of the balls in a crisscross pattern with a fork. Bake at 375° for 15 minutes.

PEANUT BUTTER COOKIES–2

These are not gourmet food, but although you CAN eat just one, you cannot eat just two or three!

1 N'egg
1 c. Sucanat
1 c. Smooth peanut butter

Mix all together. Scoop out level tablespoonfuls and roll into balls. Put on an unoiled baking sheet and flatten with a fork. Bake at 350° for 18 minutes. Cool on a wire rack.

BUTTERSCOTCH SHORTBREAD

1 c. Non-dairy margarine

1/2 c.	Sucanat
1/4 c.	Barbados molasses
2 1/4 c.	Unbleached white flour
3/4 tsp.	Sea salt

Beat the margarine, Sucanat and molasses together. Mix all ingredients together well. Roll out 1/4-inch thick. Cut into rounds or shapes. Bake on an ungreased baking sheet at 300° for 20 to 25 minutes.

CANADIAN SHORTBREAD

1 c.	Non-dairy margarine
1/2 c.	Sucanat
1 tsp.	Vanilla
1 c.	Unbleached white flour
1/2 tsp.	Baking soda
2 c.	Rolled oats

Beat the margarine, Sucanat and vanilla until fluffy. Combine the flour, baking soda and oats. Add to margarine mixture and mix well. Chill an hour or more (or freeze for later use). Roll out to 1/4-inch thick. Cut into rounds. Bake on an ungreased baking sheet at 350° for 10 to 12 minutes.

VARIATION: Form dough into 1 1/2-inch balls and flatten them rather than roll out and cut out rounds.

MONASTERY SHORTBREAD

We serve this to every one of our visitors.
Many have asked for the recipe but we have kept it as a trade secret. Now I give it to you!

3 c.	Unbleached white flour
1/4 tsp.	Sea salt
3/4 c.	Non-dairy margarine
1/2 c.	Genuine maple syrup
1 tsp.	Vanilla

Combine the flour and salt. Beat the margarine, syrup, and vanilla until smooth. Mix this into the flour, using your hands if necessary, until the dough is uniform and holds together. Pat into an oiled 9x13 pan. Bake at 350° 8 to 12 minutes until the edges are lightly browned. While still warm, cut into 2-inch squares. Cool completely in the pan and then remove.

SPICY HERMITS

Not quickly forgotten!

1/2 c.	Non-dairy margarine
1 1/2 c.	Sucanat
1/4 c.	Barbados molasses
1	N'egg
1 1/2 c.	Unbleached white flour
1 T.	Instant coffee powder
1/2 tsp.	Baking soda
1/2 tsp.	Cinnamon
1/4 tsp.	Sea salt

1/4 tsp. Nutmeg
1/4 tsp. Cloves
3/4 c. Raisins
1/2 c. Walnuts, broken

Cream the margarine, Sucanat, molasses, and n'egg together. Sift the dry ingredients together and add to the creamed mixture. Stir in the raisins and nuts. Drop from a teaspoon 2 inches apart on a lightly oiled cookie sheet. Bake at 375° for 10 minutes. Makes about 3 1/2 dozen cookies.

Father Philaret digs potatoes in the Monastery garden.

Pies

PIE CRUST

The secret of this is for the margarine and water to be as cold as possible.

6 c.	Unbleached white flour
1 T.	Sea salt
1 1/2 c.	Non-dairy margarine, cold, and cut into bits
1 c.	Ice water

Sift the flour and salt together. Add the margarine and stir with a fork until all is crumbly. Add the water slowly, kneading it at the same time until all holds together–then stop. Divide into balls. Roll out about 1/8-inch thick. Put in a pie pan or dish. Bake at 350° for 35 minutes.

APPLE PIE

4 c.	Apples
1 T.	Water
3 c.	Sucanat
2 T.	Barbados molasses
1/2	Lemon rind, grated
1/4 tsp.	Cinnamon
	Pie crust dough

Peel, core, and slice the apples. Put apples, water, Sucanat, molasses, lemon rind, and cinnamon in a saucepan. Simmer 10 minutes, stirring occasionally. Do not allow the apple to become mushy. Cool. Line a 9-inch pie pan with dough. Fill with the apples. Top with pie crust and seal edges well. Make a hole in the center of the top crust. Bake at 400° about 25 minutes, or until golden brown.

VARIATION: For a "Mincemeat" flavor, use ground cloves instead of cinnamon.

BANANA CREAM PIE

Luscious is the word for this!

4 c.	Cashew Milk
1 c.	Sucanat
1/2 c.	Coconut

1/2 c. Cornstarch
1/4 tsp. Sea salt
2 tsp. Vanilla
4 Ripe bananas
1 1/2 c. Soy Whipped Cream or Tofu Whipped Cream

Put the "milk," Sucanat, coconut, cornstarch, salt and vanilla in a saucepan and stir constantly while cooking until thick. Mash 2 bananas and add to mixture. DO NOT COOK. Slice the other bananas and add. Pour into a baked pie crust and chill until set. Top with whipped cream.

VARIATION: Use a graham cracker crust.

BERRY CREAM PIE

CRUST:

1 1/2 c. Graham cracker crumbs
2 T. Sucanat
1/4 c. Almonds, ground to a meal in a blender
1 tsp. Cinnamon
1/2 tsp. Ground ginger
3 T. Oil

Combine the cracker crumbs, Sucanat, almonds, cinnamon, and ginger in a medium-sized mixing bowl. Add the oil and mix well. Press the mixture on the bottom and sides of an 8 or 9-inch pie pan. Bake at 375° for 10 minutes. Cool before filling.

GLAZE:

1 c. Apple juice or white grape juice
1 Heaping tablespoon of agar flakes
OR
1 1/2 T. Arrowroot powder dissolved in 1 1/2 tablespoons of cold water

Pour the juice into a small saucepan and bring it to a simmer. IF USING AGAR: sprinkle the flakes over the juice without stirring and simmer gently 3 to 5 minutes, stirring if necessary to completely dissolve the agar. IF USING ARROWROOT: add the dissolved powder to the simmering juice while stirring briskly. Continue stirring until the mixture thickens–1 to 2 minutes. Cool to lukewarm before using.

FILLING:

1 recipe Vanilla Pudding
2 c. Blueberries
1 1/2 c. Peaches or strawberries, sliced

Prepare the vanilla pudding and allow it to cool to lukewarm. Pour it into the prebaked shell. Cover with 1 1/2 cups of the blueberries. Neatly arrange the sliced peaches or strawberries on top. Add the remaining 1/2 cup of blueberries. Spoon the glaze over the berries.

BLUEBERRY COBBLER

2 c. Fresh or canned blueberries
1 1/2 c. Sucanat

1 c.	Unbleached white flour
1 1/2 tsp.	Baking powder
1/4 tsp.	Salt
1	N'egg
1 c.	Cashew Milk
2 T.	Non-dairy margarine, melted

Place the berries in a buttered 9x9-inch baking pan. Sprinkle a little less than half the Sucanat over them evenly. In a bowl, mix together the flour, baking powder and salt. Mix the rest of the Sucanat and the n'egg and stir it into the flour. Slowly add the "milk." Then add the melted margarine. Stir vigorously until it is smoothly blended. Pour this batter evenly over the berries. Bake at 400° for 30 to 35 minutes, or until the batter is golden brown.

BLUEBERRY PIE FILLING

1 3/4 c.	Canned blueberries
1/3 c.	Sucanat
1/4 c. & 2 T.	Unbleached white flour
3/4 tsp.	Sea salt
3/4 tsp.	Cinnamon
1/4 c. & 2 T.	Non-dairy margarine

Drain berries and save liquid. Combine Sucanat, flour, salt, and cinnamon, and stir into the liquid saved from the berries. Heat, stirring constantly, until thick and smooth. Add margarine and berries.

CHERRY PIE

1 1/3 c.	Liquid from canned cherries, or water if they are fresh
1/2 c.	Cornstarch
1 1/3 c.	Sucanat
1/4 tsp.	Sea salt
4 c.	Cherries, pitted (if canned, save liquid and use in recipe)
2 T.	Non-dairy margarine

Mix some of the liquid with the cornstarch. Heat rest of liquid to boiling. Add cornstarch mixture, stirring with a wire whip. Cook until thick and clear. Stir in the Sucanat and salt. Bring to a boil, stirring. Remove from heat. Add cherries, mixing gently. Cool thoroughly. Put in unbaked pie shell. Dot the top with the margarine and put on the top crust, cutting ventilation slits in it. Bake at 425° for 1 hour or until well browned.

FRUIT PIE–1

4 c.	Fruit
1 1/2 c.	Sucanat
3 T.	Cornstarch
1/8 tsp.	Sea salt
1/3 c.	Water for blending–only if needed
2 T.	Lemon juice (*only* if fruit is not naturally tart)
1	Baked pie crust

Chop 1 cup of the fruit–not too fine. Blend the rest of the fruit with the Sucanat, corn starch, salt and water (if needed). Boil until thickened. Add the lemon juice, if needed. Cool slightly and mix in the whole fruit. Pour into the baked pie crust and let cool.

FRUIT PIE–2

4 c.	Fruit
1 1/2 c.	Sucanat
3 T.	Cornstarch
1/8 tsp.	Sea salt
1/3 c.	Water for blender, only if needed
2 T.	Lemon juice (ONLY if fruit is not naturally tart)

Set aside 3 cups of fruit . Blend 1 cup of the fruit with the Sucanat, cornstarch, salt and water (if needed). Add the 3 cups of whole fruit to mixture. Boil until thickened. Add the lemon juice, if needed. Pour into an unbaked pie crust. Cover with top crust that has slits in it to let out the steam. Bake at 400° about 30 minutes until brown.

GRAHAM CRACKER CRUST

1 1/4 c.	Graham crackers, ground
1/4 c.	Sucanat
1/4 c.	Non-dairy margarine
Pinch	Cinnamon
Pinch	Nutmeg

Combine all ingredients and press into a pie pan and bake at 375° for 6 to 8 minutes or until browned.

LEMON CUSTARD PIE

1	Lemon, quartered, seeds removed
1/2 c.	Water
2 c.	Orange juice
1 T.	Oil
1 1/4 c.	Sucanat
1/4 c.	Corn starch

Place the lemon in a blender–peel and all–with all the other ingredients and blend until it is finely ground. Place in a saucepan and bring to a boil. Simmer about 2 minutes, stirring constantly. Pour into a baked pie shell and chill.

VARIATION: Use 3 oranges, peeled and with seeds removed, instead of the orange juice. They should be blended until fine with the lemon.

PEACH PIE

4 c.	Peaches, sliced
1 c.	Sucanat
2 T.	Unbleached white flour
1/8 tsp.	Cinnamon
1/8 tsp.	Sea salt
2 T.	Non-dairy margarine

Combine the ingredients except for the margarine. Put in unbaked pie shell. Dot the top with the margarine and put on the top crust, cutting ventilation slits in it. Bake at 425° for 1 hour or until well browned.

PECAN PIE

How I used to yearn for pecan pie–but since eggs seemed a necessary ingredient I had to keep on yearning! But now I can have all I want–and so can you!

1/4 c. Non-dairy margarine, melted
1/4 c. Cornstarch or arrowroot
2 c. Cashew milk
1/2 c. Genuine maple syrup
1/2 c. Sucanat
2 tsp. Vanilla
1 c. Chopped pecans, toasted in 4 teaspoons of margarine
1/2 c. Pecan halves, toasted in 2 teaspoons of margarine
1 10-inch baked pie shell

Combine the margarine, cornstarch (or arrowroot), "milk," syrup, Sucanat, and vanilla in a blender and blend until smooth. Cook in a saucepan until thickened, stirring constantly–5 minutes. Stir in the chopped pecans. Pour into the pie shell and top with the pecan halves. Let cool.

PINEAPPLE PIE

2 c. Crushed, unsweetened pineapple
1/3 c. Cornstarch
1 tsp. Lemon or orange peel, grated
3/4 c. Sucanat
1/8 tsp. Salt

Drain off the pineapple juice and mix the cornstarch into it. Combine all the ingredients and cook until thick. Pour into a baked pie crust.

SHOOFLY PIE

1 c. Unbleached white flour
3/4 c. Sucanat
1 tsp. Cinnamon
1/4 tsp. Ginger, powdered
1/4 tsp. Cloves, ground
1/4 tsp. Sea salt
3 T. Non-dairy margarine, softened and cut into bits
1/2 c. Barbados molasses
1/2 c. Boiling water
1/2 tsp. Baking soda
1 Pie crust

In a mixing bowl, combine flour, Sucanat, spices, and salt. With a fork, work the margarine into the dry ingredients until the mixture resembles a coarse meal. In another bowl, dissolve the molasses in the boiling water. Sprinkle in the baking soda and stir until it dissolves. Add about two-thirds of the crumb mixture and stir together until the crumbs are moistened, but the mixture need not be smooth. Pour into the pie crust and top with the remaining crumbs. Bake at 375° for 30 to 35 minutes, or until the crust and crumbs are golden and the filling is set. Serve warm or at room temperature.

STRAWBERRY PIE FILLING

4 c.	Frozen strawberries
1/2 c.	Sucanat
3 T.	Unbleached white flour
1/2 tsp.	Sea salt

Drain berries and save liquid. Combine the Sucanat, flour and salt, and stir into the liquid. Heat, stirring constantly, until thick and smooth. Add berries.

Above the Monastery chapel, the distinctive cross of the Orthodox Church of South India sits atop the traditional spire of a Hindu temple in profound symbolism.

Sweet Pastry

CINNAMON ROLLS

Why comment? Enjoy!

1 T. & 1 tsp.	Cinnamon
1/2 c.	Powdered Sucanat
1	Sweet Roll Dough recipe
1/2 c.	Non-dairy margarine, melted
1 c.	Raisins or thick fruit jam

Combine the cinnamon and Sucanat. Make the Sweet Roll Dough recipe. Roll out the dough into a 8x14-inch rectangle. Brush with melted margarine. Sprinkle with cinnamon-Sucanat, and then the raisins or jam. Roll up like a jelly roll, starting at the wide end. Cut into 1-inch "slices." Place close together in an oiled pan and brush with melted margarine. Cover and let rise in a warm place until one-half again as big. Bake at 375° for 20 to 30 minutes. Let cool, then spread Confectioner's Icing (2 times the recipe) over the rolls.

CONFECTIONER'S ICING

3 T.	Water
1 tsp.	Non-dairy margarine
1 2/3 c.	Powdered Sucanat
Pinch	Sea salt
1 tsp.	Vanilla

Bring the water to a boil and immediately add the margarine, stirring. When the margarine is melted, add the Sucanat, salt, and vanilla. Stir until the Sucanat is melted. Add more boiling water drop by drop if necessary to produce a smooth-spreading consistency. Beat 2 or 3 minutes until very creamy, keeping the sides scraped down. Drizzle immediately on slightly warm baked goods.

VARIATION: Add 1/3 cup of carob powder. Lemon or other fresh (strained) fruit juice may be substituted for the water and vanilla, if desired.

DOUGHNUT SQUARES

1/4 c.	Lukewarm water
1 pkg.	Dry yeast

1/4 c.	Sucanat
2 T.	Non-dairy margarine
1/2 tsp.	Sea salt
1/2 c.	Boiling water
1/2 c.	Cashew Cream
1	N'egg
4 1/2 c.	Unbleached white flour

Pour the water in a small bowl and sprinkle the yeast over it. Let it rest for 2 or 3 minutes, then mix well. Set in a warm, draft-free place for about 10 minutes, or until the yeast bubbles up and the mixture almost doubles in bulk.

Meanwhile combine the Sucanat, margarine and salt in another bowl. Pour in the boiling water and stir with a wooden spoon until the ingredients are thoroughly blended and the mixture has cooled to lukewarm. Stir in the "cream," yeast mixture and n'egg. Add 2 cups of the flour and, when it is completely incorporated, beat in up to 2 1/2 more cups of flour, 1/4 cup at a time. Add only enough flour to make the dough smooth and not sticky.

When the dough becomes too stiff to stir easily with the spoon, work in the additional flour with your fingers. Gather the dough into a ball, place it on a lightly floured surface and pat it into a rectangle about 1 inch thick. Dust a little flour over and under the dough and roll it out from the center to within an inch of the far edge (of the *dough*, that is, not the floured surface!). Lift the dough and turn it at right angles, then roll again from the center as before.

Repeat–lifting, turning, rolling–until the rectangle is about 1/4 inch thick and at least 25 inches long by 10 inches wide. (If the dough sticks to the surface, lift it with a wide metal spatula and sprinkle a little flour under it.)

With a pastry wheel or sharp knife, cut the dough into 10 5-inch squares. Immediately deep fry them in 350° oil, two or three at a time. Turn them over with a slotted spoon as they rise to the surface. Continue deep frying, turning frequently, for about 3 to 5 minutes, or until they are crisp and golden brown on all sides. Transfer to paper towel.

When lukewarm, glaze with Confectioner's Icing.

DOUGHNUTS

Make Sweet Roll Dough recipe. Roll out to 1/2-inch thickness. Let rest five minutes. Dip a 3-inch doughnut cutter into flour and cut out doughnuts. Let rise, uncovered, on floured pans in a warm place until light (about 45 minutes). Fry in deep fryer at 370° for about 3 minutes, turning once. (They should be golden brown on each side.) Drain on paper towels. Glaze with Confectioner's Icing.

FRUIT SCONES

2 c.	Unbleached white flour
3 tsp.	Baking powder
	Pinch of salt
6 T.	Non-dairy margarine
3 T.	Sucanat
1/2 c.	Golden seedless raisins, soaked in warm water 30 minutes and drained
1/2 c.	Cashew Milk

Put flour, baking powder, and salt in a bowl. Rub in the margarine until mixture resembles fine crumbs. Stir in Sucanat and raisins, then add enough "milk" for a soft, manageable dough. Knead gently on a lightly floured surface, then roll out about 3/4-inch thick. Cut out 3-inch rounds. Place fairly close together on a lightly greased baking sheet and bake at 425° for 10 to 15 minutes, or until golden brown. Cool on a wire rack. Best to eat these the day they are made.

JELLY-FILLED DOUGHNUTS

Make as above, except cut into 2 1/2-inch rounds. After draining on paper towels, inject fruit filling. Glaze with Confectioner's Icing.

RAISIN DUNKERS

A treasure! We have relied on these through the years!

2 1/3 c.	Unbleached white flour
1/4 c.	Sucanat
1 T.	Baking powder
1 tsp.	Sea salt
1/4 tsp.	Cinnamon
1/3 c.	Non-dairy margarine
3/4 c.	Cashew Milk
2/3 c.	Raisins, chopped
1 c.	Non-dairy margarine, melted
3/4 tsp.	Cinnamon
3/4 c.	Powdered Sucanat (see the Etc. section)

Sift the flour with the Sucanat, baking powder, salt and cinnamon. Cut in the 1/3 cup of margarine. Add the "milk" and raisins, stirring to a soft dough (add more cashew milk if necessary). Turn on to a lightly floured board. Roll out to 1/2-inch thickness. Cut into strips 2 inches wide and 5 inches long. Dip in the melted margarine and place on a baking sheet. Bake at 425° for about 15 minutes, until lightly browned. Mix the cinnamon and Sucanat together. Dip the dunker strips again in melted margarine and roll in the cinnamon-Sucanat. One times this recipe makes about one dozen dunkers.

RAISIN-ORANGE COFFEE CAKE

2 T.	Unbleached white flour
3 T.	Sucanat
1 T.	Non-dairy margarine, softened
1 c.	Unbleached white flour
2 tsp.	Baking powder
1/2 tsp.	Sea salt
1/4 c.	Non-dairy margarine
1/3 c.	Sucanat
2 tsp.	Grated orange peel
1/3 c.	Orange juice
1/4 c.	Cashew Milk
1/2 c.	Raisins

Mix together the first three ingredients until crumbly and set aside for topping. Stir together the 1 cup of flour, baking powder, and salt, and set aside. In a small mixing bowl beat the margarine and Sucanat until well combined. Add orange peel and beat well. Stir in orange juice, "milk," and raisins. Add flour mixture, stirring until just moistened. Spread batter evenly in a greased baking pan. Sprinkle with topping. Bake at 350° about 25 minutes or until it tests as done. Drizzle with a glaze made of Powdered Sucanat and hot water.

SWEET ROLL DOUGH

2/3 c.	Cashew Milk

Simply Heavenly!

Pinch	Sea salt
1/2 c.	Sucanat
1/2 c.	Non-dairy margarine
2 T.	Yeast
1/4 c.	Lukewarm water
1 tsp.	Sucanat
1	N'egg
4 1/2 c.	Unbleached white flour
1 tsp.	Lemon rind, grated
1/2 tsp.	Mace

Heat the "milk" with salt, 1/2 cup of Sucanat, and margarine until the margarine melts. Allow to cool to lukewarm. Combine yeast, water, and teaspoon of Sucanat, and allow to dissolve. Add the n'egg and the yeast mixture to the cashew milk solution. Combine half the flour with lemon rind and mace, then add the liquid, beating until smooth. Mix in the remaining flour. Let it stand for 10 minutes. Knead for 5 minutes on a lightly-floured board. Place dough in a lightly-greased bowl, turning once to bring the greased side up. Cover with a damp cloth and let rise in a warm place until double. Punch down, turn over, cover, and let rise until double again. Punch down, shape into 2 balls on a lightly floured surface. Cover with a bowl and let rest 10 minutes. Dough is then ready for use in doughnuts, cinnamon rolls, or other pastries.

The view from the southeast of the Monastery. The chapel is directly under the cross tower.

ETC.

BAKED SPRING ROLLS

2 oz.	Rice vermicelli
1/2 tsp.	Sesame oil
3/4 c.	Carrots, coarsely grated
1/2 c.	Green onions, thinly sliced
1/2 c.	Water chestnuts, cut into matchstick pieces
1/2 c.	Bamboo shoots, cut into matchstick pieces
1/2 c.	Snow peas, thinly sliced
1/2 c.	Savoy cabbage, very finely shredded
1/4 c.	Sunflower seeds
1 T.	Sesame seeds, toasted
1 tsp.	Low sodium soy sauce
4 tsp.	Corn oil
8	Sheets (8 1/2-inch diameter) of rice paper

Cook the rice vermicelli in boiling water for 3 minutes, and drain. Place in a large bowl and toss with the sesame oil. Add the vegetables, sunflower seeds, sesame seeds, and soy sauce. Toss again and set aside. Place the oil in a small dish. Dip 1 sheet of the rice paper into warm water for 15 to 30 seconds, until soft. Place on a dish towel. Brush the surface lightly with oil. Spoon 1/8 teaspoon of the filling onto the bottom half of the rice paper. Fold the bottom edge of the rice paper to just cover the filling. Brush the surface lightly with oil. Fold in the edges, then roll up, brushing the surfaces with oil as you roll. Repeat with the remaining rice paper sheets and filling. Place each roll seam-side down on a foil-lined cookie sheet. Bake at 450° on the lowest oven rack for 15 to 20 minutes, turning once, until lightly browned.

BREAD CRUMB TOPPING

2 c.	Bread crumbs
1 1/2 tsp.	Garlic cloves, minced
2 T.	Parsley, chopped
2 T.	Corn oil
	Black pepper
	Tomato purée or paste

Toss the crumbs, garlic, parsley, oil, and pepper together in a bowl. Mix in just enough tomato purée or paste to add a touch of color.

BREADING FOOD FOR FRYING

The breading material may be cracker crumbs, bread crumbs, corn meal, or any "crunchy" form of grain. They may be used plain or combined with seasonings. Roll the food to be breaded in the crumbs, then dip them in n'egg and again roll them in the crumbs. To avoid sticky hands, bread with one hand and dip with the other. If breading is done half an hour before the food is fried, the crumbs will have a better chance to adhere. It is important to cover the entire surface of the food with n'egg–or dip in "milk"–before the second "crumbing."

CAROB FUDGE

How sweet it really is!

3 T. Non-dairy margarine
1/2 c. Carob powder
1/4 c. Powdered Sucanat
2/3 c. Ground almonds
1 tsp. Vanilla extract
3 T. Almonds, ground or finely chopped

Blend margarine and carob powder thoroughly. Add the Sucanat, almonds, and vanilla, and mix thoroughly. Sprinkle ground almonds on a clean dry surface and shape the fudge into a roll, coating it with almonds. Cut into bite-size pieces. Keep in refrigerator until needed.

CINNAMON TOAST

Mix one part cinnamon with three parts of Powdered Sucanat. Sprinkle on buttered toast. Place toast slices in a moderate oven or under a broiler to crisp them.

VARIATION: Instead of 1 part cinnamon, use half nutmeg and half cinnamon.

COCONUT MILK

After breaking the shell and removing the meat, pare off the brown skin. Chop or break the meat into small chunks. Measure the meat and put it and an equal measure of hot (not boiling) water into a blender and blend at high speed for 1 minute. Stop the machine and scrape down the sides with a rubber spatula. Blend again until the coconut is reduced to a thick, fibrous liquid. Scrape the entire contents of the blender into a fine sieve lined with a double thickness of dampened cheesecloth and set over a deep bowl. With a wooden spoon, press down hard on the coconut to extract as much liquid as possible. Bring the ends of the cheesecloth together to enclose the pulp and wring the ends vigorously to squeeze out the remaining liquid. Discard the pulp.

DEEP-FRYING BATTER

This is excellent for frying gluten, but works for vegetables, too.

1 tsp. Basil, powdered
1 tsp. Black pepper
1/2 tsp. Garlic salt
3 c. Unbleached white flour
2 T. Baking powder
2-3 c. Club soda

Combine the basil, pepper, garlic salt, flour, and baking powder. Add the soda until you have a batter of the desired consistency. Dip whatever you wish to fry into the batter and then deep fry at 400°.

FRENCH TOAST

1 1/2 c.	Water
3 T.	Soy flour
1 T.	Cornstarch
1 T.	Sucanat
1/4 tsp.	Vanilla
Pinch	Sea salt
Pinch	Cinnamon
2 T.	Non-dairy margarine, melted
1/4 tsp.	Tumeric

Blend everything in a blender until perfectly combined and smooth. Heat together until it thickens into a "batter." Soak bread slices in the batter and then fry to golden brown on both sides.

FRIED "CHEESE" BALLS

1 c.	Biscuit Mix
1/3 c.	Water
1 1/2 c.	Yeast or Pimento Cheese
1/3 c.	Onions, chopped

Mix everything together, form into 1-inch balls, and fry in oil.

FRUIT JAM

3/4 c. & 2 T.	Cornstarch
6 c.	Sucanat
6 c.	Fruit, mashed well

Mix the cornstarch with the Sucanat, and add to the fruit. Cook for 20 minutes. Allow to cool, and can or refrigerate.

GARLIC BREAD

1/2 c.	Non-dairy margarine
1 T.	Garlic, put through a garlic press
1/4 c.	"Parmesan 'Cheese'"
1/8 tsp.	Black Pepper

Melt the margarine, add the garlic, and let it "steep" at very low heat for 2 minutes. Mix in the "cheese" and pepper, and stir well. Spread generously on bread and toast it in the oven.

GARLIC OLIVES

Oh, my, oh, my!

2/3 c.	Olive oil
1/3 c.	Lemon juice or vinegar

1 T. Garlic, minced
1 1/4 c. Ripe olives

Combine everythings and refrigerate overnight or at least for several hours. Use whenever ripe olives are called for. Improves with age.

GLUTEN DUMPLINGS

Unflavored gluten can often add a great deal to dishes that contain a lot of liquid for it will absorb the flavors of the vegetables and seasonings. When the dish is fully assembled or boiling, take the raw (uncooked) gluten, break off small 1/2-inch pieces, roll each between your thumb and fingers and drop them in. After dropping in 10 pieces, stir so the gluten pieces will not stick to one another.

HOT "CHEESE" AND CIDER DIP

Now this is really different!

1/2 c. Apple cider
1 c. Yeast or Pimento Cheese
1/2 tsp. Sea salt
1/8 tsp. Cayenne pepper
1/4 tsp. Parsley or chives, finely chopped
Pinch Garlic salt

Heat the cider to the boiling point, then reduce to a simmer. Stir the "cheese" gradually into the cider until all is well blended. Add the seasonings.

INSTANT TOMATO JUICE

1 c. Tomato paste
4 c. Water
1 tsp. Sea salt

Mix together thoroughly. You can put it through a blender, but will have to wait until the bubbles and froth subside.

NOTE: For a tomato juice cocktail, add pepper (or hot sauce), garlic powder, and a little lemon juice to this.

INSTANT TOMATO PURÉE

1 c. Tomato paste
1 c. Water
1 tsp. Sea salt

Mix together thoroughly. You can put it through a blender, but will have to wait until the bubbles and froth subside.

INSTANT TOMATO SAUCE

1 c. Tomato paste
2 c. Water
1 tsp. Sea salt

Mix together thoroughly. You can put it through a blender, but will have to wait until the bubbles and froth subside.

"MAPLE" SYRUP

2 c.	Sucanat
1 c.	Water
1/2 tsp.	Cream of tartar
1/2 tsp.	Maple flavoring

Boil the Sucanat, water, and cream of tartar for 3 minutes. Remove from heat and add maple flavoring.

MULLED CIDER

1 qt.	Cider
3	Whole cloves
3	Whole allspice
1	3-inch stick of cinnamon
1/4	Lemon, unpeeled, thinly sliced
1/4 c.	Sucanat

Boil together for 10 minutes. Strain and serve hot.

ORANGE-GRAPE JUICE

Equal parts of white grape juice and orange juice.

PANCAKE SYRUP–1

1 c.	Water
2 c.	Sucanat
1 1/2 tsp.	Maple flavor

Combine all ingredients, bring to a boil, and immediately take off the heat and set to cool.

PANCAKE SYRUP–2

1 c.	Barbados molasses
2 c.	Sucanat
1/2 c.	Water
1 1/2 tsp.	Maple flavor

Combine all ingredients, bring to a boil, and immediately take off the heat and set to cool.

PANCAKES-1

2 c.	Biscuit mix
1 c.	Cashew milk or water
2	N'eggs

Beat the ingredients until smooth and pour by scant 1/4 cupfuls onto a hot griddle (oiled if necessary). Cook until the edges are dry, then turn over and cook until golden brown.

PANCAKES-2

1 1/4 c.	Flour
2 T.	Sucanat
2 tsp.	Baking powder
1/2 tsp.	Sea salt
2 T.	Corn oil
1 1/4 c.	Water (or 1/2 cup of cashew milk plus 3/4 cup of water)

Combine the dry ingredients. Pour the liquids into a "well" in the center of the dry ingredients. Stir together until just blended–the batter will be lumpy. (Do not overmix.) Cook on oiled griddle or skillet.

PARTY "CHEESE" DIP

2 c.	Tofu Cream Cheese
1 c.	Pimento or Mozzarella "Cheese"
1 T.	Pimento, chopped
1 T.	Bell pepper, chopped
1 T.	Onion, chopped fine
1 T.	Lemon juice
4 tsp.	Lea & Perrins Steak Sauce
2 T.	Louisiana Hot Sauce
1/8 tsp.	Sea salt

Combine all and let sit for a while to develop flavor.

PECAN PATTIES

1 c.	Pecans, ground to a cornmeal-like consistency
1 c.	Rice, cooked
1 c.	Cashew milk
1 T.	Soy flour
1 tsp.	Sea salt
1 T.	Dried parsley flakes
1 c.	Bread crumbs
1 T.	Dried minced onion
1/4 tsp.	Garlic powder

Combine all ingredients and shape into patties. Place on an oiled cookie sheet. Brush the tops with corn oil. Bake at 350° until brown–about 30 minutes.

POWDERED SUCANAT

1/2 c.	Sucanat
2 T.	Cornstarch

Combine and powder at high speed in a blender.

SELF-RISING FLOUR

1 c.	Unbleached white flour with 2 tsp. taken out
1 1/2 tsp.	Baking powder
1/2 tsp.	Sea salt

Combine well.

"SHRIMP" DIP

Don't dilute the soup but use it direct from the can.

1 can	Campbell's Tomato Soup
1/2 c.	Catsup
4 tsp.	Louisiana Hot Sauce or 2 tsp. Tabasco
1/2 tsp.	Onion juice
1/4 tsp.	Garlic salt
1/2 tsp.	Celery, minced
Dash	Paprika
Dash	Cayenne pepper
2 T.	Non-dairy margarine

Combine everything except the margarine, and beat together well. Chill. Just before serving, blend in the margarine until the mixture becomes smooth.

SPICY TOMATO JUICE

7 c.	Tomato juice, made from fresh tomatoes
1 tsp.	Sea salt
1/8 tsp.	Cayenne pepper

Simmer together for 15 minutes. Cool and refrigerate.

SUNBURGERS

3 c.	Water
1/2 c.	Low sodium soy sauce
1	Onion, chopped, or 1/8 cup of dried onion flakes
1/8 tsp.	Garlic powder
1 tsp.	Thyme
1/4 tsp.	Liquid smoke
1/4 c.	Sunflower seeds
3 c.	Quick oats
1 T.	Corn oil

Put all the ingredients except the oats in a large saucepan and bring it to a boil. Add the oats slowly, stirring constantly and gently, until it is mixed. Turn the heat to low and simmer for a few minutes, being careful that the oats do not burn. Remove from heat, cover and set aside until the mixture is cool enough to handle. Form into patties about 1/2 inch thick and 3 1/2 inches in diameter. Bake at 350° on an oiled baking sheet for 20 minutes. Turn the patties over and bake for 20 more minutes.

VARIATION: Fry on a griddle.

UNCOOKED APPLESAUCE

This is a wonderful surprise! Having tried it, you will never want the canned goop!

8 c.	Granny Smith apples, peeled, cored, and quartered
2 T.	Lemon juice
1 c.	Sucanat

1/2 tsp. Cinnamon
1/8 tsp. Nutmeg

Purée the apples in a blender until just smooth. Add rest of ingredients, mix well, and chill.

VEGETARIAN DOG FOOD

This was formulated by a veterinarian for his dogs, and we have raised several healthy dogs using it as their basic food. However, you should obtain Dogs and Cats Go Vegetarian, *by Barbara Lynn Peden, for a full picture on vegetarian dogs and cats and their nutritional requirements.*

1 gal. Leftover vegetables, peels, ends, etc.
Water to cover
2 T. Baking yeast
4 c. Soy beans
6 c. Rolled oats

Save the peels, ends, etc., from vegetables when you prepare your food, and keep them refrigerated, UNCOOKED, until you have 1 gallon, or just put in what extra vegetables you may have to make up the amount. If need be, cut the vegetables into chunks. The night before you are going to make the dog food, put the soy beans in water and let them soak overnight. The next day grind them in either a food mill or a blender. (If there is any corn among the vegetables, that should be ground, as well.) When ready to cook, put the vegetables, soy beans and yeast in a large pot and cover with water. Bring to a boil and simmer/low boil for about 2 hours. Add the rolled oats and cook until they are done.

In monasteries, too, someone has to do the dishes!

Heavenly Simple!

Top Secrets From The Monastery Kitchen

Because of time limitations, we use the other recipes in this book only on Sundays and special days. The rest of the time we use those in this section which we developed specially for ease of preparation.

In cooking, as in music, genius often manifests through simplicity. That is true of these recipes. We literally use them every day, and never get tired of the results. Rather, we comment continually on how good they are. Vegetables that I do not care for any other way I enjoy prepared with the Basic Vegetables recipe.

In all these recipes the addition of gluten is an excellent variation.

If you are interested in trying our way of doing things, it is quite simple. At our noon meal we always have a salad and some type of dried beans cooked according to the Basic recipes given here. Sometimes we vary that with Lentil Pot or one of the Split Pea Soups found in the Soups section. For the evening meal we usually have two dishes of Basic Vegetables along with a "starch base" that we can mix them with–such as potatoes (baked or boiled), pasta, grains, or bread. Sometimes we have one Basic Vegetable and one Basic Gluten dish.

I have made no individual comments on these recipes because each one rates a string of superlatives.

BASIC VEGETABLES

2 c. Onion, chopped
1 T. Garlic, minced or sliced
1 T. Jalapeño peppers, minced or sliced
2 T. Corn oil
6 c. One or more vegetables, cut up if need be
1/2 tsp. Sea salt
1 tsp. Total of one or more herbs of choice, such as:
Basil
Oregano
Rosemary
Thyme
Savory
Bay leaf
Dill weed
Italian Seasoning
OR 1 tablespoon of curry powder
1/4 tsp. Cayenne pepper
1/2 tsp. Paprika
1 1/2 c. Beef-like or Chicken-like Broth

Sauté the onion, garlic, and jalapeños in the oil. Combine everything in a pot, bring to a boil, lower the heat, cover and cook gently until the vegetables are tender. Nutritional yeast may be stirred in at the end for added flavor and nutrition.

BASIC VEGETABLES–CAJUN STYLE

4 c. Vegetables, coarsely chopped
6 T. Corn oil
1/3 c. Unbleached white flour
2 c. Onion, chopped
1/2 c. Bell pepper, chopped
1 T. Garlic, crushed
1 1/2 c. Canned tomato sauce
1 1/2 c. Beef-like Broth
1 1/2 c. Tomato juice
3 1/2 c. Canned tomatoes, crushed and drained (use juice in the amount above)

1 T. Louisiana Hot Sauce
3 T. Lea & Perrins Steak Sauce
1/2 tsp. Cayenne pepper
1/2 tsp. Sea salt

Steam the chopped vegetables and set them aside. In a heavy saucepan or skillet combine the oil and flour and cook slowly over low heat, stirring almost constantly to prevent burning, until it turns dark brown. Add the onion and bell pepper and cook for 5 to 10 more minutes–until they become soft. Add the garlic, tomato sauce, broth, and tomato juice and cook, stirring constantly, until it becomes smooth and "sauce-like." Add the rest of the ingredients and cook for 20 to 30 minutes, until it thickens, adding extra liquid (juice or broth) if it becomes too dry.

BASIC "CREAMED" VEGETABLES

2 c. Onions, chopped
1 T. Jalapeños, chopped fine
2 tsp. Garlic, minced
3 T. Non-dairy margarine
4 c. Thick white sauce made with Chicken-like or Beef-like Broth
6 c. Vegetables–one kind or mixed–chopped if need be and steamed or boiled

Sauté the onions, jalapeños, and garlic in the margarine. Add to the white sauce and cook for 5 minutes. Add the sauce to the vegetables and cook 5 more minutes, adding more cashew milk if the mixture gets too thick. (Remember, this will thicken when it cools some, so it should be a little on the "loose" side when cooking.)

VARIATION: Add 1 1/2 cups of mushrooms, stemmed and chopped coarsely.

BASIC VEGETABLE SOUP–1

1/2 c. Onion, chopped
1 tsp. Garlic, minced or sliced
1 tsp. Jalapeño peppers, minced or sliced
3 T. Corn oil
6 c. One or more vegetables

1/2 tsp. Sea salt
1 tsp. Total of herbs of choice, such as:
Basil
Oregano
Rosemary
Thyme
Savory
Bay leaf
Dill weed
Italian Seasoning
OR 1 tablespoon of curry powder
1/4 tsp. Cayenne pepper
1/2 tsp. Paprika
4 c. Boiling water or Beef-like or Chicken-like Broth

Sauté the onion, garlic, and jalapeños in the oil. Combine all in a pot, bring to a boil, lower the heat, cover and cook gently until the vegetables are tender. Thicken with the Soup Thickener if desired. Nutritional yeast may be stirred in at the end for added flavor and nutrition. Pasta or rice–already cooked–can be added if desired. Tomato paste or sauce may be used if desired.

BASIC VEGETABLE SOUP–2

3/4 c. Onions, chopped
2 tsp. Garlic, minced
3 T. Corn oil
1 c. Cooked dried beans
3 c. Beef-like or Chicken-like Broth
2 c. Tomatoes, chopped
3 c. One or more of the following vegetables, chopped:
Potatoes
Bell peppers
Green beans
Lima Beans
Corn
Okra
Squash
Cabbage
Brussels sprouts

1/8 tsp. Cayenne pepper
1/2 tsp. Basil
1/4 tsp. Oregano
1 Bay leaf

Sauté the onions and garlic (also bell peppers, if used) in the oil. Combine with rest of ingredients and cook.

BASIC VEGETABLE SOUP–3

3/4 c. Onions, chopped
3 T. Corn oil
6 c. Vegetables, chopped if need be
3 c. Tomatoes, chopped
5 c. Beef-like Broth
1/8 tsp. Cayenne pepper

Sauté the onions in the oil. Combine ingredients and cook until the vegetables are done.

BASIC "CREAM OF" SOUP

1 1/2 c. Vegetable of choice, chopped or pureed
1/3 c. Onions, chopped
1 1/2 tsp. Garlic, minced
1 c. Beef-like or Chicken-like Broth
2 c. Medium White Sauce made with Beef-like or Chicken-like Broth
1/8 tsp. Black or white pepper

Cook the vegetables, onions, and garlic in the broth until tender. Stir in the White Sauce.

VARIATION: Sauté 2 tablespoons of curry powder with the onions.

BASIC DRIED BEANS–1

2 c. Cooked beans–pressure-cooked in 5 cups of water with 1 tsp. of sea salt
2 c. Flavoring Broth of choice, made with 1 tsp. less of salt
3 T. Onions, minced

1 tsp. Garlic, minced
1/8 tsp. Cayenne pepper

Combine all ingredients, including the bean cooking liquid, and bring to a boil–adding more flavoring broth if needed to make it "soupy." Simmer for 20 minutes, uncovered.

VARIATIONS: Add 2 cups of tomatoes (canned preferred). Add 1 teaspoon of liquid smoke.

BASIC DRIED BEANS–2

2 c. Pinto or pink beans, DRY
2 tsp. Sea salt
3/4 tsp. Crushed red pepper
1/2 c. Onions, chopped
2 tsp. Garlic, minced
2/3 c. Bacon, Ham, or Sausage Gluten, cubed, or Imitation bacon bits
3 T. Corn oil

Pressure cook the 2 cups of beans with the salt. Drain. Cover with water. Add rest of ingredients and bring to a boil. Simmer for 30 minutes.

BASIC DRIED BEAN SOUP

3 T. Onions, minced
1 tsp. Garlic, minced
4 1/2 tsp. Corn oil
2 c. Cooked dried beans, drained (keep liquid and use in cooking if needed)
Pinch Cayenne pepper
1 1/2 c. Beef-like Broth
1/2 tsp. Savory, whole, or 1/4 tsp. ground
1/4 tsp. Sea salt

Sauté the onions and garlic in the oil. Combine all ingredients, bring to a boil, and cook for 10 to 20 minutes, adding bean water or more broth if needed.

BASIC PASTA SAUCE

1 1/2 c.	Onion, chopped
1 1/2 c.	Mushrooms, thickly sliced
1 1/2 tsp.	Garlic, minced or sliced
1 1/2 tsp.	Jalapeño peppers, minced or sliced
3 T.	Corn oil
4 c.	Canned tomatoes with juice
1/2 tsp.	Sea salt
1/2 tsp.	Basil
1/4 tsp.	Oregano
1/4 tsp.	Fennel seed

Sauté the onion, mushrooms, garlic, and jalapeños in the oil. Combine all in a pot, bring to a boil, lower the heat, and simmer, uncovered, for 1 hour, adding more tomato juice if it gets too thick. Nutritional yeast may be stirred in at the end for added flavor and nutrition.

BASIC GLUTEN

6 c.	Flavored Gluten, cubed
2 c.	Onions, chopped
1 T.	Garlic, minced
1 T.	Jalapeños, minced
1 c.	Bell pepper
1/4 c.	Celery
3 T.	Corn oil
2 T.	Unbleached white flour
1/4 tsp.	Sea salt
3 c.	Flavoring Broth of type of gluten being used

Deep-fry the gluten and set aside. Sauté the onions, garlic, jalapeños, bell pepper, and celery in the corn oil. Stir in the flour and salt and cook for 1 minute, stirring constantly. Slowly add the broth, while stirring. Add the gluten and simmer for 15 minutes. Add more broth if this gets too dry.

BASIC GLUTEN–CAJUN STYLE

4 c.	Flavored gluten, cubed
6 T.	Corn oil
1/3 c.	Unbleached white flour
2 c.	Onion, chopped
1/2 c.	Bell pepper, chopped
1 T.	Garlic, crushed
1 1/2 c.	Canned tomato sauce
1 1/2 c.	Beef-like Broth
1 1/2 c.	Tomato juice
3 1/2 c.	Canned tomatoes, crushed and drained (use juice in the amount above)
1 T.	Louisiana Hot Sauce
3 T.	Lea & Perrins Steak Sauce
1/2 tsp.	Cayenne pepper
1/2 tsp.	Sea salt

Deep-fry the gluten and set aside. In a heavy saucepan or skillet combine the oil and flour and cook slowly over low heat, stirring almost constantly to prevent burning, until it turns dark brown. Add the onion and bell pepper and cook for 5 to 10 more minutes–until they become soft. Add the garlic, tomato sauce, broth, and tomato juice and cook, stirring constantly, until it becomes smooth and "sauce-like." Add the rest of the ingredients and cook for 20 to 30 minutes, until it thickens, adding extra liquid (juice or broth) if it becomes too dry.

INDEX

BEEF SUBSTITUTES AND DISHES
Beef Gluten 98
"Beef" and Mushroom Étoufée
"Beef" with Rice and Tomatoes 99
Chinese Pepper "Steak" 99
Company Pride Hash 99
Continental Stroganoff 100
Gluten Roast 100
Gluten Roast "Beef" 100
Goulash 100
Saucy "Steak" Skillet 101
Soy Grits "Beef" 101
"Steak" Étouffé 101
Stir-fry "Beef" 102
Swiss "Steak" 102
Tamale Pie 103
Tangy "Meatballs" 103
BREAD AND SUCH
Anadama Bread 42
Apple and Banana Bread 42
Apple Icing Bread 43
Baking Powder Biscuits 43
Biscuit Dumplings 43
Biscuit Mix 43
Biscuits 44
Breadsticks 44
"Buttered" Bread Crumbs 44
"Cheese" Bread 45
Corn Bread-1 45
Corn Bread-2 45
Corn Bread-3 45
Corn Chips 45
Corn Tortillas 46
Cranberry Bread 46
Drop Biscuits 47
Flat Bread 47
Flour Tortillas 47
French Bread 47
Fried Cornmeal Cakes 48
Garlic Bread 48
Garlic Croutons 48
Hamburger Buns 49
Herb Bread 49
Herb and Onion Bread 49
Hush Puppies 49
Oatcakes 49
One-Hour Whole Wheat Bread 50
Onion Bread 50
Pocket Bread 50
Pumpernickel Bread 51
Puris 51
Soy Bread 51
Sweet Muffins 52
Toast Points 52
White Bread 52
Whole Wheat Bread 53
Yeast Biscuits-1 53
Yeast Biscuits-2 53
CAKE
Carob Cake 297
Christmas Fruitcake 297
Cottage Pudding 298
Crazy Cake 298
Date-Nut Cake 298
Devon Apple Cake 299
Fruit Cake 299
Gingerbread 300
Lemon Cake 300
Mexican Fruitcake 300
Molasses Cake 300
Orange Gingercake 301
Pineapple Upside-Down Cake 301
Shortcake 302
Uncooked Fruit Cake 302
Vanilla Cake-1 302
Vanilla Cake-2 302

Index

Velvet Crumb Cake 303
CASSEROLES
Baked Curry 171
Broccoli and Corn Scallop 171
Broccoli and Potato Casserole with Chives and "Cheese" 172
Bread Dressing 172
Cabbage Un-Rolls Casserole 172
Carrot Roast 173
Cajun Eggplant 173
Cauliflower Au Gratin 174
"Cheese" and Potato Bake 174
"Cheese" Enchiladas-1 174
"Cheese" Enchiladas-2 175
"Cheese" Pie 175
Company Casserole 176
Corn and Spinach Casserole 176
Corn Bake 176
Corn Tamale Pie 177
Corn-Bean Pie 177
Creamed Broccoli 178
Creamed Cabbage Casserole 178
Creamed Potatoes with "Cheese" 178
Creamed Spinach, Mushroom, and Onions in "Cheese" Sauce 179
Creole Rice Casserole 179
Crunch-Top Potatoes 179
Eggplant and "Cheese" 180
Eggplant Casserole with Tomatoes, Garlic, and Rice 180
Eggplant Lasagne 180
Eggplant Parmesan 181
Fresh Corn and Tomato Casserole 181
Golden Vegetable Bake 182
Green Bean Casserole 182
Green Beans in Tomato Sauce 182
Green Beans Supreme-1 183
Green Beans Supreme-2 183
Green Chili Corn Casserole 183
"Ham" and Potato Casserole 184
Italian Eggplant Casserole 184
Layered Casserole 185
Left-Over Vegetables with "Cheese" 185
Lima Beans with "Cheese" 185
Mexican Lasagna 185
Mexican Lima Bean Casserole 186
Noodle Casserole with Zucchini, Tomatoes, and "Cheese" 186
Onion Tomato Sauce 187
Paella-Limas 187
Piffel 187
Cream of Piffel 188
"Pimento Cheese" Loaf 188
Polenta Casserole 188
Potatoes au Gratin 189
Potatoes Scalloped in Margarine 189
Rice Dressing 189
Rumbledethumps 189
Scalloped Broccoli 190
Scalloped Carrots and Potatoes 190
Scalloped Eggplant 190
Scalloped Peas and Squash 191
Scalloped Potatoes-1 191
Scalloped Potatoes-2 191
Scalloped Potatoes and Mushrooms 191
Shepherd's Pie-1 192
Shepherd's Pie-2 192
Soy Grits Casserole 192
Soy Grit Enchilada Casserole 193
Spicy Potatoes 193
Spinach and Herb Potato Casserole 194
Squash and Macaroni Bake 194
Squash Casserole with Tomatoes, "Cheese," and Rice 194
Squash Creole 195
Squash Tamale Bake 195
Tomato and Corn Scallop 196
Tomato Eggplant Bake 196
Tomato Rice with "Cheese" 196
Triple Layer Casserole 196
Vegetable Casserole with Tomatoes and Rice 197
Vegetable Crumble 197
Vegetables Parmesan-1 198
Vegetables Parmesan-2 198
Zucchini Casserole 199
Zucchini Casserole with Tomatoes, Cheese, and Rice 199
Zucchini Creole 199
Zucchini Parmigiana 200
COOKIES
Apple Cakes 304
Carob Chip Cookies 304
Coconut Cookies 305
Colossal Cookies 305
Crunchies 305
Fig Bars 306
Frosted Apple-Date Bits 306
Fruit Bars 307
Ginger Snaps 307
Gingernuts 307
Maple nut chews 308
Molasses Cookies-1 308
Molasses Cookies-2 309
Molasses Cookies-3 309
Oatmeal Chewies 309
Oatmeal-Raisin Cookies 310
Peanut Butter Cookies-1 310

Index

Peanut Butter Cookies-2 310
Butterscotch Shortbread 310
Canadian Shortbread 311
Monastery Shortbread 311
Spicy Hermits 311

CRACKERS
Crackers 77
"Cheese" Crackers 77
Coconut Crackers 78
Graham Crackers 78
Rye Crisps 78

DAIRY SUBSTITUTES
Almond Milk 79
Cashew Cream 79
Cashew Milk 79
Cashew Sour Cream 80
Mock Cheesecake 80
Mozzarella "Cheese" 80
Parmesan "Cheese"-1 81
Parmesan "Cheese"-2 81
Pimento "Cheese"-1 81
Pimento "Cheese"-2 82
Pizza "Cheese" 82
Soy Milk 83
Flavoring Soy Milk 83
Soy Whipped Cream 83
Tofu Buttermilk 83
Tofu Cottage Cheese 83
Tofu Cream Cheese-1 84
Tofu Cream Cheese-2 84
Tofu Ricotta Cheese 84
Tofu Sour Cream 84
Tofu Whipped Cream 84
Tofu Yogurt 84
Yeast "Cheese" 85

DESSERTS
Apple Crisp 288
Blueberry Cheeseless Cake 288
Carob Custard 289
Carob Pudding 289
Coconut Rice Pudding 289
Date and Apple Squares 290
Fruit Cocktail Bread Pudding 290
Fruit Shortcake 290
Fruit Squares 291
Lemon Cheeseless Cake 292
Lemon Cheeselesscake Deluxe 292
Lemon Custard 292
Maple Pecan Cheeseless Cake 293
Pineapple Pudding 293
Spiced Bread Pudding 293
Steamed Irish Raisin Pudding 294
Vanilla Pudding-1 294
Vanilla Pudding-2 294

DRIED BEANS AND LENTILS
Baked Beans-1 202
Baked Beans-2 202
Baked Lentils 202
Barbecue Baked Beans 203
Barbecue Beans 203
Bean Burgers 203
Bean Enchiladas 204
Bean Loaf 205
Bean Pot 205
Beans Bourgignonne 205
Black Bean Chili-1 205
Black Bean Chili-2 206
Black Bean Soup-1 206
Black Bean Soup-2 207
Black Bean Soup-3 207
Black Beans with Tomatoes 207
Budapest Bean Soup 207
Buckaroo Beans 208
Campfire Red Beans 208
Chili Beans-1 209
Chili Beans-2 209
Chimichungas 209
Cowboy Beans 209
Cream of Pinto Bean and Tomato Soup 210
Dal Soup 210
Dried Bean Patties 210
Garbanzo Creole 210
Garbanzos Bombay (Kabuli Channa) 211
Garbanzos 211
Herbed Beans 212
Hummus 212
Kerala Dal 212
Lentil and Tomato Soup 213
Lentil Patties 213
Lentil Patty Sauce 213
Lentil Pot 213
Lentil Soup-1 214
Lentil Soup-2 214
Lentil Soup-3 214
Lentil Soup-4 215
Mexican Bean Pot 215
Mexican Garbanzos 215
Pease Porridge 216
Refried Beans 216
Simple Cassoulet 216
Southern Pinto Beans 217
Soy Fritters 217
Soyburgers 217
Soyteena 218
Special Garbanzos 218
Split Pea Soup-1 218
Split Pea Soup-2 219
Split Pea Soup-3 219

Index

Swedish Brown Beans....219
Tortilla and Tostado Filling-1....220
Tortilla and Tostado Filling-2....220
Tuscan White Bean Casserole-1....220
Tuscan White Bean Casserole-2....221
Vegeburgers....221
White Beans with "Bacon"....221
White Beans with Tomatoes-1....222
White Beans with Tomatoes-2....222

ETC.

Baked Spring Rolls....323
Bread Crumb Topping....323
Breading Food for Frying....324
Carob Fudge....324
Cinnamon Toast....324
Coconut Milk....324
Deep-Frying Batter....324
French Toast....325
Fried "Cheese" Balls....325
Fruit Jam....325
Garlic Bread....325
Garlic Olives....325
Gluten Dumplings....326
Hot "Cheese" and Cider Dip....326
Instant Tomato Juice....326
Instant Tomato Purée....326
Instant Tomato Sauce....326
"Maple" Syrup....327
Mulled Cider....327
Orange Grape Juice....327
Pancake Syrup-1....327
Pancake Syrup-2....327
Pancakes-1....327
Pancakes-2....328
Party "Cheese" Dip....328
Pecan Patties....328
Powdered Sucanat....328
Self-rising Flour....328
"Shrimp" Dip....329
Spicy Tomato Juice....329
Sunburgers....329
Uncooked Applesauce....329
Vegetarian Dog Food....330

FLAVORING BROTHS

Chicken-Like Broth....132
Beef-Like Broth....132
Fish-Like Broth....133
Ham-Like Broth....133
Sausage-Like Broth....133

GLUTEN-FOR GOODNESS SAKE!

Baked Cubed Gluten....89
Baked Cubed Gluten Casserole....89
Baked Gluten....88
Barbecue Gluten....90
Basic Gluten....87
Cooking Method 1....87
Cooking Method 2....87
Cooking Method 3....87
Gluten and Cabbage Casserole....90
Gluten and Corn Casserole....90
Gluten and Green Beans Stir-Fry....91
Gluten and Potato Hash....91
Gluten and Rice Casserole....91
Gluten Chow Mein....92
Gluten Curry....92
Gluten Dumplings....93
Gluten Enchiladas....93
Gluten Hash....93
Gluten Jambalaya....94
Gluten Loaf....94
Gluten Paprika....94
Gluten Piquant....95
Gluten Pot Pie....96
Gluten Salad....96
Gluten Sandwich Spread....96
Gluten-Vegetable Casserole....97
Hearty Gluten Bake....97
"Instant" Gluten....88

GRAINS

Barley....221
Cracked Wheat....226
"Cheese" Rice....222
Creole Rice....222
Dirty Rice....222
Flavored Rice....222
Fried Rice....222
Green Rice-1....223
Green Rice-2....223
Millet....221
Pilaf Imperial....226
Rice....221
Rice Jambalaya....223
Simple Risotto....224
Spanish Rice-1....224
Spanish Rice-2....224
Spanish Rice-3....225
Spicy Bulghur Pilaf....226
Spinach Risotto....225
Tabouli Wheat....227
Vegetable Fried Rice-1....225
Vegetable Fried Rice-2....225

GRAVIES AND SAUCES

Barbecue Sauce-1....235
Barbecue Sauce-2....235
"Beef" and Tomato Sauce....236
Beef-Like Gravy-1....237
Beef-Like Gravy-2....237
Brown Sauce....237

Index

Blender Pizza Sauce....245
"Butter" Sauce with Herbs....238
Cajun Catsup....238
Cajun "Beef" Gravy....238
Catsup....239
"Cheese" Sauce-1....239
"Cheese" Sauce-2....239
"Cheese" Sauce-3....239
"Cheese" Sauce-4....240
"Cheese" and Onion Sauce....240
Chicken-Like Gravy....240
Chili Sauce....240
Cocktail Sauce-1....240
Cocktail Sauce-2....241
"Cream Cheese" Spaghetti Sauce....246
Creole Sauce....241
Golden Sauce....241
Ham Gravy....241
Ham-Like Gravy....242
Hamburger Gravy....242
Italian Pasta Sauce....242
Maitre d'Hotel Butter Sauce....242
Mary Krieger's Sure-to-Please Spaghetti Sauce....246
Mushroom Gravy....243
Olive Sauce-1....243
Olive Sauce-2....243
Onion Sauce-1....243
Onion Sauce-2....244
Onion Sauce for Spaghetti....246
Piquante Sauce....244
Pizza Sauce-1....244
Pizza Sauce-2....244
Sour Cream and Chive Sauce....245
Spaghetti Sauce....245
Spanish Tomato Sauce....249
Spicy Barbecue Sauce-1....236
Spicy Barbecue Sauce-2....236
Taco Sauce....247
Tartar Sauce....247
Tomato Sauce-1....247
Tomato Sauce-2....248
Tomato Sauce-3....248
Tomato and "Cheese" Sauce....248
Tomato and Onion Sauce....249
White Sauce....250
Yeast Gravy....249
Zucchini Spaghetti Sauce....247

HEAVENLY SIMPLE!
Basic "Cream Of" Soup....e
Basic "Creamed" Vegetables....c
Basic Dried Bean Soup....f
Basic Dried Beans-1....e
Basic Dried Beans-2....f
Basic Gluten....g
Basic Gluten-Cajun Style....h
Basic Pasta Sauce....g
Basic Vegetable Soup-1....c
Basic Vegetable Soup-2....d
Basic Vegetable Soup-3....e
Basic Vegetables....b
Basic Vegetables-Cajun Style....b

N'EGGS
All Purpose N'egg....285
Pastry N'egg....285

N'ICE CREAM
Banana N'Ice Cream....295
Coconut N'Ice Cream....295
Tahini N'Ice Cream....296
Tofu N'Ice Cream-1....296
Tofu N'Ice Cream-2....296

PASTA
Baked Macaroni with Tomatoes....252
Basic Pasta....251
Basic N'egg Pasta....251
Basic Semolina Pasta....251
Calzone....252
Chili-Mac....253
Fettuchini with Spinach Pesto....253
Fried Noodles....253
Gnocchi....253
Herbed Noodles....254
Herbed Noodles with Cheese, Lemon, and Green Onions....254
Hungarian Noodle Bake....254
Lasagna....255
Lasagna Noodles....255
Macaroni and "Cheese"....256
Macaroni and Yeast "Cheese" Casserole....256
Mexican Bean and Pasta Dish....256
Noodle Bake....257
Noodles Romano....257
Pasta Shells with Broccoli....257
Pasta Snacks....258
Piroshkis....253
Quick "Cheese" Dumplings in Tomato Sauce....258
Simple Pasta....252
Spaghetti Bolognese....258
Special Spaghetti....259
Thai-Style Pasta....259
White Lasagna....259

PICKLES, RELISH, SALSA, ETC.
Cajun Catsup....277
Chili Macho....277
Chilipetin Sauce....277
Dill Pickles....278

Index

Dilled Green Beans....278
Green Tomato Pickles....279
Hot Herbed Carrots....279
Hot Stuff....279
Louisiana Hot Sauce....280
Marinated Tomatoes....280
Pickled Beans and Onions....280
Pickled Calico Vegetables....280
Quick Tomato Relish....281
Tomato Relish....281
Tomato Salsa....281
Tomato Salsa Cruda....282
Tomato Salsa Fresca....282
Bread and Butter Zucchini....282
Zucchini Pickles....282
Zucchini-Red Pepper Relish....283
Zucchini Relish....283

PIES
Apple Pie....313
Banana Cream Pie....313
Berry Cream Pie....314
Blueberry Cobbler....314
Blueberry Pie Filling....315
Cherry Pie....315
Fruit Pie-1....315
Fruit Pie-2....316
Graham Cracker Crust....316
Lemon Custard Pie....316
Peach Pie....316
Pecan Pie....317
Pie Crust....313
Pineapple Pie....317
Shoofly Pie....317
Strawberry Pie Filling....318

PIZZA
"Cheese"-Only Pizza....261
Easy Pizza Crust....261
"Meatza" Pie....261
Onion-Garlic Pizza....262
Pizza Bread....263
Quick Pizza....261
Taco Pizza....263
Tomato and Cheese Pizza....263

PORK SUBSTITUTES AND DISHES
"Bacon" Gluten-1....104
"Bacon" Gluten-2....104
"Baked Ham" Gluten....105
Barbecue "Spare Ribs"....105
Barbecue "Spare Rib" Sauce....106
Breakfast "Sausage"....107
Cajun Sausage....107
Chinese "Pork" with Water Chestnuts and Mushrooms....106
Cooking "Sausage"....105
Farmer's "Sausage"....107
Garlic "Sausage"....108
"Ham" Gluten....108
Herb "Sausage....108
Italian "Sausage"....109
Italian "Sausage," Pasta, and Bean Casserole....109
Mexican Chorizo "Sausage"....110
Pizza "Sausage"....110
"Pork" Gluten-1....110
"Pork" Gluten-2....111
"Pork" Gluten-3....111
"Pork" Chops....111
Rosemary "Sausage"....112
"Sausage" and Cabbage....112
Sautéed "Pork Chops" with Tomato and Eggplant Sauce....112
Simple "Sausage"....113
Soy Grits "Ham"....113
Soy Grits "Sausage"....113
Watkins "Sausage"....113

POULTRY SUBSTITUTES AND DISHES
Braised "Chicken" and "Chorizo"....115
Cajun "Chicken" Bake....115
"Chicken" à la King....116
"Chicken" and "Sausage" Gumbo....116
"Chicken" Casserole with Mushrooms, Tomatoes, and Rice....117
"Chicken" Gluten....114
"Chicken" Gumbo....117
"Chicken" Paella....117
"Chicken" Tetrazzini....118
Creamed "Chicken" with Mushrooms and Herbs....118
Jambalaya....118
Omelets....119
Oven-Fried Gluten....119
Roasted "Chichen" with Potatoes and "Chorizo"....120
Soy Grits "Chicken"....120
Spanish "Chicken" au Gratin....120
Spanish "Chicken" with Rice....121
"Turkey" Cutlets Piccata....121
"Turkey" Gluten....114
"Turkey" Holiday Casserole....121
"Turkey" Salad Burritos....122

SALAD DRESSINGS
Alfalfa Sprout Dressings....1
Almond Dressing....1
Avocado-Cashew Dressing....1
Avocado Dressing-1....2
Avocado Dressing-2....2
Avocado Dressing-3....2
Avocado Dressing-4....2

Index

Avocado Dressing-5 2
Avocado Dressing-6 3
Avocado-Olive Dressing 3
Avocado Mayonnaise 3
Simple Avocado Dressing 3
Bitters Dressing 3
Caper French Dressing 3
Caraway Dressing 4
Carrot Dressing 4
Cashew Cheese Dressing 4
Cashew Mayonnaise 4
Chive Dressing 5
Cream French Dressing 5
Crunchy Cream Dressing 5
Cucumber Dressing 5
Curry Mayonnaise 5
Dill Dressing 6
Dried Bean Dressing 6
French Dressing-1 6
French Dressing-2 6
French Dressing-3 7
Fresh Tomato Dressing 7
Fresh Vegetable Dressing 7
Garlic Dressing 7
Garlic and Dill Dressing 7
Green Dressing-1 8
Green Dressing-2 8
Green Gazpacho Dressing 8
Green Goddess Dressing 8
Herb Dressing-1 9
Herb Dressing-2 9
Herb Mayonnaise Dressing 9
Hot "Cheese" and Cider Dressing 9
Hummus Dressing 10
Italian Dressing-1 10
Italian Dressing-2 10
Lemon Dressing 10
Lemon Garlic Dressing 11
Lorenzo Dressing 11
Marinade Dressing 11
Mayonnaise Dressing 12
Mexican Tomato Dressing 12
Mexican Tomato Vinaigrette 12
"Miraculous Whip" 12
Nut Butter Dressing-1 13
Nut Butter Dressing-2 13
Nut Butter Dressing-3 13
Nut Butter Dressing-4 13
Nutritional Yeast Dressing 13
Oil and Lemon Juice Dressing 14
Oil and Vinegar Dressing 14
Old Fashioned Boiled Dressing 14
Olive Dressing 14
Oregano-Mint Dressing 14
Parsley Dressing 15
Potato Dressing-1 15
Potato Dressing-2 15
Potato Dressing-3 15
Potato Mayonnaise 15
Russian Dressing-1 15
Russian Dressing-2 16
"Sour Cream" Dressing-1 16
"Sour Cream" Dressing-2 16
Sweet Basil Dressing 16
Tahini Dressing-1 16
Tahini Dressing-2 17
Tahini Dressing-3 17
Tahini Dressing-4 17
Tahini Dressing-5 17
Tahini/Oil Dressing 17
Tahini Salad Dressing 18
Tartar Dressing 18
Thousand Island Dressing-1 18
Thousand Island Dressing-2 18
Thousand Island Dressing-3 19
Tofu Mayonnaise-1 19
Tofu Mayonnaise-2 19
Tofu Mayonnaise-3 19
Tomato Dressing-1 20
Tomato Dressing-2 20
Tomato-Cashew Dressing 20
Tomato Mayonnaise 20
Tomato French Dressing 21
"Vinaigrette" Dressing-1 21
"Vinaigrette" Dressing-2 21
Zesty French Dressing 21
SALADS
"Cottage Cheese" Salad-1 26
"Cottage Cheese" Salad-2 26
Austrian Potato Salad 35
Avocado Salad-1 23
Avocado Salad-2 23
Barbecue Bean Salad 23
Bean Sprout Salad-1 23
Bean Sprout Salad-2 23
Cabbage and Lima Bean Salad 23
Cabbage Slaw-1 23
Cabbage Slaw-2 24
Cajun Cole Slaw 24
Cajun Potato Salad 35
Chef's Bean Salad 25
Corn Salad-1 25
Corn Salad-2 25
Corn, Rice, and Bean Salad 25
Cucumber Salad-1 26
Cucumber Salad-2 26
Dried Bean Salad 27
French Potato Salad 35

Index

Garbanzo and Cabbage Salad 27
Garbanzo Bean Salad-1 27
Garbanzo Bean Salad-2 27
Garbanzo Salad-1 28
Garbanzo Salad-2 28
Garbanzo-Tomato Salad 28
Gazpacho Salad 28
German Potato Salad 35
Green Pea Salad-1 29
Green Pea Salad-2 29
Green Vegetable Salad 29
Guacamole-1 29
Guacamole-2 29
Guacamole-3 29
Guacamole-4 30
Guacamole-5 30
Kidney Bean Salad-1 30
Kidney Bean Salad-2 30
Lentil Salad-1 31
Lentil Salad-2 31
Lentil Salad-3 31
Lima Bean and Garbanzo Salad 32
Lima Bean Gazpacho Salad 32
Lima Bean Salad-1 31
Lima Bean Salad-2 31
Macaroni and "Cheese" Salad 32
Mexican Bean and Corn Salad 26
Mexican Corn Salad 26
Mixed Vegetable Salad-1 32
Mixed Vegetable Salad-2 33
Parsleyed Potato Salad 36
Pasta Salad Vinaigrette 33
Pea and Potato Salad 33
Pecos Bean Salad 33
Pink Beans and Red Cabbage Salad 34
Piquant Cauliflower 33
Potato Salad-1 34
Potato Salad-2 34
Potato Salad-3 34
Rice and Avocado Salad 37
Rice and Bean Salad 37
Rice Salad 36
Rice Salad Especial 37
Rice Salad Southern Style 38
Rice Salad with Blackeye Peas 38
Salad Nicoise 38
Sunshine Salad 39
Tabouli Salad 39
Three-Bean Salad-1 39
Three-Bean Salad-2 39
Tomato and Bean Salad 40
Tomato Salad 40
Tomato Slaw 40
Tossed Salad 40
White Bean Salad 41

SANDWICHES AND SPREADS
Barbecue Bean Sandwich Spread 265
Bean Sandwich Spread 265
"Cheese" Spread-1 265
"Cheese" Spread-2 265
"Cheese" Toast 266
"Egg" Salad 266
Eggplant Appetizer Spread 266
Fruit Butter 267
"Grilled Cheese" Sandwiches 266
Pimento "Cheese" Spread 267
Reuben Sandwiches 267
Saturday Night Specials 267
Sloppy Joes 268
Super "Cheese" Sandwiches 268

SEAFOOD SUBSTITUTES AND DISHES
Broiled "Shrimp" 125
Deep-Fried "Fish" 123
"Fish" Soup 124
French Fried "Shrimp" 125
Gluten Fish 123
Gluten Scallops 124
Gluten Shrimp 125
Marinated "Shrimp" 126
Mexican "Shrimp" 126
Salmon Loaf 131
"Shrimp" and Corn Soup 127
"Shrimp" Creole 127
"Shrimp" Curry 127
"Shrimp" Gumbo 128
"Shrimp" Imperial 128
"Shrimp" Mold 129
"Shrimp" Pie 129
"Shrimp" Salad 130
"Shrimp" Soup 130
"Shrimp" Stew 130
"Shrimp" with Caper Sauce 131

SEASONINGS
All-Purpose Seasoning 286
Fines Herbes 286
Garam Masala-1 286
Garam Masala-2 287
Garlic Oil 287
Special Seasoning 287

SOUPS
"Almost Instant" Vegetable Soup-1 54
"Almost Instant" Vegetable Soup-2 54
Avocado and Tomato Soup 54
Baked Bean Soup 54
Borscht 55
Broccoli, Bean, and Spaghetti Soup 55
Cabbage and Cheese Soup-1 56
Cabbage and Cheese Soup-2 56

Index

Cabbage and Tomato Soup 56
Calsoup 57
Carrot Soup 57
Chicken Noodle Soup 57
Cream of Carrot Soup 57
"Cheese" Soup-1 58
"Cheese" Soup-2 58
"Cheese" and Onion Soup 58
Chili 59
Chili with Mushrooms 59
Cold Cream of Squash Soup 59
Countryside Chili 60
Cold Cream of Tomato Soup 60
Corn and Potato Chowder-1 61
Corn and Potato Chowder-2 61
Corn and Tomato Chowder 61
Corn Chowder 61
Corn Soup 62
Cream of Broccoli Soup 62
Cream of Cauliflower Soup 62
Cream of Celery Soup 63
Cream of Pea Soup 63
Curried Mushroom Soup 63
Curry Stew 63
Dieter's Broth 64
Fresh Tomato Soup 64
Gazpacho-1 65
Gazpacho-2 65
Golden Corn Soup 65
Green Pea Soup 65
Minestrone 66
Mock "Cream of Mushroom" Soup 66
Mulligatawny Soup 67
Onion Soup 67
Creamy Onion Soup 67
Potato Soup 68
Chili Potato Soup 68
Cream of Potato Soup 68
Mashed Potato and "Cheese" Soup 69
Monastery Potato Soup 69
Potato and Mushroom Soup 69
Potato-Cabbage Soup 70
Shchi-1 70
Shchi-2 70
Soup Thickener 71
Sour Cream Tomato Soup 71
Spicy Tomato Soup 71
Spinach Soup 71
Split Pea Soup-1 72
Split Pea Soup-2 72
Split Pea Soup-3 72
"Three Sisters" Soup 73
Tomato Soup-1 73
Tomato Soup-2 73
Tomato Soup with Rice 74
Tomato Vegetable Cream Soup 74
Monastery Vegetable Soup 74
Russian Vegetable Soup 75
Winter Hot Pot 75
Zucchini-Tomato Stew 75

SQUARE MEALS
Apple Filling-1 274
Apple Filling-2 274
Barbecue Filling-1 270
Barbecue Filling-2 271
Blueberry Filling 275
Broccoli and "Cheese" Filling 271
Cherry Filling 275
Dried Fruit Filling 275
Hot Dog and Barbecued Bean Filling ... 271
Hot Dog and Sauerkraut Filling 272
How to Make Square Meals 270
How to Make Sweet Square Meals 274
"Meat Pie" Filling 272
Mexican Filling 272
Peach Filling 275
Pizza Filling 273
Spanakopita Filling 273
Spicy Garbanzo Filling 273
Strawberry Filling 276

SWEET PASTRY
Cinnamon Rolls 319
Confectioner's Icing 319
Doughnut Squares 319
Doughnuts 320
Fruit Scones 320
Jelly-Filled Doughnuts 321
Raisin Dunkers 321
Raisin-Orange Coffee Cake 321
Sweet Roll Dough 321

TOFU DISHES
"Beef" Enchiladas 232
Beef-Like Tofu 232
Chicken-Like Tofu 232
Oven Method Tofu 231
Stir-Fry Tofu and Vegetables 233
Tofu "Scrambled Eggs" 233
Tofu "Scrambled Eggs" Breakfast Casserole 234
Tofu 230
Tofu Hummus 233

VEGETABLES
Anandamayi Kitchuri 134
Baked Mashed Potatoes 135
Beans with Tomatoes 135
Boiled Cabbage 135
Boiled Cabbage Dinner 136
Boiled Okra 136

Index

Broccoli 136
Broccoli, Mushrooms, and Tomatoes 137
Browned Potatoes 137
Cabbage, Tomato, and "Cheese" 137
Cajun Peas or Fresh Beans 137
Carrots and Peas 137
Coponatini Eggplant 138
Copper Pennies 138
Corn à la King 138
Corn and Peppers 139
Corn Special 139
Cottage Mashed Potatoes 139
Country Corn 139
Country Corn and Okra 139
Country Corn Creole-1 140
Country Corn Creole-2 140
Cream-Style Corn 140
Creamed Carrots 141
Creamed Green Peas 141
Creamed Potatoes 141
Creamy Potatoes and Peas 141
Creole Okra 142
Creole Tomatoes 142
Curried Broccoli 142
Curried Green Beans 143
Curried Peas 143
Curried Peas, Carrots, and Potatoes 143
Curried Potatoes and Peas 144
Deep-Fried Okra 144
Deep-Fried Squash 145
Dutch Succotash 145
Eggplant and Tomatoes 145
Eggplant Burgers 146
French Fried Potatoes 146
Fried Mashed Potato Balls 147
Fried 'Taters 'n Onions 147
Golden Vegetable Layer 147
Greek Potatoes 148
Green Bean, Potato, and Tomato Combo 148
Green Beans 148
Green Beans and "Ham" 149
Green Beans and Mushrooms 149
Green Beans Stir Fry 149
Green Beans Supreme 149
Green Beans with Bacon 150
Green Beans with Garlic 150
Green Beans with Tomatoes 150
Green Lima Beans with Fines Herbs 151
Green Peas and Onions 151
Hashbrown Waffles 151
Jamaica Rice and "Peas" 151
"Kentucky Fried" Green Beans 152
Lazy Kitchuri 135
Lima Beans 152
Lima Beans and Tomatoes 152
Lima Beans in "Cheese" Sauce 152
Lima Beans in Piquante Sauce 152
Lima Beans with "Cheese" 153
Lima-Corn Succotash 153
Louisiana Corn and Tomatoes 153
Mashed Carrots 154
Mashed Potatoes 154
Mushrooms in Cream Sauce 154
Okra and Tomatoes 154
Okra with Cumin 155
Oriental Eggplant and Mushrooms in Garlic Sauce 155
Oven Fried Potatoes 155
Oven-Roasted Okra 156
Paella-Limas 156
Peas and Carrots 156
Peperonata-1 157
Peperonata-2 157
Potato Chips 157
Potato Chips-Spiced 158
Potato Curry 158
Potato Pancakes 158
Potato Pot Pie 159
Potatoes-Baked 159
Potatoes-Boiled 159
Potatoes in Broth 159
Potatoes in Their Own Gravy 160
Potatoes O'Brien 160
Potatoes Paprika 160
Quick Saucy Vegetables 161
Quick Sauerkraut 161
Ratatouile 161
Red Cabbage 162
Roasted Potatoes and Onions 162
Sautéed Vegetables 162
Scalloped Cabbage 162
Slumgullian 163
Spanish Vegetables 163
Spinach au Gratin 163
Spinach, Tomatoes, and Rice 163
Spinach with Tomatoes 164
Squash au Gratin 164
Squash, Beans, and Corn 164
Squash, Green Beans, and Tomatoes 165
Squash and Peas 165
Squash, Mushroom, and Pasta Pie 165
Squash with Tomatoes 166
Stewed Squash 166
Super Okra 166
Sweet and Sour Cabbage 167
Szechwan Braised Eggplant 167
Thai Style Vegetables 167

Tomatoes and Okra 168
Tomatoes and Vegetables.....168
Tomatoes, Corn, and "Cheese".....168
Tomatoes Creole 168
Vegetable Curry.....169
Vegetable Fried Rice 169
Yellow Squash Creole 170
Zucchini Plain.....170
Zucchini with Tomatoes.....170

NOTES

NOTES

NOTES

NOTES

$19.95, plus $2.50 for mailing

$1.00, plus 50¢ per copy for mailing

Available from

SAINT GEORGE PRESS
Rt. 1, Box 75 • Geneva, NE 68361

IT'S NOT OVER YET!

SUBSCRIBE TO THE

Simply Heavenly! Recipe Letter

As we continue to test and develop new recipes in our Monastery kitchen, they are made available to you through our *Simply Heavenly! Recipe Letter*.

Each issue of the newsletter is sent to you as soon as we have enough recipes to fill up a complete newsletter of ten pages.

The subscription fee for four issues is $16.00. Mail your check or money order to:

SAINT GEORGE PRESS
Rt. 1, Box 75 • Geneva, NE 68361

Subscribe Today!